A Farmer an

renewed by the latest date
other reader, you may
e (twice only). Please
charge will be made for
date due.

C0000 002 861 334

By the same author

Adam's Farm: My Life on the Land
Like Farmer, Like Son

ADAM HENSON

A Farmer and His Dog

BBC
BOOKS

1 3 5 7 9 10 8 6 4 2

BBC Books, an imprint of Ebury Publishing
20 Vauxhall Bridge Road
London SW1V 2SA

BBC Books is part of the Penguin Random House group of companies
whose addresses can be found at global.penguinrandomhouse.com

Penguin
Random House
UK

Copyright © Adam Henson 2017

Adam Henson has asserted his right to be identified as the author of this
Work in accordance with the Copyright, Designs and Patents Act 1988

First published by BBC Books in 2017
This paperback edition published in 2018

www.penguin.co.uk

A CIP catalogue record for this book is available
from the British Library

ISBN 9781785942488

Typeset in India by Integra Software Services Pvt. Ltd, Pondicherry

Printed and bound in Great Britain by Clays Ltd, St Ives PLC

Penguin Random House is committed to a sustainable future for our
business, our readers and our planet. This book is made from Forest
Stewardship Council® certified paper.

MIX
Paper from
responsible sources
FSC
www.fsc.org   FSC® C018179

*To all the wonderful dogs who have been
my loyal companions over the years*

Contents

Introduction

There are very few times in my life when there isn't a dog near to me. Sometimes I'm watching an intelligent, hard-working border collie handle my sheep at the far side of a field. Sometimes I'm sitting in the kitchen reading with a furry body pressed against my legs. Sometimes I'm bumping across the fields with the back of my truck loaded with four dogs – the collies Peg and Pearl and our Hungarian wire-haired Vizslas, Boo and Olive. Sometimes, when I'm away from home filming for *Countryfile*, I'm meeting other remarkable dogs whose relationship with their owners goes way beyond simple companionship.

Not that I ever underestimate the powerful beneficial effects of having a dog in the house simply as a pet. One in four households in Britain today is home to a dog and there's plenty of research to show that dog owners are fitter, healthier, and suffer less from depression than those who don't have them. Children growing up with pets learn so much, and also gain that simple, unconditional love that irons out so many worries and anxieties. There is nothing more reassuring for a youngster than cuddling up with a dog, who never asks questions about what kind of day you had, never judges you for not doing homework or not getting good grades, who is always in your corner when other friends are more fickle. Yes, just having a dog in the family is a wonderful thing, and our household always feels very empty when one of our much-loved dogs dies.

Although I understand the relationship between a family and its pet, I love the fact that dogs have evolved over millennia to be so much more than companions. Peg, the border collie sheepdog whose kennel is next to the back door of the farmhouse, is my partner when it comes to all the shepherding work I have to do. She makes my work possible in a way that no mechanical aids or extra humans could, and it is a role that dogs like her have filled more or less unchanged over centuries, even thousands of years. When I watch her working the flock I know there is a connection that goes right back to the evolution of dogs from their wolf ancestors: my work with Peg is something that a Bronze Age shepherd, rounding up his goats or sheep, would recognise. It was Peg's ancestors who made it possible for men to stop hunting to feed their families and start cultivating their own land and animals. They were there at the birth of civilisation as we recognise it today.

For me, the bond I have with Peg is priceless; she gives me a wonderful devotion and loyalty that is a real privilege, as well as making an enormous contribution to my farming life. Every morning when she bounds out of her kennel, eager to greet me and to get on with the work I have lined up for her, I know how very lucky I, and thousands of other shepherds and farmers, are to have these extraordinarily bright, enthusiastic dogs at our side. And we, who work the land and our flocks, are not the only beneficiaries of the extraordinary relationship between man and dog.

If Peg's ancestry goes back to the early days of dogs working happily alongside humans, there are many other dogs whose roles have evolved more recently to fit in with our changing times. There are gundogs, like the Labradors I grew up with, and the Hungarian wire-haired Vizslas like Boo and Olive who live with us now. There are assistance dogs, whose skills involve understanding modern life so much they can use cash machines, load and unload washing machines, and save the lives of their owners on a regular basis when they have serious health problems. There are guard dogs, search and rescue dogs, sniffer dogs – the list goes on.

In this book I want to introduce you to my own dogs, but also to some of the many others I have met through *Countryfile*, and whose stories have reinforced my belief that we humans owe an enormous debt to our wet-nosed, tail-wagging, snuffling, four-legged friends.

CHAPTER 1

Childhood Friends

The fairy godmother who stood guard over my cot when I was a baby, protecting and loving me in a way that only a dog can, was a gentle black Labrador called Chemmers. Chemmers was my first real experience of dogs, but I'm sad to report I have no clear memory of her. She died when I was three years old, but for those three years she felt her role in life was to look after me and my three older sisters, Libby, Lolo and Becca. Her main devotion was to Mum, who had been given her as a twentieth birthday present by a boyfriend she had before she knew Dad. In those young, single days Mum took Chemmers everywhere with her, including sailing down at Weymouth, which they both loved. Chemmers' unusual name came from one of the buoys they had to sail round.

Luckily for me and my sisters, the boyfriend didn't last long. However, Chemmers did, and when Mum met Dad it was a matter of 'Love me, love my dog'. This wasn't something Dad had a problem with, as he adored dogs from his own childhood days during the war, in particular, a Great Dane called John and a bull terrier called Barney. Sometimes Mum joked that he married

1

her for the dog: that's a long way from the truth, but he was certainly very happy to share her with Chemmers. They met in Cheltenham, where Mum was working as a teacher, and after they married Chemmers moved with them to the first farm Dad managed. When he got the tenancy of Bemborough Farm, where I was born and live to this day, Chemmers was very much part of the family, and because Mum was very attentive to her small brood of children, Chemmers joined in with her, treating us as if we were her own puppies.

It's a pity that I don't remember her, because according to Mum and my oldest sister Libby she was a truly wonderful dog: gentle, kind, well-mannered and everything that the very best Labradors can be. She accepted the rough and tumble of young children, the tiny sticky hands grabbing at her fur, the small, tottering steps taken by us as we clung to her back.

Mum got her into pup with a local dog, Barney, a promiscuous yellow Lab with a bit of a reputation as a Lothario; everyone in the neighbourhood with a female dog had to be on the lookout for Barney when their bitches were in season. He was remarkably agile, even jumping through an open kitchen window in pursuit of a mate at one neighbour's home. On this occasion he was officially sanctioned to breed with Chemmers, and he made the most of it, fathering a beautiful litter of puppies.

People who don't have Labradors are often surprised that when different coloured dogs and bitches are mated together, they sometimes produce litters with all three standard Lab colours – black, yellow and brown – among the puppies. (Incidentally, brown Labradors used to be called 'liver', but they were renamed 'chocolate' to increase their popularity.) I don't want to get all scientific about it, but it's down to genes. In the Labrador world, black is the dominant gene, but there are other genes in the mix, and depending on the combination different mixes of pups can occur. Nowadays breeders are able to have their dogs genotyped, if they are prepared to pay for it. Without the testing, the only things we know for sure is that two yellow Lab parents will always produce yellow pups, and a brown and yellow pairing will produce yellow or brown pups – sometimes both in the same litter – as will two brown parents. Pairings involving a black parent can produce a litter with all three different coloured pups in it, in all possible combinations. On this occasion, even though Barney was yellow, the pups were all born black.

Chemmers was an instinctively good mother to her litter. She was so relaxed that she accepted Libby curling up in bed with her puppies: like I said, I think she thought we were all her offspring, whether we had four legs or two ...

When Chemmers died, at a good old age, Dad took Libby with him to see a litter and to help him choose another black Labrador puppy. He and Mum both thought that a house needs a dog to really be a home and they both loved black Labs. Besides, when you are living in a fairly remote farmhouse, even though there is a sheepdog in a kennel outside, having a house dog gives a great sense of security. Although Labradors are, on the whole, a placid breed, they have a surprisingly stentorian bark. A recent survey by an insurance company tested reactions to recordings of dogs barking and, without being able to see which dog it was, the one that was voted as having the scariest bark was to everyone's surprise the Labrador, with more than half of all those canvassed guessing the Lab bark belonged to a Rottweiler. Next on the list of most scary was a Weimaraner, with the Rottweiler coming in third out of ten breeds that were tested.

So Labs make really good house dogs, and police and insurance companies believe the presence of any noisy dog is a great deterrent. Certainly, owners of dogs make fewer insurance claims for theft than non-owners, and surveys of burglars (yes, some burglars do co-operate when asked what would deter them ...) show that a noisy dog is top of the list of things they would avoid when sizing up a break-in.

The puppy Dad and Libby chose was named Tassle. The end of most Labradors' tails has slightly longer hair with a twist in it. This particular puppy had a very long twist to the end of its tail, like a little tassle, hence her name. Libby, who was six years older than me and nine at this time, adored her. Sadly, like many other pure bred animals, Labradors as a breed have inherent problems. One of the most common with Labs and retrievers (and other large breeds like German Shepherds) is hip dysplasia: it is, in fact, the most common orthopaedic disorder in all dogs. It means abnormal growth of the hip, with the ball and socket less functional than they should be, the socket restricting the normal movement of the ball. Muscles and ligaments around the joint can also be too lax to support it, so eventually the joint becomes arthritic and painful.

It's very hard to detect this problem in a small puppy, it only becomes obvious between six and 18 months old, and sometimes much later. Some dogs with dysplasia don't have much pain, but their legs are stiffer and they may become lame. Others, sadly, are badly disabled and in constant pain, irritable, not wanting to exercise. They can be treated with physiotherapy or anti-inflammatory drugs, and as an extreme resort, surgery, including hip replacement. Nowadays responsible dog owners only breed dogs with good hip scores. The score is a system of assessing the hips, and allocating each with a number. A perfect 0:0 is not very common in Labs, but the important thing is to keep the total as low as possible, with each hip being more or less the same as its pair. The highest score is 53 each side, so a total of 106, but this dog would probably be chronically disabled. The average total for both hips in Labradors is 12.

The score cannot be done until the dog is at least a year old, when a vet will X-ray the hips, and then a good breeder will decide whether the dog can be used for mating. Hip dysplasia is largely inherited, so scoring the parents is the only good way to avoid it. There are other factors, like how overweight the dog is (and Labradors never stop thinking about their stomachs and will eat everything ...) Of course genes are tricky things and a puppy whose parents have great hip scores can still have dysplasia from a throwback gene. However, responsible breeding means that the number of dogs with lifelong debilitating conditions is being reduced.

The British Veterinary Association and the Kennel Club – the organisation dedicated to promoting the welfare of all dogs – jointly introduced hip scoring in 1984, quite a few years after we got Tassle, but it was already well known that breeding from a dog with dysplasia was irresponsible. Sadly, Tassle became lame and Mum and Dad decided to have her X-rayed. It was then that it became apparent that she was suffering from mild hip dysplasia and they knew that they would never allow her to have a litter because of the high risk of passing her problems on. With that decision made, it was sensible to have her spayed. After all, they didn't want an enthusiastic rogue like Barney coming in pursuit of her ...

This is where the story becomes very sad, especially for my sister Libby. At the age of three, Tassle went to the vet for a routine spaying op, which obviously meant a general anaesthetic. Tragically, her heart gave out under the anaesthetic and she died on the operating table. In retrospect, perhaps it was for the best: the dysplasia would have eventually caused her pain, and she clearly had a heart problem, too. However it's impossible to be that rational about the death of a much loved family pet. I was only six, so any memories I have are brief snapshots, and not many of those. But for my sisters, especially Libby, this was terrible news, and for a few days the whole household was cast in gloom. Tassle may have died young, but she is remembered as a gentle, loving dog who fitted in with the family very well.

Labradors were now well and truly established as a Henson family institution, and the next one that came into the farmhouse was an older, well-trained gundog called Trudy. Along with a springer spaniel called Ben, she came from a mate of Dad's who was emigrating to Australia. The friend, a Mr Hidcote who lived near to us at Hawling Manor, was a shooting companion of Dad's, and when Dad heard that the dogs might have to be put down when he left the country Dad offered to have them. Trudy was five at the time, and in the prime of life, and Ben, a liver and white springer, was 11, so already an old boy. Mr Hidcote was convinced the dogs would not take to anyone else as he had bonded so closely with them. It took quite a lot of persuasion on Dad's part for him to agree to let Dad try. The dogs were duly delivered to our farm, and in a moment of inspiration Mr Hidcote included his own old shooting jackets and waterproofs. He was roughly the same size as Dad, and when Dad wore the clothes the dogs trotted happily at his side, quickly becoming completely devoted to him.

I know the smell on the clothes helped, but I'm not sure it is always as hard to rehome dogs as their owners like to think. We love to imagine we have a 'one person' dog, an animal that belongs just to us. And it's true that sometimes within a family a dog will have its 'preferred' owner – the person it relates to best and feels, on its own terms, that it belongs with. But dogs are pragmatists, they have a strong instinct for self-preservation, and generally they will go with anyone who feeds and loves them. That's not to say they will desert an owner for anyone who offers them treats: they are very loyal. But if their owner vanishes from their life (and, sadly, owners do sometimes die before their pets), it is, in almost every case, possible to rehome them.

A friend I know who works for a charity rehoming dogs has three dogs of her own, and she said to me: 'I always imagined that if anything happened to me, two of my dogs would adapt and go to new owners. But my little Jack Russell, I was sure, would pine away and die without me. Now I have been doing this job for a few years I no longer believe that. Dogs do miss people, and sometimes they do become withdrawn and sad when they lose an owner. But with sympathetic treatment they can all be successfully rehomed.'

There are, of course, loads of stories of very loyal and faithful dogs, some who spend years waiting for their masters to come back to them. But their loyalty always also involves being fed and looked after. There's a famous story about Greyfriars Bobby, a Skye terrier who kept guard over his master's grave in Greyfriars Kirkyard in Edinburgh for 14 years until his own death in 1872. Bobby became a popular tourist attraction and was rewarded with a meal from a local café every day, the café benefiting enormously from the trade it attracted. But, of course, the dog knew nothing of this, only that it had a place to stay and food. How much memory he had of his master after 14 years, I really don't know. But the public loved the story of Bobby's loyalty, and there was even a statue erected to him after his death (although cynics say the real dog died and was replaced with a lookalike, to keep the tourists coming).

It's a familiar story across many nations and cultures: dogs who wait by graves, or at the place they last saw their owner. Like Fido, a street mongrel from Italy who turned up at the bus stop for 14 years expecting the man who adopted him to get off the bus, when sadly he had been killed in a wartime air raid. Or Hachiko, an Akita, who made his way to a train station in Tokyo every day for nine years, at the time his master, who had died, would have arrived home. Like Greyfriars Bobby, these dogs have had statues erected to them as a tribute to their fidelity. And like Bobby, they were well cared for and fed; their devotion became part of their routine, and I suspect they would have moved on if nobody had been looking after them.

Ben and Trudy took to Dad and did not seem to miss their old owner – although, I daresay if he had walked back into their lives they would have been overjoyed to see him. Ben, in particular, became devoted to Dad, even following him up and down the rows when he was turning hay with the tractor and haybob. Old when he came to us, he grew noticeably older, as his gait stiffened and he no longer ran about the place. But he still loved being out with Dad, and one hot summer's day Dad sat down at the base of a drystone wall to eat his lunchtime sandwiches. Ben came and lay next to him, his head on Dad's legs. He fell asleep and he never woke up, dying very peacefully in the best place, in the lap of the man he loved and who loved him. If there is such a thing as a perfect death, Ben achieved it.

Although I remember Ben, I was still very young when he arrived in our household, and because of his age he was only with us for a couple of years. Yet I loved the look of him, that proud springer stance, his soft mouth, his unflagging enthusiasm. My parents noticed how much I took to him, and it put down a marker for my future ...

Trudy was much younger than Ben, and she is the first of the house dogs of whom I have clear memories. I loved taking her for long walks and she was a perfect companion for a young boy. Most of all, I was really happy when Dad went pheasant shooting, and I was allowed to go along, holding on to her until the order came for her to retrieve. It was wonderful to be trusted to be Dad's companion, and to spend time with him, and Trudy was the ideal gundog for me to learn with.

Before Trudy died, Mum and Dad returned to their first love, black Labs. They bought another puppy, Jemima. She was a very traditional-looking Labrador, with short legs, a barrel chest and an insatiable appetite. Labradors love their food, but it's really important for their health not to let them become overweight. Carrying extra pounds creates all sorts of health problems for dogs, from arthritis to diabetes, through to breathing and heart problems. A study of Labradors over many years has shown that slimmer dogs live on average two years longer than their overweight peers, have fewer visits to the vet because of health problems and need less prescribed medication. The fatter labs have an average age of 11, the thinner ones of 13.

That alone is a good reason to keep their weight down. But it's not just the length of life, but the quality of it. I feel so sorry for fat dogs waddling along with their owners. They are not enjoying life to the full, unable to run and jump, miserable on hot days because they find it harder to regulate their temperature and can struggle to breathe.

I appreciate how hard it is to keep the weight of some dogs down, and Labradors in particular have a well-deserved reputation for being greedy. But where throwing them a titbit when they look at you with those imploring brown eyes may feel like a kindness, it can actually be cruel. Dad always had a firm rule that dogs were not allowed near the table when we were eating. Our dogs were fed once a day and left alone to eat. This is especially important with visiting young children in the house, because even the friendliest of dogs can be protective of their supper and a growl can easily be followed up with a bite. I continue with the same rules in our house today. But even the most disciplined of owners can find their rules thwarted.

A friend of mine had a large extension built, so the builders were around for a few months. One young builder took a shine to the family Lab and was convinced the dog loved him above all others. What she actually loved was his sandwiches, which he shared with her every lunchtime. He also gave her chocolate biscuits until my friend realised and pointed out that chocolate can be deadly for dogs. In the time it took to do the building work, the Lab's weight increased dramatically, and my friend was firmly told to get a grip on it by a tough, funny nurse at her local vet practice, who said: 'That's a dog, not a coffee table. I could balance my mug on her back, she's so fat. Bring her back in four weeks to be weighed and if she hasn't lost weight I'll put you against the wall and shoot you ...'

Of course, Jemima never got overweight, because life on a farm involves a lot of exercise. But we were all aware that, given half a chance, she'd be sticking her nose in the bin or a bucket of pig nuts, and if anything got spilled on the floor she'd be there licking it up. Not all dogs need the same amount of food. Of course, working dogs eat more than house dogs, as a rule. But even with two dogs of the same breed leading the same lifestyle, food has to be individually tailored, as one will be able to eat more than another without piling on the pounds.

Jemima was a great friend and companion for me as a young boy. I first went away to boarding school at the age of eight and wasn't happy there. The school rules said I couldn't contact home for the first three weeks – a rule devised to help new boys acclimatise. I felt bereft, away from my family and away from my beloved Jemima. She was high up the list of things I missed, along with my family and all the routines of the farm.

I never told Mum and Dad quite how miserable I was. I knew they sent me away to school because they wanted the best for me. I was the sort of carefree, distracted child who had not followed my sisters' academic success at the local primary and they felt I would learn more in a more structured environment. So I never wanted to disappoint them, and they were right that being away from the farm made me concentrate on my studies more. But Mum knew, as she dropped me back at school in floods of tears, that I missed home more than I could say.

When I did come home for a weekend or for the holidays, Jemima seemed to sense that I needed comfort. I could bury my face in her shiny, black coat, stroke her silky ears and share all my fears and worries with her. She was an uncomplicated, loving friend: that's the wonderful gift that a dog can give to anyone, but particularly to a young child.

It was my close bond with Jemima that made Mum and Dad aware that dogs meant so much to me and it was at this time that I started to ask them if I could have a dog of my own. Jemima was a brilliant companion, but she related most of all to Dad, and I longed for my own, special four-legged friend.

CHAPTER 2

Carlo and Co

When Carlo lifted his top lip to show his teeth, you never quite knew why: to me and the rest of my family it was a smile of welcome. To anyone he didn't want to see, or was suspicious of, it was a snarl of warning. Maybe there was a subtle difference in the two expressions, but I never really saw it. All I know is, I'm really glad Carlo was on my side ...

Carlo was a very tough sheepdog. He was the dog Dad had when I was young and the first one that I remember watching at work, turning a flock of sheep and bringing them back to where he wanted them. Carlo was also a great guard dog and quite a few visitors to the farm were trapped in their cars until he was told they were 'friends' and allowed to be there. Woe betide them if they didn't wait for clearance, though! One land agent turned up to inspect the farm buildings but didn't have the sense to ring up first, or to call at the farmhouse before he started his inspection. Instead, he started wandering around the barns, unaccompanied, clipboard in hand. What was a dog to think? Carlo was in no doubt that this was an intruder, and it was clearly his job to protect the farm from him. A swift nip to the back of the man's leg sent the agent hobbling to the farmhouse, obviously expecting tea and sympathy from Mum and a fierce reprimand for Carlo. Instead, he was told in no uncertain terms how stupid he had been. What's the point of a guard dog if it doesn't guard? The dog, she told him, was only doing his job, and should be praised, not criticised, for apprehending a stranger who was inside the farm buildings without permission.

Carlo was always lovely with us four kids and would happily lie in the garden in the sun while we played, but if there was ever an opportunity to chase something he was up and away. It's an instinct with sheepdogs. He felt it was his duty to control anything that was moving as if it were an errant sheep. This meant he was forever chasing the postman's van, biting at the tyres, and even nipping the postman if he was foolhardy enough to jump out when Carlo was around.

One day Carlo was actually knocked over by the van. It clipped him as he ran alongside, sending him flying. He got up, shook himself, staggered as if dazed for a moment, and then normal service was resumed as he carried on chasing it. It didn't teach him a lesson.

Carlo was a black and white border collie with long hair that always seemed to be caked in mud and sheep muck. He didn't mind being so unkempt, but from time to time it was decided that Carlo needed to be tidied up. He hated the process, which involved cutting off the matted straggly bits which Dad referred to as his 'diggy-dags'. The only way to get rid of them was to muzzle him and then attack his coat with the sheep shears, and as soon as I was old enough the job seemed to fall to me. Although Carlo clearly hated it he didn't hold it against me, and as soon as he'd been released and unmuzzled he was his usual friendly self, just looking a bit tidier – although it was no poodle parlour job.

Dad was a brilliant farmer. He understood livestock, and could assess an animal at a quick glance. He had a great eye for a good animal to buy and was equally good at spotting, from a distance of 200 yards or more, if one of our animals was sick and needed help. I miss his guiding hand, and I always will.

However there was one aspect of farming where Dad was not perfect, or anywhere near it. And that was working a sheepdog. He loved his dogs and they adored him, and they worked well enough for him, but he was not a natural at training them. He'd probably never really been shown. My dad didn't come from a farming background. Dad's father was a famous actor and comedian, Leslie Henson, and his mother was a chorus girl and dancer. His younger brother, Nicky Henson, followed them on to the stage, but as a young man Dad turned his back on his family's showbusiness traditions and followed his own dream, to live on the land and to run a farm. So I think he simply devised his own way of training a sheepdog, which wasn't orthodox or, I'm forced to admit, particularly good. His success as a shepherd owed a lot to the dogs' enthusiasm to work and their instinctive grasp of what they had to do.

It was a different matter with the Labradors he schooled as gundogs: they were generally very obedient and well trained, but the sheepdogs were always a bit unruly. They were OK at doing what he wanted, which was usually fairly routine, but if they ever got it wrong he could be heard shouting at them, losing his rag. It was the only time I ever knew him to lose his temper: with us children and with the gundogs he was patient and kind. But a badly behaved sheepdog would be subjected to a rant – which meant not a thing to the dog except that it got the general idea it was in trouble.

So working sheepdogs wasn't his biggest skill, and as the farm grew in size he took on a succession of stockmen who did most of the shepherding. Some of them were quite good, but some were in the same league as Dad, so I didn't grow up with a really brilliant sheepdog mentor either. The stockmen often had their own dogs, so I could go out with them and I picked up the basic commands. While watching them work the sheep, I think I learned early on that Dad's approach – endlessly shouting at the dog – didn't help.

Carlo was one of the few male dogs we have ever had at Bemborough Farm – Dad preferred bitches, and so do I. I love the look of male dogs, they are very handsome animals. But when you are out with them they have an overriding interest in any nearby females who may be in season, constantly sniffing any bitches they come across, and if they get the scent it is all they can think about. They also stop and pee on almost every gate post and thistle to mark their territory. It drives me mad!

I know that a lot of top sheepdog trainers prefer dogs because in some ways their temperament is more reliable – bitches can be a bit unpredictable when they are in season. Also, there's some evidence that dogs are more competitive, and that's important in high-level trialling. If you look at the results of field trial championships, 80 per cent of the top awards go to dogs, not bitches. Breeders who make a living from their working dogs often prefer a male, which can be put out to stud at a high fee as often as he can cope with, whereas a bitch can only (responsibly) produce one litter a year, and she cannot compete in trials while in the latter stages of pregnancy or when she is nursing her puppies.

However, I don't pretend to be up with the best sheepdog trainers and I don't go trialling, so a bitch suits me better. Farmers and shepherds hardly ever have dogs castrated or bitches spayed: there's a deep-seated belief that they work better, and are tougher, if they have all their bits and pieces. There may not be any evidence, but it's generally believed that a sheepdog may become lazier and fatter if it is neutered. Personally, I like to leave my dogs the way nature intended them to be: it feels right. But here on a farm there is plenty of land for them to roam on, and I do understand why pet owners living in very different circumstances need to have the operation carried out, and as long as it is done properly at the right time the animals thrive.

The name 'collie' for a sheepdog can probably be traced back to the same root as 'coal' and 'collier', because they were originally black, or predominantly black. They have a very long history: dogs attached themselves to humans as soon as our ancestors settled in groups, scavenging for food, and soon taking on their first important role as guard dogs. But their next role came as soon as men began herding flocks of animals. Most experts believe that the instinct to herd – and it is an instinct, and one that saved Dad many times when his orders were confusing – is a natural extension of their innate need to hunt. Instead of hunting to kill and provide their own food, they learned that their best bet was to help the humans who would take care of their needs.

The work they do, and the different terrains and climates in which they have done it over the centuries, means that sheepdogs are superbly fine-tuned, with good feet, weatherproof coats, astonishing hearing (I'm always amazed at how a hill shepherd can control a dog with a whistle from three fields away with a mound between them) and excellent eyesight. They are functional dogs, not bred for their looks but for their herding skills, although to me no dog looks better than a well-set collie. But for farmers and shepherds, the reason to check a dog's pedigree is to see whether he comes from good working stock, not how photogenic he is.

There are different kinds of collies, but generally we have borders at Bemborough. After Carlo, Dad had, for a very brief time, a Welsh collie called Megan. He had been to the LLeyn peninsula in North Wales, probably to look at and buy some Welsh black cattle, and when the farmer mentioned that he had a dog for sale, already trained, Dad happily bought her, as he needed a replacement for Carlo who had died peacefully at the end of a long working life.

Welsh collies are longer legged, broader in the chest and generally have wider muzzles than border collies. But it's not the difference in appearance that matters: they have, over centuries, been bred for a different purpose. They were historically droving dogs, that were used to take sheep or cattle to market, rather than being herding dogs used to round up flocks of sheep. It's a subtle distinction, and nowadays with the need to move flocks to market by droving gone, many Welsh farmers have switched to border collies. But it's important to keep the breed going, and there are plenty of enthusiasts.

In terms of working the dogs, the difference is in what sheepdog trainers call 'the eye'. Border collies have 'a strong eye', which means they stare hard at the sheep and keep them in order by never taking their gaze from them. A 'loose-eyed' dog like a traditional Welsh collie, glances at the flock and runs around it more and is usually able to work more independently, making its own decisions. It is generally more mobile, constantly on the go rather than commanding the flock with its stare.

A loose-eyed dog is vital to move cattle, which are big beasts and can easily step on and damage a dog that doesn't get out of the way of their hooves. That's why small dogs, like Welsh corgis, were also traditionally used to move cattle; they could dart in and out.

So the Welsh collie was invaluable when the flock was being taken in one direction (along a droving road to market, for example), allowing one man and a good dog to move large numbers of animals, sometimes for miles in a day. However they were less useful in terms of splitting a flock, bringing them back, penning them. That's not to say there haven't been some absolutely brilliant Welsh collies working sheep, but for most top trainers, taking part in sheepdog trialling, the border collie is the preferred breed.

The problem with Megan, though, was not her 'loose eye'. I don't think Dad ever got far enough with her to discover whether she was any good at herding sheep or not. The problem was much more fundamental. She spoke Welsh! She had been trained in Welsh, all the commands she knew were in Welsh. No amount of yelling commands at her in English produced any response. A sheepdog only knows a limited number of commands (a family pet knows even fewer) and it certainly isn't bi-lingual. Poor Megan was as confused as I would be if someone was talking to me in Chinese or Polish. When Dad realised the problem, he knew he couldn't keep her. Even though she was a sweet-natured dog, he didn't have the time or patience to re-train her in English or to master her commands in Welsh. So Megan was returned to North Wales, where no doubt she flourished in the land of her fathers, with an owner fluent in her language.

Pat was our next sheepdog, a black and white smooth-haired border bitch. She had one big advantage over Carlo – no diggy-dags. No matter how muddy the ground, she seemed to self-clean when she got back into her kennel. She worked well, and even had her own moment of TV stardom. Dad appeared on television fairly regularly throughout my childhood, starting after he opened Cotswold Farm Park where he housed a collection of rare breed farm animals, a passion of his which I share. The farm park is on land adjoining Bemborough Farm, but with its own entrance. Due to my work on *Countryfile*, I'm away from the farm and the farm park a lot and rely on my business partner, Duncan Andrews, and our great team of managers and staff. Whenever I'm home, I spend as much time as I can working with the livestock and meeting visitors at the farm park. I'm thrilled that the farm park attracts many visitors to see the work we do, preserving traditional British breeds. When the farm park opened, Dad was interviewed by lots of journalists from newspapers and television stations. He was a natural: he had clearly inherited the family showbiz gene from his parents; something of his background remained, and it was clear he was at home in front of the cameras.

So he was recruited to do slots on Johnny Morris's popular children's programme, *Animal Magic*, and also to take part in other farming programmes. In one, called *Barnyard Safari*, he demonstrated how difficult it is to round up the ancient and rare Soay sheep we keep on the farm. Rather than flocking together, they have an instinct to scatter, confusing a dog that is used to dealing with more biddable flocks. Pat starred as the dog whose job it was to attempt to round them up.

When Pat died, Dad was given an ex-trialling dog called Queen by a retired shepherd from Northleach. She was brilliantly trained, a champion trialler with a great pedigree. She was a tri-colour – black and white with little ginger bits on her chin and above her eyes. She was a beautiful dog, well behaved and a brilliant worker. She took to Dad instantly, and was definitely the best sheepdog he'd ever had, although perhaps she secretly wondered what she had come down to, from working sheep at a very high level at trials to doing a basic shepherding job at our farm ...

When I was about 13 years old I was standing with Dad in a field while he talked to some people who were interested in buying some sheep. He cast Queenie out, gave her the simple command 'come by' and with great skill she skirted the edge of the field, making sure she picked up every sheep, and brought them to him without another command, and without him ever stopping his conversation. The potential buyers were very impressed by her, raving about what an amazing dog she was, and left with a trailer full of sheep.

Tragically, after only a couple of years with us, Dad let her out of her kennel one morning and she dashed through a gap in the hedge on to the farm drive, just as the assistant stockman was driving past in the farm's Land Rover. She went straight under the wheels and was killed immediately. We were all very upset, but Dad was devastated, as was the chap who ran her over although there was nothing he could have done to avert the accident. Queenie was so easy to work with, and at the same time a good-natured dog who really loved Dad.

The same stockman was leaving us shortly afterwards to run a flock in Saudi Arabia, and he gave Dad his own sheepdog, Bill. Bill was a big, shaggy-haired, thick-headed black and white collie, more like Carlo in temperament and attitude. He didn't work well for Dad, who was constantly exasperated by him, and could be seen running up and down the field yelling 'Bill, Bill!' with little success in getting him to do what was needed. Again, he could perform the basic functions of a sheepdog, but nowhere near the brilliant Queenie.

Although I really love sheepdogs – there's nothing better than watching a collie working well, and a dog that loves its work makes a great companion – sheepdogs are not the best choice as a family pet in an urban environment and sadly a large number end up having to be rehomed. Collies as a breed have high levels of energy, stamina and enthusiasm. They are also intelligent, and need mental stimulation almost as much as physical exercise. Owners who don't choose a pet carefully may find that a sheepdog with that inbuilt instinct to round up will chase whatever it can uncontrollably. They may also find if the dog is cooped up all day it becomes stressed and agitated, developing bad habits like chewing, barking and nipping.

There are three main reasons why collies end up in an animal shelter. One is that they were bought by farmers and shepherds to work with sheep but simply do not have the right herding instincts. These dogs can make good pets when they are sympathetically rehomed. They still need lots of exercise, but they can make happy, well-balanced family dogs.

The second common reason for them being rehomed is that they don't necessarily fit in with little children. A small child running down the garden is like a sheep escaping the flock to a collie, and its instinct is to round the child up by running in front and turning to stare at him, perhaps barking. This can frighten the child, who tries to run away, and the dog instinctively runs after him, perhaps even nipping at his heels. Disaster! The family assumes it has a nasty dog, but in fact the dog is only behaving in the way its nature tells it.

But the biggest reason collies end up looking for new homes is that their owners find them 'hyper'. According to Border Collie Rescue, the charity which helps rehome unwanted border collies and collie crosses: 'Most people are not willing, prepared, or able to put in the large time commitment it takes to adequately exercise a border collie ... Herding sheep is an all-day activity and often entails miles of running and sprinting across uneven farmland.'

I visited the charity for a *Countryfile* programme, and was shown around by Ben Wilkes, a retired policeman who has spent many years volunteering for the Trust. When I was visiting, there were 26 dogs on site.

'We see so many dogs, coming from a variety of sources,' Ben told me. 'Sometimes it is a bereavement, sometimes families find they have a child who is allergic to the dog, sometimes it's a matter of people having to work long hours and not having enough time with the dog, and in recent years we've seen a steep rise in people moving into rented accommodation where they're not allowed to keep a dog.'

Often it is simply because a collie needs so much mental and physical stimulation that they are not an ideal pet unless owners can devote time and energy to them.

'Farmers breed for their own needs, not for the characteristics that a domestic dog owner is looking for. People buy on impulse, and then the problems develop later,' said Ben.

The Trust does an amazing job, looking after these very special dogs, and I'm a great supporter of their work. There will always be collies that need rescuing, often for very good reasons. But the work of the Trust would be easier if families looked more carefully at what they want from a pet dog, and what they can offer the dog.

My advice to any potential dog owner is always: find a pet who fits in with your lifestyle. If you live near open land and have time to get your collie out there for an hour or two a day, he may be the perfect pet for you. If you want a dog to train for agility classes (see chapter How Bright Are My Dogs?) a collie may be the right choice. But there are many other breeds which require far less exercise and are better adapted to living indoors with young families.

Choose your dog carefully.

CHAPTER 3

Nita

It was Christmas 1974, and I was eight, nearly nine years old. My older sisters and I were, like all kids on Christmas Day, scarcely able to contain our excitement. As per usual in most farming households, we children had to wait for our present-opening session until Dad had finished seeing to the stock. Animals first: they had no idea it was a special day, and needed to follow their usual routine of being fed and checked to ensure all was well.

My sisters and I would often go with Dad and the dogs to help out. I am not sure whether we were more of a hindrance than help, but it was great fun and gave Mum some space in the house to prepare the Christmas feast. Once back, washed and changed, we would settle down to the main event. Not the big lunch, which was always great as Mum was such a fantastic cook but, of course, the presents. That year was a Christmas of special presents for all of us. Mum and Dad had decided to push the boat out and give us all a larger, more expensive gift than we were normally given. There was a bike for Libby – hard to wrap up so we had a good idea it was coming. Lolo got a flute, which she had been learning to play at school, and Becca a saxophone, as she loved Ska music.

As they were all oohing and aahing over their presents, I looked around the room wondering where mine was, but trying to be brave and not make a fuss. There was nothing left under the Christmas tree, and the room was awash with colourful discarded Christmas wrapping paper and the sound of the girls trying out their instruments. The only object that wasn't normally in the room was a battered old tea chest in the corner – a big, square plywood box, bound on the edges with metal. The top was covered with a sheet of bright red Christmas paper.

'And here's your present, Adam,' said Dad, a broad smile on his face. I went to the chest, not sure what it could possibly be, tore off the wrapping and there, nestled at the bottom on an old blanket, was the best present I could have dreamed of: a small liver and white puppy, looking up at me with as much wonder in her big brown eyes as I had in mine. As we looked at each other I felt a rush of love for this tiny creature, and I believe she recognised it and felt the same. It was love at first sight for me.

She was eight weeks old and tiny: probably the smallest from the litter. Mum and Dad knew I wanted a spaniel, because I'd always said I liked them and I still do: they are fantastic dogs.

Dad was very fond of his aunt Benita, so in honour of her, and partly for Ben, his old spaniel, Benita became the puppy's registered kennel name, but she was always known as Nita. I can still remember the moment when Dad lifted her out of the chest and put her into my arms: she instinctively snuggled against my chest. Later I had to be reluctantly separated from her to join in with the traditional Christmas lunch, but no amount of crackers, turkey and pudding could distract me from her, and as soon as was decently possible I left the table and joined Nita on the floor.

There were strict rules in our house about dogs: they were not allowed on the furniture and they were definitely not allowed upstairs. Only one dog was ever allowed to break this rule – Nita. On the first night, when she was bedded down in the kitchen, I reluctantly went to bed. But I could not sleep for thinking about her, and when I heard her whimpering, I sneaked silently down the stairs, took her in my arms – whispering to her to keep quiet – and carried her up to my bedroom. She was soon snuggled up next to me and we both fell fast asleep. Mum found us the next morning, and I pretended to be asleep in fear of getting told off. She didn't have the heart to lay down the law thankfully, and neither did Dad: from that moment on, when I was home from school, Nita shared my bed. Dad pretended to be disgusted by a dog on a bed, but he always let me get away with it.

I'd been at boarding school for a year by the time Nita came into my life, and although I hated leaving my family at the start of every term, I was growing more used to it and had settled into the life of the school. But leaving Nita was agony, and I extracted firm promises from Mum and Dad about how she was to be looked after while I was away (as if they needed any advice on caring for dogs!) Phone calls home were always peppered with questions about her, and the most thrilling dates in the school calendar were the rugby fixtures when Mum and Dad came to watch me play. Of course, I was delighted to see them as I missed them badly. But I was delirious with happiness when they brought Nita with them. It was wonderful to see her on the touchline.

I know Nita loved and bonded with me above all others, but I also know that when I wasn't at home – and there were long spells when I wasn't – she was happy with Mum and Dad and my sisters looking after her. But when I was there, it was my legs she snuggled against when I sat down, and at night she took up her usual place at the bottom of the stairs, waiting to be invited up to share my bed, which she always was.

There's a very special relationship between children and dogs, and I first experienced it with our black Lab Jemima, and then, in spades, with Nita. I'm not surprised that we hear so many stories of dogs helping children with problems, whether it's conditions like autism, Asperger's, family break-ups, or terrible traumas. You can bury your face in the coat of a dog and feel accepted and loved, whatever is happening in the rest of your life. Not that I needed Nita to make me feel loved, but I know that wonderful feeling of emotional completeness that a dog brings. Everyone has times of being sad, angry, excited, happy: a dog shares it all. Nita was my best mate, always enthusiastic about trailing around the farm with me, full of energy, but also there, cuddled up to me, if ever I needed reassurance.

Jemima was firmly established as the house dog when Nita arrived. After the usual stand-off between an older dog and a puppy, she came to accept the little one. It's always difficult introducing a new puppy into a home with other dogs and even when they are bitches you should never assume that the maternal instincts of older dogs will kick in. The best advice is to monitor them, never force a puppy on another dog and let them establish their own relationship. After snapping at Nita once or twice to put her in her place and to instil due respect for her elder, Jemima and Nita settled down happily together.

Like all springers, Nita had an incredible energy and enthusiasm and a brilliant sense of smell. Once when I was in my early teens, I took a shotgun to go pigeon shooting. Pigeons can be a real problem on the farm, particularly when they eat young oilseed rape plants, and from time to time we try to deter them by shooting. Nita was never the sort of dog to sit patiently in the hide with me: she was so inquisitive that she couldn't resist nosing around, which would scare off the pigeons before I had chance to take aim. So I left her at the farmhouse, shut into the kitchen. I walked half a mile down the farm road, then skirted around the boundary of several fields carrying my shotgun. I erected a simple camouflage hide, put out some decoy plastic pigeons to attract the real birds, and settled down to wait.

Looking back towards the farmhouse I saw an amazing sight. Someone must have left the door open, because Nita was out and she had one mission: to find me. I could see this small liver-and-white splash of movement. I watched her, nose to the ground, go out of the farmyard, down the drive, turn left at the gate, up along one hedge, round another hedge, along the top of a big field, following my scent. Then she was at the hide, and she knew I was inside despite the camouflage. She'd achieved her target, finding me, but I didn't achieve mine: needless to say, I didn't bag any pigeons that day ...

But if she stopped me shooting the pigeons on that occasion, she was very useful on conventional pheasant shoots. I took her with me when I was working as a beater. She would flush the birds out of even the thickest of brambles and then retrieve them for me.

Nita actually spent more of her long life apart from me than with me. I was away at boarding school until I was 16, then I had two blissful years when I was studying A-levels locally, when she was welded to my side whenever I was out and about on the farm. I was no different from most boys of that age: I hated getting up in the morning. No longer at boarding school, I discovered the joys of beer and girls so, after arriving

34

home in the early hours, I was even more reluctant to be dragged from my warm, comfortable bed. Nita was my ally. Whenever anyone came into the bedroom to rouse me, she would growl protectively and not let them near me. I owe many a good lie-in to Nita's guard dog instincts.

After A-levels, I spent a year working on the Chatsworth Estate in Derbyshire. Then I was at agricultural college in Devon for three years, and only home in the holidays, and after I went travelling for a year with my good friend (and now my business partner) Duncan Andrews. But despite all these long separations, Nita knew she was my dog. She was fine with everyone else, and didn't seem to pine for me, but the minute I was back she related totally to me. She lived with our separations, accepting that I would come and go, and adapted her life to my absences. Going upstairs to sleep on a bed only happened when I was home: she never presumed to try it with anyone else and accepted without question that she slept in the downstairs toilet the rest of the time.

The downstairs loo at Bemborough Farm always seems to have a dog bed in it, that's why I point guests upstairs when they visit! There is a flagged passageway entrance to the farmhouse, leading into the kitchen, with the loo off it. When dogs track mud into the house (and they do all the time when you live on a farm), then the passage and loo are a good place to confine them until they dry off. Otherwise Mum would have spent her whole time mopping mud from the kitchen floor. Spaniels have large, well-feathered feet – in other words, very hairy, and a real sponge for picking up mud and debris. Nita was very used to plopping down on her bed until she had dried off, when she would be allowed into the kitchen.

Springers have a very long history as gundogs, and although they were not recognised as a Kennel Club breed until the early twentieth century, there's lots of evidence that they, or very similar dogs, have been around for centuries. The name 'spaniel' is generally accepted to come from the word used by the Romans for Spain, Hispania, or perhaps the French term 'chiens d'Espanol', which means they almost certainly originated in the Iberian peninsula. But they spread across the globe long before anyone started to categorise dogs. There's a reference to spaniels in the 1576 book *The Treatise of Englishe Dogs*, but it was not until 1801 that springers and cockers were separated into two types: 'the springing, hawking or starter' and the 'cocking or cocker' spaniel.

At that time there was no attempt to breed them separately. It was simply a matter of sorting through a litter and making the small ones 'cockers', their name coming from hunting woodcock, and the larger ones 'springers', who could spring and flush out birds to be caught by hawks or falcons, and later by men with guns. Nita was certainly a springy dog, always ready to jump up and take part in anything that was going on.

There are some highly questionable references to springer spaniels in history, including a tale that one travelled to America with the Pilgrim Fathers. I love the story that William Wallace, that icon of Scottish history played by Mel Gibson in the film *Braveheart*, had a springer by the name of Merlin MacDonald way back in the thirteenth century. But there's no real evidence as to the type of dog he had (or even that he had one), and the film makers left Merlin out of their Hollywood blockbuster, much to the annoyance of some springer fans. But though the dog wasn't in the film, I was. Dad was asked if he could provide some traditional-looking livestock for the movie, including a pair of longhorn oxen to pull William Wallace's dead father's body back from the battlefield. An old college mate joined me and, dressed up in kilts and ginger wigs, we worked with the actors to control the oxen, so my claim to fame is that I have been directed by Mel Gibson. You'll have to look closely to spot me, but it was good fun.

What we do know, reliably, about the history of springers, is that when George Stubbs, famous for his paintings of horses and dogs, painted a 'land spaniel' at the end of the eighteenth century, the dog looks more like a liver and white springer than a cocker, although not quite the same around the ears.

There are lots of other variations on the spaniel breed, notably the King Charles and Cavalier King Charles (much smaller dogs bred by mating small parents, and for other distinctive characteristics like their flat noses). Others are known by their place of origin: Norfolk, Sussex, German, Russian spaniels, and Irish water spaniels.

Naturally, the type of spaniel that appealed to me – and to my dad – was a springer, because of their ability to retrieve, as well as to flush. They have beautifully soft mouths, like all good gundogs. This is important so that they don't crunch down into whatever they are carrying, as often the shot prey is for human consumption. They have an easy temperament, are quick to learn and like working hard, all of which makes them the perfect dog for hunting with, but also a great companion.

As well as working as gundogs, the sniffing ability of springers, which I saw first-hand when Nita tracked me through the fields, has been recognised – alongside that of Labradors and other breeds of spaniel – and they are used by police forces and military organisations across the world in drug and explosive detection. Jake, a springer working with the Met police, was deployed to search for explosives after the London bombings in 2005. Another springer, Buster, is estimated to have saved more than a thousand lives in his work as an explosives detection dog, serving with the RAF in Bosnia, Iraq and Afghanistan, earning a chest full of campaign medals. I'm happy to say he had a happy retirement with his handler, and died peacefully at the age of 13.

Jemima died peacefully at a good old age and I think Nita missed her old house mate. Dogs are unpredictable when it comes to mourning their companions. Some dogs take the departure of a familiar friend without showing any sign of grieving. On the other hand, sometimes some dogs are so closely bonded that one deeply pines when the other dies, perhaps going off their food and becoming lethargic. I've known a dog lie on the bed of her departed friend for hours, a place she never previously went, and I've heard of a dog who escaped the garden of her home at every opportunity to lie on the front door step of the house next door, the place that her best friend had originally lived before being adopted into her family eight years earlier. She still seemed to believe he would come bounding out to greet her.

Mostly, dogs appear to be able to move on without too much disturbance. Mum, though, missed her gentle black shadow and was very happy when Dad suggested we get another puppy. That's how a bundle of black fur called Raven came into our lives. She was given her name while she was in the litter: the breeder insisted all the puppies born that year should have names beginning with the letter R. The Guide Dogs for the Blind Association, which is the world's largest breeder and trainer of working dogs, follows the same rule, choosing names with the same initial letter for each litter of puppies.

Nita, by now a stately middle-aged lady, was a little bit apprehensive about the boisterous ball of energy who invaded her space, especially as Raven was allowed to sleep curled up in front of the Aga while she was confined to the passageway and loo. Not fair! And the new arrival seemed to be getting a lot of attention: there's nothing cuter than a Labrador puppy, so there was a lot of fuss from visitors. Nita's nose was out of joint at first, but she soon mellowed towards the puppy and accepted her into the family.

Raven grew to look like a replica Jemima, with a round body that looked podgy even though she was very fit, and she loved working as a gundog. All our house dogs are able to roam freely around the farm yard. We are lucky enough to live a long way from the road and they quickly learn to avoid tractors and other farm vehicles, so they are fairly safe. If we want them home, then shouting their name, or a whistle, soon brings them trotting back. Like Jemima, and most of her breed, Raven loved her grub to the point of being gluttonous, which sadly, led to her early death when she was only eight years old. While out and about around the farm buildings she unfortunately came across some spilt rat poison, which she snaffled down. Farms need to control vermin, but Raven's death underlines how important it is not to leave poisons in an accessible place.

It's not just poisons: there are lots of innocuous-seeming human foods that are dangerous to dogs. Most people know that chocolate, especially dark chocolate, should be kept well away from pets, and increasingly, more and more pet owners are aware that grapes (and raisins) can be a serious problem. A friend of mine had a greedy Labrador/springer cross that managed to eat half of a Christmas cake. If he hadn't been very, very sick, and vomited the whole thing out, he would have needed to have his stomach pumped.

Other foods that are dangerous to dogs include avocados, coffee, alcohol, onions, garlic and the kind of synthetic sweetener often used in low-calorie chewing gum. Responsible owners have a duty to keep all human foods out of reach of their dogs, but these in particular. Even the best-behaved dog will be tempted if left alone with the enticing smell of something that is well within his reach.

I firmly believe dogs should be fed a very good quality food designed for them. I was fascinated to find, when I made a programme for *Countryfile*, that the first pet foods came on to the market in the 1860s. Before that dogs and cats lived on scraps and anything they could scavenge, and naturally their lifespan was much shorter. The first proper dog food was made by an American electrician called James Spratt, who saw dogs scavenging for food in the London docks when he arrived in this country. He realised there was a market selling food to the rich English gentry for their shooting dogs and came up with a complete dog food that combined wheat meal, vegetables and meat all bound together with beef blood.

Today the pet food industry is vast, with £3 billion spent in Britain every year. Dog trainer Richard Clarke demonstrated to me for the programme just how important it is to check the quality of the food we give to our dogs. He showed me a tin of appetising-looking meaty chunks in gravy, only to reveal that actually the tin contained 80 per cent gravy and a lot less meat than I expected from the picture. He also poured out a portion of complete dry dog food with bits in green, brown and beige.

'Dogs are colour blind: the colours are designed for the owners, and the colours are artificial additives. The same additives and preservatives are in this food as are in a can of fizzy drink.' he said.

We talked about how a poor diet can affect a dog's behaviour, as well as its general health. Going to a supermarket and looking at the array of dog foods on sale can be, we agreed, a bit of a nightmare.

'It's about balance,' Richard said. 'The cheaper the food, the cheaper the ingredients. Look at the list of ingredients on the label: the one that comes first will be the one that accounts for the biggest proportion, so if it is cereal, avoid it.'

My dogs are a vital part of my working life, but I know that even if they were just family pets I would feel the same: I want to fuel them well. Just as I know my children need a balanced diet, so do my dogs. I also know the risks of feeding them titbits and extras: in a survey of 2,000 dog owners, Forthglade pet foods found that 60 per cent of owners fed their dogs part of their Christmas lunch, even though over half of all owners know that human food is harmful to pets.

I was shocked to be told that 15 per cent of all dog owners needed to take their pet to the vet, or get advice from a vet, on Boxing Day. Spurred on by this alarming statistic, I made a film for Forthglade to make owners aware of the problems their dogs face if they are too indulgent. It may feel like you are giving them a treat, but it is much better to be cruel to be kind, and ignore those pleading eyes. It is far better to treat your dog with an extra helping of affection and some play.

It's also important to check that the food you give your dog is appropriate for its age: puppies, adult dogs and senior dogs have different dietary requirements.

If Nita felt a bit put out by Raven's arrival in the family, another intruder, Tammy, caused a much bigger upset. Tammy was also a liver and white spaniel, although not identical to Nita because she had patches of ginger fur above her eyes. Technically, that made her a tri-colour spaniel. She belonged to my sister Libby, and was a bit of an impulse buy. Mum and Libby had been to visit our Auntie Nancy in hospital, and on the way back they saw a sign on a gate: 'Spaniel puppies for sale'. On the spur of the moment, they made the rash decision that it was time for the Henson household to have another springer, and this time it would be Libby's.

Tammy was a typical puppy, full of beans and into mischief, which didn't go down well with Nita, who regarded her as a tiresome nuisance. The puppy was not particularly well trained, mainly because Libby soon went travelling and then worked in America. Tammy grew up to feel that she was in no way subservient to

Nita, and the two jostled to be top spaniel. If I was around, the position automatically went to Nita, and then in my absence, when Libby was in residence, Tammy would strut around as top dog. There was no natural head of the pack, which normally happens when dogs live together.

The most difficult time was if both Libby and I were there together. On one occasion, the dogs started to fight, both determined to exercise their authority. Libby blamed Nita for the scrap and started shouting at her. This was a red rag to a bull for me, as I was definitely on Nita's side. In the end, as Libby and I railed at each other, I settled the argument by picking Libby up bodily, carrying her out into the farmyard and dunking her in the water trough. Luckily, we can look back on it now and laugh, although I'm not sure Libby was laughing at the time ...

When I returned from my travels with Duncan in Australia, New Zealand and America, which was the longest continuous time I was away from Nita or my family, the change I saw in her was dramatic. Within that year, she had aged: she was 14 when I got back, which is a good age for any dog, and particularly for a springer (their average age is 10, and only a few live to 14). Nita looked like a real old lady. I realised, with a lump in my throat, that while I was growing up, she was growing old.

She was thrilled to see me, shuffling to me as fast as her stiff old legs would allow, pushing her way to the front of the reception committee of family and friends who welcomed me home, and her tail never stopped wagging for the first couple of days. She followed me as I worked in the yard, always by my side, snuffling at the familiar scents, and brushing her unkempt coat against my legs every so often to remind me that she was there. I fondled her shaggy head, and made a note to myself to give her a makeover: I resolved to groom her and cut her nails. Her coat was duller and curlier than before, and there were grey hairs around her muzzle. Although she was slow and no longer had that spring that gives the springer its name, she was so happy to be with me, pottering about the farm.

One thing she could not manage on her arthritic legs was to come upstairs to my bed, and she accepted this, no longer waiting at the bottom of the stairs for my summons. So at times, as if to even the score, I got down and cuddled her on her bed. We both felt the same, unbreakable bond we made when our eyes first met as I peered into the tea chest. She was mine, and I was hers, but I realised sorrowfully that our time was running out.

Three weeks after I came home I found her one morning, peacefully curled up on her bed. She did not respond to the sound of my feet or my voice gently calling her name. I crouched down and realised she had died in her sleep: like Ben, she had the kindest and most peaceful death any dog can have. It was the perfect way to go, and I was grateful for it. She had lived well beyond the usual span for a springer, and it was as if she had kept herself going until she saw me again. Some uncanny sixth sense let her know that I was heading for home, and she waited for me. Then, having renewed our old, deep companionship, she allowed herself to go, happily and quietly.

The tears poured down my cheeks as I dug her grave at Buttington Clump, a group of trees not far from the farmhouse where all our family dogs are buried, and lowered her shaggy body into it. I knew I was saying farewell to the best and most faithful friend any young boy could ever have. I have now said goodbye to many wonderful dogs, but Nita was the first dog that was so personal to me, and I still well up when I think about her.

CHAPTER 4

My Aussie Mates

B ob is a dog who made a huge impact on me. I met Bob during my gap year, when I was travelling around the world with Duncan. Duncan and I met at agricultural college and became great friends, and we now work together as business partners at Bemborough Farm. Back in 1988, though, we were young lads with no responsibilities, who decided to see a bit of the world before we settled down to full-time work. Being farmers was a great help: it's not too difficult to find jobs on farms if you are happy to be a labourer and get stuck in. If you add in some skills, well, you can earn enough to keep funding your travels when you move on.

That's how we arrived in Katanning, a small town two hours' drive from Perth, Western Australia. We'd worked ourselves into the ground for six weeks with a sheep-shearing gang, travelling to different farms to help the shearers. It was exhausting, hot and pretty relentless work.

So we were hoping for something a bit easier as we rattled into Katanning in our beaten-up, ancient Ford Falcon XB (a model only made in Australia) and made our way to a farm which we had been told was looking for seasonal staff. The farmer had one question for us: did we prefer livestock or machines? It wasn't difficult to answer. I, like my dad, have always been a livestock man. Duncan is the arable man, and that's the machine part of farming (it's how we still divide up the farm work to this day). On this occasion Duncan certainly made the right call, and found himself having an easier time than I had working with the sheep. He spent all day driving a huge, state-of-the-art combine harvester, with a lovely air-conditioned cabin.

I, on the other hand, was asked to drench 16,000 Merino sheep. That number may not mean much to a non-farmer, but if I say I have a flock of 700 sheep at Bemborough now you get an idea of the scale of these outback farms or 'sheep stations'. (The largest has about 60,000 sheep – imagine going to sleep counting that lot!) Drenching was a familiar process to me: you have a pack on your back full of the necessary liquid worm treatment and a pipe with a gun on the end with which you squirt a dose down the throat of every sheep. But 16,000? I couldn't imagine any flock so vast.

Nowadays drenching is scientific; we take dung samples from our sheep that are dissolved into a solution so they can be examined under a microscope to assess what is known as a faecal egg count. An expert is then consulted on exactly how much of what chemical to use to treat our sheep. Back then, it was a matter of getting a dose of worm treatment into every single sheep, and without Bob I simply wouldn't have been able to do it. It would have been a two, or possibly three, man job, so Bob, who worked for nothing more than his daily feed, definitely earned his keep for the farmer. Bob was an Australian sheepdog, known as a kelpie. He was not the first I had seen on my trip, as the farmers rounding up their flocks for the shearing gang used them to help pen the sheep, and I'd watched in awe as these agile, enthusiastic dogs moved the sheep around quickly and expertly.

Kelpies are great yard dogs, handling huge mobs of sheep (the Australians talk about 'mobs', not flocks, and, with the numbers they handle, it's a good word ...) Kelpies are brilliant at moving the sheep and packing them into pens. They can bark on command and when they are penning the sheep they jump up on to their backs, moving from the front to the back of the mob barking and packing the animals in tighter.

At every sheep station we went to with the shearing gang, the farm owner (known in Australian slang as 'cockies', because the early settlers, like the cockatoos, made their homes along the edge of water courses) used their own dogs to get the sheep into the sheds for shearing. The shearing sheds over there were purpose built, with stands for as many as ten shearers (we generally have shearers who bring their own mobile stands, with a maximum of two or three). As roustabouts, or unskilled labourers, we had to do everything apart from the actual shearing: picking up the fleeces as soon as they were off the sheep, lying them flat on a table, picking out the dirty bits, then rolling them up and throwing them into the right bin for their grade, which was determined by a professional grader. It was hard work keeping up with the shearers, but if there was ever a pause we were expected to sweep up the shearing area, so that it was spotless and clear of any locks of wool.

The cockie would use his border collies to bring the sheep in from the paddocks, and Duncan and I would push the sheep into the catching pens. That was when I first saw a kelpie jump on to the back of the sheep. I'd heard about it, but never seen it. They squeezed the sheep in, but with pens containing as many as 500 sheep the dog had to be brought out quickly: if his presence made the sheep rush to one side they could crush each other.

I was fascinated and really impressed by the dogs' skill and hard work. Kelpies look a bit like dingoes and lots of Australians believe they are indeed descended from the ancient wild dogs that have lived on the Australian continent for at least 3,500 years. However, it's actually more complicated than that. Kelpies are almost certainly descended from collies brought over by early settlers, but there is scientific evidence that dingoes interbred with them, probably way back in the early nineteenth century when Australia was newly colonised. The interbreeding may have been accidental at first, but seeing the result some shepherds and farmers probably deliberately bred dingo into the mix. There is no real way of knowing because keeping dingoes or dingo-cross dogs was illegal, so nobody ever owned up to doing it. When sheep were introduced to Australia the dingo found them easy prey, and was therefore public enemy number one. There was a bounty for killing them, and a hefty fine for any farmer keeping a dingo cross. So naturally farmers were deliberately vague about their dogs' pedigree.

But DNA tests in recent years have shown that modern kelpies have 3–4 per cent dingo genes. That's only a small percentage, but perhaps enough to account for the differences between traditional collies and kelpies. Bill Robertson, a well-known breeder who organised the DNA testing, believes the dingo contributed 'the spirit, the grit and the ability to handle heat' to the character of the kelpie. I think most of us who love collies would be reluctant to credit the dingo with the spirit and the grit, as we see plenty of those qualities in our dogs, but the ability to handle heat is a vital addition to working dogs in Australia. If, as most experts believe, the first kelpies were collies brought over from Scotland (the word 'kelpie' means water spirit in Gaelic), the searing Australian heat would be something they needed to adapt to, and a dash of dingo blood almost certainly helped.

Bob had plenty of grit, but even he rebelled against the heat at times, retreating to the shade under the ute (utility vehicle) whenever he got the chance. As it was regularly 35 to 40 degrees as we worked together, I couldn't blame him.

The sheep I was drenching were Merinos, which have very valuable wool. Over in the UK, the fleece is generally a by-product of sheep farming and we earn very little from the wool. Our wool is coarser, because of the climate, and we farm sheep to produce lambs for meat, rather than specialising in wool, but Merinos produce wonderful white fleeces, the best in the world.

Merinos are stocky, strong sheep, with claims to be one of the oldest domesticated breeds of sheep around today, coming originally from Spain but thriving in the Australian climate (other breeds brought in during the early years of colonisation simply couldn't survive the conditions). They proved to be very good foragers, finding food in the scrubbiest, most parched landscape where the grass is brittle and doesn't look as if it has any nutritional value. The rams have big, spiralled horns, and are tough old characters, as I learnt from experience. The sheer size of the Australian landscape means that these sheep are left to their own devices most of the year. They grow so much dense, close, fine, valuable fleece that it has become a major export for Australian agriculture. As a farmer working with livestock you often get covered in manure and interestingly it was noticeable how Australian sheep smelt differently from our sheep back home. Their dung is dryer due to the parched pastures that they graze on, and it is a smell that still sits in my memory.

Pete Dewar, the farmer's son, took me out on the first day of my mammoth task to show me the ropes. Back home in those days when we wanted to drench the sheep we gathered them and brought them to our permanent handling pens in order to treat them. So it was a novelty for me to see the mobile handling pen that Pete towed behind the old Suzuki ute, a pick-up with a flat-bed back, and I made a mental note to tell Dad in my next postcard home how useful it was. We used to walk the sheep miles across fields to our permanent pens, which was stressful for the sheep, time consuming, and knackering for the dogs. This more efficient way of doing it was made necessary by the vast acreage of the sheep station, but I could see it would also be very helpful even on our English farm.

Pete and I drove out to one of the paddocks, set up the pen in a corner of the field and started to round up a mob of sheep. I was accustomed to paddocks of ten or twenty acres, but out there they were more like a thousand acres.

We circled the paddock in the ute, zig-zagging to gather the sheep together, Bob on the back of the ute barking. Because of the noise he made the sheep would draw together. We skirted the perimeter to make sure there were no dead or injured ones and then Bob, who was a lovely red colour with a thick coat, took over. He jumped off the vehicle and worked behind them very naturally, moving them along without any commands from me, doing his job. He didn't need the standard sheepdog commands for 'left', 'right', 'lie down', and there were no whistle commands like we use with our collies, but if a sheep or two broke away the command 'Go back' sent Bob off to round them all up again. To the postcard I was mentally writing for Dad I added, 'We really need one of these amazing dogs.'

Bob's next job was to get the sheep into the pen, and then he leapt on their backs to the command 'Get up on them', packing them in tight, and funnelled them through into a narrow race, where I could drench them one by one. On the command 'speak up' he would bark, which underpinned his control of the sheep, and 'That'll do', told him to stop immediately. It was a very efficient system: without him I would have been running up and down in the baking heat trying to push them through by myself (which is why it was a job that one man would not be able to do on his own).

Occasionally, if the sheep were too far apart, Bob would fall into the race and instead of leaping from back to back towards me, he would end up having to weave under their legs as the sheep leapt forward to avoid him and often ran over him. He would let out a whimper as he made his way through them, but still managed to pack the sheep in tight. As soon as they were in I shut the back gate. Bob would clamber out and flop in the shade under the ute until I called him out to help me fill the race again. It was easy to drench them when they were so tightly packed as they couldn't move away from the drench gun. This made it easier to put the gun into their mouths and helped stop them leaping about, which could have caused damage to their throats. It is a very labour-intensive job but needs to be done carefully and accurately for the welfare of the sheep.

After the first day with Pete showing me what I was expected to do, I was on my own. I had a map, and Pete told me which paddocks I'd find the sheep in, I had the ute and I had Bob. It was exhausting work in that interminable heat, and with flies hovering around the sheep and me. Flicking away flies is known as the Aussie salute, also known as the Barcoo salute (after the Barcoo River) or the Bush salute. It's an automatic gesture to keep bush flies away from the nose or mouth – or at least, that's what you hope.

I had to wear long sleeves and trousers tucked into my boots. I also wore an Akubra, the traditional wide-brimmed hat made of rabbit fur felt, named after the aboriginal word for 'head covering'. I needed to protect myself carefully from sunburn, not just the flies.

Driving out to the paddocks where Bob and I worked was an incredible experience. In the throbbing heat of the day – and it was hot from dawn onwards – the hard, dry ground shimmered, the noise of the parrots was a raucous din, and the sight of them was blinding in the harsh light. There were flocks of galah cockatoos with their vivid pink faces and breasts and soft grey back plumage chattering constantly and calling to each other, and smaller flocks of sulphur-crested cockatoos.

These are white with soft yellow feathers under their wings and on their tail and a flash of acid yellow on the crest of their head, and every bit as noisy as the galahs. They flocked on to the ground pecking around for seeds and insects, or perched on the silvery eucalyptus trees. As we bumped along in the ute I'd see grey kangaroos, hopping along beside or in front of us. For a young man in his early twenties alone in this landscape this was all amazing, and made even better by the constant presence of my mate, Bob.

If the noise from the birds was deafening, the din was increased by Bob's excited barking. He loved working and he couldn't wait to get started. His racket drove me mad every morning, but by the time we returned after a hard, hot day working, he would simply lie down and keep quiet behind me on the flat bed of the ute.

On my first day I drank the whole of my water supply from its big polystyrene container by midday: this was a mistake I didn't repeat, as I was a couple of hours' drive away from my base and couldn't pop back for more. I made sure from then on to fill more of the huge plastic containers to sling on to the ute every day. When I took a break of any sort, even to just have a swig of water, Bob made his way to the shade of the ute and in the hottest part of the day I had to coax him out to carry on working.

Most of the sheep were ewes, like a flock here, but there were also mobs of wethers, which are large, castrated males who were kept solely for the huge, valuable fleeces they produced each year. Castrating them was supposed to make them calmer and easier to handle, but they were still big beasts with minds of their own. At least they and the ewes did not have sharp horns like the rams, who really were my toughest customers.

One day I was drenching a hundred enormous rams in forty-degree heat, and I literally found it impossible to touch their backs, the fleece was so hot. They did not want to move and Bob was more stubborn than usual, refusing to come out from the shade of the vehicle. The flies were driving me mad and I genuinely feared I would die of heat stroke.

That was when I realised that perhaps Bob was trying to tell me something. The old Noël Coward song (which no doubt my famous grandfather, the actor and comedian Leslie Henson, sang sometimes) about mad dogs and Englishmen being the only creatures foolish enough to go out in the midday sun was clearly true, and Bob was certainly not happy being cast in the role of a mad dog, however bonkers the Englishman was. I loaded him back into the ute, bumped across the rough paddock back to the shack where Duncan and I were living and settled in the shade until about 5pm, when the heat was abating. At this time of day Bob jumped willingly on to the back of the pick-up, and off we went again, working late until the job was done.

I never asked the Dewars whether without me they would have done the job in the cooler evenings; perhaps they laughed at me attempting it earlier. From then on, I was on the late shift.

Dotted around the massive station were deep man-made ponds, which were called dams. At over 30 yards long by 15 yards wide they were more like small reservoirs and were built to provide water, a very precious commodity, for cattle and sheep. Despite the fact that the water was pretty dirty and slimy, it was very tempting. At the end of a long day in the heat I often plunged into the cool, if filthy, dam that was closest to our home. It was big enough to have a good swim, as long as you weren't too particular about the colour of the water. At the end of a long, dusty day, it felt great.

The dams were full of crayfish, or 'yabbies' as the locals called them. They were regarded as a pest because if they burrowed into the walls of the dams the water would leak away. But they were a treat for Duncan and me. Pete Dewar taught us how to catch them. The yabbies were meat eaters with a great sense of smell and so were attracted to lumps of meat wrapped in a net. When this was thrown into the dam on the end of a rope and weighted down the yabbies would try their best to get to the meat, getting their claws tangled in the netting, so all you had to do was leave it for an hour and then haul them out. We would catch them, cook them and eat them with relish.

Our home was a shack, about the same size as a mobile home but raised on stilts, at the side of the farmhouse. There's an established tradition in the outback for building raised homes because they are better ventilated and cooler, as well as deterring some of the snakes and spiders (although not all ...) There were fly screens at the windows and door, and we soon learned to keep these closed. We had two bedrooms and more or less all we needed. We cooked our own food, which meant a fairly basic repertoire of chilli and spaghetti Bolognese, so the yabbies were a welcome change. We had to do our own shopping, but the nearest town was a good drive away, so the farmer's wife would sometimes take a list of what we needed and bring it back when she fetched her own supplies.

Bob slept in the yard with the other dogs: there were a couple of other kelpies and a couple of border collies. They were kept on long chains, and had barrels to sleep in out of the heat and trees to give them shade. Dog pellets were thrown to them, and sometimes they got raw meat – chopped up sheep or kangaroo meat.

For the month I worked with Bob, I came to adore him. He wasn't a demonstrative animal, but I think I earned his respect. He worked devotedly for me and I realised how impossible it would have been without him. Our weeks at Katanning passed very quickly, as Duncan and I were both working long and hard, and the time to move on came quickly.

Back home from our adventures, Dad was very receptive to my new ideas. He was always very open to new advances in farming and, besides, I think he wanted to encourage me, as he relished the idea that I would one day take over Bemborough Farm. He could see that I loved the place as much as he did, and that my travels may have broadened my farming experience but they had also cemented my conviction that this was the place I wanted to live and work.

We bought a quad bike and the mobile handling pen system. Next on the list was the kelpie, and that was down to me. If it was to be my dog I had to research and find it. At that time, in 1989, there were not too many kelpie breeders in England, but I saw an advertisement for a new litter in Hampshire. I drove down and instantly fell in love with a little red bitch, choosing red because she reminded me of Bob. The mother of the litter had been imported from Australia, so this little one was a first generation English kelpie.

I called her Bundy, naming her after the famous Australian Bundaberg rum – I'd enjoyed a few rums while I was out there, and she was a lovely dark rum colour. She was a smashing dog from the first day I had her. I taught her to 'speak', and she was an excellent yard dog, and great at getting the sheep into the pens. She was not so good out in the fields: some kelpies are on a par with collies in the paddocks, but it's rare to get one that does both jobs equally well.

By the time I bought Bundy I had moved out of the farmhouse and into a bungalow on the farm. It had been previously used by the stock manager, but when he left there was no need to replace him, as I was now working full time and Mum and Dad wanted to give me some more independence.

Bundy moved into the loo. Just like Nita had spent many happy hours sleeping in the downstairs toilet at the farm, Bundy accepted that her bed was next to the plumbing in the bungalow. Unlike the kelpies in Australia and the sheepdogs on our farm, she slept inside, but she never ventured into the living rooms. She was half-house dog, half-outside dog: house-trained and great company, but definitely a working dog, who liked nothing better than joining me at the crack of dawn to get on with my farm chores.

She was very good natured and quickly got on with the other dogs on the farm, Raven and Bill, working well alongside Bill. Dad and I both thought she was a real success and I was keen to breed from her. There were not too many kelpies in Britain at the time, but I found a kelpie dog living not too far away and he served her. I didn't take her to be scanned: I realised she was pregnant because she was getting bigger and coming in to milk. When I knew she was near her time I didn't take her out to work with me, but left her curled up on her bed.

When I got home she wasn't there, and I realised I had left the door from the kitchen into the rest of the bungalow open. Normally, Bundy would not have gone through, but on this occasion she had found her way into my bedroom and was under my bed. I'd left a book I was reading on the floor next to the bed and

Bundy had ripped it up and made a nest for herself under the bed, where I found her proudly licking one, really large, puppy.

I searched around all the other bedrooms and the living room to see if there were any others. Then I sat with her waiting for more puppies to come, although she was showing no signs of still being in labour. After a couple of hours I rang the vet and he told me that it was possible for a bitch to have one large pup, although it's not common. It's a great credit to Bundy as a mother that she raised her pup really well: I now know that singleton puppies can have a hard time, not having the warmth of their litter mates and sometimes gorging themselves because there are no others competing for the mother's milk. Apparently, there is a risk of such a large puppy getting stuck during the birth and a Caesarean being the only answer. But Bundy had delivered him on her own, showed no signs of having had a bad time, and was looking after him devotedly. What a star.

We called him Red because he had the same colouring as Bundy, and when he was old enough to leave her I gave him to Duncan. Duncan, like me, really liked the kelpies we met in Australia. At this time, he had a farm tenancy on Bryher, the smallest of the inhabited Scilly islands, with his wife Becky. Red took to his new life with enthusiasm: the island is only one and a half miles long by a mile wide, and Red regarded it all as his territory. He was a lovely, friendly dog, and everyone on the island knew him. He would go down to the quay to greet the boatloads of tourists when they arrived and stood proudly on the bow of Duncan's launch when they went to St Mary's to go shopping.

Red eventually moved back to Bemborough Farm when Duncan and I took over from my Dad and his partner, John Neave (who was known to me and my sisters as our lovely 'Uncle' John throughout our childhood). By this time the farm had expanded, after I'd convinced the landowners that I was serious about remaining at Bemborough. My private life had also changed: the bungalow had gone from being a scruffy pad that I shared with two mates in which I often had late-night parties, to the first home for me and my girl-friend Charlie.

With Dad and John both looking forward to retiring and with Cotswold Farm Park rare breeds centre to run as well, I needed help. Rather than employ someone, I knew that the best move was to go into partnership with Duncan, who was not only a great mate but also had all the skills needed to complement mine. Before Duncan moved to the Scilly Isles he had worked for an agricultural mortgaging corporation and got a really good grounding in business management and financial budgets, something I have to admit is not my strength. He was also happy to take on the arable side of the farm while I ran the livestock and Cotswold Farm Park. After spending a year travelling with him, living in each other's pockets, I knew we would work together well, an instinct that proved to be completely right.

He and Becky and their two children were happy to move back to the mainland, and Red came with them. He did not spend too much time on the farm (the usual problems of a dog among bitches ...) but I was surprised that when he and Bundy met, neither of them showed signs of recognising the other – or perhaps I was just not tuned in enough to see it.

By the time she met Red again, Bundy had had another two litters. Again, when I decided to breed from her, there was the problem of finding a suitable father. Wherever I went, if I met anyone who was interested in or had kelpies I discussed it, and one day I met a chap from Northumberland who agreed with me that the best way forward was to import kelpie semen from Australia and to get our bitches pregnant by artificial insemination. As a farmer I'm familiar with artificial insemination in animals, and I wasn't worried about it. We contacted an Australian breeders' association and we both bought some straws of semen (narrow PVC tubes into which semen is sucked, and then frozen in liquid nitrogen). We chose semen from a dog called Bonang Tommy, a black and tan dog from Bonang, Victoria, with a list of trialling wins to his credit. His CV said he was good at backing (jumping on the sheeps' backs) and at barking on command, and that he had a good breeding history.

The straws of semen were flown to Edinburgh, where they were stored at a laboratory that has the facilities and specialises in artificial insemination, waiting for Bundy to come into season.

When she did I was about to contact the lab to supply me with my straws and the vet to book in the insemination. In the meantime, I took all the sensible precautions, locking her in the bungalow when she was not by my side, but I underestimated the determination of a testosterone-driven dog. They can scent a bitch in season from as far away as three miles in the countryside, and one whiff and they are transformed from obedient, gentle dogs into crazed, lustful creatures who will stop at nothing to get to the object of their desire. In this case, a wooden back door was no deterrent to a black and white collie belonging to one of our neighbours: he simply gnawed his way through it until he had a hole big enough to get through to Bundy.

I was really annoyed, but I didn't rush her to the vet for a scan and an injection to end the pregnancy: I let nature take its course, crossing my fingers and hoping the marauding dog had not scored a bullseye. Of course he had, and nine weeks later Bundy gave birth to a litter of ten kelpie–collie crosses. I was relieved that it was a large litter (kelpies normally have between four and seven pups), as it meant the one single pup she had first time was not a pattern. They were delightful, Bundy coped very well with them all, and I didn't have any trouble finding homes for them. Nowadays, kelpie–collie crosses are sought after by shepherds and farmers, but back then the kelpie was still a little-known element. I let my neighbour know what I thought of his dog, the father of this litter, but the truth is that I understand how hard it is to physically restrain a dog when there is a bitch in heat in the area. It underlined to me why I prefer bitches.

As a responsible owner, I couldn't breed from Bundy again until the following year: bitches should be given at least one season rest between litters, and only irresponsible owners (and dreadful puppy farms) would put a bitch through birthing again in less than a year. When the time came, I kept her very safe until I could get her to the vet for insemination. I'm used to seeing it done with cattle, when the insemination takes place vaginally, but the vet explained that with smaller animals like dogs the best way was to anaesthetise her, cut her open and put the semen straight into her fallopian tube. She said it was more efficient, and it certainly worked.

Bundy gave birth, this time to 12 pups. A really big litter; some red, some black and two yellow ones. I hadn't seen yellow ones in Australia, and I wondered if somewhere in the past either Bundy or the father had some yellow Labrador genes. I rang Pete Dewar in Australia and he put me straight. Apparently yellow is a perfectly normal colour for kelpies, but they are not popular in Australia because their skin is pinker, more susceptible to sunburn, and their pale pads and noses can get sore in the sand and dry ground. Yellow ones, as a result, are usually not kept.

But the heat wasn't a problem in England and I so liked the look of my little yellow pups that I decided I would keep one of them. I called her Ronnie, full name Ronnie Barker, even though she was a girl.

Then I faced a dilemma. Twelve was a lot of puppies to feed, and Bundy only had the usual eight teats. How would she cope? I rang the vet and he said the best option would be to keep six or eight, and to be fair on Bundy I should get rid of some.

So I got two washing baskets, put all the puppies on the kitchen table, and started to sort them out. The ones I was keeping would go into one basket; the others, who were going to be put down, would be consigned to the other. I favour bitches, naturally, so they had a good start. Clearly the bigger ones had a better chance of survival, and so the small runty ones had to go. It was agony, as I debated their futures, changing my mind over and over again.

In the end, I had four 'rejects', all boys, and I found myself muttering my apologies to them. 'Sorry, little one, I wish I didn't have to do this.' They were tiny, blind, nuzzling each other as they squirmed around looking for their mother's teats.

It seemed so wrong, and I hated being the one who decided their fate. Although I am used to dealing with the deaths of animals, it doesn't come without senti- ment, and I had a lump in my throat as I looked at the little ones whose life was going to be over so soon.

'I can't do this to you,' I finally said to one little black fellow, lifting him up and putting him in the other basket. Then, when I looked down at the last three, I said: 'D'you know what? I'm putting you all back with your mum. It's survival of the fittest, and you are going to have to take your chances ...'

They all snuggled up to Bundy straight away, and she was delighted to have her brood back, licking them enthusiastically.

'It's up to you now, old girl,' I said to her and I went off to bed, leaving her to it. I expected that some would not survive, but at least it would not be my choice.

Why did I doubt her? Bundy was a natural mother, and when I came into the kitchen the next morning she had her pups neatly sorted into two groups, six of them feeding from her and the other six asleep. She must have been exhausted, because no sooner was one shift of pups full of milk and drowsy than the other lot were waking up and demanding food.

I told the vet what was happening, and he advised me to start feeding some of them with a pipette, as he was afraid Bundy would not have enough milk to keep this up. She hardly had time to feed herself, let alone rest. So I bought a pipette normally used for feeding kittens, and some powdered puppy milk replacer. Now I was also part of the feeding production line, on duty every four hours to top up those hungry little pups.

At this time Charlie and I were serious about each other, but she was still living and working in London, coming down to stay with me at weekends. It was hardly a lovely romantic time, as she was also roped into the feeding rota. On the vet's advice, as soon as the pups could lap from a bowl we weaned them. Every single one grew into a healthy, good-sized dog, and I was able to sell them all – apart, of course, from Ronnie Barker.

One of the pups, Sledge, went on to be a renowned sheepdog locally, and I would bump into him and his owner at various times. I shudder at the thought that he may have been one of the boys I put into the 'wrong' basket ... Another one I kept in close touch with was a little bitch called Tui, named after a kiwi beer, who went to the stockman who was working on the farm. Some of the others went to nearby homes, so I saw them from time to time. The other little yellow one went to a guy who eventually bred from her, so Bundy's line definitely lives on.

A little time afterwards it occurred to me that I was paying to store the rest of the imported semen at the laboratory in Edinburgh. I did not intend to breed from Bundy again: she'd had three litters, which I feel is enough for a bitch. Nowadays the limit imposed by the Kennel Club is four litters over a lifetime, but at the time I was breeding with Bundy it was six, which most reputable breeders felt was too many. I was never into breeding as a living: I breed from my dogs because I feel it is good for the bitches to have a litter, and because I like the idea of keeping the genes of these wonderful dogs going, for myself and to share them with others. Of course, I do sell them as it covers the cost of breeding.

I would never be able to use the semen on my next kelpie, Ronnie, as it wouldn't be sensible to get her in pup to her own father. So I put an advert with my phone number in *Farmers Weekly*: For sale, kelpie semen. Two or three evenings later the phone rang and Charlie answered it.

'It's for you. It's about the kelpie semen,' she said, handing the phone to me.

'Oh, great,' I said. In my usual way I launched into an enthusiastic description of the semen.

'It's from a really good dog in Australia, Bonang Tommy. He's won lots of trials, he's got a great breeding record. We've had a wonderful litter from the semen, twelve healthy pups ...'

The man on the other end of the phone tried to interrupt, but I babbled on. Finally, I said, 'Tell me about your bitch. What colour is she?'

He spoke flatly, finally able to get a word in edgeways: 'I don't have a dog. I don't want to breed dogs. I've been trying to tell you. I'm your Dell PC man, I'm coming to install your computer ...'

Kelpie semen / Dell PC man ... It was an easy mistake to make. But it must have sounded very bizarre to the computer expert, and he gave us a couple of odd looks when he eventually came to install the new PC.

Bundy lived to a good age of 12, but eventually, following numerous operations to have lumps removed from her mammary tissue, she became seriously ill and passed away. I grieved for her: she'd been a great mate, a good worker, all I have ever wanted in a dog.

Ronnie was a smashing little pup, and she, too, grew into a great dog. She was not quite as good as her mother when it came to working the sheep, but handy enough, and a good companion. She and I bonded well, and I still feel emotional when I remember that we nearly lost her when she was two years old.

Ronnie went to the vet for her annual injections, and in retrospect it's clear she had an infection and was running a temperature at the time. The injections then caused a complete breakdown of her immune system: Vaccine Induced Autoimmune Disease is recognised by vets, with the symptoms being triggered or exacerbated by the vaccines. It happened very quickly after her vaccination and she went into a major decline the following day.

Our vet referred her immediately to the Bristol School of Veterinary Science, where they have state-of-the-art facilities and all the most up-to-date treatments. They had seen cases like hers before, but I was told it was rare. I was also warned that her survival was touch and go, and it was with a very heavy heart that I drove back home after leaving her there. She looked so weak and helpless. She spent two weeks there, on steroids, and all the time I was expecting the phone to ring with bad news. The house felt so empty without her.

At last, thank goodness, I was able to bring her home. She was skin and bone; she'd lost all her weight and muscle tone. I had to tempt her to eat, and I tried different foods: cooked chicken, beef mince, eggs and milk, rice, anything of which I could to get her to take more than a mouthful or two. It was a slow, steady recovery, and I very gradually weaned her off steroids, reducing the dose incrementally.

It was while we had Ronnie that Charlie and I had our two children, Ella and Alfie. Alfie, in particular, bonded with Ronnie; they were like two little mates. I loved seeing Alfie toddling around the farmyard with his faithful yellow shadow by his side. Ronnie, in the tradition of my dogs, also slept in the loo, and like Bundy she was half house dog and half farm dog; a pet but one who worked. I don't remember teaching either of them to be house-trained – they were both naturally clean and it happened without much effort on my part.

Ronnie lived until she was ten, but she had a sad ending. She was coughing and wheezing, and was given a course of antibiotics by the vet. Then, to my dismay, she started passing blood, so I took her to the vet where an X-ray showed she had swallowed a needle which was causing internal bleeding. The vet wanted to operate immediately, but admitted there was no guarantee that the needle would be located.

I was reluctant to rush her into having a general anaesthetic and so decided to get a second opinion from the senior vet, who I knew well. He ordered a scan which included her chest and it revealed a large tumour, which was obviously the reason for her breathing problems. He told me that there was really no hope: she had four or five months left at the most, and that she would be increasingly uncomfortable and in pain. I didn't vacillate. It was a very tough decision, but I knew it was the right one: I asked him to put her down. As with every dog I have had put down, the procedure is simple and they die painlessly. I held her in my arms, muttering goodbyes to a faithful, kind, hard-working dog, everything any owner could ask for. Then I carefully drove her back to the farm, for burial among all those other wonderful dogs at Buttington Clump. I cherish the fact that the dogs are buried on the farm: it feels right. This was their home in life and it is where they remain.

Alfie, who was four at the time, was very upset, and he really missed her. But farm children learn the cycle of life early, seeing animals breed, and then, eventually, seeing them die. For Alfie it was his first experience of grieving for a dog to whom he was very close, and I felt for him. But I also knew it is something we all have to learn to accept. I loved Ronnie, and missed her cheerful little snout pushing its way into my hand. But she had a comfortable end, and the alternative was not good.

CHAPTER 5

Three Wonderful Dogs

Six months after I bought Bundy I acquired another sheepdog, this time a traditional border collie. I have now had a succession of border collies, but that doesn't mean I have turned my back on kelpies. One day, when I am doing less television work and have more time on the farm, I'd like to have another of those wonderful dogs. Our livestock manager has a kelpie–collie cross, which is another great option, with some shepherds classing them as the best of both breeds.

I bought Fenn from a great friend of mine, Dick Roper, who manages a farm not far from mine. He's an acclaimed sheepdog trialler, winning the *Countryfile* One Man and His Dog competition for England in 2016. The competition involves teams of a senior handler and a junior handler from Scotland, Wales, Ireland and England, and for many years has been a huge TV hit, now having its own slot on *Countryfile*.

I'm going to describe Dick as the doyen of sheepdog trainers, because he'll enjoy the joke. When he first heard the word 'doyen' he went home and looked it up in the dictionary, to find it means 'outstanding in his field'. So he reckons it is a description that fits him (and all shepherds) because he spends his days out, standing in a field.

'Outstanding' is a good description of him, especially as he won the championship despite having lost the sight in one of his eyes, which is a real handicap in trialling. But he's a cheerful person whose attitude to life is, 'Yes, I'm sad to have lost the sight of an eye, but on the other hand, at least it's not a red wine allergy ...'

I first met Dick when I joined Dad and Uncle John on the farm and I went on a sheepdog training course organised by the Agricultural Training Board. I took Bundy, and that was the occasion when Dick made his unforgettable judgment on kelpies, something along the lines of: 'Sell her and get yourself a border collie ...' He stands by that opinion.

'Collies are accurate in the way they work. They stare at anything that is moving, which is why puppies who live on a farm will chase vans and bikes before they get near to sheep. They don't run around like headless chickens, they run with purpose and balance, and that's what makes them so good at their job. The amount of "eye" they have governs how close they can work the sheep, how they can make the sheep go in the direction they want.' (As I've explained, eye is the ability of a dog to fix its stare on a moving object, essential when working sheep at a high level.)

I'm afraid Bundy had no eye; she was scatty. She wanted to work, but she never had an accurate point of balance. She was just as happy chasing the sheep away as rounding them up and bringing them to you, but with no style or accuracy.

'And that's the difference between collies and nearly all other types of working dogs. They have eye, and they'll work anything moving – they'll work the water coming out of a hose pipe,' said Dick.

Clearly, I defer to Dick in all things to do with collies. But I think he was a bit harsh on poor Bundy: she wasn't great by his standards out in the paddock, but she was a wonderful yard dog. Dick particularly loves border collies, but, despite his criticisms of kelpies, he recognises the abilities of other strains of collies. Bearded collies have less eye, but are still very good with sheep. One of our assistant stockmen bred beardies and he handled sheep well with them, but they would never reach trialling standard. They are lovely strong dogs, though, which is sometimes a great advantage.

Welsh collies have no eye, but they can still work sheep and are more versatile because they are also good at moving cattle. Dick admits he was very impressed when he was judging trialling in Brazil and he found the same dogs being used in the sheep classes and the cattle classes.

'It was very exciting watching them moving half-broken Aberdeen Angus steers around, and then seeing them working a flock of sheep. But you cannot use a good border, with real "sticky eye", with cattle because they are too stationary and will get kicked or trodden on, so you need a free-flowing dog like a Welsh collie.'

Dick has trained all sorts of dogs: Labradors, spaniels, German shepherd dogs among others. He believes that collies have brains that are wired differently, almost completely controlled by their eyes.

'The whole thought process of a collie is different. Other breeds are great at other tasks, but for working a flock of sheep, give me a collie every time. There's something about the German shepherds that makes me think they have a bit of collie in their breeding, but not enough ...'

Dick is often asked to help out with dogs that are not behaving well, and he says the first thing to consider is their circumstances. I know, because I've seen it myself several times, that the very best of dogs can be ruined by owners who don't understand the animal and it becomes unruly and even nips people. Dick cites the example of a serviceman based at a nearby RAF station who was worried about the behaviour of his collie.

'It never takes its eyes off the budgie,' Dick was told. The owner and his wife had a new baby, and they were worried that the collie now seemed to be watching the baby with the same fervent attention as it focussed on the budgie.

'I told them that the dog was 99 per cent guaranteed to be the best protector their baby could ever have, but there was a 1 per cent chance it would nip, especially if it was bottled up all day without enough exercise or mental stimulation. They gave the dog to me and I rehomed him with a shepherd who found him to be a really great worker.'

One reason for the problem of collies going to the wrong homes, which I've talked about, is that people see Dick and all the other great sheepdog trainers on television, they read that collies are so intelligent, and they think they would like to own one, without any consideration of what they can offer the dog. Some collies thrive as pets, particularly if they are taken to agility classes, especially flyball competitions. Flyball is a sport where competing teams of dogs race across hurdles, then release a tennis ball which they have to carry back before the next dog in the relay team can set off. It's fun to watch – they have competitions at Crufts – but it is also stimulating enough to keep a collie's brain and limbs busy. But so many get nothing more than a half-hour walk in the park and spend the rest of their day confined inside.

So it is from Dick that I have learned most of my sheepdog training – and unlearned the bad habits I developed growing up!

When he expressed his disdain for Bundy, I was, at first, determined to defy him, and prove that I could train Bundy to round up sheep the way I wanted her to do it. I still had the image of Bob, the kelpie in Australia, in my mind. But after a while I realised that my best plan was for Bundy to work the sheep in the pens and to get another dog for out in the fields, because rounding up sheep was not her greatest talent. Dick, I was forced to admit, was right.

I rang him up and he told me of a litter of puppies, bred from one of his own trialling dogs and a mother who was kept as a pet. The sire was Dick's dog Cap, who was a national champion sheepdog four times, so I was keen to see the puppies. We looked at the litter together and Dick helped me choose the right one for me. His rule of thumb for choosing a good pup is to look for a brave and curious one, with good 'eye'. Dick likes to get a broom and see which ones in the litter chase it as he moves it around, showing that they have a natural inbred herding instinct and a fascination with anything in motion. He also drops an empty metal feeding dish, making a loud clatter. Any dog that doesn't run away may well be deaf or stupid, so he ignores that one. Then he looks for the pups who come back to the source of the noise quite quickly, with curiosity, not too frightened but naturally wary.

I knelt down on the floor with the puppies. There were two bitches I liked, but one of them came up to me, taking more interest in me than the others, jumping to try and get on my knees. As Dick says:

'A puppy chooses you, not the other way round. It's an old adage, but it's true: a puppy will choose the right owner if it has the chance. You can't hide your character from a dog, they can judge you in a few seconds. It's part of their history, from when they lived in packs and had to understand the hierarchy very rapidly. They learn, as puppies, which ones to get on with, which to back off from, which to scrap with. You rarely see a major fight in a pack, because they each understand their position. And that's how they quickly judge humans, knowing instinctively who they will get on with.

'It's because they make instant judgments that they are also good guard dogs, sensing which human beings are friends and which are foes.'

Predictably, like everything people like Dick and me know instinctively, there has now been a university study to confirm it: scientists in Japan have demonstrated that dogs are good at working out who their masters' friends are, and similarly they remember anyone who has not shown kindness to their owner. The scientists' conclusion is the same as Dick's, that dogs are very quick to sort out who is who in a pack, and will be ready to protect the animals (or people) who look after them. It demonstrates, they concluded, that dogs show sophisticated intelligence and make use of their observations 'to reach a decision about which individuals to interact with or to avoid'.

As Dick says: 'Puppies will go to a person they like, automatically, and a confident dog will go to a confident person. A subservient puppy can still flourish, but will be much happier with a gentler owner.'

If Dick is interested in a litter, he tries wherever possible to make his choice when the pups are seven weeks old, which he believes is the right time to assess their characters.

'There are lots of odd myths around choosing a sheepdog, but one that is true is that at seven weeks a dog's eventual character is established. They may go through a mad teenage period between seven months and up to 12 or 14 months, but then they will revert to the personality they had at seven weeks.

'Many police forces also make their selection from litters at seven weeks, choosing the dogs best suited to police work and rehoming the ones whose personalities don't measure up to the criteria they need. At one time, far more puppies went forward for training only to fail at a later date, which was expensive. By choosing well at seven weeks the failure rate is cut back, and the other puppies go on to work that suits them better, perhaps security work, or simply to be pets.'

Dick also judges pups by the position of their tails. He doesn't like dogs who keep their tails up – another strike against Bundy, who always worked with her tail up.

'In a collie if the tail is up it is a sign that they are tense, under pressure, or even that they are simply thick. I like a tidy tail. If it is rammed under their body that is just as bad, as it means they are wound up or scared. What I look for in a border collie is a nice relaxed tail, because that signals a relaxed dog. Other signs of tension are when they eat sheep droppings, or when they yawn.'

The little pup I chose was beautifully marked, even at ten weeks old, which was when I saw her for the first time. She was adorable and seemed to like me too, and I was very happy to take her home with me. Of course the first thing you need to do when you have a new puppy is choose a name. With a dog I am a strong believer that it needs to be something short and snappy, ideally with one syllable. That's why many sheepdogs are called names like Fly, Pat, Meg or Ben, so that they can be said quickly and clearly with no chance of mis-understanding. For my little puppy I wanted something a little bit different to the ordinary and went for the name Fenn.

It didn't take Bundy long to accept her, which was probably easier because Fenn was kept outside in a kennel, as working sheepdogs are, and Bundy slept in the loo. At first Fenn had a lamp in there to keep her warm. Our kennels are large, with a comfortable bed for the dogs. Working sheepdogs housetrain themselves very quickly: a young pup will mess in its kennel but it soon learns to keep its own home clean.

Fenn was a beautiful black and white bitch. If you asked a child to draw a sheepdog, the result would be Fenn. She looked exactly the way everyone thinks a sheepdog should look, and her behaviour didn't let the side down, either.

The first thing any dog of any breed needs to learn is its own name, and to come to its owner. It needs to come not in answer to a polite request, but on command, obeying an order. If it doesn't come at once, don't shout at it or punish it. You can do this with a disobedient older dog, but a puppy has to feel that being by your feet is the safest and best place. Teaching a dog to come to you is the most essential, but also one of the hardest, lessons. When the dog obeys, even if not straightaway, it should be rewarded with a stroke and some words of approval. The dog will know from the tone of your voice that you are pleased with him. Dick's advice is to ration stroking and fussing over a dog, so that when you do it really knows that it has earned your praise. Much harder said than done! I'm nowhere near as strict, and I'm happy to stroke and fondle the ears of my sheepdogs on greeting them every morning. I treat them a bit like when you see a pack of wolves on a natural history programme, when they wake in the morning and they all fuss around one another, whimpering, wagging their tails and saying hello. This is all over in a matter of minutes and then it is off for the hunt. I do the same with my dogs, a lot of fuss to say good morning and then it is off to work.

The importance of having control of your dog and being able to get it to come or stop on a sharp command is obviously fundamental. Every parent knows that a child who doesn't obey first time can end up in danger, touching something hot or walking into a road. So it's something that every dog owner, even if the dog is a pet who will never work, needs to be able to do.

Fenn was easy to train. At six months old she met the sheep for the first time, and she instantly took to them and the job. I knew she would: I'd seen her trying to round up the chickens in the yard. It always amazes me how the instinct is there in sheepdogs, thanks to selective breeding down the centuries. The herding instinct is part of natural hunting behaviour, but these dogs have learnt not to follow through and kill their prey, but to try and please their owners by bringing the prey, in this case sheep, to them.

If a dog is really difficult to teach to come (or any other behaviour problem) Dick told me his method of bringing it into line: 'Dogs are pack animals, and even if you only have one dog it feels part of a pack with you. So the worst thing that can happen is to be excluded from the pack. You do this by ignoring them, making it clear you don't want anything to do with them. If you are in a field, simply walk away and shut the gate. When the dog attempts to follow you, ignore it, leave it there. If you speak to them at all, tell it to clear off. It sounds harsh, but you'll find that it quickly picks up on the fact that it has to come when it is called.'

Of course, Dick is training sheepdogs, and it is much easier to enforce rules when the dog lives outside, which explains why most working sheepdogs are kennelled (plus the fact that they are often covered in mud and muck). The same rules apply to family pets, although it is much harder to enforce them within a family. I may be trying to ignore the puppy, but that doesn't mean that Charlie, Ella and Alfie will ignore her ... puppies get mixed messages, especially if they are living inside with several family members.

I am a strong believer that the family should decide what the rules are for the dog in the house and everybody should make their best efforts at sticking to them. At home we don't allow the dog to have titbits from the table as this leads to begging when you are trying to eat, which drives me mad. Our dogs are never allowed upstairs, so even one paw on the bottom step is out of bounds. Many people let their dogs upstairs, even sleeping on their beds, but when you live in a muddy farmyard it really doesn't work. I also think that a dog should have its own bed and as it views you as the alpha male/female, it does not have the right to sleep on yours. A bit of dog psychology, which I am sure is right. For a similar reason, our dogs aren't allowed on the furniture. It is always important to scold a dog at the moment it breaks the rules so that it can identify with what it has done wrong. We all use the same commands so there is no confusion, and simply say the word 'No'.

Trialling dogs like Dick's, of course, have to learn so much more even than a working dog on a farm, like Fenn, and the amount of time given over to training them has to be so much greater. I never took up trialling when I was younger. Partly because trials take place at weekends, and, back then, weekends were for playing rugby ...!

Also, if I am honest, I don't think I would ever have been good enough. But I love watching sheepdog trials, and I'm full of admiration for the experts like Dick, just as I'm full of admiration for hill shepherds who control

My sister Libby with Chemmers, the first dog in my life, and her puppies

Nita was the only dog allowed upstairs – Mum and Dad turned a blind eye

My kelpie, Bundy

Red, Bundy's first pup

Grown up Red enjoying life on Bryher, where he lived with my friend Duncan and his family

Bundy was a natural mother, rearing this huge litter

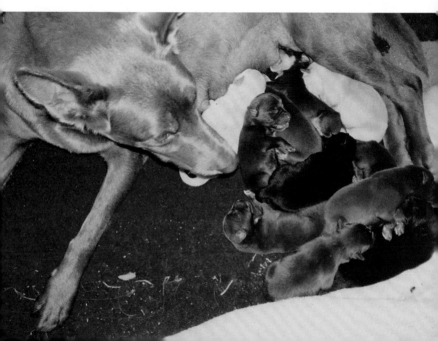

Fen, a great sheepdog
and a great companion

Ella with a loving guardian, Fen

Little together: Ella with
one of Fen's puppies

Ronnie Barker, my lovely kelpie

'The cold doesn't worry us, we've got fur coats.' Maud and Pearl love romping in the snow

Two lovely mates, Maud and Pearl

A boy's best friend: Alfie with Ronnie

Dolly as a pup

On top of the world: Me, Alfie, Dolly and Boo

a dog in a howling gale from one and a half miles away. It's awe inspiring to watch them.

I started training Fenn with the sheep by walking her along the edge of the field and then taking her into the corner with a small group of sheep (I used Bundy to round them up). Then, because her instinct was to be on the other side of the sheep, I made her sit before giving her the command to go to the right of the sheep – 'Away'. When she mastered it we went to another corner to learn the 'left' command – 'come by'.

We practised for 15 to 20 minutes every morning and every evening. I learnt from Dick that if she got it wrong the worst thing I could do was to show anger. I had to walk away, put the dog back in the kennel, let my steam out, have a cup of tea then go back later. Different dogs take different amounts of time: sometimes weeks, sometimes months. Fenn was very good, and she learnt the voice commands and whistles within days.

After mastering right and left, I moved the training to the middle of the field, where I erected a circular pen out of hurdles and stakes. (It's interesting that dogs, like humans, have a natural preference for left or right. They'll obey the commands, but if simply sent out to round up some sheep they'll tend to choose their own favoured way.) I used Bundy to round up some sheep and pen them, and then I walked around the pen with Fenn. I didn't let Fenn run with Bundy all the time, although that is a method used by some farmers and shepherds. There's always the risk that the puppy will learn bad habits from the older dog and will end up watching the other dog instead of listening to you and watching the sheep. And besides, Bundy wasn't the best model for the kind of work I wanted Fenn to do.

I took Fenn back to Dick after I had been training her for a few months to refine some of my techniques and sort out a particular problem I had. I probably started working her with sheep too soon, before I had perfected a strong 'stop' command with her. Dick stresses that you need to be able to stop your dog before it works with sheep 'otherwise you end up chasing behind it, ranting and raving, in a bad temper, and the dog recognises your temper but it doesn't understand what you want it to do.'

Dick sometimes introduces a puppy to sheep before he teaches 'stop', but he does it in an enclosed space with a few sheep, so that they cannot scatter and run away. He taught me that when you have a particular problem with a dog, as I did, you go right back to basics, and start teaching 'stop' in the yard, until she has it.

'Do it at five yards away, fifty yards, a hundred yards, and bring it back if it doesn't obey. You are going to have to control your dog from a long distance away, so you need to be sure and confident in what you are doing. A dog quickly senses when you are not confident.'

If you ask Dick how he knows he can stop his dog at a thousand yards distance he simply says: 'Because I know it's going to stop and therefore it will stop.' Confidence is the key.

A general tip that Dick gave me about training dogs, and which I always remember, is never to overdo it.

'Sometimes a dog seems to have mastered a command, then it loses the plot and goes backwards. My advice is to stop training for a few days,' he says. 'Dogs, especially those being trained at a high level, sometimes need a bit of thinking time to absorb what they've learnt. If you are trying to teach too much at once, it can all go to pieces.' It helps having their own kennel, their own space, in which to reflect and not be distracted by everything going on in a busy house full of people.

Dick says the warning sign that a dog is worried and overstretched by training is that it will begin to act out of character, perhaps chasing its tail, carrying things in its mouth, eating sheep poo. Obviously, lots of dogs carry sticks all the time; it is only a sign of stress if it is outside their normal behaviour.

Fenn developed into a really useful working dog and was happy to work for our stockman, John King, as well as for me. John had his own border collie, and they worked well together. This was really important for me, because although the idea of 'one man and his dog' is very appealing, on a working farm a dog should respond to other masters. This doesn't mean she wasn't first and foremost my dog, but I could happily go away and leave John to it, knowing she would do everything he wanted her to do.

When I have a good dog like Fenn, it is natural for me to want to breed from her, to keep her genes going. I arranged for her to be served by one of Dick's dogs, and she had a litter of six puppies.

It's easy to know when a bitch is ready to conceive: it happens three or four days after they finish menstruating. They start to get overexcited. Generally, the bitch is taken to the dog, and usually they have a bit of fun running around together. When he eventually mounts her they get 'dog tied', because he swells inside her and for up to about 20 minutes they are tied together, until he deflates and it's all over. Often it's wise to follow up with a second visit to the dog a couple of days later, just to be sure.

The owner of the bitch pays for the service, either in money or by giving the owner of the dog the pick of the litter. Our sheepdogs have their litters in the stables and it is really fantastic fun: there's nothing better than seeing those adorable little bundles of fur finding their way about, playing roly-poly with each other. It's especially nice if a litter is born in spring, because they will be with their mother for ten to twelve weeks and if the weather is good they can have more freedom running around in the garden and exploring.

We kept one of Fenn's pups, another little black and white bitch called Maud. Charlie and I chose the name for no particular reason except that we both liked it. Maud worked out very well, but I didn't put as much time into her training as I did with her mother, so she never quite lived up to Fenn's standards.

Fenn lived a long and active life, but eventually, when she was really old and in semi-retirement from work, her back legs gave out. I took her to the vet who told me her spine had prolapsed, and there was nothing we could do. I made the decision there and then, and he put her down. I took her body back for the usual burial at Buttington Clump, driving with tears filling my eyes. I was very sad to say goodbye to her, but I knew her time had come and she had lived a great life, doing what she loved best. If I can, I always bring the vet to the farm to put down an animal so that they feel at home, away from the alien smells of the surgery and in familiar surroundings with a familiar, loving hand to hold them. It's hard to suppress tears, but I never let them flow until the dog is dead: I never want to unnerve them in those last few minutes by showing my own sadness.

With Fenn gone, Maud became my top dog and she was proving really useful. I had started working for *Countryfile* but was still very busy with the livestock on the farm, and my loyal, hardworking sheepdog was invaluable. During foot and mouth when we couldn't have any cloven-footed animals on Cotswold Farm Park – i.e. sheep, cows, pigs or goats – I started to give sheepdog demonstrations using ducks and taking them around a course to entertain the public. Maud was brilliant at this and the skill came into its own for

Countryfile, as you will read in Chapter Seven, Other Kinds of Sheepdog.

With Maud doing so well I was keen to breed from her, too. I took her to a friend of Dick Roper's and she successfully conceived and gave birth to a lovely litter of six puppies: three bitches and three dogs. We chose one bitch that we called Pearl, John our stockman had another and the rest were sold to local farms.

When Pearl was still quite young, about a year old, I made a stupid mistake that I will never make again. I allowed Pearl to ride on the back of the quad bike with her mother, Maud. She was too young, and I should have been more sensible and only had one dog on the bike. As I went round a corner, Maud slipped and Pearl fell off the side going straight under the wheel of the mobile handling system I was towing. Thankfully she wasn't killed but her leg was badly damaged. It is not uncommon to hear about dogs getting run over on farms, usually due to the farmers rushing around in their very busy lives. Our daughter Ella was particularly close to Pearl and I knew she would be devastated if she couldn't be saved, so we invested quite a lot of money having the vet pin her leg back together with a Meccano-like structure. I was under strict instructions for her to be rested in her kennel, with only gentle exercise on a lead. The accident occurred just at the peak of her training, and the long layoff, coupled with what turned out to be a permanent limp, meant she was only ever half trained – a useful dog to have as an extra but I rarely used her on her own, or for anything difficult. She has lived to a ripe old age, over 13, quite deaf and a little bit stiff, but still game for pottering around the farmyard. She sleeps in the stable and is always there, ready for a walk, when Charlie takes our family dogs out.

Maud also lived a long life, reaching 13, which is above the 12-year average lifespan of a border collie. She spent all those years as my constant companion in the field, and it is hard to think of a better life for a dog bred to love working.

CHAPTER 6

Finding Peg

With Maud gone and Pearl becoming older, slower and more deaf, it became apparent that I really needed a fit, young replacement. So I went in search of a new border collie. I knew that my requirements were going to be tough to satisfy. As I was now away from home quite regularly working on *Countryfile* I knew I would not have time to train a puppy, which would be my usual method of taking on a new dog, and is something I have always enjoyed in the past. I was looking for a middle-aged bitch – so about five or six years old – who was well trained, but who would also work for other members of my team when I was away. As we run Cotswold Farm Park and have lots of visitors, it was very important that she would be kind natured, good with children and definitely didn't nip like old Carlo. I also wanted to be able to take her away filming with me when the opportunity arose, so I wanted a dog that was happy to travel and stay away overnight, and who would not be fazed by a variety of different situations. Yes, I know, this was a big ask.

The first time I saw Peg was in photographs and I have to say she was quite an unusually marked border collie, and I was unsure about her. But if you are a working farmer like me, you don't judge a sheepdog on its looks, and when I met her, I realised what a beautiful dog she is.

Peg was a highly trained, successful trialling dog whose life had been overtaken by tragedy. Her owner, a dedicated sheepdog trialler called Steve Barry, had died of a sudden, unexpected heart attack while he was out walking his dogs. He was living alone and nobody in his family wanted to take on a sheepdog, so a very good friend of Steve's, Meryl Fox, became temporary custodian of his two dogs, a puppy and a trained trialling bitch, Peg, who was just beginning to win prizes. Meryl set about finding permanent homes for them.

This was in 2014, and at roughly the same time, I asked my great friend and the expert I always turn to, Dick Roper, if he knew of any sheepdogs that matched my difficult requirements. I knew it was a long shot, as fully trained dogs rarely come up for sale – if they are good the farmer or shepherd wants to keep them, and if they are getting rid of them there may well be a problem with them.

Of course, top breeders do sell trained dogs, and at the sheepdog auctions really good dogs can command high prices. The record is just under £15,000, but that's exceptional, with a good dog costing £2,000–£3,000. I wasn't in the market at those kind of prices and, besides, I wanted a working dog to help on my farm, not a top trialling dog. Although that's exactly what I now have in Peg ...

Dick looked at a couple of collies for me but felt they weren't right. Then he heard about the plight of Peg. He suggested we might be a perfect match, but first of all I had to be carefully vetted by Meryl. She was very keen to make sure that Peg went to a really good home, and so she wanted to see me with Peg, to see how we reacted to each other. She brought Peg to the farm to meet me, and we immediately hit it off. There was something in the set of her head, the intelligent, inquisitive eyes and the good nature that brought her straight up to me, even though I was a stranger. Dogs, as I have said, have a sense that tells them which human beings are going to be their friends and which to be wary about: I always find when I'm visiting someone's house that their dog will make a beeline for me and settle down pressed against my leg. But there was something a bit extra about Peg, as if she recognised a kindred spirit in me. I knew without hesitation that I wanted her, and I crossed my fingers that Meryl, who took the vetting process very seriously, would think I was a suitable new owner for her.

With Meryl's agreement, and after a two-week probation, I bought Peg and she came to live at Bemborough. She and Steve had been very close; apparently she sat on his lap while he was driving his quad bike. She would also run towards him and then jump up into his arms for a cuddle when he asked her to. When she lived with Meryl she slept inside the house, but as she is a working dog I wanted to kennel her outside. So I bought a new, roomy kennel from Timberbuild and installed it by the farm back door, so that I could let her out and spend time with her with ease. The right kennel is very important: it needs to have a good-size run to give plenty of fresh air and a warm, dry area to sleep in at night. At the end of Peg's kennel there is an insulated boxed area where she can curl up in the straw, snug against frosty nights. On a hot summer's day she can sit on the top of it, in the shade, to keep cool.

I spent quite a bit of time for the first few days sitting with her in her kennel, letting her build confidence and trust in me. I was aware that she'd been through major changes in her life, losing Steve and then settling with Meryl before coming to me, so I gave her extra attention to help her settle in.

She's now very happy in her kennel – collies love having their own space. She also likes to wander into our kitchen, which most sheepdogs don't do, but which she was allowed to do when she lived with Steve and so we let her continue (there's an old saying that when a sheepdog is brought into the house to lie in front of the fire, it knows its days are numbered). She gets on with our house dogs, and the kids and Charlie love her.

There was only one big problem with Peg when she first arrived. Every sheepdog is trained to the voice commands and whistles of its owner, and although there are some standard ones, with perhaps a few variations on each, the whistles in particular are very individual. Although plenty of people had seen Steve running Peg at trials, there wasn't any video of him and nobody could be exactly sure of Steve's whistles and commands. Steve was a very good whistler, with his fingers not a metal whistle, and I'm OK at whistling, but I'm not in his league. As for voice commands, Steve had a loud, booming Welsh voice, and I admit I have tried to imitate it when I'm out with her in a field far away from anyone hearing me ...

Meryl had discovered how to make Peg go left, right and stop, but she wasn't performing as well as she could, because she clearly was a bit hazy about the commands. We tried out the standard ones, with mixed success.

OK, so here are the basics. Stop, walk-on, left and right. For stop you can use the verbal command 'sit' or 'lie down' or 'down', or even 'stop'. After a few goes, I discovered 'lie down' was what she reacted to best and for the whistle a straight blast and she would drop to the ground. For walk-on she responded well to what I have used with my other dogs; simply saying 'on' or two short, sharp whistles. Run to the left was the standard 'come by'. My other dogs just go on 'by'. Right is usually 'away', and an extra command when you want to pick up some sheep that have been left behind is 'look back'. These were my usual verbal commands, and Peg generally reacted well to them.

But the trouble is, when a dog is working at the far side of a field and there's a wind blowing, you need the whistle command because they won't hear you shouting. With my sheepdogs I've trained from puppyhood, like Fenn, Maud and Pearl, I have simply made up my own whistles, and all three worked to the same ones. But these improvised whistles didn't work with Peg.

Apparently Steve had a very strong whistle, using his teeth rather than the plastic mouth whistle that many shepherds use. I can whistle with my mouth but my whistle is not that strong. What I had to do was try and work out the whistles that Peg understood for 'come by' and 'away'. Despite standing in the field with her trying various different pitches and tones, I wasn't really getting anywhere.

So Meryl and I took Peg to see Dick.

Dick whistles brilliantly with his mouth, like Steve did. He claims it is due to his slightly crooked front tooth that got knocked about when he played rugby. Dick experimented with various whistles until he found the ones that worked for her. They are fairly standard whistles, although not ones that Dick himself normally uses. As soon as she heard whistles she recognised, you could almost see her relief, and she was very keen to get out in the field, working the sheep.

When Dick had her running well, I took out my phone and recorded him whistling. He and Meryl thought it was very funny that it took me a few minutes to work out how to use my phone to record: they teased me that, as I make TV programmes, I really ought to understand the technology better. But in the end I had a good recording, which I played to myself in the car and practised as I was driving for several weeks until I knew them. Duncan, my business partner, thought it was really bizarre when he rang me one day and after we finished chatting I somehow left the phone line open, and all he could hear at the other end was me whistling the commands ...

I got there in the end but it hasn't been easy. Under pressure, when something dramatic is happening with the sheep, I sometimes automatically revert to the whistles I used for the other dogs. For instance, to send them right my usual whistle is low and up, with a tail, but for Peg it has to be low and high. So in a crisis I make matters worse by giving a whistle she doesn't understand.

Dick's advice to me, and the problems of taking on a ready-trained dog, made a good feature for *Countryfile*, and we filmed Dick putting me though my paces with Peg. He told me off for gesticulating so much: sheep-dogs should not be looking at the shepherd, but using their ear to hear the commands. So me flapping my arms about was at best pointless, and at worst a distraction. I'm a person who naturally uses my arms when I am talking, and I have also been taught to use my arms to give commands to gundogs. So it went against nature for me to stick my hands in my pockets while controlling Peg, but that's what Dick made me do.

Luckily for me, my dogs have always obeyed the voice and whistle commands and taken no notice of my arms. But there's a danger that a dog can become 'hand trained' rather than voice trained. Dick had one young lad who came to him for training and every time he told the dog what to do, the dog did a full pirouette before setting off. Dick realised that he was taking no notice of the voice command and was watching for the hand signal. When Dick told the lad to put his hands in his pockets the dog could not perform at all. As he was a mature dog, it was probably too late to retrain him, and he worked well enough if he got a clear hand signal. But that limits the distance at which he could work, as he always had to have a clear sight of his master, and meant there was inevitably a delay while he twizzled round, plus he wouldn't be able to work for anyone else.

Dick also taught me that the strength of my whistle or my voice command is another way of communicating with the dog. A strong command or whistle means 'Do it now, fast'. A softer one means 'Let it happen more moderately'. For example, the 'stop' command can change from a flat out 'drop down NOW' to 'slow down, canter, trot, then down'. I had been struggling to get Peg to go down quickly, and that was because my command was too weak.

I haven't got these new whistles off to perfection: sometimes my right hand whistle makes Peg look back over her shoulder, as if to make sure of what I meant. She doesn't ping off immediately, as she would have to in trialling, but that's not what I'm trying to achieve, and we are working well enough together.

Dick can fine tune the commands he uses with his own dogs. For instance, if the dog is going wide he can put an accent into his whistle which tells it to go wider. He has so many little additions, and seeing him work his dogs is like watching a masterclass, which is why he's the best in the country.

You need a very good, brainy dog to be able to work at that level. It's also a question of personality. A schoolboy who hates exams will go into a funk in the exam room and fail the exam even though he has done all the revision and knows all the answers. In the same way, some dogs are sensitive and can't cope with too many commands. They have done all the training, know all the commands, but they will only ever be good working dogs, not top level trial dogs, because they can't cope with working in different environments and with strange sheep. Like the rest of us, dogs have their limits. Dick knows dogs that have been brilliant in training, learnt all the commands well, have the speed, the fitness and everything a great trialling dog needs, but their temperament is just not quite right, and they blow up under pressure.

'Another dog will seem at first to be a very basic sort of character, but he'll train and train and turn out to be a top dog. I'm always wary of dogs who are too brilliant too soon,' he says. 'There's a fine line between brilliance and madness in a collie.'

I know that Peg is good enough to get back to trialling, which she did with her first owner Steve. If she spent three or four weeks with Dick she'd be up to that standard again; she's a brilliant dog. But I'm not that skilful and my understanding of dog psychology is not at that level. I recognise my own abilities and limitations. I was a good rugby player and always managed to get into the first team for the local clubs wherever I was in the country, but at the same time I always knew I was not international standard. It's the same with dog training: I know my limits, and I also know what I want and need my dogs to do.

Peg is very happy working on the farm. She gets enough stimulation and satisfaction from what she has to do, and she loves doing it. If there is a day when no work with the sheep is needed, she'll happily go out for a walk with Charlie and the other dogs. She's got her own eccentric little habit: she loves jumping into the water trough. She has a very thick coat, and she clearly loves cooling down in the water, but she'll do it even on a day when the weather is bitterly cold, and you would think a soggy wet coat is the last thing you'd want. If there isn't a water trough around, she'll lie down in a puddle, and when there's ice on the ground she pulls herself along on her tummy, like a seal. She clearly doesn't feel the cold at all, but you need to stand clear when she leaps out of the trough, if you don't want an icy cold shower when she shakes herself.

Many of the jobs for a dog on a farm like ours are routine, rounding up the ewes and their lambs, bringing them to me. But Peg is well up to doing anything out of the ordinary, and when she's working, the sheep know who's in command. It's the slightly unusual tasks that test a working dog, and often result in the shepherd shouting 'Damned dog, stupid sheep!'

When you are working a sheepdog you have to be in the dog's head, but also in the head of the sheep. You have to be able to look at a sheep and understand why she has stopped. Is she ill? Is she being awkward? Or is there an obstacle she doesn't like, like a puddle of water? Water will always stop sheep. If there is a puddle at a gateway they won't go through, or an obstacle they won't go past, or you are trying to load them into a lorry when they don't want to go, the best way to deal with it is catch one and pull it in front of the rest of the flock and they will usually follow. Shepherds have always found it very useful that they follow each other – just like sheep in fact ...

Dad always said: 'A farmer who calls a sheep stupid is a farmer who has been outwitted by a sheep.' Sheep are definitely not brainless, and they have their own personalities. As a dog handler, I have to be aware which sheep is the leader, which one is likely to break away. A really good collie shares the ability to suss out where the problems are without help, but the shepherd should never rely solely on the dog, instead anticipating the problem and giving the right command.

I was lucky enough to go to Australia with *Countryfile*, and I was asked to help round up some cattle on horse-back, which isn't my favourite mode of transport, and I was quite nervous about the prospect. I don't regard myself as a good rider and this horse was a spirited animal, so I wasn't completely confident. The farmer agreed to take the horse round the cattle to 'knock the sting out of her', as he put it. He galloped flat out downhill with the kelpies barking, cracking his whip, and the noise was enough to keep the herd of cattle running in front of him, with dust everywhere. It was an amazing sight, like something out of the movies. I always fancied being a cowboy as a child and now was my chance. The farmer pulled the horse up next to me, jumped off and said: 'Right, it's your turn.'

I replied: 'Crikey, what if she bolts under me?'

He said, 'Just head for the fence and hopefully she'll stop.'

The fence was huge and topped with barbed wire, which didn't make me feel any happier ...

I managed reasonably well and the horse was surprisingly well behaved. As we moved the cattle to the corner of the field, trying to get them into the pens, I could see that one of the calves was going to make a break for it. I could tell from the way she was moving and looking to the side, which is a sense you acquire after years of working with stock. A good dog would have acted to head the calf off as soon as I gave the command, and a very good dog would have spotted it before me. In the seconds that I was thinking about the problem, the horse took off, heading in exactly the right direction to turn the calf back to the herd. I've wondered about it since: did the horse feel the slight pressure of my knees as I looked at the breaking calf? Or did it have the same instinct as a good dog– did it understand the cattle in the same way a collie understands sheep? A horse isn't a natural predator of cattle, with the instinct to chase that a dog has. But having worked with cattle for years, perhaps it had simply assimilated a deep knowledge of what they do, and how to recognise the signs. Just as I, as a stockman, could see what was going to happen, perhaps the horse also recognised it. Thankfully I was ready for the sudden move, otherwise I could have ended up in a heap on the floor and looked a right buffoon, especially with the cameras running.

Importantly, Peg works for anyone else on the farm who needs a sheepdog. I'm away a lot, so I don't get to work her as much as I would like to, but she still gets out to the sheep most days.

She's also a brilliant dog to take on location for *Countryfile*. She's happy being filmed, and when we have to repeat the same scene over and over again, she's up for it and never complains.

I'm hoping to breed from Peg soon. She's got a good pedigree, and she's such a great worker that I'd really like to keep her genes going. I'll take her to one of Dick's dogs when the time is right. Peg is now not only part of the farm workforce, but also part of the family, and I love her to bits. I feel hugely grateful to Meryl for having trusted me to take her on and also to Dick for recommending me and for helping me out with her. I can

certainly reassure Steve's family that Peg is well cared
for and very happy, and I like to think that Steve would
approve of her new owner. She has become well known
due to her appearances on *Countryfile*, and has pride of
place on the front cover of this book.

CHAPTER 7

Other Kinds of Sheepdog

D ad sparked my interest in farming, but he also sparked something much deeper in me. It was his work, pioneering the Rare Breeds Trust and setting up Cotswold Farm Park that started my lifelong fascination with the history of the animals we see around us every day as we drive through the countryside, or even as we walk in city parks.

Dad loved animals of all sorts, and he cared particularly about preserving the breeds that are in danger of extinction. In his early farming days, when he and his partner were running a mainly arable farm because they didn't have much money and arable was the most cost-effective way to establish themselves, Dad bought a couple of Gloucester Old Spot sows and two Gloucester cows, more or less as a hobby. He loved the idea of breeding pedigree livestock.

In 1969, when I was a lively little three-year-old, Dad was asked to join a working party set up by the Royal Agricultural Society and the Zoological Society of London to find a home for a collection of rare breed farm animals that had been kept at Whipsnade Zoo. The zoo needed the space for more exotic animals.

When he saw them, Dad knew he had to save them. That's when he had the idea for Cotswold Farm Park, a safe place for the animals to live. By opening the park to the public he hoped to fund the cost of keeping the animals, but, more importantly, he wanted to educate people about the need to conserve these wonderful breeds.

Two years later, the first rare breeds farm park in Britain (possibly in the world) received its new residents: a small flock of Jacob, Soay and Portland sheep, with one lone Norfolk ram, plus five different breeds of cattle: Highland, longhorn, White Park, Belted Galloway and Dexter.

Cotswold Farm Park was, from the day it opened, a great success. As well as educating the public about the precarious survival of these beautiful animals, Dad always made time to talk about them to me and my sisters. We all had animals that we had to look after: mine were a couple of Exmoor ponies. We were in charge of buying and selling the stock for our breed, with half the profit going into our piggy banks. It was a brilliant way to motivate us, and I loved going to market with him to buy new animals.

A couple of years after Cotswold Farm Park opened its doors, Dad helped to found the Rare Breeds Survival Trust, and became its first chairman. The members of the Trust wanted to stop rare breeds disappearing: between 1900 and 1973, 26 native breeds of farm animals became extinct. Now they publish an annual watchlist of endangered breeds and encourage farmers and other enthusiasts to keep these heritage animals going. Today the Trust has 10,000 members, and Prince Charles is its patron.

At about the same time as he took on his work with the Trust, Dad's TV career was launched properly, with a guest appearance on the very popular *Animal Magic* show on children's television, presented by Johnny Morris. Dad was a natural, and from then on he appeared regularly on a variety of animal programmes. I was very proud, never dreaming that he was also sowing the seeds of my other career (I already knew I wanted to be a farmer – well, I quite liked the idea of being a cowboy in the Wild West, too ...)

So, because of Dad's work on Bemborough Farm and the farm park, from a very early age I developed a strong interest in the history of domesticated animals. It fascinates me how breeds have evolved – and how some have been completely discarded – to fit with modern farming methods.

For many animals you can easily see the origins: the wild boar is clearly recognisable in today's pigs, even though wild boar became extinct in Britain by the twelfth century. Way back in time it originated in North Africa and Eurasia, and it was probably humans who spread it further, domesticating it more than three thousand years ago. A couple of efforts were made to reintroduce it, but it was not until the 1980s that boar were re-established here. At the farm park we have Iron

Age pigs, the only animals we have which are not pure bred, but rather are a reconstruction of the type of pigs our ancestors first herded from the wild during the Iron Age. They were created for a BBC television programme where the producers wanted to see how people coped living like Iron Age people, with the same clothing, houses and livestock. We mated a Tamworth sow (the oldest of the existing British breeds) with a wild boar.

We also have Highland cattle, which are the closest descendants of the massive Auroch cattle that appear in Neolithic cave paintings. Attempts have been made, and are being made, to re-establish Aurochs by breeding for their characteristics, or by sequencing their DNA from remains and comparing the genome with existing breeds. As well as Highland cattle, we also have White Parks at the farm park – another breed that have these ancient genes.

Goats have claims to be the earliest animal to have been domesticated as there is evidence that Neolithic men had herds of primitive goats. The first evidence of them in Britain is 5,000 years ago, and there are still pockets of feral goats dotted around the country who are descended from these early goats. Among the breeds we have at the farm park is the Bagot, which legend says was brought to Britain when Richard the Lionheart returned from the Crusades.

Naturally we have rare breed sheep: 14 different old breeds, with at least a couple who still have the genes of the earliest known sheep in the world, the wild mouflon.

Sheep are in contention with goats for the position of oldest domesticated animals, and their value was recognised more than 10,000 years ago in Asia as producers of meat, milk and wool – all valuable commodities. When I look at our small herd of Castlemilk Moorits or our Soays, which are unchanged from Viking times, the history of sheep is right there in front of me: I can see the way our modern breeds are descended from these hardy pioneers. The Merino sheep I became so familiar with in Australia are another breed with genes from the wild mouflon, although there have been centuries of refining the breed since.

But the animal whose history intrigues me even more, and who is not represented in our rare breeds park, is the animal I work with every day: the sheepdog.

Experts are agreed that dogs are descended from wolves, and the process of domestication was more the choice of the dog than of the humans who took them into their camps. Towards the end of the last Ice Age, men survived by hunting and gathering. They had no domesticated animals and they grew no crops. The wolves who learnt to forage around the human camps for bones and left-over food became useful as guard dogs, warning of predators and enemy incursions, and there soon developed a symbiotic relationship: the wolves/dogs stayed around for food and warmth at the fires, the men encouraged them for protection and also, after some time, to help with hunting. I expect, by taking in young wolf cubs, they managed to befriend them even more. The wolf gradually evolved physically but, more importantly, in its characteristics, to accept that hunting with a pack included a human pack.

Eventually, individual dogs became attached to families or groups of humans, even to one specific man. The 'ownership' of dogs by man had begun and has continued down the millennia. With the domestication of other animals – goats and sheep mainly – the dogs had another vital function, to guard and preserve the flock on which their human masters relied for food and skins. I've heard it argued that, given that man is the most successful animal on the planet, the dog is the second most successful, because it has learnt to have all its needs catered for simply by being useful to its masters.

As we all know, dogs have evolved into all sorts of different shapes and sizes, and have now been subdivided into breeds. There are dogs to sit on laps, dogs to race round tracks, dogs to guard our homes and premises, dogs to help us in specific ways, and even more dogs whose sole role in life is to be a good companion to its human owners. Despite how different they look – a St Bernard is one hundred times bigger than a Chihuahua, for example – they have a lot more in common than their appearance sometimes suggests.

All the different breeds of dog we know today evolved over centuries of selective breeding from the dogs who did the kind of work I still do with my dogs. If dogs had not become 'sheep' dogs, it is possible that no other domesticated breeds would exist. When I look at Peg or Pearl, I can see the history of all dogs before me, as they are where it all began. Their body shape may have changed, but the job they do is still principally the same as it was when Bronze Age men ran flocks of sheep, goats and pigs to feed their communities, using dogs to herd, guard and drive their livestock. Although today's sheepdogs do look different in some ways from the remains that have been found of their ancient predecessors, they are much closer in appearance to their forebears than any of the ornamental breeds. Farmers and shepherds have always wanted functional dogs: we don't judge them on their looks but on how well they can do the job. So there have been no excesses of inter-breeding, and a sheepdog is about as close as we can get today to an ancient breed.

There are, though, different types of livestock working dogs that have evolved. As we've seen, there are sheepdogs like Peg, who work rounding up and moving sheep, using all the attributes I described in the last chapter, and will tell you more about in the next. There are droving dogs, like the Welsh collie, who were used to take cattle and other livestock long distances. And there are pastoral dogs, who lived with the herd to guard it from predators and are still used in some parts of the world.

First, let's look at droving dogs.

For centuries, before railways and long-distance travel became normal, the people who moved around the countryside for miles and miles at a time were mainly drovers, taking cattle, pigs and sheep to market. Great cavalcades of drovers with their flocks would block the routes of the stagecoaches and horseback travellers for hours on end – not too different to being stuck in a motorway jam today.

To farmers like me, used to loading our livestock onto trailers and lorries, it's difficult to imagine how important drovers were. But in days gone by I wouldn't have been able to leave my farm for weeks at a time and so would have relied on a drover to take my flock to market and bring the money he got for selling my livestock back to me. It was a vital job, and every drover had at least one dog. Flocks of sheep as big as 6,000 strong, collected from different farms, would be taken to markets all over the country, even making journeys from the Pennines to the famous Smithfield market in London. The drovers would team up on the road, working together and using their dogs as a pack. For days, weeks and occasionally even months, the drovers, who were sometimes mounted on hardy horses used to rough terrain, but would often travel on foot, would steadily move their charges onwards, settling them at night in fields specially reserved for them. The dogs were vital for keeping the sheep together, keeping them going, and separating the different flocks when they got to market. Usually the flock or herd would wait for a few days before making the final few miles to market, to allow the sheep or cattle to rest and fatten up. At this point the drover's dog turned into a guard dog, fighting off any predators, including thieves and village dogs. Sometimes the enormous trains of animals in a drove would be accompanied by hunting dogs, which were used by the drovers to provide hares and rabbits for food on the journey: these dogs are the ancestors of today's lurchers. The droving dogs were fed on anything left over when the men had been fed.

A description from a book published in 1800, *Cynographia Britannica* (a very early description of different dog breeds), says about these remarkable droving dogs:

'He is sagacious, fond of employment and active; if a drove is huddled together so as to retard their progress, he dashes amongst and separates them till they form a line and travel more commodiously; if a sheep is refractory and runs wild, he soon overtakes and seizes him by the foreleg or ear, pulls him to the ground. The bull or ox he forces into obedience by keen bites on the heels or tail, and most dexterously avoids their kicks. He knows his master's grounds and is a rigid sentinel on duty, never suffering them to break their bounds, or strangers to enter. He shakes the intruding hog by the ear, and obliges him to quit the territories. He bears blows and kicks with much philosophy.'

What a dog! He was loyal and hard-working, and when he and his master finally delivered their charges to the market he was often turned loose to find his own way home, even if this was a journey of a hundred miles or more. He would scavenge for his own food on the way, saving the drover from having to feed him. If he never made it, the drover would simply acquire another dog, or use one from the small pack he bred especially for the job.

The drovers (like shepherds) were not concerned with how their dogs looked; they were breeding them for working qualities, not to win beauty contests. As Iris Combe, a renowned historian of herding dogs, wrote:

'To define a droving dog would be impossible, for they were a collection of canines of every shape and size, make and colour, each selected by the drover for its natural instincts and to deal with the specific type of livestock to be transported. The requirements for a drover's dog were a stout heart, good lungs, rock-hard feet, great physical courage and a strongly-developed instinct for self-preservation. The framework which housed these qualities was of relatively little importance.'

Sadly, not all the drovers were kind to their dogs, which usually lived short lives, due to exhaustion, accidents, ill-treatment and neglect. If a bitch gave birth to pups on the journey, the pups were often left to die, although there are heartening stories of bitch and pups being left at the nearest farmhouse and collected when the drover returned.

The routes the drovers used formed a criss-cross network across the countryside, which can still be seen today as the old droving roads are rediscovered and preserved as routes for walkers. They did not necessarily go in a straight line: the main roads had toll gates, and the cost of taking a whole herd through was too high for the drover who was paid a flat amount by the farmer. So routes were devised that bypassed the tolls.

Even when railways spread across the country in the mid-nineteenth century, droving dogs were still in demand. They no longer had to make the weeks-long droves all the way to the markets, but they were still needed to get livestock from the farms to the holding sheds at the railway stations, which could be journeys of many miles.

It wasn't only sheep and cattle who were escorted across the country by the drovers: flocks of geese and turkeys were also driven, with dogs urging them on and keeping them in line, often for several days at a time, to get to market. Just as cattle were usually shod like horses to protect their feet on long journeys, turkeys wore leather boots and geese were first herded through wet tar, followed by sand, to give their feet a protective coating. The dogs had to drive them through the tar – not something the geese were very willing to do – and the dogs hated the job because they ended up with tar on their own feet.

To illustrate the hard life the drovers led, I followed an old drover's road for three long days for *Countryfile*, taking 40 geese across the Brecon Beacons to the market town of Llandovery. We couldn't use sheep because of the strict movement licences that are now in place when you transport these animals from farm to farm, but geese are free from these restrictions. Nor could we walk them through tar – the RSPCA would not have approved. Before we set off, and at regular intervals along the route, my little flock were checked out by Peter Laing, a vet who caught up with me whenever we stopped for long.

My adventure was shown over three episodes of *Countryfile*, leading up to Christmas: geese were very popular in the Christmas markets in Victorian times. I dressed for the part, in a long drover's coat and a wide-brimmed hat, which I was very glad of when the rain swept across the open heathland.

We weighed a sample three geese before I set off, because, as a good drover, my employers would expect me to get the geese to market in good condition. An important part of my job, as well as covering the distance, was to take care that my charges were well fed, got plenty of rest, and plenty of access to water. Every couple of miles we stopped for 20 minutes, which was all the geese seemed to need to feel refreshed and ready to go.

My sheepdog at the time was Maud, and she was very happy to switch her attention from sheep to geese, having already herded geese and ducks in front of visitors at Cotswold Farm Park. She wasn't fazed by them, and understood the slow pace they needed to waddle along at. I was nervous that one of my flock would get lost or hurt, but Maud was vigilant.

As well as Peter the vet, I was also joined along my route by Richard Moore Colyer, a historian who has studied the ancient droving routes and the men who travelled along them.

'There is evidence of drovers moving animals in Saxon times, and probably earlier,' he told me. 'But the heyday was from the sixteenth century to the end of the nineteenth century. Wales had poor quality pasture, so the cattle the farmers bred were taken to lusher pasture in England. Lots of animals, including geese, were taken to the markets at Llandovery.'

The whole area I was walking was honeycombed with drovers' roads, and in days gone by I would have met up with many other men in charge of flocks and herds of animals, but I'm pretty sure I was the first drover to walk this way in the past hundred years or so. Halfway through the first day the rain came down, the geese looked muddy and bedraggled, and I could feel trickles of cold water running down my neck. But if I was feeling sorry for myself I only had to remember that at least my coat and hat were made of waterproof material: the old drovers, with their heavy woollen coats, would have been a lot wetter than I was.

The first night we stopped at the village of Caio, which was an important droving centre in the eighteenth and nineteenth centuries, when the population was three times larger than it is today. Richard told me about a famous drover, Dafydd Jones of Caio, who lived between 1711 and 1777, who didn't fit the usual image of drovers, who were known as hard-drinking, hard-womanising, wild men. Dafydd Jones spent his hours on the road composing hymns and translating English hymns into Welsh. In one of his hymns, Richard said, he compares souls going to heaven with all the cattle and sheep converging on Caio.

Our first night was spent in a tent, while the geese were corralled in a sheep pen lined with a generous amount of straw. Because of the rain, we built a tarpaulin shelter to keep them dry. I was exhausted and also worried about the safety of the geese, as there were foxes about. We'd travelled across some difficult open country, and it was a bit disappointing at the end of a hard day to find that my drover's rations were a hunk of bread, a piece of cheese and a raw onion. The geese, on the other hand, got a generous helping of barley for their supper. I tried not to think about the luxury of a warm dry bed as I settled down for the night, cold and wet.

Maud loved the luxury of sleeping in my tent with me and I was glad of her company, but I know the original droving dogs would have been expected to live in the pen with the geese. The drovers in fact would not have had tents – they slept in barns and haylofts, and, if the weather was reasonable, underneath hedges, with nothing more than blankets to protect them. The drovers faced many dangers. On their way to market there were rustlers intent on stealing their livestock, and on the way back the risks were even higher, because they were now carrying money, often gold sovereigns, for the farmers whose stock they had transported. Highwaymen, sometimes operating in armed gangs, would target them, which was another reason that the best drovers did not release their dogs but kept them alongside to alert to danger and to attack human predators just as enthusiastically as they saw off foxes.

The next morning I was relieved to count all my 40 geese present and correct, and almost all looking fit and healthy. There was one goose I was worried about. She was struggling a bit the day before, always lagging behind. This morning, while the others had preened their feathers and were now pure white again, Jemima (I called her after Jemima Puddleduck, the Beatrix Potter character) was still muddy and wet. I caught her and dried her with a towel. Peter had a good look at her, because I was worried about whether she could continue.

'She's not got such good feathers as the others, but she's healthy, her eyes are bright,' he said.

Thankfully, the weather was dry, so I was able to light a fire, brew some tea, and have a good breakfast of fatty bacon cooked over the fire. I'd hoped for some eggs from my flock, but Peter explained that they would not lay in the bad weather we had overnight.

We set off again over open moorland and I asked Richard why the drovers didn't follow the roads.

'Most of the roads had turnpikes, which meant that you had to pay twopence for every animal that went through. If you had a large herd or flock, that represented a lot of money. The drovers had to balance the cost against getting the animals to market quicker and probably in better condition.

'The drovers also had to avoid mixing their sheep, cattle and geese with other animals also being driven to market. If a drover had a very large number of animals he may have had to hire other men to help him.'

As I strode out, I carried poor old Jemima for some of the way. She was so valliant, trying to keep up with the others when it was obviously hard work for her. Without Peter or Richard to accompany me I felt isolated on the big wide open hillside. But I didn't feel lonely: hundreds of drovers and millions of animals had trodden this path, and somehow their spirits felt alive to me.

Maud really came into her own as she had to drive the geese down some hazardous, narrow hill tracks. She was ducking and darting, keeping them safe. I was worried one would disappear over the edge, but I should have had more faith in her: she brought them all through brilliantly.

It was late when we stopped for a lunch break, because we had to keep moving down the dangerous track. We were all exhausted, and once again I was on bread, cheese and raw onion, and beginning to fantasise about a good hot meal. The geese enjoyed a swim on the next leg of the route, with only Jemima needing a helping hand to get in and out of the river.

We stopped that night in the village of Cilycwm, another droving centre in the old days. There used to be five pubs catering for these wild men who drove their animals through, but today there is only one left. Luckily, I was staying there, so a warm bed, a pint and a hot meal were in sight.

Lots of villagers came out to see me and my flock arrive – I'm sure they thought I was a harmless eccentric. But Richard explained that in times past when the drovers came through, locals would 'lock up their daughters, their mistresses, their sisters and everybody else. They definitely had an eye for the ladies.'

While we were happy to relax over a pint, the drovers were known for kicking up a fuss, with records of them appearing at Quarter Sessions and being bound over to keep the peace, or fined for being drunk and disorderly.

Still worried about foxes, I arranged for my geese to spend the night in a stable. When he checked them the next morning Peter said they looked so fit and relaxed 'they could be on a holiday cruise'.

On our final day we covered most of the distance by road, and I admit we cheated a little bit by loading the geese into a trailer because we were causing such a tailback of traffic. But only for a short distance: we faithfully walked the rest. Richard broke the journey for me by walking with me to explain that geese were not just a valuable foodstuff, they also provided feathers for pillows and mattresses, goose grease for mothers to rub on their children's chests to ward off the cold, and even fuel for lamplighting.

When we arrived in Llandovery I was fascinated to see a plaque outside Lloyds Bank, commemorating one of the first banks established in Wales. Not only did the drovers have money on them from selling animals, they were also used to transport deeds and documents. For example, on the journey from Wales to London with the cattle and sheep, they often carried rents from Welsh farmers for their English landlords and taxes levied by the government. So in both directions they were targets for villains. If, instead of gold, they were given credit by banks, they were no longer such a target, and that's why the banks were established.

Enterprising men like David Jones, a farmer's son who worked as a drover, set up the Black Ox Bank in Llandovery in 1799, using his own savings and the substantial sum of £10,000 (£800,000 in today's money) which he acquired when he married his wealthy wife. The name 'Black Ox' came from the depiction of the Welsh Black cattle, the local breed, on the bank notes. In one year, 1800, the Black Ox bank lent over £6,000 without any security for the purchase of cattle, sheep and geese. That's about half a million in today's money. In 1909 Lloyds Bank acquired all the branches of the Black Ox bank, ending the existence of the last and largest of the independent banks in Wales, and one that made life so much safer for so many drovers.

We were given a great reception as we arrived in the town, and, to keep up the spirit of droving, I delivered a letter from the satchel I was wearing to the mayor, a scroll commemorating our historical trip and thanking the town for welcoming us. Despite the crowd that turned out to greet us, and all the cameras being aimed at them, my geese remained calm and dignified and Maud kept them in check. When we retired to a quiet field to feed and rest them, Peter reweighed the same three we weighed at the beginning, and to my astonishment they had all put on weight, one of them even putting on three pounds.

It was an amazing three days for me. I felt I had stepped back in time, and got a real taste of what it was like to be a drover centuries ago. My life today, and the life of all farmers and shepherds, is very different from the life they lived. But one role hasn't changed in all that time: the job of the sheepdog. Maud worked brilliantly, doing exactly what her predecessors would have done. During the filming, as we went from farm to farm, one shepherd who saw her working was so impressed he wanted to buy her. Of course, it didn't matter how much money he offered, she was definitely not for sale ...

Now to another type of sheepdog, the ones who lived with the herd to protect the livestock from predators. They're sometimes called pastoral dogs, although that definition strictly means all breeds working with animals, so it is more accurate to refer to them as guardian dogs. There are many different breeds, developed in different countries, and with different names – sheepdogs, mountain dogs, mastiffs – but all with the same job.

When I was little we had, for a short time, a lovely Old English sheepdog called Guinevere. She was huge, especially to me as I was only five or six at the time, and I still remember her massive paws and the density of her thick coat. Because of Dad's interest in old breeds, he liked the idea of having an Old English sheepdog and so he bought one for Mum as a present, getting her from a local breeder at Rissington. She was a beautiful puppy, just like the one in the Dulux adverts, but in a muddy farmyard she was constantly filthy. When she was fully grown we clipped her a few times to keep her cool in summer and cleaner in winter. Unfortunately, she hated being separated from Mum, and whenever Mum was down at the farm park, Guinevere, who was left behind in the farmhouse, became a brilliant escapologist, nipping out of the back door at any opportunity. Then she would bound a quarter of a mile over the fields to be reunited with Mum. The problem was solved eventually when the breeder lost her own dog and offered to have Guinevere back, giving her a lovely home where she lived to a ripe old age.

The thing is, although her name includes 'sheepdog', Guinevere no longer had a working role on a farm like ours. Back in time, she and all the other huge breeds were vital to farmers and shepherds. They lived outside with the sheep, and any predators who turned up during the night were given short shrift by these large, tough dogs. In some parts of the world, close relatives of the Old English sheepdog are still working as flock guardians, sleeping and eating alongside the livestock, spending all their time guarding them, but it's a dwindling number.

The flock-guarding dogs developed alongside their smaller, more agile cousins, the collies, who could herd and move animals. The guardians needed to be big and fierce, as thousands of years ago and in different parts of the world they had to be prepared to fight lynx, lions, wolves, jackals, tigers, leopards, cheetahs, foxes and huge eagles. They needed to be brave and strong, and they had to have a well-developed instinct to protect. They did not need to be able to hunt, or to herd. Their sole job was to live with the flock of sheep or goats and see off any predators. Often they simply needed to bark, from the centre of a flock, for a predator to turn tail; a bit like a pet dog's barking can make a burglar go elsewhere. Their size also meant that they could carry large fat reserves, which helped them survive the worst weather and protected them from bitter cold, which a smaller dog couldn't survive.

Although we no longer use them – in England today there are few natural predators of sheep – there are times when I feel they could still be useful, especially when I hear of rogue dogs worrying sheep, or even of rustlers stealing them. Luckily I farm in an area of the country that has not been badly affected by rustling, but I really feel for the farmers and shepherds in the north of the country and in Northern Ireland, where rustling offences are up by nearly 200 per cent in the last five years, with about 90,000 animals stolen each year, probably to be illegally butchered and eaten. The word 'rustling' can sound amusing and even romantic, with connotations of the Wild West, but for a farmer who has spent decades building up the bloodlines in his flock and investing money and time in his animals, it is devastating to lose them.

Unlike my working dogs, the collies, these flock guardians did not work to commands, and often did not have or know their own name. In some parts of the world they lived with the flock from birth: pups were put among the sheep before their eyes were open. Charles Darwin, the most famous naturalist ever, noted when he was in South America that shepherds would teach pups to be suckled by ewes and the dogs slept in a bed of sheep's wool. They were trained to go to a set place every day for meat, but the rest of their life was spent exclusively with the flock, and when sheep were sold it was usual for the dog to be sold with them.

The breeds of dog developed differently according to the parts of the world where they were used, so in the harsh climate of northern Europe, where they often worked on mountainsides and open steppes, they developed thick, waterproof coats. In more temperate areas they had smoother coats. But common to all was the thickset body and powerful legs that Guinevere had. They lived tough lives, sleeping outside in snow and icy winds, giving birth to pups in a hole in the ground.

Many different breeds still exist, but many more have sadly been allowed to become extinct. Some have found other uses, like the St Bernards used in mountain rescue and the German shepherd dogs and related breeds which have become excellent guard dogs in a completely different context, working with police and security firms.

Nowadays, some of these ancient breeds are reared for their appearance and for showing. Old English sheepdogs are endearing to look at and in personality, and as a result they have their own niche in books, films and, famously, advertising the Dulux brand of paint. Nana, the dog who looks after the children in the story of Peter Pan, is sometimes depicted as an Old English Sheepdog, as is the Colonel in the film and book *One Hundred and One Dalmatians*. Yet a couple of years ago these magnificent animals were on the endangered list, but now I'm happy to say there has been a surge in popularity, and they have been taken off the list.

Several breeds of guardian dog are white, selectively bred over centuries to camouflage them in a flock of sheep. One of these is the Maremma sheepdog, originally bred in central Italy, and still used to this day to protect the dwindling number of sheep that are over-wintered by shepherds in the Maremma marshlands.

They've spread across the globe, having been used as livestock guardians in the USA, Canada and Australia.

I've been lucky enough to meet some of these huge, friendly dogs, which from a distance look like small polar bears. A group of owners arranged to meet up at Cotswold Farm Park for a most unusual fund raiser, which really fascinated me. So with Charlie, Ella and Alfie I took a stroll across to the farm park to chat to them, and we were enthusiastically greeted by about 12 boisterous, adorable dogs, probably averaging about 40 kilos in weight each (for comparison, Boo, our wire-haired Vizsla, is probably about 20 kilos, and Peg the border collie only about 14).

The Maremma Sheepdog Club of Great Britain had organised the money raiser to give support to a touching initiative in Australia, where these woolly giants of dogs have been protecting an endangered species – a subject close to my heart, of course.

The smallest penguin breed, known originally as the Fairy penguin and now as the Little penguin, colonises an uninhabited island, Middle Island, off the coast near the town of Warrnambool, in South Victoria. The penguins are only 30 to 40 centimetres tall, so definitely little.

There used to be hundreds of them on Middle Island, until an enterprising fox discovered that at low tide it was possible to cross to the island, only a matter of a 150 metres off the mainland, without even needing to swim, just getting his paws a bit wet. He told all his mates and in a very short space of time the population of penguins was almost completely wiped out. The problem started in about 2000, when the sea's natural current shifted and there was an increased build-up of sand, and it rapidly got worse as the fox population escalated with this free and easy source of food. Foxes also kill for the thrill of it, not necessarily just to eat, and in the space of two nights in 2005 around 360 corpses were found on the island by the Penguin Preservation Project monitors.

Patrols were set up to shoot the foxes and poisoned bait was laid for them. Sadly nothing was very effective, and it looked as though these delightful little birds were not going to survive in this spot. It wasn't going to be the end of the Little penguin species, as there are other colonies around the coast of Australia and New Zealand, but it was desperately sad for local conservationists. Finally, only four Little penguins were surviving on the island.

Step forward local free range chicken farmer Alan 'Swampy' Marsh. Alan was using a Maremma to protect his chickens, having successfully trained her to regard them as her 'flock'. He suggested his dog, Oddball, might be able to see off the foxes on Middle Island. There was a lot of scepticism, and even downright opposition (some people suggested the dog would attack the penguins), but as nobody had a better idea and the penguins were almost wiped out, Oddball was dispatched to the island.

She stayed there for three weeks before swimming back to the mainland to be reunited with her master. But her presence had done the trick: the foxes had been scared off by her barking and her scent. The Preservation Project monitors saw no more fox pawprints on the island.

Two more Maremmas were trained up to take over from Oddball, and since 2006 there have been a succession of dogs. They stay on the island during the warmer months when the sandbar appears, and volunteers feed and check on them each day. They are trained to regard the penguins as their friends and the island as their own territory, barking if anything suspicious happens. They have never had to kill a fox because, since their arrival on Middle Island, the foxes have beaten a hasty retreat. But their trainers have no doubt they could and would kill a fox if they had to, just as their ancestors did to protect sheep. The population of penguins has increased to 200, and not one has been killed by a fox since the project began.

Oddball sadly died recently, but she'd reached the grand old age of 15, well above normal life expectancy for such a large breed. A children's film was even made about her and Swampy, her owner: it was called *Oddball* and was popular in Australia, sparking an influx of tourists to the area. They go to meet the Maremmas that are in training and to do a tour of the island.

Buying and training dogs is expensive, and that was why the Maremma owners who met at Cotswold Farm

Park were raising money. I'm pleased to say they were able to send £200 to the project as a result. It was a lovely day, with the sun shining, and the dogs and owners were able to go on the farm wildlife trail, which is where we caught up with them. A sudden shower drove us all into the café where these lovable dogs, who seemed mischievous while we were outside, settled down obediently.

I know that guardian dogs like Maremmas are used not just for sheep and goats, but for turkeys, chickens, deer and even alpacas in areas of the world where there are still predators, but I had never heard of them being used to protect penguins before. The local council, which had to be convinced reluctantly to give Oddball a chance to protect the penguins, is now talking about erecting a statue in her memory.

So that's two types of sheepdog: the droving dogs and the guardian dogs. In the next chapter I will look at the history of the ones I am very familiar with, herding dogs.

CHAPTER 8

My Kind of Dogs

I never imagined I had much in common with Queen Victoria but it turns out I do: collies. She loved them too. This was, naturally, very influential, because before she became devoted to them, collies were a Cinderella dog in the fashionable world. They weren't lap dogs or sporting dogs, they were dogs who worked for a living and were treasured by their owners – shepherds and farmers – for their great skills, not for their looks. Their history stretches back to the beginning of civilisation.

So does mine: I'm very proud to call myself a shepherd. It's one of the oldest professions in the world – yes, I've heard all the terrible jokes – but herding sheep and goats really does go back to primitive times. Hunters came first, of course, but it was the shepherds who tended livestock and the farmers who planted crops who moved civilisation on, and made it possible for men to put down roots, build permanent homes, and feed their families in safer, better conditions than their nomadic forefathers.

The men who rounded animals up, domesticated them, moved them from pasture to pasture, bred them to provide even more meat and better wool, are the men who laid the foundations of life as we live it today. As I go about my livestock work on the farm, or meet other shepherds through filming for *Countryfile*, I know that I have a connection that extends all the way back to the beginnings of domestication, about 15,000 years ago. I am part of a very long tradition, and by my side my dog Peg, and all the other sheepdogs I have known, are just as much a part of that tradition.

There are shelves full of old books about spaniels, setters, pointers, beagles, foxhounds and gundogs, but relatively few books about herding dogs. The men who owned them were rarely even literate, and so not likely to go into flights of fancy about their wonderful dogs. A shepherd will describe a dog as great if it can round up sheep, divide them, pen them. He doesn't care about its colouring, the colour of its eyes, whether its ears are a perfect match. When they win prizes today, it is for their agility and intelligence, both of which they have in spades, and both of which are reasons they are so vital to me and all others who depend on them daily. A working shepherd in the market for a new dog is keen to know how well its parents were able to work, not how many rosettes they won at dog shows, and the dogs that sell for huge sums at sheepdog sales are bought for the working history of their forebears and the signs of ability they show.

The history of sheepdogs, as I have said, is as old as the story of domesticated animals, but it came relatively late to Britain. Domestication of animals began in western Asia, and that's where dogs are first believed to have been used to herd animals. It was another 10,000 years, during the Bronze Age, that farming really began in Britain, with dogs guarding and then herding the flocks.

Herding dogs worked alongside the guardian dogs, the ones who lived with the flock, and then really came into their own after the need for protection dogs receded as wild predators disappeared and flocks could be moved around for better grazing. Now shepherds could turn their flocks loose and allow them to wander, but they needed to be able to round them up again. Dogs with an instinct to herd were highly prized, and breeding for the purpose began. Herding dogs are smaller than the guardian dogs, more agile, and, most important, they are able to be trained to respond to their master's commands, whether it's voice or whistle. They are not directly descended from the large protection dogs who would have been difficult to train for this job, and would have caused havoc if they had tried to move a flock by herding.

The ability to herd – to cast wide and round up a flock of sheep – developed when great swathes of the country were covered in forest, and sheep and goats would be left to crop the vegetation among the trees. The shepherd needed a dog that worked silently, out-flanked the animals and nudged them together simply by his presence, but did not chase or attack the animals.

Most importantly, the dog had to be able to respond to its master's commands when it could not see him, because of the trees. It also needed, at times, to work on its own initiative when it spotted a problem – a sheep making a break, say – that its master could not see. Over generations this specific, gifted sheepdog evolved. The hills and forests of Scotland and the border country was a good breeding ground, but all across the country sheepdogs with traits peculiar to their particular area were being bred, all of them for the same purpose.

Agriculture in Britain developed massively in Roman times, when many independent farms were established with shepherds tending their flocks in different terrains and weather conditions across the country, including on remote hill farms, where even today the living is still bleak, tough, and essentially unchanged over the centuries. The farmers supplied the Roman forts and camps with meat and wool, and as the soldiers were often stationed in forts for years at a time, many of them, too, became part-time shepherds, with their own flocks and their own dogs. Sheep and goats were imported to Britain by the Romans from Spain and North Africa, where herding was well established, and dogs and herdsmen often came with the flocks. As the climate and terrain here proved to be good for sheep, the wool trade became a very important part of the Anglo–Roman economy, so the flocks grew, and so did the role of herding dogs.

The value of sheepdogs was recognised by the Roman writer Marcus Terentius Varro, who wrote: 'Be careful not to buy dogs from hunters or butchers, for the dogs of butchers are too idle to follow the flock, and hunting dogs, if they see a stag or a hare, will chase after it instead of after the sheep. Thus the best is one that has been bought from a shepherd, and has been trained to follow sheep ...'

The wool trade became the backbone of the economy of this country until the late fifteenth century, and to this day the Speaker in the House of Lords sits on 'the woolsack' – now a large wool-stuffed seat but originally a bale of wool – a reminder of the huge importance of wool to the nation's wealth. The very name of my area, the Cotswolds, comes from the word 'cot', an enclosure for sheep, and 'wold' for hill, so it literally means sheep enclosure on the hills. It was well known throughout Europe in the Middle Ages for the quality of its wool, from sheep known as Cotswolds Lions which have long lustrous coats and a faintly golden hue to their wool. They remained very popular until after the First World War, when their numbers declined so much that they became a rare breed. Of course, we have a flock at Cotswold Farm Park, and their numbers are now building up well. I am proud to continue breeding these wonderful historic animals that have called this area home for many centuries.

Wealth from the sheep trade largely went to the church in the Middle Ages, which owned vast flocks of sheep, and to rich merchants. These merchants made enormous contributions towards the building and expansion of fine churches, known now as 'wool churches'. (They are spread across East Anglia, another prosperous sheep area, as well as the Cotswolds.) The story is that they believed that endowing churches would help buy them an easy journey to paradise after their deaths. The legacy for those of us who live in the area is wonderful, architecturally important, church buildings around us.

Of course, wherever there were sheep in large numbers, there were also dogs in large numbers. A good working dog was a precious commodity. The word 'collie' for a working sheepdog has been around for many years, and there are arguments as to where it originated: it could come from a Gaelic word meaning 'useful', which these dogs certainly are, or, as I've mentioned before, it could be a version of 'coaley', a Scottish word possibly referring to dogs working with the black (or coal) faced sheep of Scotland and the border countries, which is still the most common sheep breed in Britain. These Scottish collies spread across the country, especially in the second half of the nineteenth century when Scottish sheep farmers and shepherds moved to East Anglia, bringing some livestock and, more importantly, the dogs used to handle the flocks.

The word 'cur' became a derogatory description of an ill-behaved mongrel of very mixed parentage, and in years gone by an insulting word for a scoundrel. But the name derives from the word 'curtail', which means to cut short. In the seventeenth century, taxes were imposed on dog owners. The only exemptions were for shepherds and others who needed working dogs for ratting or other jobs. To claim the exemption the dog must have a docked tail, or 'curtul'. This led to all working dogs becoming known as 'curs'.

Although shepherds and farmers were not normally the sort of educated people with time on their hands to wax lyrical in print about their wonderful dogs, there are exceptions, the most notable being a man called James Hogg, who became known as the Ettrick Shepherd, and who, in the early 1800s, published poems and magazine articles about his amazing sheepdogs. He was a shepherd in the border countries from an early age and educated himself through reading, eventually becoming a well-respected writer and friend of the literati of the day, including Sir Walter Scott and William Wordsworth. But it is his stories about his real-life dogs which endure, and which any shepherd today will recognise.

He had a dog called Sirrah, who he bought from a drover who was starving him and treating him badly. Sirrah had not been trained as a sheepdog, 'and he knew so little of herding that he had never turned a sheep in his life; but as soon as he discovered that it was his duty to do so I can never forget with what anxiety and eagerness he learned his different evolutions. He would try every way deliberately till he found out what

I wanted him to do, and when I once made him understand a direction he never forgot it again ... He often
astonished me for, when hard-pressed in accomplishing
the task that he was put to, he had expedients of the
moment that bespoke a great share of the reasoning
faculty.'

Hogg told the story of 700 sheep which escaped their
pens in the middle of the night, scattering in three different directions, and could not be found in the dark.
Eventually he and his assistant gave up, but Sirrah did
not return when called. The next day they found Sirrah
holding the entire flock in a deep ravine, not one injured
or missing. He had been there for several hours.

The status of collies shot up when Queen Victoria
adopted them as her all-time favourite dogs – quite an
accolade, because she was a renowned dog lover. When
she and her husband Prince Albert built Balmoral
Castle in the Scottish Highlands in the 1850s it triggered
a fashion for all things Scottish, and that included collie
dogs. The queen already had kennels at Windsor Castle
with several dogs, but it was in Scotland she met and
fell in love with collies. Many dogs were given to her –
what do you give to a queen who has everything? Well,
another dog never goes amiss, and with so many
children, she could hand them all on.

The queen herself especially loved smooth-coated
collies, and as a result these became the fashionable
choice for carriage dogs for aristocratic ladies (not a
job an active, intelligent collie would relish, but I guess

they had servants to make sure the dogs got plenty of exercise before being taken out for stately trips in a carriage!) The queen's favourite, called Sharp, lived until he was 15, and there is a statue of him on his grave in Windsor Home Park. After Sharp, she had Noble who lived for 16 years, and in his final illness was attended by the queen's own physician, who also had to give her a sedative because she was so distressed. He, too, has a statue on his grave. Next came Roy, who was with her until she died. Although she had many other dogs these three were special: they lived inside her palaces with her, and from pictures and the statues, I'd definitely describe them as border collies, although that name was not used until later, in the early years of the twentieth century (border collies were not recognised as a breed by the Kennel Club until 1976).

Partly influenced by the royal patronage, wealthy Americans were also impressed by the cleverness of these dogs and breeding for commercial purposes began, with canny Scots farmers and shepherds selling their best-looking dogs (but never their best working dogs). Scouts went around country markets buying up dogs, purely for their looks.

Two things happened at roughly the same time. Although local farmers and shepherds had for a long time held competitions among themselves, properly organised sheepdog trials began to spring up across the country. The first was held in Bala, North Wales in

1873, with ten dogs competing. The following year there was a trial in Scotland, and they quickly spread.

Today, I'm really pleased to be involved in the *Countryfile* coverage of One Man and His Dog, a competition between England, Scotland, Ireland and Wales, with a junior and senior member in each team. I've always loved watching trials, and I'm constantly amazed by the highly refined skills of these super dogs. So it's terrific to get to meet the competitors, both two-legged and four-legged.

Coincidentally, showing dogs became popular at much the same time as trialling began to emerge, and breeders started to turn their attention to how the dogs looked. The first Crufts dog show was held in 1891, with 2,000 dogs competing. Nowadays, Crufts is a four-day event with classes not simply for the appearance of competitors, but for obedience, agility, flyball and heeling to music. Nonetheless, the overall champion is awarded for the dog which best conforms to its breed standards. In the 104 shows held since 1905, it's interesting to see that collies have only won three times, the first being a 'Scotch' collie in 1906, probably as a result of them still being popular with the royal family. (Queen Victoria's daughter-in-law, Queen Alexandra, was very keen on rough-coated collies, and bred them at Sandringham House.) Despite their few years in the fashion sun, they have resolutely remained as working dogs, proving themselves in agility and flyball rather than parading round the ring being assessed for their looks.

In the early days of dog shows an interesting challenge was issued to the show fanciers from working dog owners: a competition to demonstrate that show dogs very quickly lost their ability to work, by setting them a task of rounding up sheep. That's exactly how it turned out: the show collies barked, yelped and lost control of the sheep. The winner of the sheep herding was a working collie called Maddie, who may not have had the looks but certainly had the ability to move sheep around. I'm not sure it meant the show dogs had 'lost' the ability to work – they had never been allowed to work, and had no training. What a shame for them: as you know by now, I personally believe dogs are happier if they work, and literally thousands of years of breeding by shepherds and farmers have made sheepdogs what they are today, finely tuned to the demands of the job, without so much as a thought for how they look.

Today there are many different types of herding sheepdog: Welsh collies, rough-haired collies, Shetlands, smooth-haired collies, border collies, kelpies and Huntaways, plus lots of continental breeds. Some breeds are no longer used for their original purpose, but they all have their origins in the proud tradition of the working dogs of farmers and itinerant shepherds, who relied on them for a living.

When I look at Peg, and at any of the sheepdogs I meet as I go about my work as a farmer or filming for *Countryfile*, I know I am looking at hundreds, even thousands of years of history, and it's a history I love being part of.

I enjoy all the stories we feature on *Countryfile*, but naturally the ones that speak to me most are the ones where I meet shepherds and farmers who are doing the same job as me, but in wildly different terrains and climates. I love watching them work sheep, and I am full of admiration for what they achieve. The way some of them live and work makes life at Bemborough Farm look like a walk in the park ...

Perhaps the most spectacular was when I joined the shepherds of the high Alps in Switzerland to bring a huge flock of black-nosed sheep down from their summer grazing near the Aletsch glacier, a journey which involved herding them along a precarious mountain path and across a narrow bridge over a thundering, icy river. I had to travel up to the village where the sheep belong, Belalp, by cable car, as there are no roads. The annual movement of the sheep is spectacular, and it was a privilege to see it, but, boy, did those shepherds earn my respect as they clambered across this rugged territory to bring their livestock more than a thousand metres down the steep mountain to winter in kinder pastures.

I helped out with similar challenging missions to round up and move animals in difficult terrain here in Britain when I visited Devon for the annual check-up carried out on the feral goats of the Valley of the Rocks, near Lynton. They lived up to the name 'mountain goat' by running away from us up near-impossible rocky inclines. Then again, I helped introduce sheep to the magical island of Tintagel in Cornwall for the first time since 1896. With some difficulty I assisted the Tintagel property manager, Matt Ward, and assorted helpers get a small herd of Soays along a wooden path, across a bridge and up 148 steps, so that they could graze the land around the ruins of the castle built on what legend says was the home of King Arthur and his knights of the Round Table.

In all of these cases it was decided not to use dogs as they may have chased the animals too close to the cliff where either dog or livestock may have fallen to their death, so the herding was all done on foot by humans. This can prove very tricky, particularly as the animals you are trying to round up are far more agile and quicker than you.

The reason the Soays, a hardy Scottish breed of sheep which I know well because we have them at Cotswold Farm Park, were introduced to Tintagel is to help manage the land and preserve rare species of plants. The sheep graze on the coarse grasses which, left untended, would out-compete and eliminate the valuable, diverse plant life. Matt told me that he was hoping the sheep would increase the number of wild flowers from hundreds to thousands of different species.

The use of sheep and other animals to manage and preserve the landscape is a common theme in the shepherding programmes I've made for *Countryfile*. It makes so much sense. But I was taken by surprise when I filmed a flock of sheep on a beach at Ainsdale, because I had no idea that sheep could live on sand dunes.

Ainsdale is a 13-mile stretch of beach and dunes between Southport and Formby, on the north-west coast. It's a wide, sandy beach area that was once used by locals to run rabbit warrens, when rabbit was an essential animal for the family pot. Sadly, the rabbits were wiped out by myxomatosis in the 1950s, and it was only some time later that ecologists and other experts realised what a good job they had been doing of managing the dunes, chomping away at the vegetation to keep it in check and allow different species to thrive.

Now the 253-acre site is maintained by Natural England as a National Nature Reserve. There are way-marked paths for the public to use, but because of the diversity of rare animals and plants, people are not allowed to wander all over.

But one creature that is allowed to wander in the winter months is a flock of 250 Herdwick sheep. I'm a great fan of Herdwicks: they are tough little animals who live on the Lakeland fells, so they are accustomed to rain, snow, sleet and anything else mother nature throws at them. They stand as solid as rocks, unde-terred by howling gales and blinding rain. Flocks from remote and difficult hill farms are often sent to kinder pastures to over-winter, so I wasn't surprised by the fact that these fell dwellers go away for a holiday each year. But a holiday to the beach?

I took Peg to Ainsdale, hoping she could help out rounding up the flock. Peg was new to me at the time and this was the first long journey we'd done together. She was great, travelling peacefully and sleeping in the back of the truck outside the hotel where I and the film crew were staying. She was such an easy companion, and I couldn't believe my luck in having her. Because I don't know much about her early years, I had no idea if she had ever been to a beach or seen the sea before. So prior to linking up with Dave Mercer, the senior reserves manager for Natural England who is overall head of the conservation project on the dunes, I took her across the sand to the sea. She went in up to her waist when I threw a stick, but she never went out of her depth and she seemed a little bit nervous of the waves. Collies are not renowned as water dogs, so I wasn't surprised that she jumped a bit when the waves swept in, but I already knew she was a brave little dog and she didn't seem at all fazed by it.

It was a beautiful day, with a wintry sun taking the edge off a chill breeze, and the view of the dunes was impressive. What surprised me was the amount of vegetation.

Dave explained: 'If left alone this area would be a birch forest, or even an oak forest. But a forest is not as rare as an open dune landscape, so we're halting the degradation of the dunes with our four-legged lawn-mowers, the sheep. This area has a European designation as a special area of conservation, and if we want to keep the diversity of the plant and animal life here, we have to hold the dominant vegetation at bay.'

The dunes are a natural sea defence that prevent flooding and maintaining them means keeping the right sort of grass, the type that binds the dunes together. Dave told me that the dunes are home to a really large population of Natterjack toads, with as many as 50 per cent of the British population living on this coastline in some years. They are so noisy that they are known as 'the Birkdale chorus', Birkdale being the neighbouring stretch of the sand dunes. As well as the toads there are great crested newts and sand lizards.

There are also 473 different species of plant, including the heath dog violet, which is the food source for the very picky caterpillar of the Dark Green Fritillary butterfly. Other rare flowers include dune helleborine, seaside centaury, yellow bartsia and sticky stork's-bill. The plants encourage all sorts of insects to live and thrive on the dunes: it's an inter-connected web of life, and I can appreciate how tricky it is managing the area for the benefit of so many different creatures.

That's where the sheep come in. They've been grazing here for over ten years, starting with a small group to see how well they survived and whether or not they had the right impact on the vegetation, which had been uncontrolled since the rabbit population disappeared. The flock is contained in a wide parcel of land, and when they have exhausted the grazing there they are moved on to a different area. And moving sheep is a job for sheepdogs, so I hoped Peg was going to be useful. It was going to be a real test for her, as she would be operating among the dunes and for much of the time not able to see me, just responding to my whistles and shouts. Dave gave me a tip: climb to the top of a high dune so that I could keep an eye on her as much as possible.

Easier said than done: the sheep were roaming happily among the dunes, but Peg and I made heavier weather of it, unused to walking on sand and constantly sticking our feet into hidden rabbit holes and tripping over the rough scrub. Peg was, as ever, very eager to work, and she shot off like a bullet when we sighted some sheep, going round them and encouraging them to flock together. They disappeared from my sight behind a sand dune and so did she, but I knew she was still working, using her own brain. Sheep have an amazing instinct to collect together whenever they see or hear a dog, or hear a shepherd's whistle, and they were soon running in from all around, funnelling through tight gaps in the dunes, and heading down to the gate we were trying to get them through.

Peg wasn't the only dog rounding up the sheep. Tony Meadow, the reserve warden, and his assistant Sophie Bray, were also there with Molly, a five-year-old collie, and Tato, another collie who was retired from his working life, but more than happy to help out. They worked together as a team and we drove the flock on to fresh grazing.

The sheep are on the dunes from October to April, and they thrive, returning to the Lake District well fed and with none of the foot problems sheep can get in winter, because the sand is so dry. Herdwicks have proved to be the best breed for the job: when some Icelandic sheep were brought in they were a lot less successful, not being used to being moved by dogs and not thriving in the damp of the north west of England.

While I was there I saw another animal that has been brought in to crop the dunes. Seeing sheep was a big enough surprise, but it was even more bizarre to see five rare breed Shetland cattle, which were being trialled as another way of managing the vegetation. Since my visit a couple of years ago the breed of cow has changed and the dunes are now host to a small herd of Red Poll cattle, who, like the sheep, come to the dunes to spend the winter months keeping the vegetation in check. It's a win-win situation: the dunes are maintained, and the farmer gets his sheep or cattle looked after without having to provide any winter fodder.

It was a similar conservation project that took me to Snowdonia a few months later, real hill-farming countryside. But there are special habitats for wildlife and plants here, too, and it's a juggling act getting farming and conservation to work hand in hand, in a way that benefits both.

The farm I visited, Hafod y Llan, was bought by the National Trust in 2000 with the aim of preserving the mountainous area that was being overgrazed by the sheep. After reducing the number of sheep from 4,000 to just under 2,000, it was clear there were still problems. The Trust did not want to reduce sheep numbers further, but after looking at the conservation work of hill farmers in the Alps and the Pyrenees, they decided the way forward was to actively manage the sheep with a shepherd on the mountain with them all the time between May and September, moving them away from sensitive places where overgrazing was damaging the plant life.

It is a five-year project, and the aim is to have flower-rich mountain tops with grazed valleys below. The problem is that the sheep that live on this land are, like most sheep on hill farms, hefted. This means they have a particular area of the mountainside which belongs to them and their own small group of sheep. The lambs are taught by their mothers that this is their patch, and the ewes teach them the terrain, where to find shade, where to find water and all the pitfalls to avoid. To move them to different 'hefts' or 'heafs' (the word changes depending on which part of the country you are in; the Welsh word is 'cynefin') is going to take a long time and careful management.

I went up there when the project had been going for a year, and when the farm had just appointed a second shepherd to help cover the long hours that have to be spent up on the mountainside with the sheep. It's a lonely job, but very fulfilling for the right person who loves sheep, has a good four-legged companion and doesn't mind his own company.

I met Arwyn Owen who manages the farm for the National Trust and I asked him why the sheep needed this special, full-time attention. He explained that the sheep need more management.

'They are not always eating what we want them to eat, and without intervention they linger in some areas and graze the vegetation too closely. These are areas where the wildflowers and plants need to be safe-guarded. So we've gone back to the way things used to be, with a shepherd actually on the hill with them all the time in daylight hours. He leads the sheep to the areas that need to be grazed.'

With Peg by my side I climbed up the mountain to where the latest recruit to the shepherding project, Daniel Jones, was going about his job of checking where the sheep were cropping. There were about 800 Welsh mountain sheep. They're a lively little breed whose thick, coarse wool protects them from the harsh Snowdonia weather. In different parts of Wales there are derivatives of the same breed with various Welsh names: as well as white Welsh mountains, there are Torddu, or Badger Face, with a white body and black belly. Torwen are the reverse – a black body and white belly. Black Welsh are, as the names suggests, black all over, and the little Balwen have black with white socks and a white tip to the tail and are the only one of all the Welsh sheep considered a rare breed.

The flock were dotted around us and I realised how difficult Daniel's job is. It's not like moving a flock: he has to monitor individual sheep and move each one when it's in the wrong place. I commented that he must be fit; Peg had romped up the hill but I was breathless by the time I reached him. He described his job as 'awesome', and said he had learned a lot in the six weeks he had been there.

'There's a lot of walking, and without dogs we'd be pretty useless up here. They're an essential tool, and we couldn't work the sheep without them.'

I noticed a small box attached to the collar of Dan's dog, which I recognised as a GPS tracker. Dan explained that it records where they have been working and how many miles they have covered. There are also fixed cameras dotted around the hillside which monitor the movement of the sheep. Combining both technologies shows where the sheep are grazing the most.

Dan was happy for me to let Peg have a go bringing a few sheep down from an area above us where they were not supposed to be. Working individual sheep on steep slopes was not something either she or I are used to, and I'm afraid Peg in her eagerness did move the sheep a little bit faster than Dan wanted, the ewes charging down the mountain at a bit of a lick. Unlike me moving a flock, when speed helps, the art here is to be able to move individual sheep so gently that they don't realise they are being nudged. I reckon Peg and I would get the hang of it if we practised ...

I was amused when Dan told me he knows by sight several sheep that are persistent offenders, always grazing in the wrong places. He even puts a blue mark on the naughty ones so that he can pick them out more easily.

Although it is clearly an idyllic and ancient way of life (if you don't count the trackers and cameras), I wondered how the project was going in terms of saving rare plants, so I met up with Sabine Nouvet, who is the National Trust conservation ranger for Snowdonia, and who is monitoring the project.

'It's very encouraging. We have plants like heather and bilberries that are starting to recover, and we're hoping that the new shoots that are appearing now will survive.'

She led me further up the mountain, to show me the little green bilberry fruits, and heather with new shoots.

'Bilberries respond very quickly to a change in grazing,' she told me. 'We had some heather flowers last year and we are hoping for more this year.'

She also explained that it wasn't simply a matter of saving the plant life: the sheep are also benefitting, because the diversification is bringing back plants that are more palatable and nutritious for them. The sheep and the ecology of the mountain are both gaining from the project.

For me, the most satisfying thing was seeing a shepherd working in the old-fashioned way, alone with nothing but his dog and his sheep, upholding a very ancient tradition.

Another very traditional shepherd I met for *Countryfile* is a young woman called Ashley Stamper, who works on the Cheviot Hills of Northumbria in the harshest of conditions. The work she does very much follows the old, largely unchanged, routines of centuries of shepherding, with her dogs by her side and only a quad bike and some good waterproof clothing to distinguish her from the men and women who ran flocks on this land for generations past.

Yet in some ways, Ashley is very different from those shepherds of yore. For a start, she's not from a farming family. In fact, quite how she has ended up living in the lee of the Kielder Forest and working a flock of north of England Blackface sheep on the Otterburn ranges, where the landowner is the Ministry of Defence, is, to me, a surprising story, and hearing it made me think of my dad, who also had no family background in farming. I recognised in Ashley something that he must have had: an urge to work outdoors, close to nature, at one with the land. Something that they both intuitively knew, without having any experience of the life, as I was lucky enough to have as a child.

Ashley's mother and father both work in different branches of the beauty business, her mum as a beauty therapist and her dad running a company that has developed and sells tanning machines. As a child, the only connection Ashley had with the great outdoors was her love of horses.

At her school near Edinburgh, Ashley was studying for her Highers (the Scottish equivalent to GCSEs) when her parents bought her a beauty salon. She was 15 at the time, going to school in the morning, and rushing out to run the salon at lunchtimes and after school in the afternoons, putting herself through courses in accountancy, beauty therapy, massage, reflexology and holistic therapy, managing staff who were many years older than her. She even opened a wedding dress shop at the rear of the salon.

So far, so very girlie, and clearly Ashley had a good career laid out for her when she finished school. But she wasn't happy. She'd sold her pony to a farmer and to keep in touch she spent a few school holidays helping out on the farm, and she realised that these were the happiest times of her life.

So, despite having won accolades as one of Scotland's youngest entrepreneurs, and as the world's youngest salon owner with a good wage coming in from the salon, at the age of 17 Ashley decided she would never be happy working inside all day, and beauty therapy wasn't what she wanted to do for the rest of her life.

'Dad said I was mad, and told me I needed to knuckle down and get on with the business. But I was adamant: I wanted to go to university to study horses. When I looked into it, though, horses wouldn't take me far enough, and I realised what I needed to do was take a degree in agriculture.'

Without enough qualifications to get on to a degree course, Ashley went to college for two years to get Scottish Vocational Qualifications, combining her time studying with working on the farm where she had spent school holidays. She'd gone from having money in her pocket every week to working on the farm free in return for board and lodging, staying with her grandparents while at college, and relying on her mum for subsidies.

'But I was so happy, I knew this was what I wanted to do for the rest of my life. The people I was working for, Pam and Paul, taught me lots, including how to train a sheepdog. I also found some local contracting work to help out financially.'

The first year of her four-year degree course was in Dumfries, and the following three years in Edinburgh. She had a beaten-up £300 car, she didn't go out socialising and she got stuck into her studies, getting excellent results.

When I met her she was still in the final year of her degree, attending uni only a couple of days a month and studying at home, with the rest of her time spent working on a large farm up in the hills looking after sheep. It's clear she loves her job, and when I watched her loading sheep onto a lorry for market, I could see she has the calm personality that you need around animals.

Where she works on the Ministry of Defence ranges where the army test heavy artillery and rockets, the landscape is constantly changing because of the explosions and there is only so much work she can do with a quad bike. 'Thank goodness for the dogs, I couldn't manage without them,' she said. Because nobody is allowed on the ranges when firing is in progress, she often has to get up there at 4.30am to check on the sheep, and be off by 9am.

It struck me as a very tough life, but Ash told me she prefers being up on the hills to having the sheep down in the valley.

'It changes all the time. You think you've learnt the hills and then one morning the fog is down in front of your face and all of a sudden you've no idea where you are. When you are on the hills by yourself and the mist is in and it's just you and your dogs, it feels very special.'

Ashley rents a small cottage from another local farm, where she lives with her three border collies, Dot, who is a quarter kelpie, Jim and puppy Mo.

'I'm very lucky, everyone helps me out,' she says.

'When I could no longer stay at the farm where I was working for nothing, because I needed to earn money, Mum said "Come home". It was tempting, it would have been very easy. But I knew I couldn't leave this valley, the people here, the sheep. At the same time I was homeless with three dogs and two horses. Luckily by then I had a boyfriend, James, and his family let me stay for a while, then I was offered the cottage. Another friend had a garage full of furniture she did not need, two friends took my horses and one horse now has a loan home. It was a real community effort.'

One chunk of very welcome help came from the Prince's Countryside Fund, a charity set up in 2010 by the Prince of Wales to improve the prospects of family farm businesses and the quality of rural life. One of the major worries for the future of farming in this country is that the average age of farmers is 59, so in conjunction with the car manufacturer Land Rover the Countryside Fund launched an initiative in 2016 to give five young people under the age of 35 the chance to drive a Land Rover Discovery Sport for a whole year to help them in the difficult early years of their career. It was the head of agriculture at her university who told Ash to apply.

'I had to put in a one minute video of why I needed the Discovery to help with my work. I was in Edinburgh, without my dogs, and I was up against the deadline to apply. So I borrowed a collie from Mum's next door neighbour, a pet dog who has probably never seen a sheep, and I had a couple of feedbags and medicine bottles in the back of my old car. We filmed it pretending it was 5am and I was hauling myself out of bed for work. I'm really surprised I got through the first round, because the dog was so fat I had to lift her in and out of the car ...'

Luckily, after interviewing Ashley over the phone and visiting her on the farm where she works, the team from the Countryside Fund and Land Rover could see how she would make great use of the car, especially commuting from Northumbria to Edinburgh.

'I put the two people who came to assess me on the quad bike and took them up on the hills where I work. I think they were impressed by the vastness and hardness of it all, and the long hours we work. They could see my little car was overflowing with feedbags, medicine and dogs.

'The only sad thing is that I only get to keep the Land Rover for a year. Then it will be back to another old banger, I guess. I've been a bit spoilt, having such an amazing car.'

One of the things about Ashley that intrigues me is that she has chosen, for her university honours project, to study sheepdogs. As she told me: 'There's not much data that shows how much work these dogs do, so I'm looking at energy consumption, comparing working dogs with non-working dogs.'

It will be useful to have some scientific data – although, I must say, I don't need any stats to tell me that my dogs, and dogs like Ashley's, are burning a lot more energy than the average family pet. Her project has two other parts; one on how dogs gather sheep, to assess whether they could ever be replaced by drones (like me, Ashley thinks this will never happen, but she's carried out an impartial study). The other part is an attempt to analyse the behaviour of dogs competing at sheepdog trials.

Ashley told me she was nervous about meeting me, because my dogs look so well behaved when they feature on *Countryfile*. She was worried hers would let her down. But I reassured her that mine are not perfect and sometimes the same scene is shot over and over until they do it right. I must say, working with her, I think she is doing really well with her dogs, and they are lovely animals.

Does she ever wish she'd stuck with the beauty business? 'When it's 4am and howling with wind and rain outside, it takes a bit of strength to get out of my bed. But I never seriously think about changing my job. I've never wanted to go back. Sometimes when Mum has to attend a big beauty show in London, I'll go with her to help her out – I owe her for all the support she has given me. So I wear a dress and makeup, do my hair. I like being girlie sometimes, and I sometimes give friends a massage, or do waxing, but I don't miss doing it every day, and I do miss the farm whenever I'm away from it.

'People tell me that with a degree I should go after a graduate job, earn a lot more than I do as a shepherd. But it's the part of the job I love most, and find constantly challenging: it's a lot trickier for me starting a tractor and picking up a bale of hay than it is writing 3,000 words on the protein requirements of ruminants. I know that if I took an inside job, after a couple of days I would crave the hills, the farm, the dogs.'

As I met Ashley and her dogs just before Christmas, filming for a *Countryfile* Christmas special, she and I popped in to hear the choir at a local chapel, Bowden Kirk, practising for their Christmas service. Lay minister Pam Walker explained to me why dogs are welcome in the church.

'It's a tradition in the borders, especially at times of festivals like Christmas, for sheepdogs to come to church. Dogs are part of the family as well as working companions, so shepherds would naturally bring them along to church.

'It was a bit strange for travelling priests, not used to the area, who were puzzled as to why their congregation was not standing up at the appropriate times in the service. But if they did stand, the dogs would get up, assuming they were off home. So it was easier, and kept the atmosphere more holy, if everyone stayed sitting down.'

As the choir sang, appropriately, 'While Shepherds Watched Their Flocks by Night', Ashley's three dogs settled down very contentedly and never stirred. It's wonderful to think of those old shepherds whose bond with their dogs was so strong that they went everywhere with them, even to church. And it's wonderful, too, that the church welcomed them.

Ashley is a fine example of a young person who has been attracted into shepherding, and I'm passionate about enthusing other young people to take on the job. If the average age of a farmer in Britain is 59, we need as much young blood as possible.

So I was very happy to travel with Peg up to Cumbria, to visit Newton Rigg college, which is a few miles from Penrith in the rugged, high fells of north Lakeland, where an exciting new course has been launched, the only one in the country dedicated to sheepdog handling.

The course, which has attracted 15 enthusiastic young students, is run by Derek Scrimgeour, a top dog trialler and sheep farmer. When I caught up with him he was impressing on the students how important it is for a shepherd or dog handler to stay calm.

'The dog buys into your mood. If you are loud, excited and rushing about, the dog will be the same. It's a technique you learn. I'm not a naturally calm person,' he confessed, 'but I can act calm.'

Derek enjoys passing on tips and skills to the youngsters, particularly the things he had to learn through making mistakes when he was their age.

Matt Bagley, from the college, was instrumental in getting the 20-week course off the ground and he believes as passionately as I do that we need to encourage the shepherds and farmers of the future in any way we can.

'It is fundamentally important because the bond between a dog and a handler is so special, and if we don't harness it in young people we may lose these skills. In this terrain a quad bike is of little or no use. You need a dog to do the job quickly and efficiently. When you buy a tractor, you get a manual, but not when you get a dog. All dogs and all handlers are different.'

The youngsters I met that day all seemed to be enjoying themselves, and knuckling down to learning their whistles.

One student at Newton Rigg college who doesn't need to do a sheepdog-handling course is 16-year-old Tom Blease. Tom was partnered with my old friend and mentor Dick Roper in the 2016 One Man and His Dog competition, and they were the winning team.

Tom now combines his studies at the college with an apprenticeship on a sheep farm near Ullswater, and he's intending to do more trialling. He says, 'I am earning a bit of money to pay for my own sheep and for when I can start driving, and I'm doing something I really enjoy,' he told me.

That's the key thing: enjoying the work. It's what gets us all, me included, out of bed on cold, wet mornings and outside into the fields. I'm thrilled that at *Countryfile* we've established a Young Farmer of the Year Award, for under-25 year olds, because these youngsters are the future of farming in this country.

I can't leave the subject of herding dogs without looking at New Zealand Huntaways. I've been to New Zealand twice, but on my first visit, when Duncan and I were making our way around Australia, New Zealand and North America on next-to-no money, I didn't get much chance to see Huntaways at work. Then, we spent a month pruning kiwi vines and the rest of our time driving around enjoying the breath-taking scenery. I'd heard of this special breed of New Zealand dog, and after working with Bob the kelpie in Australia, I was interested to see them. But I was slightly put off because I was told they barked from the moment they were let out of their kennels in the morning until they went back at night. I now know that this is not the case; although barking is an important part of their skill set, they are taught to do it on command, not incessantly.

The farmer who generously gave me and Duncan somewhere to stay did have a Huntaway, a remarkable three-legged dog that brought the cows in for milking in the morning, but because I was not working with livestock I didn't see a Huntaway working sheep.

I went back to New Zealand to make four programmes for *Countryfile* at the end of 2016, and this time I saw Huntaways working. They are beautiful black and tan dogs – they look like great big Labradors with a dash of hound in the mix. Nobody knows their exact heritage; they were first mentioned by the 'huntaway' name in the late nineteenth century. They were developed in response to farming in the hilly countryside. The vast sheep stations needed dogs that could work for days on end on steep, rough terrain, covering great distances. The sheepdogs brought by the settlers from Britain worked silently, but occasionally one would bark, and this was seen as useful, because the dogs had to work out of sight of the shepherd. So barking traits were deliberately bred for, as well as the agility, stamina and the intelligence needed for a dog that can work to some extent independently of his master.

A Huntaway does exactly what its name says: they hunt away, and they are not used for rounding up sheep. Their job is to take the huge flocks of sheep that are farmed out there up the mountains or along the valleys. In New Zealand it is normal for one man to handle a flock of 2,500 to 3,000 sheep, compared to here where it's usually one man to at the most a thousand. The dogs are therefore vital, each one doing the work of a couple of men.

The sheep in New Zealand are very hardy Romney sheep, which originated on the Romney marshes in Kent. They have been toughened up out there by natural selection: if a ewe can't lamb on her own or rear her lambs, they and she will die. Only the fittest live, so the surviving flock is naturally strong. Also, through careful genetic selection, the New Zealand farmers have bred sheep with worm resistance, foot-rot resistance, good growth rates and other desirable traits. So the sheep may have originated back here in Britain, but now we import them from New Zealand. At Bemborough Farm we buy New Zealand rams to put on our Romney ewes.

People sometimes ask why New Zealand lamb is so cheap: they have the advantages of very low overheads, with vast flocks and limited manpower, plus their grass grows all year round, not seasonally like ours. And much of that low production cost is down to these fantastic dogs. A collie wiggling about at the back of such a large flock would not be seen by the hundreds of sheep at the front, but the booming bark of the huntaway tells all 2,000 of them that there is a dog around, and the shepherd can work them from as far away as two miles. It's really impressive, watching one of these Huntaways zigzagging at the back of a huge mob of sheep, barking and controlling them.

During the *Countryfile* trip I also saw Huntaways driving a herd of Welsh black cattle, which were owned by an 83-year-old farmer who was as tough as his dogs. He lived in an old, very remote farm bungalow, two hours' drive down a forest track. I genuinely thought I was lost and was considering turning back, when at last I came to the farm. He works with his two grandsons, two collies for rounding up sheep, and two Huntaways, which get up behind the cattle and push them in the direction he wants them to go. I could see how responsive they were, and how quick to avoid getting too close to the cows. The farmer used whistle commands, and he had a whistle that told them to 'speak up', or bark.

He also had a remarkable little black and white Jack Russell, called Rhondda, who would travel about on the quad bike and hang out with the working dogs, occasionally dashing away to catch a rabbit. He lived outside the bungalow in a box he shared with a cat, and they curled up together. If the men went away for a few days they left food and water and both the cat and Rhondda fended for themselves outside. I asked one of the grandsons: 'What does the dog do when you're not here?'

'I don't know – I'm not here,' he replied, pragmatically.

Much as I admired Huntaways, because they are really lovely looking dogs, and I thrilled to the sight of them working, I wouldn't want a Huntaway back here. I simply wouldn't be able to use it to its full potential. We have small fields, and we don't need to drive enormous flocks over long distances.

While I was out in New Zealand, I heard about Pig dogs. They are cross-breeds with some qualities of herding dogs and border collies, with a touch of hound so they bark and have a good sense of smell, and genes from pit bull terriers so that they are brave and have strong jaws. The end result is a dog that barks when it smells pigs and will hunt them, but rather than chase them away it rounds them up back towards the dog's owner. Once the pig stands its ground the dog will grab hold of it. I recognise the skill of the dog but I'm rather glad I never witnessed it. Hunting wild pigs is a popular pastime, especially in the more remote areas. It is talked about as a great night out at the weekend in the same way that people here talk about a night down the pub. Whole generations of families – fathers, sons and grandsons – turn out together with their dogs. Pig hunting for sport also happens in America and Australia. The New Zealanders still have a bit of a frontier attitude, but sports like this in the UK were banned centuries ago.

CHAPTER 9

Have You Thought About Hungarian Wire-haired Vizslas?

After Ronnie died, our house felt very empty. Charlie and I both believe that a house needs a dog living in it, but for a few months all we had were the sheep-dogs kennelled outside. There was no welcoming snuffle when you came through the back door and nearly tripped over Ronnie on her bed in the passageway. There was no feeling of the comforting, unquestioning, non-judgmental presence of a dog to rush up to you with a wagging tail, delighted to see you even after the worst of days. There is nothing more relaxing than a dog pressing itself against your knee while you absent-mindedly stroke its head.

And there was no furry companion for Ella and Alfie, who were nine and five when Ronnie died. I'm a great believer that children thrive when they have a dog to love and be loved by. Of course, Ella had Pearl, but Pearl, despite her tricky start, was a working sheepdog and had always lived outside. We all felt the loss of Ronnie acutely, because the house felt strangely empty.

So there was no question: Bemborough farmhouse needed a dog. We'd also had a couple of break-ins on the farm, and we know that a barking dog is the best protection you can have against thieves, especially as we live in a fairly isolated place. When you go to sleep at night, it's reassuring to know there is a dog downstairs that will make all the right noises and make sure a burglar thinks twice about trying to get in, but neither Charlie nor I wanted a proper guard dog, like a German shepherd or a Rottweiler. We wanted a dog with a good bark, to alert us if necessary, but we also wanted a gentle family pet, and, for me, the bonus would be if it was also a gundog. So the big question was: which breed of dog should we go for?

I have fond memories of the Labradors I grew up with, but I know how gluttonous they can be, and how it's always necessary to check there is nothing within their reach that they may decide to devour, which can be tiresome. I also vividly remember the death of Raven after eating rat poison, and I don't want to experience something like that again.

Of course, after Nita, I'm a fan of springer spaniels, but Charlie is not so keen on them. They can be neurotic and non-stop, which can get irritating in a busy household. I considered German pointers, which are good gundogs, but I was told they are highly strung – like spaniels only with longer legs – so I crossed them off the list. So we faced a blank canvas, with all the many dog breeds – the Kennel Club recognises over 200 – to consider. We discussed it endlessly, and somehow no dog that we came up with completely suited all our needs, or appealed to us. There was a lot of talk of various small breeds but I like a larger dog that you don't have to bend too far down to pat, so the search went on.

Until, that is, the day I was filming for *Countryfile* in Norfolk and I was interviewing a gamekeeper, Tracie Rickman, about the way warreners used to keep rabbits in enclosures. The rabbits were such a valuable commodity that the warreners had fortified buildings in which to butcher them for meat and for their pelts. We were filming ferrets being used to catch rabbits in an area where the soil is sandy and riddled with rabbit warrens.

When we were on a break I talked to Tracie about our dilemma, explaining our reservations about the obvious candidates, Labradors and spaniels.

'Have you thought about Hungarian wire-haired Vizslas?' she asked.

I had literally never heard of Vizslas and had no idea what they looked like or what temperament they had.

'Come and see mine,' she said, after filming was over. So I went back to her home and was met by four big, gingery, long-haired dogs, who barked loudly when I first arrived but settled down when she told them to. She explained that they were good gundogs, easily trained, and excellent house dogs, guard dogs and companions.

They ticked all our boxes and I fell for them straight away. Friends later joked that I chose a Vizsla to match my own hair colour, but the main attraction for me was that they had the right combination of attributes that we were looking for.

Charlie's birthday was coming up later in the month, and as this dog was to be mainly hers, a house dog, I emailed her a link to a Hungarian wire-haired Vizsla website and asked if she liked the look of them. She replied enthusiastically. Like me she had never heard of them: there weren't that many around back then, although in the years since I have seen more and more at agricultural shows, both smooth coated and wire haired.

Before I left, I asked the gamekeeper if she knew anyone who was breeding wire-haired Vizslas and who might have puppies. She told me about Clint Coventry, who lives in West Sussex with his partner Anita Scott. They are renowned and well-established owners of Hungarian wire-haired Vizslas.

Before I committed to buying one, I read up about them. The wire-haired Vizsla is now recognised as a different breed from the Hungarian Vizsla, which has a smooth coat. But the wire-haired ones are actually close descendants of the smooth-coated ones: they were bred from traditional smooth-coated Vizslas crossed with German pointers. They were only recognised as a distinct breed in Hungary in 1966. So much of their heritage and history is intertwined with their smooth-haired cousins.

The cross-breeding, which began in the 1930s, was done by two Hungarians, one a breeder of Vizslas and the other of German wire-haired pointers, with the express intention of creating a dog the same colour as the Vizsla but with a bigger, stronger frame, with a wiry double coat, better suited for working in cold weather and retrieving from icy water, which they get from the German wire-haired pointers. The undercoat is dense and water repellent and the outer coat is long, harsh and wiry. They also have thicker hair on their tails and ears than the original Vizslas. They are a very fast breed, running at a top speed of 40mph (the fastest dog is a greyhound, with a maximum speed of 43mph, so not too far adrift ...)

During the Second World War, there was more inter-breeding and it's possible there is some Bloodhound, some Irish setter, some English pointer and even some standard poodle mixed in there, all contributing more assets to the eventual Hungarian wired-haired Vizsla that is now the breed standard.

So that's a relatively short history. But the original Vizsla, the smooth-coated one, goes back a very long way. Yellow hunting dogs arrived in Hungary with the first settlers in the country, the Magyars, who came from Asia in around AD 900. The Magyars had two types of dog: one for guarding their flocks and another for hunting and water fowling, and this second one was the ancestor of the Vizsla. The name comes from a tiny hamlet in Hungary, and has been in use since AD 1100. Traditionally the dogs were used for boar hunting and hunting with falcons, and later, after firearms were invented, for retrieving game and flushing out birds.

These were the dogs of barons and warlords, owned only by the land-holding aristocracy, who jealously protected their breeding. There's a story that during the Second World War, both the British and the Americans made plans to capture the Crown of St Stephen, the historical symbol of power in Hungary, as a major psychological blow to the Nazi regime, which was ruling the country. The Brits got there first, with an MI5 officer, Derek Peters, parachuted into Hungary with plans to get into the castle in Budapest, shoot the two guards who he believed were keeping vigil, and escape with the crown. Unfortunately for him the two guards were Vizslas, who hurled themselves at him and pinioned him to the floor.

Peters was imprisoned by the Nazis, and saw more of the reddish-coloured dogs, which were being used to guard the prison. Despite the way they had foiled his plans, he became a great admirer of them, and when he finally got back to England after the war he made his mind up to import the breed. By this time Hungary was behind the Iron Curtain, and Peters could not legally bring dogs out. Clearly not frightened of risk, he smuggled himself into the country again, but this time was dealt with ruthlessly when he reached the border on his way back home: his body was found riddled with bullets, and beside him, shot through the head, a handsome male Vizsla. Such is the pull of these beautiful dogs.

To me, the extra assets of the wire-haired breed make them a better choice than their smooth cousins. They are generally confident dogs – not aggressive but they'll take a stand if they have to. They have an easy nature, they're good company and easy to train (apart from housetraining, as I was to find out ...) One of the facts I read, that really endeared them to me, is their nickname 'Velcro dogs', earned because they have great loyalty to their owners and love to stick close to them. They've also been described as 'a dog for all reasons', because of their multi-purpose skills. There's been quite a discussion about the correct description of the colour of their coats: 'yellow'; 'golden rust'; 'amber'; 'brownish amber'; 'the golden colour of bread crust'; 'russet gold'; 'copper'; and 'dark sandy gold' have all been suggested.

Anyway, with Charlie as keen as I was about these interesting dogs, I made contact with Clint, who had a litter of puppies just weaned and ready to leave their mother. We had a long chat over the phone and arranged to meet up in a layby on the Warwick bypass as he was attending an event near there. He brought the bitch and one of her female puppies, so that I could see them together.

Meeting in a layby, or a car park, or at a motorway service station, is something dog owners are advised never to do. It's the way ruthless puppy-farm owners get round showing their puppies in the terrible conditions on the farms where they were born. But this was very different. I knew that Clint was a responsible and very well-respected Vizsla breeder, who runs a very good set-up. He is not a professional breeder, only having a litter when he wants a puppy for himself, and he laid down strict rules about me not breeding from our puppy until she was at least two. I signed a contract that said that if we decided we did not want her, he would have first refusal on having her back. So I was satisfied with him, and he knew enough about me from the many questions he'd asked me on the phone to be sure I would be a good owner for her. He brought all the paperwork that I needed, including her vet certificates to show she'd been wormed, her pedigree, insurance documents and a certificate of microchipping.

Puppy farms often sell dogs that are cross-breeds (especially tiny handbag-type dogs) to avoid having to give pedigree details, and they either don't have, or even forge, veterinary certificates, and they are frequently reluctant to give receipts. Bowled over by the cuteness of the doe-eyed pup, new owners either forget to insist, or don't even know what paperwork they should have. Often the consequences are dire, with puppies that are really sickly being passed on to unsuspecting owners who end up with vast veterinary bills or, worse, a puppy that is not healthy enough to survive. A reputable breeder like Clint will provide a record of the dog's first visit to the vet, of the first of his two vaccinations and the flea and worm treatment he has had. Since 2016, all puppies are required by law to be microchipped by the time they are eight weeks old. However, good breeders like Clint were doing it years ago. Breeders like him also make sure they know what kind of home the dog is going to: obviously, I'm very experienced with dogs, but if I was new to owning puppies Clint would have wanted to inspect our home to make sure we had the right facilities and the right degree of knowledge for bringing up a puppy. It's an old adage, but it's true: a dog is for life, not just for Christmas.

I knew there was no risk with buying a puppy from him. And, of course, I fell for the wriggly little pup who was put into my hands. I don't claim to be a dog expert, but I have handled enough animals in my life to know a sickly one, and this little girl was as healthy as could be. The only surprising thing was that, next to her shaggy mother, she was remarkably smooth looking, more like the traditional Vizsla except for the flatter head and stronger build of a wire-haired. She didn't have a lot of hair, but what she had was smooth.

'Don't worry,' Clint assured me, 'the longer hair will come in as she gets older.'

It never did, and it became a standing joke between me and Clint. 'The hair's in the post,' he would say. And I used to reply that I was expecting a discount if I ever bought another one from him. But I know he was slightly embarrassed by having sold me a wire-haired who didn't have wire hair ...

In fact, there is a wide range of hairiness in wire-haired Vizslas. Some are quite smooth, others have a coat that is more woolly than wiry. And the wiry hair can come in for up to four years after birth. Dolly, as we decided to call her, appeared on TV with me quite a lot and I was always having to tell people that she was one of the wire-haired breed.

Clint is an interesting character. He uses his Vizlas for hunting. He goes to pheasant shoots like many people with gundogs do, but also has a more unusual hobby. Clint and his partner Anita hunt with eagles all over Britain and across Europe. He has two eagles, a young male and an older, mature female. He tells me the females are always larger and more aggressive and if his two were ever released together the older female, Galina (which means chicken in Latin and Italian), who weighs 9lbs 6ozs, would kill the 7lb 6oz boy. This eagle doesn't have a name – eagles apparently are not called by their names, and are frequently not given one. He's not fully grown yet, and may put on another half to one pound, but he'll never be as heavy as the female.

The eagles hunt hares and sometimes the dogs are used to flush out the quarry. But not always: an eagle could easily attack a Vizsla. There is a shortage of hares in the UK, and so most of Clint's hunting is in the Czech Republic, Hungary, Germany, Austria, Slovakia and Croatia. Every year he goes to a big meeting in Opočno, in the Orlicke mountains in the Czech Republic and meets up with eagle hunters from all over the world, some flying in from America and Canada. Some of the really big female eagles hunt and kill foxes and deer, and Clint even knows a Croatian falconer who uses his eagle to take jackals (there is a strain of jackal, the European jackal, that thrives across Eastern Europe). There are, Clint estimates, only 30 to 50 eagles in the UK that are being flown.

It's a passion Clint has had since he was a teenager; working up from flying a kestrel, then a buzzard and a falcon. It took him 20 years to get up to a golden eagle. It's a dangerous sport, but he loves it. He wears a heavy glove on his left hand and arm, but as he takes hold of the leather straps (jesses) dangling from the eagle's ankles with his right hand, he has on more than one occasion felt it sink its talons into his unprotected hand, once being manacled by an eagle for 30 minutes. He knew that struggling would make the bird aggressive, so he simply waited, in pain, until it released him.

'Luckily I've never had a talon in a joint, like an elbow, so I've never needed hospital treatment,' he says. 'But my right hand and arm have taken a lot of punishment over the 20 years I've been flying eagles. I've had a talon go right through a finger and out the other side.'

When I ask why he does it his answer is simple: 'There is nothing like watching these magnificent birds in flight. It's not about the kill, or any kind of blood lust: most eagles only catch prey once in ten flights, and they are the least productive birds in all falconry. What makes all the work worthwhile is watching a wonderful, graceful creature fly free. It's such a thrill.'

I've only ever caught glimpses of golden eagles in the distance when filming in Scotland, so to see these awesome creatures up close at Clint's home was great. Clint loves his birds deeply, and talks movingly of a bird that was poisoned (inadvertently, by another eagle hunter) and which lay with its head on his lap, and which he held tenderly when it had to be put to sleep, which reminded me of the final minutes of my dogs.

Clint discovered Vizslas by accident. He was using German wire-haired pointers to pick up at pheasant shoots and he bought a puppy he thought would work well with his eagles. But the eagle attacked the bitch and Clint discovered the dog had been stealing the bird's food. The relationship was never going to work, so the puppy went back to her original owner, who told Clint he could borrow a young Vizsla for a hunting trip he was making to Scotland.

At the time there were fewer than 150 wire-haired Vizslas in the country, and Clint had never heard of them. The one he borrowed, Lady, was a very withdrawn dog who had no energy, but gradually she came out of herself, and he found her to be loving, loyal and hard-working, a very special dog.

'I wish I'd discovered them 20 years earlier,' Clint says.

Lady had a litter, and one of her pups, Emmie, was the mother of our new little one, Dolly.

Charlie and the children were just as besotted with her as I was when they saw her and she quickly became Charlie's dog. If she was attached by Velcro to anyone in the family it was Charlie, and although I fed her and took her out around the farm with me she'd choose Charlie first every time. Dolly was the first house dog we had owned together, which made her extra special.

I soon realised that Vizslas as a breed are far more sensitive than the collies and spaniels I had previously trained, and that the main ingredient needed for their training is love, not discipline. It took longer to house-train Dolly than I expected, and I admit I was probably a bit too strong with her. With a spaniel you need to show them who is boss and you can be quite tough with them, yelling at them when they have done wrong and left a puddle in the house. Dolly would be broken for a whole day if she was spoken to harshly: if you raised your voice at her or went to grab her to carry her outside for a wee, she would whimper and cower away. Throughout her life she was a bit insecure and very sensitive.

Once, when she was still very young, she was lying near the Aga when I took a boiling saucepan of peas off the heat. As I moved it a tiny droplet of water fell onto her back and she yelped. It didn't burn her or cause a blister, but it obviously stung her. From then on, whenever anyone started cooking she would leave the room. She never forgot that tiny incident.

We wanted to breed from Dolly, so she went to stay with Clint and Anita to run with one of their dogs. It turned out Dolly was completely frigid: she wouldn't let the dog anywhere near her. She just wasn't having it. When a bitch refuses to breed there's not a lot you can do, but we were disappointed because we had planned to keep one of her litter. Most disappointed of all the family was Alfie because we told him that he could have the puppy we kept as his own dog. He was really excited when Dolly went off for her romantic assignation in Sussex and crushed when she came back resolutely not pregnant. He'd even chosen a name: his puppy was going to be called Boo.

We were thinking about what to do when I was chatting to a friend, Jon King, who used to be our livestock manager, one day shortly after Dolly's return and he mentioned that he had heard about a litter of wire-haired Vizslas that were ready to find new homes. The breeder lived in Gloucestershire, not too far from us, so Charlie, Ella and I headed off to see them. It was early May, and Alfie's tenth birthday was only a couple of weeks away, so we planned to get a puppy for him, although we didn't mention it to him because we didn't want him to be disappointed again. Some of the pups in the litter of six were already spoken for and they all wore a different-coloured collar to make sure the right ones went to the right new owners. We played with them in the garden, threw toys for them and I checked them over looking for any health problems. In the end, we settled for the one with the red collar.

On the day of Alfie's birthday, we had arranged for Charlie to pick up the puppy on her way back from her job in Bristol where she worked in television, as it was only a short diversion from the motorway for her. It meant that Alfie didn't get his main present until late in the afternoon. He had a few presents in the morning before we all raced off to work or went to school and Alfie was told he could open the others in the afternoon when we were all back, and then we'd cut his birthday cake.

It was a sunny day, spring was slipping into summer and the garden was looking green and lovely. Ella, Alfie and I were sitting outside, but it was late afternoon by the time I heard Charlie's car, and I know Alfie was beginning to fear his longed-for present wasn't going to materialise.

'I was sort of expecting it, because we'd talked about names for a puppy when Dolly tried to have puppies,' he says. 'But it was getting late and I began to think it wasn't going to happen.'

When I heard Charlie's footsteps approaching I cupped my hands over Alfie's eyes. As she walked into the garden with the little bundle nestled in her arms I uncovered his eyes and we all shouted: 'Boo!' And there she was, his very own Boo, a little bundle of joy.

Alfie's face beamed with the biggest smile you have ever seen, and for a few moments I relived that wonderful Christmas when I first set eyes on Nita, snuggled in the old tea chest. Alfie was, literally, speechless. He took the puppy in his arms, and that was the start of a deep relationship between the two of them. As Nita was my dog, as Dolly was Charlie's, as Pearl is Ella's, so Boo is Alfie's. If we are walking around the farm together and Alfie heads off in a different direction, Boo never hesitates: it is him she goes with, not me.

Boo has grown into an excellent gundog, with the softest of mouths. Gundogs need soft mouths because they must never bite into the game they are retrieving. No one wants to eat a pheasant or partridge that has been chomped into by an over-zealous dog. Boo's mouth is so soft that one day Charlie saw her in the garden with wings sticking out from either side of her mouth. There were loads of birds fussing round the bird table and clearly Boo had caught one. Charlie shouted to her to let go, and when Boo opened her mouth a blue tit flew out, completely undamaged.

A good gundog will carry an egg without breaking it, and Vizslas have proved to be every bit as good as the more traditional Labradors and retrievers. From childhood I have loved watching gundogs work. Before I went to agricultural college I spent a year working on the Chatsworth Estate of the Duchess of Devonshire, and although I missed Nita, who stayed at home, there were dogs all around and I was in awe of these highly trained gundogs. Ours at home were really good field dogs, but these were trained to an even higher level, and each gamekeeper would have his own – perhaps as many as four or five – mainly Labradors and spaniels. I was full of admiration for the control they had: a gamekeeper could send one of his dogs to fetch a pheasant and the others would sit and stay.

Of course, to a gamekeeper a well-trained dog is a tool of the trade, and must be kept in good condition like any other tool. The dogs on the Chatsworth Estate needed to be very well controlled because it was a very professionally run estate and there was no place for an unruly dog.

The head gamekeeper also had a German shepherd. It had been trained as a police dog and he used it to deter poachers. He had fantastic control over it. It was a lovely, soft dog, who would play with me and muck about – until he put its collar on. The minute the collar went on it was just like turning a switch and the dog was in work mode. It was a lesson to me in how well trained dogs can be, if you have time and effort to put into it.

I'm sure our Vizslas could work at that level: the breed is capable of it. But from my point of view, all that is required is that they are competent and willing retrievers of game, and the rest of the time are affectionate family pets.

We bred from Boo while she was still young, at three years old. I heard about a lady in Bristol, Rebecca Bye, who has a dog called Frost, and we arranged to get them together here at the farm. It was a bit of a palaver: Frost got over excited the first time and swelled up before he was inside Boo, but they had another go when he had calmed down and this time he hit the jackpot. Rebecca brought him back for a follow-up mating, just to be sure.

I took Boo to the vet a month later and she was scanned, which showed she was having six or eight puppies (it's hard to tell on a scan with so many of them wriggling around). The scanning was filmed for *Countryfile* to be included within one of the 'Adam's Farm' pieces, telling the story of everyday life on the farm.

We borrowed a whelping box from a friend, which is a box big enough for the bitch to lie down but designed so that she can't squash or smother her own puppies. Then we waited for it all to kick off, which it did a day or two later. I heard her whining, panting and padding around the kitchen at 4.30am so I went down to her, took her outside for a wee and settled her in the box. It was 6am when the first puppy showed its head, but I could see it was stuck and Boo was panting and distressed. I've helped lots of lambs being born and I've seen puppies being born, so I had no hesitation in helping her, by easing it out. She yelped a little bit as the first puppy popped out, but she was not at all aggressive towards me for helping, which some bitches are.

Her firstborn was a lovely little girl pup, and she instantly licked her all over. I knew at that moment that Boo was an instinctively good mother, even though the whole process must have felt alien to her this first time. After that, she gave birth to another puppy every half-hour to 45 minutes, and it took all morning for the full litter of six to be born. The vet had told me that if any of the pups took more than 45 minutes I should ring for help, but I didn't need to – although I was watching the clock with a couple of them.

Boo was brilliant. I helped them latch on, and they were happily suckling as soon as she had licked them clean. They were all the Vizsla reddish colour, but a bit stripy at birth, which is normal. Ella loves the theatre, so she gave them all Shakespearean names: Beatrice, Romeo, Rosalind, Desdemona, Gertrude and Ophelia, completely ignoring my preference for one syllable names! They had different lengths of hair, and as they got older it was clear that Romeo and two of the little bitches had shorter hair, more like Dolly, and the other three were as hairy as Boo herself.

We sold them all to local people: I think Dolly and Boo were good ambassadors for this special breed of dog and, having met them, there was no shortage of people wanting to take one. I copied Clint's example and gave them all similar contracts to the one he gave me. Because the new owners lived locally it was easy enough for me to ensure they all went to suitable homes.

We decided not to keep one as we fully intended to have another litter from Boo a couple of years later, and keep one of those puppies so that, as Dolly grew old, there was another little one in the house.

Tragically, our plans were overtaken by Dolly's death, which I will talk about in the next chapter. Now we regretted not keeping one of Boo's litter because we were down to one dog in the house, and we like to overlap them so that we have a little one growing up alongside the older ones. We could not breed from Boo again so soon, so we rang Clint on the off-chance he may have some pups. Clint told me his bitch was pregnant and he would, of course, save us a bitch pup if there was one.

By coincidence, I was filming down in Sussex, so when they were born I went to see the new litter of puppies, and in particular to see the parents. The dog was one that Clint had imported and was very hairy and really lively. Clint let him out and he bounced around full of beans and clearly adored Clint. We took him out into the field where Clint had his chickens – the dog stalked one and then went on point, freezing to the spot. Clint explained he was a brilliant working dog. I was slightly worried that his excitable temperament may be a bit too much for me to handle, though, if it was inherited by the pups. Next I met the bitch who had a shorter coat than the dad, with sweet, loving eyes and a gentle nature. Clint explained that she, too, was brilliant at working and very intelligent. I really hoped we could get one like her.

A couple of weeks later Charlie and I went down together to choose another little girl wire-haired Vizsla. There were six pups, two dogs and four bitches. Clint had chosen a little bitch pup for himself and that left us three to choose from. Clint was away in Hungary with his golden eagles when we visited, and so his partner Anita looked after us. We popped all those that weren't available into the kennel, leaving the three prospective pups running around. One immediately went to the corner of the run and sat there looking very shy and insecure. For me this meant that it wasn't the sort of character I was looking for. The other two bounded around and jumped up at us. The first one Charlie picked up nestled into her arms, holding its head back and pressing it under her chin. I could see in Charlie's eyes that she was quickly falling in love with this one. I picked up the other one and checked its teeth, feet and nipples to ensure they were even, in case we wanted to breed from her in the future – that's the farmer coming out in me. The one Charlie was cuddling was quite small with shorter hair. Charlie and I swapped pups and again the one she was holding nestled into her with as much love and affection as the first. What an impossible decision to make. Two gorgeous puppies, either would do us well. The final decision was made because we really wanted a reasonably sized dog with a similar coat to Boo, not too long but not too short. Out of the two puppies, the one I was originally holding was probably the best option for us. Anita confirmed to us that we had made a great choice and as she has seen dozens of puppies over the years, I trust her judgment. So we had our new puppy.

She wasn't ready to leave her mother, and I was just about to set off on an amazing three-week trip to Australia and New Zealand, filming for *Countryfile*. But as soon as I got back, Charlie drove down and collected her: the latest addition to our household, who we have called Olive.

At least, the rest of the family chose Olive. I'm all in favour of a dog having a one-syllable name, as a short, sharp name is easier for them to learn and better when you are training them. But I was outvoted, and now that she's here, very much part of the family, Olive seems very appropriate.

Alfie said he was going to train her: 'I was very young, just ten, when I got Boo, so I probably didn't work hard enough at her training. But I'll put in more time with Olive.'

Olive is certainly a very sweet-natured puppy, and she loves other dogs almost as much as she loves us. The first thing she does when I open the back door in the morning is to run over to Peg's kennel to say hello. Peg is very tolerant with her.

There are so many dangers on a farm that it is important to acclimatise her nice and slowly. I've been taking her around with me on certain routine jobs, getting her used to travelling in the back of the Polaris 4x4. When she was four months old I introduced her to sheep for the first time. They can be very flighty and it's important she learns to respect them. She has behaved very well with them so far: on that first meeting, which was filmed for *Countryfile*, I put her down near them. She was clearly a little bit nervous, but her reaction was perfect: not over-excited, backing off when the sheep approached her.

All dogs, not just those that live on a farm, should be taught to be respectful around sheep and kept on a lead at all times when they are being walked through fields with sheep, especially pregnant ewes and ewes with lambs. A dog that is loose can worry sheep, at worse attacking them or causing them to abort. It's every shepherd's nightmare: a rogue dog, following its instincts to prey on sheep, causing havoc with the well-being of the flock and the livelihood of the shepherd.

It's also important that Olive learns to be patient and quiet in the back of the trailer, so I left her in there for a while with the other dogs and she was very good. To introduce her to the cattle I put her on a lead – cattle can be inquisitive and aggressive around dogs, and as she's going to see a lot of them for the rest of her life, it's vital she knows how to react to them. The first time she met the cows she barked a bit, not very loudly, and I made sure I kept the encounter short. Gradually she has been introduced more and more to the animals and the routines of the farm.

Living on a farm is exciting and scary for a puppy, but one thing is certain: she'll never be bored. And I enjoy her company – having a puppy around always brightens up my day.

CHAPTER 10

Losing Dolly

Dolly was the loveliest, gentlest dog you can imagine. Her own sensitivity meant that she was, in turn, very sensitive to the needs of those around her and she always seemed to know intuitively whenever one of us was low, or had problems.

For example, when Dad died in October 2015, the whole family was plunged into grief. It seemed impossible to imagine life at Bemborough going on without him, even though he and Mum no longer lived at the farm. After his death, in the days before his funeral, we all coped with our grief in our own ways, and Dolly was always there, with a comforting wet nose to push into your hand, a gentle pressure on your legs as she leaned into you. It was her way of telling us she understood, and wanted to give her support. If I was sitting, quietly, going through my memories of Dad, she'd put her head on my lap.

Grief rolls over people in waves and we were all up and down in our emotions. Dolly seemed to sense exactly which member of the family needed her most at any time. When my sister Libby, fighting back tears, took herself away for a contemplative walk through the

fields she had known since childhood, and which sym-
bolised Dad to all of us, without being summoned Dolly
rose from her bed in the kitchen and attached herself to
Libby's side – a comforting presence on a tear-stained
walk. She knew that Libby was, at that time, most in
need of a gentle, undemanding companion.

About eight months after Dad's death I was absent-
mindedly stroking Dolly when I felt a lump on her
ribcage. It was very small, but it grew rapidly until it
was about the size of a golf ball; a smooth lump raised
on her chest. She was only nine years old, so I hoped it
would be a lipoma, a benign fatty lump of the sort that
I was familiar with because Labradors are prone to
them (as are Doberman Pinschers, miniature schnau-
zers and larger mixed-breed dogs). But it's always
advisable to get a lump checked out, so I took Dolly to
the vet, which of course she hated because she associated it with sterile smells and needles.

The vet didn't seem to share my optimism about the
lump, which was harder than a lipoma, and he kept
Dolly in for a biopsy that involved taking quite a large
slice of the growth. She came home the next day, the
stitches came out and she seemed as happy and energetic
as ever. But the bad news was that the biopsy results
showed that Dolly had an aggressive soft-tissue
sarcoma. Cancer, and one that would progress fast
through her body if it wasn't checked.

She went back to stay at the vet's and this time had
major surgery: not only was the lump removed but an

area of tissue around it was also taken, including between the intercostal muscles of her chest. The vet warned us that, although he hoped he had got rid of the tumour and enough tissue around it to halt its spread, there was a chance that it could come back. Dolly came home with a large scar and a shaven chest but she was soon back to normal, ready to come out around the farm with me in the mornings, always up for a long walk with Charlie.

When I took her for a check-up about a month later, I could feel a few tiny nodules on her scar, but the vet was hopeful that these were just scar tissue. She seemed so well in herself that I optimistically believed he was right.

Charlie, the children and I were due to go on a fortnight's holiday to Italy a few days later, and we went without any worries about Dolly, as she was trotting around happily and did not seem to be even slightly off colour. Doris, a good friend of ours, stays at our house to look after our menagerie of animals while we are away, and Dolly adored her.

When we got back, though, we could see that the lump had returned, and I took her to the surgery again. Yes, the vet said, the cancer had returned. To operate again, and be sure it was all removed, he would have to take away two or three of her ribs, and rebuild her ribcage with a wire mesh. It was a difficult operation and she would need a long, slow recovery; she would almost certainly never get back to the level of exercise she enjoyed. On the other hand, he told me, it might stay the way it was (it was clearly not bothering her) and not get any worse.

She was nine years old, and although that is short of the life expectancy of a healthy dog (the Kennel Club lists the life expectancy of a wire-haired Vizsla as 'more than ten years') she was already approaching old age. So we decided to go for the second option: take her home, give her the life she so much enjoyed, and hope for the best.

Charlie was very upset. Dolly was almost like a third child to her. They adored each other. At first it seemed to be going well: Dolly was her usual self, charging around on the farm. A few days later Charlie went to see a friend and they took the dogs for a long walk, and Dolly was every bit as energetic as she normally was. We were beginning to be hopeful.

But that evening she was lying on an old easy chair in the living room. (Despite my edict that dogs don't go on furniture, we have an old chair, covered with a blanket, that they can lie on. So much for my strict rules ...) As she lay there the swelling on her chest suddenly blew up. You could virtually see it getting bigger. She could hardly move and was clearly in pain.

We let her sleep there overnight. I crept down in the small hours to check on her and thankfully she was sleeping peacefully. I got up even earlier than usual and was downstairs at 5.30am to find that the whole of her side had expanded and she struggled to walk. I managed to get her out into the garden to wee, but it was costing her a massive effort.

I broke the news to Charlie, then I rang the vet and asked him to come to the farm, and to be prepared to put her down. While we were waiting for her to arrive, Charlie stayed with Dolly and I walked up to Buttington Clump to dig another grave: I knew that her end had come. When the vet came, she told us the cancer was rampaging through her body. I sat with Dolly in the garden while Charlie took refuge in the house, and we were both grateful that Alfie and Ella were away with friends. I held Dolly in my arms, keeping my emotions in check so as not to alarm her. The vet gave her a large dose of anaesthetic and after a few seconds I felt her beautiful body go limp. I carried her reverentially to the clump and buried her.

It was a sad time, especially for Charlie. She and Dolly went everywhere together. A few months after her death, when I was at the Bath and West Show, I met a charming artist called Sophie, who had studied at the Royal Agricultural University in Cirencester before deciding to turn her hobby of drawing into a profession and starting up Sophie Cotton Limited. I was very impressed with Sophie's work and commissioned a portrait of Dolly for Charlie's birthday. Sophie works from photographs, using fine graphite to create intricate portraits, and Charlie was delighted with her present. The drawing now hangs on the wall outside the living room door, and we pass it every time we go into the living room or upstairs – it's a lovely reminder of the beautiful dog we still miss.

We had Boo, Pearl and Peg, but there was a Vizsla-shaped hole in our lives. After six months we knew we had to do something, so that's when we got Olive.

The story of Dolly's death was used on *Countryfile*, with archive film of her walking through the farmyard with me, to introduce an item I did about cancer in dogs, and the way new treatments are being developed. After the programme I received an amazing number of letters of sympathy and support, with many dog owners sharing their own similar experiences. As I said in the introduction to the programme, treating cancer in dogs has always been notoriously difficult, but technology is giving more and more dogs a chance of life, and as long as an animal is young enough and fit enough, some owners are prepared to give it a go.

I went to meet TV's 'Supervet', Professor Noel Fitzpatrick, who founded the Fitzpatrick Referrals hospital at Godalming, Surrey, in 2005. As anyone who has seen *The Supervet* programmes knows, Noel has pioneered an amazing array of treatments for animals, things that would not have been available even ten years ago. The hospital is at the forefront of cutting-edge technology, which is combined with genuine care for the sick patients. His team treats orthopaedic and neurological conditions in small animals, and the hospital is a world leader in joint replacements for animals, including, to my amazement, hip replacements for cats.

I can't imagine anyone being able to perform such a delicate operation, but it happens here. All spinal and neurological conditions are treated, and prosthetic limbs are fitted to any animal that needs one.

But, because of Dolly's recent death, what interested me was a new hospital, Fitzpatrick Referrals Oncology and Soft Tissue hospital, opened just a year earlier and dedicated to the cure of cancer in animals. In that year, more than 1,000 furry patients have received cancer treatment there. It was there I met Noel, as well as the hospital's clinical director, Professor Nick Bacon. The two hospitals employ over 200 staff, 40 of whom are vets, and the operating theatres are constantly busy.

Before I went to see the work they are doing, I met a dog and his owner who have both benefitted from being referred to this highly specialised unit. Anne Rogers, a farm manager from Hampshire, has a lovely collie cross called Monty. On Christmas Day Anne had a friend round for Christmas dinner, and when Monty sat on her lap for a stroke, Anne's friend noticed a small lump on his leg.

When Anne's local vet examined it and sent a sample away for testing, the diagnosis was cancer. The only option available to the vet was to remove Monty's leg, but Anne wanted to give him another chance, as he was a young dog. At this point she was told about Noel's hospital.

'Monty's a very important part of my life. I spend a lot of time on my own in the day and he is with me from dawn to dusk, checking round the farm. He's a pet and a work companion,' Anne said.

Monty was referred to the hospital at Guildford in the hope that he could be treated without a radical amputation. He was successfully operated on, recovered fully, and when I met him he was full of beans, a lovely, healthy dog: you'd find it hard to imagine he had been through such a tough time.

The hospital itself is a state-of-the-art building, and Noel is as charismatic in person as he appears on TV. I was not surprised when I learned later that, after training as a vet, Noel had a spell when he combined veterinary work with acting, appearing on TV in popular dramas like *Heartbeat* and *Casualty*. Thank goodness he didn't find acting stardom: thousands of animals owe their lives to his decision to give himself full time to his first love, being a vet. And not just any vet ... But I'm guessing the acting gives him the confidence to appear in front of the TV cameras in an unselfconscious way, and adds just enough showmanship for him to be able to explain his work so clearly to those of us who don't have degrees in veterinary science.

Noel is passionate about his work. He loves cars but once sold an Aston Martin to pay for an extra vet, that's how dedicated he is. Some people are ready to criticise pet owners who spend thousands on their animals, but Noel understands the pure, unconditional love that owners have for their pets. He knows that for many people the value of a pet in their life is incalculable.

He points out that every advanced medical drug treatment used in humans has been tested first on animals before being declared safe for us, so why shouldn't we give something back to them, now that we have the technology and the skills?

My first question for Noel was, 'Is cancer more prevalent in animals than it used to be?' He explained that it has always been there, but with modern diagnostic techniques owners are hearing about it more.

He introduced me to Archie, a dog with a tumour in his jaw, which was bursting through his gums. It looked very nasty to me, but Noel explained that it was operable, and that Archie would soon be back to his old self.

Noel told me that the hard statistical fact is that half of all dogs over the age of ten will die of cancer. After accidents and trauma, cancer is the biggest single canine killer.

'People used to say that nothing can be done when an animal got cancer,' Noel said. 'But today that's not true. We can cure some cancers, and we can give good palliative care for most, so that the quality of their lives is good. Dogs can have all the treatments that humans can have. It's a game changer.'

The treatments the hospital provides include surgery, chemotherapy, immunotherapy, radiotherapy. Surgery alone cures more tumours than any other treatment, or combination of treatments. The same anaesthetic drugs, surgical equipment, instruments and suture (stitch) materials are used as in any human operating theatre.

The chemotherapy drugs are also the same as those given to humans, but in lower doses to keep life as normal as possible for an animal that can't understand what's happening. Anti-sickness drugs are used to make sure they keep their appetites.

'Our chemotherapy goal is for your pet to look so well that none of your family or friends would know they were on chemo,' I was told.

Having just had to make the heartbreaking decision to end Dolly's life, I said to Noel: 'It must be very difficult for the owner to make a decision on how much they want to put their dog through, and how much the vet thinks the dog can cope with.'

'In every case,' Noel said, 'all we can do is promise the family hope, but not in the absence of reality about their situation, and that includes the possible financial costs and the moral implications of what we will put the dog through. 'I feel very, very strongly that it's not enough to be able to do something, it has to be the right thing,' he said.

Every pet owner who comes to the hospital with a sick animal is given a copy of *The Little Book of Cancer*, which explains the nature of the disease, the different types of cancer and the treatments available. One section that struck me was the page headed 'What would you do if it was your pet?' This is a question often asked of Noel and the other vets – and is probably familiar to every vet in the country. Anxious owners, unable to make the decision themselves, turn it back on to the vet.

'Many factors come into the decision: the type of tumour, its growth rate, the tumour location, if it has spread, how far you live from the cancer centre, what your own personal experience of cancer is, your financial situation and your pet's character – to name but a few. What we promise is that we will carefully explain the pros and cons of various options and patiently work with you to find the one that feels right. We do not judge, we do not criticise and we do not coerce. We are on your team.'

I went through the door marked 'Dog Ward' to meet up with Nick Bacon and one of his patients, a gorgeous Labradoodle (a Labrador/poodle cross) called Fudge, who had come from Cardiff with his owner Andrew. Andrew wanted to know if the cancer in Fudge's leg had spread to other parts of his body, so the dog was gently sedated before being given a CT scan. As his limp body went into the scanner, Nick explained to me how it works, with a rapid series of X-rays being taken and then built into a 3D image, enabling the vet to look inside the dog's organs for traces of the cancer.

'It can find much smaller things, much faster,' said Nick.

I asked him if the future for Fudge would depend on whether or not more cancer was found, and where: 'If, say, you found tumours in the lungs, would that affect his treatment?'

'In that case,' Nick said, 'we would look at ways of making him feel good for as long as possible, but we probably wouldn't do surgery.'

For me, it was extraordinary seeing human technology used on dogs, and I think it is brilliant that a hospital like this can now give owners a real choice about the future of their animals based on scientific evidence of what is going on inside their pets. Before technology made this level of diagnosis available, most dogs with cancer would be given a very slim chance of survival.

Another dog I met while I was there was Lola, a Labrador and a working gundog. Lola is a success story: she was back at the hospital for a check-up after an operation to remove a tumour earlier in the year. Lola reminded me of the Labradors, also working gundogs, I grew up with at the farm. She was only three and a half when the cancer was diagnosed.

'She was such a young dog,' said Sharon, who explained that Lola had trained beautifully to work in the field with her husband, who works her three times a week. 'We felt we couldn't throw all that away, and we wanted to give her the best chance of survival. It would have been a different discussion if she was eight or ten years old. But she was very young, she'd done so well in training.'

I understand how close owners are to their working dogs: after all, that's my way of life, too. But Nick explained that it is not just owners of working dogs who will go the extra mile – and extra cheque, if they don't have pet insurance – to save the lives of their dogs and cats.

'For Sharon and Lola it's a working relationship, for some people their pet is company on a quiet night, for others the pet has seen them through their own emotional turmoil and is more than a pet – it's a member of the family. It's a very rewarding job, being able to help them.'

He was preaching to the converted: I know full well how much we all want the best for our animals, and how close to them we are.

Before I left the hospital, I got a progress report on the dogs I had met. Lola had passed her final check-up with flying colours. Archie had the operation on the tumour in his jaw and was making a full recovery. And luckily for Fudge and Andrew, the cancer in Fudge's leg had not spread, and Nick was confident that he could remove the tumour and save the leg.

It was an inspiring visit, and I really admire the pioneering work done by vets like Professor Fitzpatrick and Professor Bacon, as well as being totally in awe of their skills. I never doubted that we made the right decision for Dolly because of her age and the widespread cancer raging aggressively through her body. But I totally sympathise with owners who are prepared to travel miles and pay out large amounts to save their dogs, especially young ones. As every owner I spoke to said: 'Whatever the outcome, by coming here we feel we have done everything we possibly could do. We've given our dog the best chance.'

That's what we all, as dog owners, want.

CHAPTER 11

Dogs at War

I crouched down in a muddy trench, rain spattering my shoulders, and fumbled with a small green felt bag tied to the collar of an alert, patient Airedale terrier. Opening the bag, I stuffed a folded piece of paper into it.

'Go, Earnie, go!' I whispered to him.

As soon as I released his collar, Earnie, a typical curly-haired brown and black Airedale, took off at speed. He leapt out of the trench and tore across the field to another trench, where his owner, Karin Schnichels, was hiding. Spotting her immediately, Earnie leapt straight down into the trench to deliver the message.

We were filming for *Countryfile* as part of a special edition that went out on Remembrance Sunday; dedicated to the way life in the countryside was affected by the First World War. The programme covered the regeneration of the countryside where the battles were fought, the cemeteries of the war dead that are so beautifully maintained and the development of the first tanks in Lincolnshire, among other topics.

I found filming my segment was very moving: I looked at the way dogs, particularly Airedales, were used in the First World War to carry important information from the trenches back to headquarters; risking their lives to save human lives, acting with incredible bravery as shells whined around them, dodging the holes left by the heavy artillery bombardment, tearing their flanks on jagged barbed wire, racing on despite being hit by snipers' bullets. I felt very humble in the safe surroundings of a farm field near Ipswich demonstrating how those amazing dogs worked, and I was well aware that I was many miles and lifetimes away from the harrowing, appalling conditions of the French battlefields where so many young soldiers perished.

It's important, a hundred years on, as we remember the horrific conditions of that terrible war, not to overlook how crucial dogs were to the war effort and how courageously they worked – unquestioningly obedient and willing to give their lives for mankind. Hearing their stories, I was deeply moved by how much we owe to these remarkable creatures – the dogs we have taken into our lives and who reward us with loyalty beyond imagination. I know, from working every day with my own dogs, how valuable they are in my life, and in the lives of any shepherd or farmer, how loyal they are and how much they want to please. But my dogs have comfortable beds to sleep in at night, if they have an accident they are whisked to a vet, and they live long, fulfilled lives.

These trenches dogs, the ones who saved so many lives, were far from the comfort of their homes, their

'Go on, throw it again'. Ella with Boo and Dolly

Dolly: I commissioned this lovely line drawing by artist Sophie Cotton as a birthday present to Charlie, after Dolly passed away

One man and his dog: On a walk with Dolly

'Don't I look smart? But have they forgotten I'm a girl?' Boo does some modelling for the clothing brand, Joules

A beautiful litter of puppies for Boo

Six hungry pups

The latest edition to the family: Olive makes herself at home

'Come on, play with me.' Olive wants Boo to pay attention

Stand back! Peg cooling down in her water trough

Ashley Stamper with her sheepdogs

On location in New Zealand with *Countryfile*. Rhondda the terrier sits on the quad bike with the Huntaways

Clint Coventry, hunting hare with his eagles

Earnie, the Airedale

Allen Parton with Endal and EJ

Alan Stewart and his sled-dog team

Myrtle the whippet

A farmer and his dog

injuries were tended in rudimentary fashion, and as soon as they were fit they were back at the front line. Thousands died on active service, and thousands more were killed at the end of the war; put down when their help was no longer needed.

I didn't know of the work of dogs in the war until I made the programme, but it is one episode of *Countryfile* that has made an indelible impression on me. I interviewed author Isabel George, who has written extensively about the use of animals in warfare, and it really struck home when she told me that it was men like me – farmers, gamekeepers and shepherds – who were mainly chosen by the army to handle the dogs in the trenches, for the obvious reason that we work with dogs all the time.

We chose to stage the recreation of how messages were carried by dogs with an Airedale because that was the breed used more than any other. When I heard this, my immediate question was: why? Today we don't particularly think of Airedales as a popular working breed, but I was soon to learn what made them the right choice for the war effort 100 years ago.

At the start of the First World War, the British had not yet cottoned on to the idea that dogs were useful on the battlefield. There was only one working military dog, an Airedale with the 2nd Battalion of the Norfolk Regiment, and he was being used as a sentry. By contrast, the French army had 5,000 working dogs and the Germans 6,000. Ironically, many of the German army dogs had actually been bought in Britain in the years leading up to the conflict. As early as 1895, the German government was sending agents to Britain to buy large numbers of dogs, particularly collies, because of their intelligence and natural willingness to train and work.

The most important man in this story is Lieutenant Colonel Edwin Hautenville Richardson, who pioneered the use of dogs here (and whose training methods were taken up by the US army in turn, and who still influences dog training today). Edwin Richardson was the son of a gentleman farmer, so he grew up with a close knowledge of the land, and in particular, of dogs working on the land. He knew from an early age, as I did, that dogs are a vital extra worker, sometimes doing the work of more than one man around a farm. He also loved them, and I completely agree with the words he wrote in his book, published in 1920: 'As a family we have a way with dogs and all animals. What this exactly means is extremely difficult to define, but there seems to be in people this sense, a certain sympathetic confidence, to which the animal responds with a like attitude. This comradeship is very delightful, and brings much sweetness and happiness in life. One feels really sorry for those people who do not possess it, as certainly they deny themselves an immense amount of pleasure and innocent fun.'

I can't improve on what he said: he was clearly a man after my own heart. As a young man he was well educated, being sent abroad to become fluent in both German and French, and then on to Sandhurst to become a British army officer. After he married, Lt Col Richardson and his wife Blanche bought a farming estate in Scotland, where they raised their two sons in a household shared with lots of dogs.

It was while he was out shooting with friends before the war that Lt Col Richardson saw a shepherd selling one of his dogs to a German, and when he spoke to the foreigner he discovered he was going round the countryside buying up dogs for army service back in Germany. Intrigued, and already very keen on dog training, he and Blanche set about training their own dogs. Richardson made contact with dog-training schools in France, Belgium, Holland and Germany. He even went over to Germany to see collies being trained as Red Cross dogs for finding wounded soldiers. He bought one of the dogs and brought it back.

Convinced that dogs would be useful if Britain were to find itself at war, Lt Col Richardson started training his own dogs to carry messages, find wounded men on the battlefield, guard objects and act as sentries. There were army camps nearby, and he was able to train his dogs, unofficially, with the soldiers – all at his own expense.

The dogs were so good that various officers from the camps wrote to the War Office about their usefulness.

Other countries recognised how good these dogs were: when Russia went to war with Japan their army bought several Airedales from Lt Col Richardson, which resulted in him being awarded a Red Cross medal and given a gold watch by the Czar. He went on to supply dogs to Morocco, Bulgaria, India and Italy and even sent sentry dogs to guard the harem of the Sultan of Turkey!

However, back in Britain, despite many recommendations, including from Queen Mary, by the time the Great War broke out, he had only one Airedale working officially in military service, with the Norfolk Regiment. The police were gratefully recruiting dogs from him, including bloodhounds, collies and Airedales. But when he offered the services of his dogs to the army he was rebuffed: the War Office was too busy organising the shipping out to Europe of vast numbers of men, equipment and supplies, and there was no time or money to spend on dogs. The Red Cross were willing to use them, however, and found them an immense help leading them to men who were wounded, among the many dead.

Lt Col Richardson did not give up his belief that dogs had more to give; continuing to train his dogs and travelling to France to see how the French were using their dogs on the front line. He was constantly fighting to convince military bosses that dogs would be formidable allies for men fighting on the front line. Eventually, halfway through the war, he was asked to set up a training school for war dogs at Shoeburyness, Essex, and within a month 30 dogs were in the trenches – most of them collies, but also Airedales and German shepherd dogs. (It was during the First World War that German Shepherds became known as Alsatians, because anything with 'German' in the name was associated with the enemy.) Soon, the Airedales were performing so well that they became the breed most in demand.

Which brings me back to my question: what is it about Airedales that made them so suitable for this work? They are not a breed I had encountered much before, and I had no idea of their history.

Airedales are the biggest of the terrier breeds, known to their fans as the 'king of terriers'. They originate from the Aire Valley, in West Yorkshire, where, in the mid-nineteenth century, miners competed to breed a dog that was the best hunter and the best fighter. By selective breeding the Airedale evolved into a strong, brave, intelligent dog, loyal to his masters but quick to see off anyone he regarded as an enemy. It was a multipurpose dog, very useful for retrieving during hunting (or poaching) expeditions, very happy to work in water, and with some herding skills, as well as its supremacy in dog fights. The downside is that they are not the easiest breed to train: you have to start early and persevere, so they are not recommended as family pets for anyone who is not prepared to put in the time and effort. But once they've been trained, they work superbly and willingly.

The main reason that Lt Col Richardson favoured them is because they are fearless. He assessed this by feeding all his dogs once a day, and a few minutes before their grub was served he threw several grenades into a nearby pit creating a loud noise. When the noise stopped the food was removed. For the first couple of days the dogs went hungry, until the bravest left their kennels and ran to the food. The ones who did well in this test, and were actually waiting for the noise that signalled food, were then trained to run through smoke, barbed-wire fences, across hurdles, through hedges and to work with the constant scream of shells from practice batteries, with heavy army vehicles passing to and fro. Local people volunteered to be the wounded, and as the dog approached they were told to fire blank cartridges.

Many other dogs showed as much courage as the Airedales, but no other breed was so consistently reliable. They are large enough to be able to leap wire, agile enough to dodge shell holes and their brown and black colouring was good camouflage in the mud of no man's land. Richardson found retrievers and Labradors were too compliant, not independent enough, and other breeds were too playful and could be distracted. Whereas Airedales, once given a task, were single minded and determined.

Once the War Office approved, the first two Airedales went out to France: Wolf and Prince, who carried messages for a battalion of the Royal Artillery. They were so successful that Richardson was inundated with requests for more.

The dogs travelled out to the battlefield with their handlers – known as keepers – who were the only ones allowed to feed them. This gave the dogs a huge incentive to get back to their handlers, who were based at headquarters, from wherever they were taken to on the front line. They were released with messages, and would run through the worst of conditions to make it back. Field telephones existed in the First World War, but reception was poor and the booming of artillery and wailing of shells made it impossible to hear. Men who carried messages had a very short life expectancy as they were a natural target for snipers. So dogs, when they finally arrived with the British troops, were invaluable.

One of the most difficult problems was to stop the soldiers in the trenches petting and feeding them: the presence of a dog in a trench was a huge boost to morale, lifting the spirits of young, homesick soldiers, as the dogs pushed wet noses into tired faces. But it was vital that the dog was kept alert and ready for duty, and any soldier caught sharing his rations with a dog was in serious trouble. There was a rule that no dog would spend more than 12 hours in a trench, to prevent him becoming too hungry and too comfortable with the soldiers there.

There are many tales of canine heroism, but the most famous is the story of Jack, an Airedale who rescued an entire battalion of the Sherwood Foresters that was surrounded and cut off without supplies. The message for help and reinforcements was put into his leather pouch, and off he went, running full pelt through the carnage of the battlefield.

A piece of shrapnel smashed his jaw, a shell tore open his back, and finally his forepaw was shattered by a sniper's bullet, but still he kept going, dragging himself the final three kilometres. When he reached headquarters he collapsed and died, but his message had got through, and reinforcements relieved the battalion. Many, many lives were saved by his incredible bravery and determination. I'm staggered when I think of it: how tempting it must have been to lie down and give up, but something inside him, some indomitable force, made him keep going. It's very moving to think of his remarkable determination.

While Jack's is perhaps the most spectacular story, there are many more of dogs who fulfilled their missions, time after time. One dog keeper recorded in his log: 'Boxer, a staunch, reliable Airedale, went over the top with the Kents. He was released at 5am with an important message. He jumped at me at 5.25am. A tip top performance, about four miles. Great dog!'

Another keeper wrote that his dog, Tom, was gassed and hit by shrapnel, but only needed two weeks to fully recover and be back at his post.

Because of my own close affinity with sheepdogs, I particularly like the story of Tweed, a large rough-coated sheepdog. When he arrived at the military dog school, Lt Col Richardson was not impressed as Tweed was slow to pick up the training and the colonel dismissed him as dim-witted. It was Blanche, the colonel's wife, who took over his training and in the end he served for six months, surviving Passchendaele. In May 1918, the Queen Victoria's Rifles were caught off guard by a surprise German attack near Amiens and pinned down by heavy shelling. If they did not hold the line, the Germans would break through and take Amiens, but they were low on ammunition and badly needed reinforcements. They stuffed a message into Tweed's leather pouch, and he sprinted off into the night. His keeper wrote later: 'He came through a Boche barrage, three kilometres in ten minutes. The French were sent up and filled the gaps and straightened the line, otherwise Amiens would be in the hands of the Germans.'

Six days later, Tweed made three night runs carrying messages that alerted headquarters that the Germans were preparing a raid. Lt Col Richardson said he was 'a dog not easily forgotten'.

After the War Office recognised the immense value of dogs on the battlefield, demand soon outstripped supply. Dogs were originally recruited from Battersea Dogs Home and other dog shelters, but eventually appeals were made to families to give up their pets. More than 7,000 family dogs were donated, a substantial contribution to the 20,000 dogs who served in the war. Sadly, because of the expense of keeping a dog, during the war when food was scarce many healthy dogs were put down, to Lt Col Richardson's annoyance: he felt that more would have been given to him if their owners had been told about his training school. Quite a few that did come to him were not in good enough health to be used. In his final dispatch of the war Field Marshal Haig, the British commander on the Western front, acknowledged their vital importance to the victory.

To quote Lt Col Richardson again: 'The trained dog regards himself highly honoured by his position as a servant of His Majesty, and renders no reluctant service. From my observation along this line I have, in fact, come to the conclusion that a dog trained to some definite work is happier than the average loafing dog, no matter how kindly the latter may be treated. I certainly found it to be the case with the army dog.'

Again, I can only agree: my sheepdogs are always ready and eager to work and seem to definitely prefer days when they have a job to do on the farm to simply being taken out for a walk. I've never owned a dog that does not have a purpose, whether it's for retrieving or working with sheep.

With the help of Earnie the Airedale we were able to illustrate the work of the amazing messenger dogs who worked in such terrible conditions for *Countryfile*. While obviously we could not reproduce the real conditions those dogs worked in, Earnie was able to show how fast and how obedient a well-trained Airedale is.

Earnie and his owner Karin Schnichels live in Surrey, and Karin takes him and her other three Airedales to obedience classes, where they compete against other breeds. Karin confirms my prejudice in favour of collies by admitting that when collies are in the competition, it is rare for any other breed to win, but she loves Airedales for their feisty spirits.

When Karin was asked why she thought Lt Col Richardson preferred Airedales to other breeds, she said: 'They are bloody-minded individuals, they like to do what they think is appropriate.' She believes they act on instinct and with bravado, never thinking about their own safety. 'They are tenacious, determined, brave, stubborn, agile, alert ... everything you would want from a dog that was going to war.'

When I met Earnie, and another of Karin's dogs, Denzell, who came along as an understudy for the filming, they immediately took to me, and I felt the same about them, with their tough, wiry coats and their intelligent faces. Denzell was so excited to meet me he bounced round me, wrapping his flexi lead around my legs, while seven-year-old Earnie was busy drinking a cup of tea which someone had unwisely left on the ground. I asked Karin about the background of Airedales, and she told me they were bred from Waterside terriers and Otterhounds: I can see the Otterhound in them.

Before we started filming, Karin made us all laugh when she pointed out that she is of German nationality, so that we were actually sending a message to a German trench. We were filming at Trench Farm, near Ipswich, in Suffolk, where there is a set of re-created trenches. Earnie stayed with me in one trench, which was built with similar wooden supports and duckboards as those that were used in the war, while Karin made her way to the other set of trenches lower down the field. Karin had made a green pouch, very similar to the ones used in the First World War, and I placed a note inside it, then told Earnie to go.

He shot out of the trench, covering the distance by the most direct route, avoiding the obstacles littered across the field to simulate the wartime conditions, and then leapt into the narrow trench where Karin was crouched. He virtually dropped like a stone, six feet down through the small opening. Unfortunately, the camera crew were expecting him to go to the sloping end of the trench, not leap in. We filmed again, and the second time he crashed into the crew in his determination to get to Karin as quickly as possible. Third time lucky, and we got the shots we needed.

Yes, I was only too aware of how staged and sanitised this was. But Earnie did his bit, and it was clear why Airedales had the characteristics that were needed for this vital work. There was one final, very poignant, moment, when I went across to Karin's trench and took the note out of Earnie's pouch, reading it with a lump in my throat.

'I have given my husband and my sons, and now that he is required, I give my dog, too.'

This was a real letter, sent by a woman who donated her pet dog to the training school for military dogs. Her sacrifice is almost too great for comprehension.

Lt Col Richardson continued to train dogs after the First World War, and by the outbreak of the Second World War there was no need to convince the military authorities of their worth in a theatre of war and they were used for detecting explosives, patrolling and guarding ammunition. Some were even parachuted into France during the D-Day landings under heavy artillery fire. Three thousand three hundred dogs served with the British military, and more than 200 were killed in action. Another 1,500 were put down after their military service ended. But the bravery of the dogs was recognised when, in 1943, the PDSA introduced the Dickin Medal, the animal equivalent of a Victoria Cross, to be awarded to the most courageous.

On the home front, the government again appealed to owners to give up their pets for war service, and a large number responded. For many of them, feeding a dog while living on reduced rations themselves was very difficult, and also very controversial: neighbours who were struggling to feed families were often openly critical of pet owners, believing dogs were eating valuable resources, and a great many dogs were put down.

I know about this for the most poignant of reasons. My dad, who throughout my life was my mentor and my hero, came into farming from an unusual background – so unusual that I and my sisters did not know the full story until after he had retired from the farm. We'd heard bits of it, but somehow it had never been very clear: no wonder, because it was a tangled and very moving story. After a little prompting, Dad wrote a long, detailed letter, with copies for me and my three sisters.

Dad's parents were an actress whose stage name was Billie Dell, and a very famous actor and comedian, Leslie Henson. My grandmother's fiancé had been recently killed in a motorcycling accident. Leslie, who was married at the time, swept into her life when they appeared together in a West End production, and he filled the gap in her life. When Billie became pregnant with my dad, Leslie rented a home for her, later buying a house. But he wasn't able to leave his wife, the actress Gladys Henson, even though he regularly spent time with Billie and their son.

Eventually, aware that Leslie (who was known to Dad as Lally) was never going to divorce his wife and marry her, Billie moved away, down to Bournemouth, and it was there that Dad acquired his first dog, a lovely big Great Dane called John. Dad adored John, and was completely devastated when, during the Second World War, his mother decided to hand him back to the kennels he came from because she couldn't stand the constant criticism from neighbours and passers-by for keeping a big dog when food was rationed. It must have been a very sad day for Dad.

There was some compensation, though, because by this time Billie had met and married my father's stepdad, Cyril, a fine man who Dad grew to love, and who after John was re-homed bought a little brindle bull terrier pup, Barney. This was another four-legged friend Dad became very close to. After the outbreak of war, Barney went with Cyril when he became a Bristol Blenheim bomber navigator, living with him at the RAF base but coming home on leave to Dad, who was eight or nine at this time, and Billie.

I'm going to quote from Dad's letter: 'One day, which I will never forget, the postman called with a telegram for Mum. Cyril was reported missing. Mum collapsed in tears and I held her in my arms, telling her that he was only missing. She seemed to know that she would never see him again.'

When Cyril's possessions were collected from the base, among them was Barney. Dad and he became inseparable and spent hours roaming together. Barney was a scrapper and Dad had to hold him tight on his lead when another dog came towards them. After a fight with a German shepherd he was reported to the police and an officer called at the house. Barney, who had been devoted to Cyril, loved any man in uniform, and made such a fuss of the constable that he was let off with nothing more than a warning to Dad to keep him under control.

On one occasion he probably saved Dad's life when they wandered on to the beach together. Barney went ahead, turning and barking at Dad leading him through the sand dunes. When they reached the road Dad saw the sign 'KEEP OUT. HEAVILY MINED.' Barney had guided Dad through, avoiding the mines.

Sadly, one day when Dad's father Lally was visiting, Barney attacked another dog so ferociously that Lally had to hit him with a stick to get him to let go, and Lally then insisted that Billie get rid of him. But it worked out OK for Barney: he was given to a seaplane pilot in the Fleet Air Arm, another man in uniform, and Dad and Billie later heard that he used to swim out to sea after the seaplane until it took off.

Leslie Henson finally divorced and married Billie in 1944, and Dad's birth certificate was changed to acknowledge Dad as Leslie's son. He and Billie had another son, the actor Nicky Henson, Dad's brother.

It's comforting to know that in Dad's tumultuous childhood, so very different from the secure idyll he and Mum gave to me and my sisters, he had the companionship of dogs. However, the stories of John and Barney underlined to me just how difficult it was to keep dogs as pets during the war. As I have learned to say goodbye to dogs when their lives come to a natural end, he had to say goodbye in very different circumstances. But I'm sure those early experiences with dogs as his companions – and the rabbits, chickens and geese he and his mother kept during the war – were the building blocks of his love of the outdoors and farming, and took him on a route in life that would never have been predicted by his show business family.

The *Countryfile* programme I made brought the story of how dogs are used in the armed forces right up to date. I visited the Defence Animal Centre at Melton Mowbray, where they carry out some of the most sophisticated military dog training in the world. The centre opened in 1946, initially to train dogs for the army, but now it also trains them for the RAF and the navy. So Lt Col Richardson's lesson was well learnt: dogs are an essential tool of modern warfare, and also for peacetime duties with all sections of the armed forces. Not just the military, either: the centre trains dogs for the UK Immigration Service, HM Prison Service, HM Revenue and Customs and other UK government agencies.

More than 250 dogs are trained there every year, with 150 there at any one time. After being cleared through security (and, yes, my car was given a thorough once-over by a sniffer dog), I met the officer in charge, Major Tom Roffe-Silvester, and, as I looked round the state-of-the-art facilities I commented that it was a far cry from the school that Lt Col Richardson set up, but that he would be proud to see his legacy.

I asked Major Roffe-Silvester whether dogs were still relevant today and he assured me they were needed more than ever. No amount of technology can completely supersede their skills. Just as quad bikes were once tipped to take over from sheepdogs, but are now recognised as a great addition to have on a farm, but certainly not a replacement for a dog that can work away from the shepherd and use its own initiative, so it is with military dogs. As Major Roffe-Silvester told me: 'We use dogs alongside the latest technology, and together that builds up a great toolbox in operations. Nothing can replace a dog's ability to follow a scent, and they are also more mobile.'

Nowadays, we have sophisticated ways of transmitting information, so dogs are no longer required to carry messages, but they are used to search vehicles for arms and explosives, to guard military bases, and to give soldiers warnings of IEDs (improvised explosive devices), ambushes and possible suicide bombers. As Dad realised after Barney led him safely through a minefield, dogs are brilliant at threading their way through danger, and one of their most valuable roles in conflict is to tell soldiers where bombs have been planted. Their sense of smell is off the scale compared with ours, and they can be trained to alert to almost anything.

The dogs most commonly trained for defence work are the Malinois, a type of Belgian shepherd, which look very similar to German shepherds but finer, and an alert, intelligent and strong breed. German shepherds are also trained for the same work. Springer spaniels, Labradors and a few cocker spaniels are used to search for explosives, drugs or other contraband. Training takes between nine weeks and 18 months, which impressed me: I know how many hours I put into training my sheepdogs.

I watched a demonstration as one of the Malinois was given the 'Attack' command, and immediately went after a man who was running away. The target was wearing a heavily padded 'bite arm', designed for these demonstrations, so that when the dog grabbed him it didn't do any damage. But I could easily see that without the protection the dog would have practically taken his arm off.

I asked his handler, who had him under complete control: 'How come the dog went for him, and not for me?'

'Because I pointed him at the target,' was the reassuring reply.

To get the dog to release the arm, the handler squeaked a little toy, and the dog immediately returned to his side. Another dog, also a Malinois, demonstrated sniffing out IEDs, the deadly improvised explosive devices which have caused so much loss of life and injury to our troops in recent years. He was on a long rope lead and he walked in a dead-straight line down a 40-metre sandy track, where a tiny piece of electrical wire had been hidden two inches down in the sand. The dog stopped, sat down and stared at the spot until his handler called him off with another squeaky toy. I was very impressed.

I was told how dogs have been used in every theatre of war since the Second World War, including the recent conflicts in Iraq and Afghanistan. I was thrilled to meet JJ, a boisterous, friendly yellow Labrador who was injured in Afghanistan. JJ was deployed to Afghanistan in 2011 with his handler, Corporal Phil Corlett, who trained alongside him at the Defence Animal Centre. JJ's job was to sniff out roadside IEDs. While he was working he fell down a deep well, breaking his back.

Unlike the dogs who served in the two World Wars, who would have been immediately put down, JJ was treated, flown back to Britain and given extensive physio at the veterinary and rehabilitation facility, which is on the same site as the training centre.

To the delight of both JJ and Phil, they were reunited as soon as he got back – a 'hugely emotional' moment, Phil says.

Now, happily, JJ has been adopted by Phil and his girlfriend Gina and is a very contented family pet, who likes nothing more than splashing through streams (well, he is a Labrador ...) on his daily walks. I was amazed to see how well he has recovered from such a severe injury, and relieved that we are now treating our hero dogs so well.

I ended my part of the Remembrance Day programme with the words:

'One hundred years later, the legacy of Lieutenant Colonel Edwin Richardson lives on.'

Dogs are still saving lives, day after day. We owe them so much. In the next chapter I will tell you about the remarkable work of two civilian dogs I have met who every day make their own contribution to keeping their owners safe and well.

CHAPTER 12

Assistance Dogs

I'm sure by now you've picked up that I think the world of my working sheepdogs. But I'm prepared to admit that they are not, in all cases, the right breed for every job, and that there are other dogs whose abilities in their own fields are up there with those of an elite trialling collie.

These are dogs who have been trained to help human beings in remarkable ways: assistance dogs. It blows my mind when I hear about dogs that have turned the lives around of so many people. Anyone who owns a pet dog knows the therapy value of having a wet-nosed, waggy-tailed mutt gazing up with eyes brimming with love. It is a statistical fact that people who have dogs are four times as likely to recover from cardiovascular disease, and dog owners have significantly smaller increases in heart rate and blood pressure in response to stress. Couples with dogs are less likely to split and divorce than non-dog owners. But these are just normal dogs, pet pooches with no special training, nothing but instinctive devotion and love for their owners. Imagine the impact if this instinct is harnessed to specific training?

Guide Dogs UK was the first dog-training charity I, and most people, became aware of, as we occasionally saw a steady, unruffled Labrador or retriever guiding a person with little or no sight through crowded streets, negotiating round all sorts of obstacles, patient and never distracted, even by other dogs. Today there are many more assistance dogs for a whole range of disabilities.

The first guide dogs were trained in Germany immediately after the First World War, to help ex-servicemen blinded in the trenches. It was not until 1930 that Britain began training its own dogs, a year after the idea took hold in America. And it was a lot longer before the idea of assistance dogs expanded to cover other disabilities. Now there are over 7,000 people in the UK who have a specially trained dog to help them with their disabilities, including deafness, epilepsy, diabetes, autism, stress, including post-traumatic stress, Addison's disease and life-threatening allergies. I've been privileged enough to see assistance dogs in action, and watching a dog work demonstrates their value much more effectively than any statistics.

From time to time, I am invited to give talks to different organisations, sometimes about my farming life, sometimes more specifically about my relationship with my working dogs. One such invitation came from the Vets4Pets organisation, which represents many vet practices across the country.

I gave my talk to a full house and was pleased with the reception I received. But I'm more than happy to admit that my contribution was completely eclipsed by that of the man who spoke after me. Everyone in the hall was bowled over by his story, and as I looked out from the stage I saw lots of tissues wiping away tears. I was not ashamed to have to dab at my own eyes, as his story was so moving. All the time he talked, a gentle yellow Labrador lay at his feet.

Allen Parton was badly injured in an explosion on board a ship in the first Gulf War in 1991, where he was serving as a naval officer. He had a catastrophic head injury, which paralysed him from the waist downwards: he could no longer read or write or talk, and, perhaps most important, he was unable to remember anything that happened before the explosion. He did not recognise his wife, Sandra, and had no knowledge of his two children. It was devastating for him and equally so for his family. When his children, Liam and Zoe, who were six and four at the time, visited him in hospital he did not know them, had no interest in them, and was trapped in an angry and despairing mood.

Despite five years in hospital and a long period of rehabilitation, during which he made two major attempts at suicide, Allen's condition showed no sign of improving, and his wife Sandra was, he says, a saint for looking after him. When he was in the rehab hospital one of the staff told Sandra that he would never speak again and suggested she should divorce him and get on with her own life without him, but she refused.

Eventually, Allen was living at home but going to a day centre for rehab, but there was little progress and the children became used to tiptoeing around his irritable temper.

Unable to work because of her full-time caring duties, but with the children in school and Allen at daycare, the house was calmer and Sandra decided to volunteer as a puppy walker for the charity Canine Partners, which pairs dogs with disabled people to help them perform everyday functions. Once a week she had to attend the local centre with the puppy she was helping to train.

'One day the bus that was taking me to daycare didn't turn up,' said Allen. 'Sandra was understandably annoyed that she was going to miss her puppy class, so she bundled me into the back of the car and took me with her. I was left in my wheelchair, completely unresponsive, at one end of the hall while the puppy walkers went about their training.

'At the other end of the hall was a yellow Labrador that had been returned to the centre for a career change – he wasn't working out as an assistance dog because he had a bit of an attitude problem. If he was asked to pick something up he'd give a look, as if as to say, "Why don't you do it yourself?" He was going to be socialised and rehomed as a pet.

'While I was slumped in my wheelchair, immersed in my own miserable world, the dog, Endal, picked up a toy and brought it to me, dropping it in my lap. He expected praise or a reward, but he got no reaction from me. It clearly hacked him off, so he went to the mocked-up supermarket (where the puppies are taught to help their disabled owners to shop) and he took a tin of beans off a shelf and dropped it into my lap. Still nothing. He brought more toys, more shopping. I did not respond, I did not know how to respond. This was a challenge to him.

'Eventually, as I and my wheelchair slowly disappeared under a mountain of things that the dog brought, I smiled. It was the first human reaction, apart from anger, that had crossed my face since the injury. Somehow, Endal had seen and unlocked in me something that no amount of rehab had managed.

'He came home with me that day and he stayed with me for the next 14 years, completely transforming my life and the life of my family. He broke my miserable, unhappy world apart with his waggy tail.'

Allen explained that Endal had no advanced training, but that he instinctively knew how to handle Allen's problems, eventually learning more than 900 different commands – far more than any sheepdog needs, even the best trialling dogs. He learnt to put Allen in the recovery position and cover him with a blanket if he collapsed. Endal would bark for a neighbour to help, and if nobody came he would go and find someone. If Allen became unconscious in the bath Endal would leap in and release the plug. For the first time since Allen came home from hospital, Sandra could go out and leave her husband, knowing he was in good paws.

It was after Allen involuntarily burped, which seemed to excite Endal, that Allen stuttered his first words.

'Endal did what five years of speech therapy had not achieved,' said Allen, who today talks fluently.

But much more than any physical help he gave, he 'found' the old Allen, the good-natured man who Sandra and the children knew before the injury.

'Before Endal came I was on a perpetual short fuse, angry with the children if they disturbed me, or if they smeared chocolate on my trousers. But Endal released the goofy, funny side of my personality. He once dragged a rhododendron bush into the house that had only been planted the day before, and I just laughed. I'd have gone ballistic before he came.

'One by one, he brought back my emotions. I learnt to hate, because I began to hate people who were cruel to animals. And I learnt to love again, not just him but my family. I had no memory of marrying Sandra, and it was important to me to do it again. Endal was my best man.'

Allen and Sandra could have had their marriage blessed in church, but Allen insisted he did not want a blessing on something he could not remember. It took an effort to get permission to marry again, with a complete ceremony, but they achieved it.

But the story that brought sobs from the audience was what happened one night, after Endal and Allen had been giving a demonstration at Crufts to raise awareness of the charity Canine Partners. They were staying at a hotel and Allen took Endal out to the car park for a final chance to relieve himself before bed, when they were both knocked down by a hit and run driver, and left unconscious.

'I know what he did because it was all recorded on CCTV,' said Allen. 'But I was unconscious throughout, so I wasn't aware of it at the time. When Endal came round he was clearly dazed, but after a few seconds he pulled me into the recovery position, and then fetched a blanket from the back of my wheelchair to cover me. Then he crawled under a car to retrieve my phone, and tried to rouse me. When he got no response he went to the hotel and raised the alarm, barking and leading people to me.'

Endal was voted Dog of the Millennium by the PDSA, and given the Dickin medal, commonly called the animal's VC, and normally awarded for valour in wartime. 'He qualified because my injuries were sustained in war,' said Allen.

One day, when Allen was struggling at a cashpoint machine, Endal jumped up, took the card, the money and the receipt and handed them to Allen. This became part of their normal routine. One day, a newspaper photographer was behind them in the queue and asked for permission to snap Endal doing it, and he featured in a national newspaper, becoming a star. He was used to launch chip and pin machines when they were introduced, taking all the fuss and flashing cameras in his stride. He was the first dog on the London Eye and the first dog to be invited into the cabin of a commercial aircraft. He even picked up a Gold Blue Peter badge.

For Allen, a wonderful moment came when his children, who are now grown up, invited him to speak at their school.

'I think until I got Endal I was an embarrassment, a father whose speech and behaviour were not normal. But Endal was the catalyst, he made them proud of me.'

Eventually, when he was nearly 15 years old and very arthritic, Endal had a fit and lost his balance. Allen phoned the vet who said he would come the following day. That night Allen stayed downstairs with the dog who had changed his life.

'I was cuddling him, telling him how grateful I was for the incredible journey he had taken me on. He had given me back my wife, my children, my life. When I left him asleep on the sofa you could almost see him thinking, "Thank goodness, now I can get some sleep ..." The vet came in the morning, and I held Endal on my lap while he died, peacefully. He had given me so much, and in his death he gave me another enormous gift. I cried like a baby, and it was the first time I had been able to cry since my injury: another emotion he had released in me.

'My life was like a jigsaw puzzle that was smashed to pieces in the Gulf War, and every day Endal patiently found a bit of the missing puzzle and put it back. I still can't walk, I still have problems, I still have days when I feel miserable, but everything positive that I have, I owe to that remarkable dog.'

When Endal died there was a young, 11-month-old puppy called EJ in the house, starting his training as an assistance dog. He had come to live with Allen when he was eight weeks old, and had learned from Endal to pick up his bowl, and all the other help that Allen needs on a regular basis.

'That day, the day of Endal's death, EJ picked up Endal's collar and his assistance dog jacket and he brought them to me. He knew it was his turn. And he has become a great addition to our family. He can do everything that Endal did, even using an Oyster card on the London underground.'

It was while thinking about the amazing second chance he got with EJ, a dog who took over from Endal so smoothly, that Allen came up with the idea for a charity to provide dogs just for injured servicemen, and that's how the charity Hounds for Heroes came into existence.

'I looked back at what a miserable, unresponsive lump I was. I didn't want to sit back and think "I'm alright, Jack". I realised how much I had been given by these two dogs, and how incredibly lucky I was to have a second dog of such quality. What made me special? There are 9,000 injured servicemen and women in the UK today. And I know from my own experience that not all the injuries are the ones you can see: there are physically fit men and women who are crippled with post-traumatic stress disorder, and for them a dog is just as much a lifeline as it is for those of us who struggle with a cashpoint machine.'

Allen's charity now has more than ten dogs out in the community, helping ex-servicemen, and there are more dogs being trained.

'Although I'm a Lab man myself, we also train golden retrievers because they are more sensitive. Labs career in with great enthusiasm and gusto, which is what I needed from Endal, but it's not always the right approach. There are men and women who have been injured so badly that there is not enough skin to stitch up the holes in their bodies, and they need very, very gentle dogs.

'One chap, a double amputee, came to our HQ with his mother and grandmother, who had persuaded him to come. He didn't want to be there and he said, "I don't want a dog near me". One of our best dogs, Rookie, who can put keys and pens into someone's mouth, can operate pedestrian lights, and knows 938 commands even from an electronic voice, quietly went up behind him and put his head on the guy's lap without him realising it, while he was still protesting about dogs hurting him. He changed his mind.'

Allen was a vice chairman of Canine Partners for 15 years, and Sandra worked there for 20 years.

'We are not in competition with them or any other charity. We just feel we give servicemen something they can relate to. We use military language: the puppies are "cadets", and they have names like Juno, Monty, Colonel, Flanders. We joke and banter in the way that service people are used to: there's plenty of black humour.

'We get a lot of support from the armed forces, and from people connected with them. It was very touching when a widow sold her husband's Second World War medals and his gold watch chain and gave us the proceeds.'

EJ has raised more than two-and-a-half million pounds for the charity, happy to appear in endless photoshoots, as well as taking care of Allen every day. The charity fully funds the costs of the dogs, never wanting a dog to be a luxury some injured serviceman cannot afford. By paying for food and vet's bills, they know the dogs are being well cared for. They get sponsorship from Petplan, the animal insurance company, and they get free medical supplies and food donated to them. The hotels where they hold conferences and training events have all given them the use of rooms free.

'I'm gobsmacked by how kind people are to us,' said Allen.

The charity places dogs with injured firemen, policemen, paramedics, and prison officers. 'We don't think the word "hero" exclusively applies to the military.'

Like I said, there wasn't a dry eye in the house when Allen told his story. He finished his talk by telling us: 'Endal picked me up from an abyss of despair, and took me to where I am now: confident, able to talk to anyone. I wouldn't be here talking to you if it wasn't for the love of a dog.'

I was so moved by what I heard, that when I got home I nominated Hounds for Heroes as our latest charity to be sponsored at Cotswold Farm Park, where we display collecting boxes. I couldn't think of a more deserving cause, or a better ambassador for it than EJ, who gave me an affectionate nudge when he came on stage with Allen.

The story of dogs like Endal and EJ make me realise how adaptable dogs are. My sheepdogs are working in much the same way as their ancestors, going back centuries. Despite modern technology, their role has hardly changed: they run across fields and hills, rounding up sheep. Yet assistance dogs have had to learn all about life in the twenty-first century, to be able to help with the everyday aspects of life for their human partners.

Another assistance dog I met is Archie, a miniature poodle (although he's large for the breed). He is a smashing chap, friendly but always keeping an eye on his owner, William Stavert, who was born profoundly deaf and uses Archie as his ears. I met them when I went on the Great British Dog Walk organised by the charity Hearing Dogs for Deaf People, where they were also walking, raising money for the charity which has helped him so much. I went on the walk with Charlie and Boo.

William says he knew as soon as he met Archie that there was a bond between them, and it's easy to see that they have become a very close partnership.

'Archie's an independent dog, he only comes to me for strokes and cuddles occasionally. But when we are outside he never leaves my side or lets me out of his sight.'

He has twice alerted William to potentially life-threatening situations: once when a faulty toaster was burning the bread and close to setting fire to it, and another time when William forgot that he had put something in the oven. After pawing at William to alert him, Archie is trained to lie down flat if the smoke alarm is going off.

'The kitchen was full of smoke, goodness knows what would have happened if Archie hadn't alerted me.'

Archie's training is for specific sounds. Every morning when William's alarm goes off, Archie wakes him. He also tells William when the doorbell rings, when the timer for the oven goes off and, most importantly, if the smoke alarm sounds.

He also alerts to fire alarms in public places. When William was working in a college his colleagues forgot to tell him that the fire alarm would be sounded to tell them all it was time for the two minutes' silence on Remembrance Day. Archie naturally barked and pawed at William when the alarm went off, and William, as usual, shouted 'What's that?' Archie lay flat, to signal it was danger: the fire alarm. It was only when a colleague signalled to them to be quiet because they were disturbing the silence that William realised what it was.

'If they'd told me first, I'd have taken Archie out of the room!' he said.

Archie even understands some of the sign language William uses every day – he knows the signs for 'food', 'bed', 'walk', 'car'.

As well as helping with William's inability to hear, Archie has brought other benefits to his life.

'He is a great companion. He makes me go out, and he helps me to meet people. I'd be completely lost without him. He gives me confidence. I love Archie.'

Before Archie came along, William had not had an easy life. He was at school at a time when sign language was not encouraged, and was even banned. The authorities believed that deaf children would do better in life, and be more included in society, if they could lip read and talk. It meant that William was sent away from his home in Malvern at an early age to a boarding school for deaf children, where signing wasn't allowed.

'But we did it in the evenings, when the staff weren't around,' he said. 'Then if someone came in we'd switch to speech.'

Today, he tells his story with the help of a British Sign Language interpreter, Deb Watkins. Deb and the other BSL interpreters are special people, completing a long and difficult training to become accredited. They are a vital link between deaf people and a hearing world, and Deb has interpreted in some unusual places, including an operating theatre, laboratories, sports fields, cruise ships and behind the scenes at weddings and funerals.

When William left school at 17, he was taken on for an engineering apprenticeship with the Ministry of Defence, at the Royal Signals and Radar Establishment. He says, 'It came as a shock, moving into a hearing world. I was only used to deaf peers, and I didn't know how to make friends or communicate.'

He received no help as he tried to learn alongside hearing apprentices, who often mocked him and were cruel. 'Even the lecturers refused to turn round from the blackboards so that I could lip read.'

After a near breakdown, social services became involved and helped William find a teacher for the deaf to interpret for him in college. He became the first person in adult education at that college to have specialist support.

He completed his apprenticeship, passed with flying colours, and worked at the RSRE for 18 years, until a round of redundancies led to a career change and he went to work as a deaf role model for deaf students in college.

'The students were as lost as I had once been, and I helped them adjust to living in a hearing world. All the tutors were hearing, so I would intervene in lectures to help deaf students understand.'

He also spent half his time working in a school with younger deaf pupils, until his role was phased out and he was made redundant. By this time, he had Archie, who was very popular at the school and the college, and created a lot of interest in hearing dogs. Being a poodle, Archie does not moult: this was vital when he was chosen for William, because working in a school meant that William could be in contact with pupils who might be allergic to dog hair.

It was William's sister who first persuaded him that having a dog would give him more independence. Her husband is blind, and consequently she knew about guide dogs and other assistance dogs.

'I wasn't sure, but it turned out to be the best thing ever,' said William.

Every year, Hearing Dogs for Deaf People places over 150 dogs with people who need them, and they are aiming to increase the figure to 200 by the year 2020.

Jay Elcock is a training team leader at the charity, and has worked there for the last ten years. 'We train the dogs to physically touch the people they are working with in order to alert them. It's the only reliable way, especially if the deaf person has their eyes closed. With big dogs it's a nose nudge, with smaller dogs they sit on the ground and put two front paws up onto the person's legs.

'When they have been alerted by the dog, the deaf person will use a hand gesture, which means "Where?" Then the dog leads them to the sound, or in the case of danger, like a fire alarm, a burglar alarm or a carbon monoxide detector, they will lie flat on the floor.' Just like Archie did.

Those who have hearing dogs are encouraged to use a portable timer for the cooker, so that the dog doesn't have to lead them to a potentially dangerous situation.

Jay recalled one dog owner who commuted into London to work every day, and on the way home, like so many others after a long day at work, had the habit of falling asleep on the train. So he set the timer every day so that it would go off and his dog would wake him up just before they got to the right station. After a while he realised that other people were regularly getting into his carriage, because they too wanted to be woken up and not go beyond their stop.

Another dog was desperately trying to alert its owner to danger, but she could not see anything wrong. Then she looked out of the window and realised that the burglar alarm at the next-door house was flashing, and she phoned the police. The dog had heard the alarm.

Dogs also help those who live with a deaf person. One deaf woman was alerted by her dog when her father, who was upstairs, suffered a heart attack. She phoned for an ambulance and got him to hospital in time to be saved.

A profoundly deaf mother of three children was able to let them play in the garden on their own for the first time after she got a dog: before that she had to be with them, because she would not hear them cry if they fell over. Now the dog fetches her whenever she is needed.

All the hearing dogs are taught to a high level of obedience and manners. I noticed that when I was walking with them there was no skittish misbehaviour, as you often see on dog walks. Of course, they all have to know how to behave in shops, cafés, on public transport – not the normal places for a pet dog.

The most popular dogs for training are the reliable breeds: Labradors, cocker spaniels, poodles and crosses, like cockapoos. Jay believes that any dog could be taught to do the job, but clearly some breeds are happier working than others, so it makes sense to train those.

I really approve of the way the charity trains and looks after its dogs. All the puppies stay with their mothers, living with foster families, until they are eight weeks old, then they go to live with a puppy socialiser, who introduces them to all the normal situations they will encounter with their deaf recipient: walking through a busy town street, going into public places like libraries and so on.

At about ten months old – it varies from dog to dog – they meet their potential new owners and begin their specific training for their lifestyle. They may have to get used to a household with children, or cats, they may have to go to an office every day and lie quietly. The next part of the training is a two-day overnight stay in their new home to see if the pair bond. If it all works out well, the deaf person does a week's course at a placement centre, working with their dog, and at the end of the week they go home together. There's more support at home – in fact, all the 800 dogs that the charity has working in Britain today are supported whenever they need help.

I learnt all this about the charity during the walk and at the end we saw an amazing demonstration, which brought home to me just how well these dogs work. The charity has a team of demo dogs, specially trained to work in front of crowds of people and even in television studios, but they essentially do the same job as a dog in a normal home.

A ring was set up in a field, with a room setting with a bed, a chair, a doorbell, an alarm clock, a telephone and a timer. I watched in wonder as an enthusiastic cocker spaniel alerted to every different sound, leading the person to the right noise every time, or lying flat in the general 'Danger!' alert.

I know how to train dogs to sounds: that's what shepherds do with their dogs. We teach them voice commands and whistle commands. These dogs were reacting in exactly the same way that Peg does when I tell her to 'come by', or 'stop'. She hears the sound, and she obeys.

But if a sheepdog gets it wrong, the worst that happens is a few swear words from the farmer or shepherd and another go at it. These dogs can never get it wrong, because the people they live with depend on them so completely, and sometimes they are saved from life-threatening situations by them.

I am full of admiration for these dogs, and all the other assistance dogs who have transformed the lives of so many people. They do it out of devotion and loyalty, and they enjoy it: that's the most striking thing about all working dogs. They love to be needed and wanted, and they are happy when they have a job to do.

CHAPTER 13

How Bright Are My Dogs?

I didn't watch a lot of television when I was a child as there were always far more interesting things to do outside, following Dad around the farm. But on a wet afternoon there was one programme I really enjoyed: the TV films about Lassie, the amazing dog that always came to the rescue, performing feats of great daring and endurance to bring help when it was needed.

It never occurred to me that the dog's skills were exaggerated, and achieved by clever editing. After all, I lived with highly intelligent sheepdogs, and I had no doubt they were capable of similar exploits should the occasion arise. If ever I was going to round up a gang of baddies, a dog would fetch help for me. If ever I was stranded by a raging torrent, a dog would swim for help. If ever I needed a dog to leap through the air and knock down a criminal, or drag an injured person from a burning building, a dog could do it for me. And that dog, of course, would be a collie. We had Labradors as house dogs and gundogs, but I knew from a very early age that collies were the ones with the brains, who would share these amazing adventures with me. Just like Lassie.

Lassie, as she appeared on screen, was a rough collie. At least, from her first appearance in cinemas in 1943 through to her last appearance in 2007, she was played by many rough collies, most of them direct descendants of the original, Pal, who shared the screen with a very young Liz Taylor, and most of them male. 'She' starred in nine feature films, a TV series that ran for 18 years, a radio series and animated cartoons.

Why was a collie chosen for the part of this amazing dog? I'm not exactly impartial, because of my love for the breed, but even without my bias, it's a no brainer. It's an accepted fact in the canine world that collies are the brightest, most intelligent and agile dogs. There are now dog shows that hold agility and flyball classes labelled ABC, standing for Anything But Collies, in order to give other breeds a chance. If there's a collie or two in the class – and up to 95 per cent of the entrants to the large dog category at agility shows are collies – they invariably take the top spots. They are fast, the right shape, and good at jumping, plus they are the brainiest of all the breeds.

But how do we know this? I have my own experience to go on, but that's not scientific. I understand my own dogs and what they can do, but I don't understand how their intelligence works, and whether or not it can be compared to human intelligence.

So when *Countryfile* wanted to look into a new intelligence test for dogs, I was very happy to take Peg, my super-bright sheepdog, and our Hungarian wire-haired

Vizsla, Boo, a lovable buffoon of a house dog, along to be put through their paces. To make up a threesome for the trial, I also took Millie, our collie/kelpie cross farm dog. They made up a good cross section: Peg who (not really thanks to me, but because of her previous owner) is a highly trained ex-trials dog; Millie, who is a sweet, good-natured hardworking sheepdog trained to the level we need on a farm, but not as refined as Peg in her abilities; and Boo, who is completely lovable, knows how to behave, but has never struck me as particularly bright.

The test has been devised by Dr Rosalind Arden, who is a research associate at the centre for Philosophy of Natural and Social Science at the London School of Economics. Rosalind normally researches cognitive abilities (known to you and me as intelligence) in humans, but she is very interested in exploring differences in intelligence in non-human species, like dogs.

She told me why she has chosen to work with dogs, rather than other animals: 'Dogs are charismatic, they are not stressed by working with us, they are easy to work with, fun, and they enjoy doing the tests.'

The intelligence test involves giving the dogs six different tasks, and under scientific conditions each task would be carried out twice by each dog. But my dogs were doing the tests as a demonstration for the cameras, so we only put them through five of the tests; enough, Rosalind said, to get a relative score for their intelligence. Her major university study, done with 68 working border collies, set out to demonstrate that the bright dogs who excel at one task will also be reasonably good at the other tests, even though the tests are completely different. This tallies with how intelligence works in humans, and has long-reaching implications for the study of the relationship between high IQ and dementia (dogs can also get dementia in old age).

More relevant for me and others who rely on dogs for work, the tests will also be able to give a guide to how trainable a dog will be, from a very early age.

Apart from the scientific importance of the test results, I was simply intrigued to see how my dogs would fare. I was pretty sure Peg would come out best, but she did not get off to a flying start ...

The first test set out to see how long a dog faced with a bowl of food behind a mesh barrier would take to work out that it needed to go round the barrier to get its reward. It sounds simple to us, but dogs see the world differently, and this 'Detour Barrier Test' is a good starting point.

To my great surprise, Peg appeared to linger, looking around, before making her way round the barrier to the food. In contrast, both Millie and Boo did it very quickly, and scored better times than she did.

'My guess is that Peg is being very vigilant, looking around in case she should be heading off to round up sheep,' said Rosalind, as we were in a field where there are often sheep grazing. 'That's why we need to do other tests.'

It is true that collies are cautious by nature, always looking for possible problems. That's part of their intelligent makeup, and it has saved many a shepherd who has not spotted a problem that the dog has seen, and taken steps to solve without any human command. But it meant Peg, surprisingly, came last in this test, probably because she had higher priorities on her mind than food.

The next test was similar, but with a much longer mesh barrier between the dog and the food, necessitating a much longer detour. Peg and Millie both did it in a very impressive 12 seconds. Boo decided to run off with a stick, and it took her twice as long – that's my girl ...

The next test demonstrated whether dogs react to social cues. In other words, do they take instructions from human beings, by watching what the person wants them to do? I had two bowls of food, one either side of me, and I pointed firmly at one of them. When Peg was released she went straight to the bowl I was indicating. Millie appeared to be more confused, and ate the food in the other bowl. Boo came good, following my pointing hand and eating from the bowl I was gesturing towards.

In fairness to Millie, she is not a dog I work with regularly or feed, although she knows me well enough around the farm, so perhaps the other two had the advantage of being more used to me serving their grub.

But in the next test, again Millie didn't do too well, and this one was nothing to do with her familiarity with me. Two bowls of food were put down, one containing substantially more food than the other one. The test aims to show if dogs can discriminate between quantities. Peg went straight to the fuller bowl, whereas Millie went to the smaller amount and began eating it. Boo, who likes her food, made sure she went for the larger portion.

The final test was the hardest, a lot more elaborate. Two hay bales formed a passageway into a three-sided mesh cage. In front of the cage was a plate of food. Each dog was led into the cage, and then when released had to go backwards out of the cage, around the hay bales and round to the front of the cage to get the food. It took a lot more working out.

Peg sorted it out in a flash, and backed out, ran round and scoffed the food in five seconds flat. Millie, after a very slight pause, did the same, clocking a time that was only a second longer than Peg's. Boo showed her true colours, jumping on the hay bale as I led her in, then looking very confused when she saw the food. It didn't take her too long – she reversed out and ran round – but in her enthusiasm ran beyond the food and had to come back to it. All in all, nine seconds, four more than Peg.

Now the results were in, and Rosalind did the maths and gave me the final scores: Peg, nine; Millie, seven; and Boo not far behind with six.

It was exactly the order I thought they would come in, and it confirmed my belief that Peg would do very well. But I was agreeably surprised that Boo didn't completely lose the plot.

'Boo doesn't have a terribly low IQ, does she?' I asked Rosalind.

'No,' she replied, not too convincingly. 'Besides, IQ is only one thing, and we love our dogs for lots of different reasons.'

That's true, and we didn't choose our wire-haired Vizslas for their MENSA ratings. But putting the dogs through the test was fun, they enjoyed it, and I discovered how their skills vary. I'm all for anything that helps us understand dogs better, because the more we know the better we can work with them, and if Rosalind and her colleagues can use their studies into dog intelligence to help human beings, that's great.

Rosalind explained to me that scientists have known for some time that brighter people tend to live longer, but it is tricky to investigate because human beings make so many different lifestyle choices, like whether we smoke, how much we drink, the amount we eat and whether or not we exercise.

'Dogs, on the other hand, are basically teetotal,' she said. 'They don't touch pipes, cigars or mess around with recreational drugs – lots of things that muck up our findings in human reports can be very much better studied in non-human animals.'

By studying a cohort of border collies, all working dogs, it's a good chance to get a fairly even playing field. And because dogs, like humans, can get dementia, which interferes with their behaviour and brain structure, it could lead to a better understanding of why some dogs are more likely to get it than others, with possible ramifications for humans.

Of course, this work is very much in its infancy, and Rosalind and her colleagues at both the LSE and Edinburgh University are working on perfecting the IQ test. But so far their findings show that dogs that do best on the detour tests – finding their way round the barriers to the food – also did better on the choice tests, when they chose a fuller bowl of food or when they chose to interact with the human pointing them to one particular bowl. So those dogs are overall more intelligent, not just suited to one task, and the hope is that this will lead to more understanding of the evolution of intelligence.

As for me, well, I'm just delighted to have my faith in Peg confirmed.

Stanley Coren, a Canadian Professor of Psychology and the author of *The Intelligence of Dogs*, has done a lot of work on how dogs think and why. His interest was triggered when, as a student, he saw an example of a dog's ability to reason. The family pet, Penny, a boxer cross, had done something wrong and Stanley's mother was so angry with her she hurled a bunch of keys at the dog, hitting her in the rump and causing her to yelp. Stanley, who walked into the kitchen at the end of this scene, rescued Penny by suggesting she come with him to his room. As they were leaving the kitchen Penny made a wide detour round the keys, which were lying where they had fallen. As she reached the doorway, she dashed back, picked up the keys, carried them to another room and hid them behind a sofa, pushing the keys with her nose until they were out of sight.

Professor Coren concluded that Penny was actually using reason. She was hiding the keys that had been used to punish her, having reasoned that they could be used against her again. At the time that Stanley Coren watched Penny's behaviour, the general belief in the scientific community was that dogs don't have conscious reasoning abilities, even though many pet owners have similar stories to demonstrate that they do.

I'll quote just one, and it's not about a pet dog, but about a stray bitch who gave birth to nine puppies. When they were two weeks old the forest where the puppies were born, in Chile, was engulfed by a forest fire. Unable to carry all of her dogs to safety, the mother dug a deep hole, placed all the puppies into it, then dragged a sheet of metal from a nearby landfill site and covered them. She stayed close by, and when the fire was brought under control she led firefighters to her underground shelter. After publicity, all the pups were adopted. But, again, the mother showed a great deal of insight and reasoning.

Lots of research has been carried out on perception, awareness, memory and learning in dogs, and experts have found that dogs have very high interpersonal intelligence, higher than that of other intelligent mammals like the great apes and much higher than their own wild relatives, like wolves.

Interpersonal intelligence shows that a person, or an animal, has social skills and can relate to others. Dogs definitely relate to the humans around them, often showing preferences, and a recent study in Japan has shown that dogs even remember people who have been unfriendly towards their owners. They look to humans for help when they face a problem they cannot solve, whereas captive-raised dingoes do not, even though they are just as smart as dogs at solving the other problems.

Of course, other animals, including apes and wolves, live in societies where they relate to each other because there is a pack order, and they all know and accept the hierarchy. They learn from each other: a puppy set a simple task with a reward at the end of it will learn the task 15 times more quickly if an older dog demonstrates it than if left to its own devices, and it's roughly the same success rate if a human demonstrates it.

But the relationship between domestic dogs and humans goes beyond the pack mentality. Dogs are the only animals that can discriminate emotional expressions on human faces. Without being aware of it, humans tend to look at the right-hand side of another person's face, because that's the side that most expresses emotion. Dogs also look at this side, interpreting signs of anger, happiness and irritation in exactly the same way that we do. The fact that dogs don't look at any particular side of another dog's face shows that they use this behaviour just with humans, where there is a point to it.

Another type of intelligence is linguistic, the ability to understand and use language. While dogs don't talk in words, they certainly understand many and can express themselves to their owners. Professor Coren estimates the average dog knows 160 words or phrases. Seems a lot to me, and I'm not sure Boo would have such a big vocabulary, but clearly many dogs do.

A border collie called Chaser is believed to have the largest vocabulary of any animal in the world. Chaser has been taught by her owner, a Professor of Psychology in America, to correctly identify over a thousand different toys by their name, and to retrieve the right one when asked to do so. I'm convinced that it's not the word they understand but the sound. As people we can understand the same word spoken in many different accents, pitches and tones, whereas a dog needs consistency of tone.

Dogs also understand body language and hand signals. Although chimps and other primates have been taught similar language skills, dogs of all breeds pick up words and gesture, often without any structured teaching.

Spatial intelligence is the ability to recognise places and remember them relative to other places. In other words, to have a mental map of the world. Dogs remember where the dog food is stored, where their bed is, which way to go when they are taken out for a favourite walk. What's more, they have a spatial memory. Take a dog back to a place it used to live, or where a relative lives, and it will instantly know its way around, even if it hasn't been there for years.

Another type of intelligence is logical-mathematical. Well, dogs clearly don't do algebra and fractions (and plenty of us humans never really got the hang of them!) but dogs are able to make logical choices – just as the dogs in Rosalind's intelligence test did when they went to the large bowl of food not the smaller one. Some dogs also have rudimentary counting skills, and it is more than likely that a bitch with pups has a mental count of them, so she knows when one is missing.

Professor Coren carried out a major study into which breeds of dog are the most intelligent. Nearly half of all the obedience judges in North America filled in a questionnaire for him and added their own comments. From their information he assessed 140 different breeds of dog, and ranked them from 1 to 79 for obedience and working intelligence. Of course, as he points out (and so did the judges) there are exceptions in any breed: dogs that do better or worse than their breed would suggest. Mixed-breed dogs are harder to place on charts, as it all depends what genes they inherited from which parents.

Different research shows that, generally speaking, a mixed-breed dog will behave most like the breed it looks like. For example, a poodle/Labrador cross that looks more like a poodle is likely to have more behaviour traits of a poodle. But of course, some dogs are 'bitzers' – bits of this and bits of that – so their behaviour and character can only be judged on an individual basis.

So for the purpose of his list, Professor Coren has only assessed pure breeds. And guess what? Top of the list, numero uno, is the border collie. Out of 199 judges who assessed the breeds, 191 put the border collie in the top ten, so there was a great deal of overall consistency. At the bottom of the list too, where the ditzy but loveable Afghan hound took the wooden spoon, 121 of the judges assessed it in the bottom ten.

How did the other dogs in my life fare? Labradors came in at number seven, and springer spaniels at 13. As for Vizslas (and the list did not differentiate between smooth and wire-haired), they came in at number 25. According to Stanley Coren, dogs ranked in the top ten will start to understand commands after less than five goes, and will remember them with ease. He said: 'These are clearly the top breeds for intelligence and seem to learn well, even with inexperienced or relatively inept trainers.'

Dogs ranked from 11 to 26 are 'excellent' working dogs, but they may respond a bit more slowly when the handler is further away: 'Nevertheless, virtually any trainer can get these breeds to perform well.'

I don't want to sound smug, but it's no surprise to me to find border collies in top place. But there is a note of caution to be sounded: the Border Collie Rescue charity says that intelligence in dogs is a double-edged sword. Working dogs like Peg are fine: they have plenty of scope for exercise and to use their active brains. But the charity warns: 'Having a smart dog means waging a continual intellectual war with your dog, trying to out-smart them. Put in a gate, and they figure out how to get over or under it.' These are dogs that can lift latches and even turn doorknobs, and they need a lifestyle that allows them to burn off their tremendous energy and work their restless brains.

Before I end this chapter, I want to share one very heart-warming story with you, that takes me right back to my early love of Lassie, and demonstrates the intel-ligence of dogs. Two rough collies (probably not pedigrees but definitely collies from the look of them) called Panda and Lucy, escaped from their home in Ukraine and spent two days stranded on a railway track after Lucy was injured and could not move. Panda, a male dog and the larger of the two, stayed close to her, and every time a speeding train approached he lay down next to her and nudged her head flat, so that the train rattled over them. He never left her side, and was so fiercely protective that locals had to call in dog rescue experts to get them off the tracks.

'I saw a train approaching, and felt sick,' said Denis Malafeyev, a volunteer from a rescue centre who was contacted by a train engineer about the plight of the dogs. 'The male dog also heard it, came close to the female and lay down next to her. Both of them pushed their heads to the ground and let the train pass. He had been doing this for two days, and keeping her warm. I don't know what to call it: instinct, love, friendship, loyalty?'

I'd say it is all of those. But I'd add bravery and intelligence. The dogs were rescued, Lucy was treated, and they were returned home. That's collies for you.

CHAPTER 14

They Also Serve ...

I set out from Aviemore in my Land Rover, bumping along a narrow, icy track, pine forest closing around me, hoping I was going the right way. Eventually, when I was beginning to seriously wonder if this was the route, I came to my destination: the Cairngorm Sleddog Centre. The centre, the home of Alan and Fiona Stewart, feels about as remote as you can get in this crowded isle of ours. It's five miles from Aviemore, but they're a lonely five miles, with no other habitation around.

As soon as I realised I was in the right place, I paused to take in the landscape. The centre is in the foothills of the beautiful Cairngorm mountains, the highest, coldest and snowiest range in Britain. The Caledonian Forest, which used to extend over much of Scotland and stopped the Roman invaders in their tracks, may now be reduced to only 1 per cent of its original size, but it is still dense here. I was struck by how crisp and clean the air is, and how the intense wintry light sharpened the colours of the hills, the snow and the pines.

Alan Stewart came out to meet me; a friendly, energetic man whose life story is just as breath-taking as the scenery. He runs the centre, and he was going to take me on one of the most exhilarating experiences of my life, riding behind a team of 12 Alaskan huskies, being filmed for *Countryfile*.

Alan is, by anyone's standards, a tough guy. He spent more than 18 years as a member of a deep-sea diving team, working all over the world as well as on the North Sea oil rigs, and he still works in the industry as a dive rep for an oil company, monitoring the dive teams working for them.

'Working under the sea, you are at the sharp end,' he said. 'If you make a mistake, you are not coming back. You work at great pressure for four months of the year. So when you are back on land it can be boring, when you are used to that pressure and excitement. I am very lucky: I found something just as exciting and rewarding to fill the rest of my life.'

That something was dog racing with Alaskan huskies, an interest that consumes Alan, his wife Fiona and their son John. Alan has been running and breeding sled-dogs for 26 years, and he and Fiona have lived at their remote home for 18 years.

'I was working in a deep saturation diving team, living at a depth of 500 feet in a pressurised container no bigger than a medium-sized van for 26 days at a time. I was reading about dogs, and luckily my super-intendent was interested, and was happy to let me have blocks of time off to go to America to learn about it properly. I went over to Minnesota and worked at the kennels of a well-known sled-dog guy. It was unpaid work, but I got six or seven weeks' training from him at a time.'

When he felt he really knew the sport, Alan started to buy his own team of dogs.

'I've always bought from the best sled-dog racers, usually from one kennels in Montana, and I know the great, great grandfathers of most of my dogs.'

While he is away working, the job of looking after the dogs falls to Fiona. She is responsible for feeding them, supervising their medical care and taking care of the pups. She runs the admin for the centre, taking bookings and liaising with local hotels. She's also, like Alan and John, a musher, and has competed at the top level in the UK. ('Musher' is the name given to sled-dog racers, and it's believed to come from the French word 'marche', meaning 'walk', used by the original French settlers in the icy wilds of Canada, where travelling with sleds and dogs was a skill learnt from the indigenous people.)

Alan's dogs are magnificent to look at, and I immediately fell in love with their wonderful thick coats and their intelligent eyes. The dogs live outside in kennels made from old whisky barrels.

'They're not domesticated. You can't train them to walk on a lead or sit. They're athletes, born to run,' he says.

Alan's dogs are all Alaskan huskies, descended from those dogs who were a vital form of transport in the wild and inaccessible terrain of North America and

Canada, and who were used by the prospectors and miners in the Klondike gold rush days of the 1890s, a time which inspired Jack London's famous novel, *The Call of the Wild*, about the tough life of a sled-dog.

The word 'husky' comes from 'huskimos', which was the name English sailors in the eighteenth century gave to all indigenous people in the far north (a corruption of the work 'eskimo'), and by the early nineteenth century the name had transferred itself to the dogs.

Alaskan huskies are mongrels, bred specifically as sled-dogs, and first recorded in the late 1800s. They are a mix of Alaskan Malamutes and Siberian huskies, with genes from pointers and Salukis to increase speed, and a contribution from Anatolian shepherd dogs to give them a solid work ethic. Some may have greyhound blood, and some are part wolf. They are smaller and leaner than other sled-dog breeds, and because of their mixed heritage they come in different colours and with different markings. On the whole they are good with other dogs and gentle with people. They are now the fastest breed of sled-dogs, and the favourites for competitive sled-dog racing.

The first sled-dogs were Alaskan Malamutes, which probably evolved in Mongolia about 30,000 years ago, when humans migrated and trained them to pull sleds carrying their belongings. Malamutes are larger and stronger than Alaskan huskies, not bred for speed but for pulling strength. They were used in rural communities in Alaska, Canada, Lapland, Siberia, Norway,

Finland and Greenland for mail deliveries, and for transporting supplies.

Other sled-dogs include the Canadian Eskimo dogs, used by the indigenous Thule people of Arctic Canada. They were used for pulling sleds, but also by the Inuits for hunting seal, musk ox and polar bears. Greenland dogs are another Eskimo breed that have high endurance, but are not noted for speed. Samoyeds, bred by the native Samoyede people of Siberia, are all-purpose dogs which haul sleds, herd reindeer and hunt. The Siberian husky is smaller than a Malamute, although there is a strong resemblance between the two breeds. They can pull large loads, but not for such long distances as the Malamutes.

The last mail delivery by dog sled was in 1963, because planes had taken over, highways had been built for trucks, and snowmobiles were being used for local transport. But the dogs live on in remote communities, and, of course, in the kennels of mushers like Alan, since dog-sled racing has become an international sport, and is particularly popular in Canada and the USA.

As well as racing dogs on snow, Alan's dogs also pull wheeled carts, which is what I rode in. There simply isn't enough snow to always run sleds, even in the Cairngorms.

Alan's dogs run in teams of 12, and he changes around their positions, so that every dog gets the opportunity to lead. The worst position is to be the wheel dogs, close to the cart or the sled, and they need to be calm and steady and not worried about the wheels immediately behind them.

Travelling at great speed behind a team of dogs through the forest tracks was a peak experience for me, something I will never forget. We moved at an astonishing, bone-shaking speed, and it was inspiring to see these strong, willing dogs straining to run as fast as they could, working together as a team and clearly loving it as much as I did, confirming my oft-stated belief that dogs are happier when they have a real job to do.

Alan has raced dogs all over the world, competing at the highest level of the sport in the USA, Chile, Argentina and Europe. He was the first and only UK musher to take sled-dogs over the UK's second highest mountain, Ben Macdui.

But the star of the family – and of all British sled-dog racing – is Alan and Fiona's son, John, who has raced and trained dogs since he was six. As a junior he dominated all the British events, and travelled with Alan to major events all around the world, spending six weeks in the remote Chilean mountains at the age of ten. From the age of 18 he has lived and worked in the USA and Canada with the world's greatest mushers. He and his wife Liz, also a professional musher, live in remote Wyoming. Prize money in the big events can be as high as $250,000, and John's greatest success to date is coming second in the gruelling 700-mile Wyoming

Open race. Like his dad, he is a commercial deep sea diver when not racing dog teams.

John has taken part in the most famous dog-sled race in the world: the legendary Iditarod. Alan suggested I might consider taking part in the race. I think I was tempted for a few seconds, then the reality of what it means hit home and I firmly shook my head. No thank you. It's a gruelling endurance test that lasts for two weeks, covers 1,150 miles, and is known as 'the last great race on earth'. Teams race through blizzards and gale-force winds that can bring the temperature down to minus 73 degrees Celsius. People have been known to veer off course, get lost and die in those conditions – not for me, thanks!

The race has been run every year since 1973, but its roots stretch back much further. The Iditarod Trail was used by indigenous people, and then by Russian fur traders, followed by gold-rush miners. Dog sleds were used all year round to deliver mail, firewood and supplies, because the seaports were closed for vicious winters which lasted from October to June.

Sled-dog racing became a popular winter sport, and in 1908 a man called 'Scotty' Allan started the All-Alaska Sweepstakes race, which covered 408 miles. Scotty is a great hero of Alan's, and the Cairngorm Sleddog Centre includes a small museum dedicated to him. Scotty was a local lad – well, he was born in Dundee, only 60 miles away from Alan's home – who was sent out to South Dakota in the early twentieth century by the local laird to deliver a valuable Clydesdale horse. Scotty saw an opportunity and stayed in the States running his own dog-sled transport business. He was an acclaimed musher, winning the race he established three times in the early 1900s, and setting up a famous breeding kennel for Alaskan huskies. He only returned to Europe to deliver dog teams to help carry supplies to the Allied troops fighting the Germans in the First World War. After the war, Scotty returned to the wilds of North America, where he became a successful businessman and politician, and never came back to Scotland.

'We brought a bit of him home,' said Alan. 'To me, he is the founder of sled-dog racing, and I wanted him to be honoured in his home country.'

Sled-dogs were also used in the Second World War, transporting munitions and laying telephone wires. Teams of dogs also towed sleds to find survivors when planes went down. As a military historian said: 'Dogs were eminently more economical than horses. Two dog teams could do the work of five horses in formidable terrain ... Although it may seem that dog sleds are an obsolete mode of transport ... sled dogs are still far superior to aircraft and track vehicles, a dog requires no repair shops or spare parts ... In one of the most desolate and inhospitable regions on earth, the dog is still a man's best friend.'

The most celebrated and moving story of mushing in Alaska, and one that is honoured every year when the

Iditarod is run, is the Great Race of Mercy, one of the most gallant feats ever performed by dogs for their human masters. In the winter of 1924–25 the small town of Nome, in Alaska, was threatened with a diphtheria epidemic. The doctor, Curtis Welch, had placed an order for diphtheria antitoxin a few months earlier, but the shipment did not arrive before the port at Nome iced up and closed to shipping for the winter. In several weeks over the winter Dr Welch treated children for tonsillitis, four of whom died. He was increasingly convinced he could have a diphtheria epidemic on his hands, and when he had two confirmed cases in children, both of whom also died, the mayor of Nome arranged an emergency town meeting, and the whole town was quarantined, to prevent the epidemic spreading. Dr Welch sent radio telegrams to all other towns in Alaska, alerting them to the threat, and also to the US Public Health Service in Washington.

'An epidemic of diphtheria is almost inevitable here. Stop. I am in urgent need of one million units of diphtheria antitoxin. Stop. Mail is the only form of transportation. Stop.'

When the serum was obtained from west coast hospitals it had to be shipped to Seattle and then on to Seward, before it could begin the journey across Alaska. But a smaller supply was at Anchorage hospital; not enough to defeat the epidemic but sufficient to hold it at bay until the larger shipment arrived. It was taken by train to Nenana, 674 miles from Nome.

Dr Welch calculated that the serum would only last for six days in the brutal winter conditions, with temperatures at an all-time low and snow drifts and high winds burying the route and making the going tough. The dog sleds would have to travel by night as well as day, and make record-breaking times to get there, on a route that offered no protection from blizzards, and included a 42-mile stretch across the shifting ice of the Bering Sea.

A relay of the best dog teams in Alaska set off. Most of the dog mushers were direct descendants of native Athabaskans, the indigenous people who were the original dog mushers, and who now worked for the mail delivery service.

It was a brutal run. One musher arrived with half of his face blackened by frostbite, having made a run of 52 miles – double the 25 that makes for 'an extreme day's mush' and the third-longest leg of the relay. Another musher had to have hot water poured over his hands to get them off the sled's handlebar. The teams travelled by day and night. One of the mushers had to take over pulling the sled himself after two of his dogs died.

The longest section was run by Leonhard Seppala with his lead dog Togo, and they travelled 91 miles into an oncoming storm with gale-force winds and a wind chill of minus 65 degrees. Twelve-year-old Togo led the team across the sea ice in the dark, using his sense of smell to keep them on course. After feeding the dogs and resting them for six hours, they set off again in the teeth of a blizzard, climbing 1,500 metres up Little McKinley Mountain, before passing the serum on to the next runner. The dogs were near collapse, and Togo was never able to race again.

The final stage was taken by a musher called Gunnar Kaasen with his lead dog Balto. When his sled flipped over in the storm he nearly lost the cylinder of serum, and had frostbitten hands through groping for it on his hands and knees in the dark. They ran a total of 53 miles, the second-longest leg.

When the serum was triumphantly delivered, not one vial was broken, and it was thawed and ready for Dr Welch to use about seven hours after arriving. The whole trip had taken five days and seven and a half hours, a world record achieved in ferociously bad conditions. Several dogs died during the trip, but the people of Nome were saved. The death toll was five or six, but Dr Welch estimated that as many as a hundred more died in the camps of indigenous people outside the town, where no medicine was available. A second run was made by many of the same mushers when the rest of the serum arrived, but the time pressure was not so acute, even though weather conditions were still appalling. Critics had argued that transportation by plane would have been better, but on this second delivery, when a plane was to be used to carry half the delivery, it failed to take off on two consecutive days because of the conditions, and even the greatest advocates of technology over dogs had to concede that the dogs were the only way the serum would have made it in time.

All the mushers received letters from the president and a gold medal. Balto became the greatest star, and there is a statue of him in New York's Central Park, with the inscription 'Endurance. Fidelity. Intelligence'. Among mushers, though, the greatest respect is given to Leonhard Seppala, who with Togo did the longest and most difficult leg of the run, and apparently Seppala died unhappy that Balto was getting the credit: 'I never had a better dog than Togo. His loyalty, stamina and intelligence could not be improved on. He was the best dog that ever travelled the Alaska trail,' he said.

The Iditarod Trail race today does not follow the route taken by the dogs delivering the serum, but the race commemorates the bravery of the men and dogs who saved the town. The Leonhard Seppala Humanitarian Award is given every year to the musher who provides the best care for his dogs during the race.

The modern Iditarod race was started to encourage the preservation of sled-dogs. The traditional Iditarod trail was becoming overgrown and forgotten, until a man called Joe Redington started clearing it to work as a hunting guide. He was depressed that the invention of the snowmobile had almost wiped out the role of the sled-dog in ten years. He and an associate, Dorothy Page, started a 25-mile race to encourage owners to keep and breed these fantastic dogs, and a few years later the race expanded, and mushers and their dog teams were running the full Iditarod.

I'm full of huge admiration for Alan's son John who has done the race, and all the other mushers who face the unforgiving conditions of the trail each year. But I think I made the right decision to give it a miss ...

When I visited Alan, as well as the huskies he had a German pointer, Buster, who used to run with the dog teams. Buster had another job: when Alan bred a litter of puppies, once they were weaned they were taken from their mothers (who went back into harness to pull sleds) and they roamed free, with the pointer rounding them up and keeping them safe. He even took them swimming in the river. Alan explains, 'No husky puppy goes into harness until it is 18 months old, and they never go on a lead. With Buster with them, I always knew they were safe.'

Alan now has another dog who also has a vital role at the centre. Arnold is an Australian blue heeler, also known as an Australian cattle dog, a breed that is used for rounding up and driving cattle in the outback. Arnold has a different job from Buster: he takes the old huskies out for walks. There are four or five old ones, no longer able to join the sled teams, so Arnold rounds them up and, with a walkie-talkie round his neck so that Alan can communicate with him, trots off with them for a walk. As soon as the old dogs spot Arnold they are ready to go. 'The walkie-talkie means I can keep my voice low, because you never raise your voice to huskies,' Alan says. Alan told me he'd wanted a blue heeler because he'd seen them when he worked in Australia years before. I'd seen them, though I'd never worked with them, but I understood why he liked them. They are a tough, energetic breed, known for their incredible loyalty to their masters. Alan intended to import one from Australia, but then he found out about a breeder in Italy. He rang her while he was out on an oil rig, and she told him he could do her a great favour if he was prepared to take a heeler who had not worked out in its home in England because it was too excitable.

Now Arnold has definitely found his niche. He lives outside Alan and Fiona's cottage, on a long line.

'We need a guard dog because we are in the middle of nowhere, and he alerts us to trouble. There is an osprey nest near to us, and we have had thieves trying to steal the eggs.'

As well as the ospreys there are plenty of other rare breeds around Alan's home: 'The cottage we live in once belonged to the man who introduced reindeer to Britain,' he says. The herd of reindeer in the Cairngorms is the only wild herd in the country.

The isolation of the life is normal for Alan and Fiona, and they both love it.

'Not many people can understand why we do it. Even the ones who want to take up sled-dog racing find it harder than they imagined. Many of them go into it because they like the look of it, but 80 per cent of the people who take it up only last two or three years. I feel sorry for people who do it as a hobby, as they miss most of the pleasure of having dogs, and I feel sorry for the dogs, because they need to run. The courses we organise are meant to show people the reality of it, so they don't go into it with romantic notions. It's hard work.'

I know better than most people the amount of time and energy that you need to have working dogs, but Alan's kennels are on a much bigger scale than anything I have ever dealt with. Because the centre is winding down, through lack of snow, Alan now has only 26 dogs, but there were 36 when I was there.

'We knew global warming was happening, but we never expected it to come this quickly. I used to have my dogs in training mode for seven months of the year, and I could take clients out all that time. Now the season is down to four months. It was too warm to take the dogs out last Christmas Day, and even John, living in Wyoming, has had to take the dog teams up to Alaska to find snow. I used to be able to take a sled across the mountains, but I can't now.'

I enjoyed my visit to Alan and Fiona so much that I seriously considered having one of their puppies. As well as the dog-sled teams, Alan showed me two-wheeled scooters that are pulled by one dog, and I loved the idea of being able to zoom about being towed by one of these beautiful animals.

When I got home I had a quick reality check. Life on a farm is always very busy, and when I add on my *Countryfile* filming, there is no spare time left. A sled dog requires regular running, and, unlike all my other dogs, it could not wander around the farm with me. I got in touch with Alan and told him that I wouldn't be able to give the dog the life it deserved and needed.

It is very sad that Alan's centre is winding down. But Alan is never going to put his feet up in front of the fire: he's found himself another high-adrenalin sport, racing specialised off-road vehicles. And sled-dog racing is such a big sport in North America and Canada that the future of these fantastic dogs is assured, at least as long as there is enough snow.

I knew before I reached Alan's remote centre that I was going to love his dogs. Not only is the breed beautiful to look at, but they are the sort of dogs I relate to: working dogs with a strong purpose in life.

But I have to admit I was very pleased when I met another breed, the Yorkshire terrier, to have my prejudices overturned. Yorkshire terriers are cute little things, with a reputation as handbag dogs, wearing ribbons in their hair and posing prettily with their little heads cocked to one side.

Not my type of dog, I thought. And then I met David Ward and his two little Yorkies, Sika and Turtle, when I was making a series of programmes for *Countryfile* on county breeds. In each county I went to, I met and found out about the animals that originate there. In Yorkshire I met Swaledale and Wensleydale sheep, a

Cleveland Bay horse, large white pigs and, finally, Yorkshire terrier dogs.

I came away with a new respect for these tough little fellows. They were originally working dogs just as much as my sheepdogs or the Alaskan huskies, although nowadays far more are kept as companion dogs. I discovered they punch well above their weight in terms of ferocity, stamina and loyalty, and they've got a big attitude for such a little dog. What's more, in a survey of dog owners, it's apparently Yorkie owners who are the happiest, so the little fellas obviously bring a lot of pleasure with them.

They were bred for ratting in the textile and woollen mills of Yorkshire. They were small enough to get behind the large looms, and brave enough to corner and take on any rodent, shaking it to death.

'They're lightning quick, and they can get into all the nooks and crannies,' David told me. 'And they are not frightened of anything. They're a big dog in a small body. They'll tackle any dog that they think is threatening them – don't be deceived by the ribbon in their hair.'

In the 1800s there was an influx of Scottish labourers into Yorkshire, looking for work. It was the time of the Industrial Revolution, and factories and mills were springing up all over the county. The labourers brought with them small terrier dogs of non-descript breeds, which were great hunters and ratters. They'd been used in Scotland for hunting animals that lived in burrows and dens, like badgers and foxes. The dogs were carried in the pockets of the hunters and then released into the dens of the wild animals, fighting fiercely with their cornered prey. They were encouraged to bark, so that the hunters would know where to dig to catch the quarry and retrieve their dogs. They were famous for standing their ground, and were so determined they would risk their lives in the struggle rather than give up.

They found a natural home in the mills, and also down the coal mines of Yorkshire. Cats were used for catching mice, but rats are often too large and vicious for a cat to handle. The dogs were also useful in the overcrowded slums that sprung up to house the mill-workers, again keeping the rat population down. There are no records of what breeds these small dogs from Scotland were, but it is believed they were Clydesdale, Paisley and Skye terriers, which interbred with other small dogs. The dogs' history and lineage was of little importance to the mill workers: all they wanted was a good ratting dog that they could take hunting as well. It wasn't until 1874 that the breed was given the official name of Yorkshire terriers, affectionately known as Yorkies.

In the Victorian era they were adopted as pets, and became the pampered pooches that many people like me mistakenly thought was their true calling. It's easy to see why they became so popular in the salons of Victorian England: they are small, cute, fond of attention and easy to train. As the breed has been bred to be even smaller, they don't need very large amounts of exercise, which makes them an ideal town dog, but they are bright, and they definitely keep their owners on their toes if they don't get enough mental stimulation. In Stanley Coren's book, *The Intelligence of Dogs*, the Yorkie comes in at number 27, an 'above average working dog', and the highest ranked of all the terriers.

David, who converted me to them, uses his when he goes shooting, to stalk deer and rabbits. He showed me how they worked in the mills by taking them into a barn and turning them loose among some bales of hay, where they darted about, looking for rats or other vermin. I could see how useful they were, and how families must have relied on them to keep rats away from their homes. Unlike my soft-mouthed gundogs, the spaniels, Labradors and Vizslas that I am used to, these little fellas have a terrier instinct to shake anything they chase down, to stop the rat or other prey biting them. You can see this in the way they shake newspapers (I've got a friend whose terrier regularly shreds her daily paper and her post) or dog toys.

Now, whenever I see a Yorkie, even if it has a ribbon in its hair, I don't dismiss it as a handbag dog, or an old lady's petted pooch: I see it for the spirited little working dog that it really is.

It's not only through *Countryfile* that I meet other breeds of dogs, and discover their histories. Just as I had never really given much thought to Yorkies before I met them, similarly I didn't know much about whippets until they came into my life through some very good friends of ours. Now I know what wonderful dogs they are, and how they have also been bred for centuries to help out their owners, including in a very surprising way.

Whippets were a multi-purpose dog to their peasant owners in the north of England and Wales. They are sighthounds, the sort of dogs that hunt by keeping their prey in view, and then overpowering it with their great speed and agility. They were very useful for bringing in rabbits for the family pot. They are able to detect motion faster than many other breeds, so the slightest rustling in a hedgerow will send them off in pursuit before their owner or another dog would have spotted anything.

The name 'whippet' comes from an early seventeenth-century word meaning to 'move briskly', which we still use in the abbreviated form of 'whip'. For example, we talk of the wind 'whipping across the fields'. Whippets look like small greyhounds, and that's exactly where they come from: when a greyhound pup was too small for the landowner to use for stag hunting, it was given back to the peasant who bred it. Sadly, the small pup was often maimed, by having a tendon in its leg cut or a toe removed, because under the forest law peasants could not own hunting dogs. The dogs defied their disabilities and were still used for poaching hares and rabbits, and ratting. When the forest law was repealed these small greyhounds became very popular, and by the time of the Industrial Revolution they were well established in northern parts of the country, where they were prized for their speed. From their basic use, providing food for the table, developed sports such as hare coursing and racing against other dogs, and a whole betting culture evolved around them. Race tracks were established and whippet racing was a very popular Sunday outing for the whole family. There is today a very well established whippet-racing calendar, all across the country.

But there was another use for whippets, which surprised and fascinated me. In the days before central heating, when bedrooms of peasant cottages or industrial slums were cold enough to have ice inside the windows, and poverty meant there were not always enough blankets to keep children warm, whippets became furry hot water bottles, put into the beds of toddlers and small children. They were perfect for the job, not shedding hair to trigger allergies, and being delighted to burrow under the covers.

It's a great tribute to the gentle nature of whippets that parents trusted them with this vital job. It must have been a huge comfort to many a child to snuggle up to sleep with their own permanent source of heat. I can remember how much I loved sharing my bed with Nita (although she never came under the covers). For these children, there was not only the companionship of the dog, but the vital warmth of its body.

It's possible the instinct to climb under the covers was bred into them, or it may simply be because they are naturally skinny, with no extra layer of fat, and their coat is thin with no soft underfur, so they enjoy the warmth of the bed covers and of the human being they are snuggled up against. It's definitely something they still want to do, as any whippet owner will tell you.

My friend David Bridgwater and his wife Lucy have actually bought a bigger bed – going from double to king size – to allow room for their whippet Molly. Now there's love for you.

David was a top horse jockey, riding over 500 winners, coming second in the Grand National and second in the jockey's championship one year, and is now a successful race-horse trainer. He and Lucy have had whippets for over 20 years, often several at a time, but until his children grew up and moved out, the dogs shared their beds. Now that George is at university and Poppy is an apprentice jockey with Andrew Balding (brother of Clare), Molly has decided that she needs to sleep with David and Lucy.

'She used to share Poppy's bed, and if Poppy wasn't around she slept with George. Now she snuggles under our duvet, right inside the bed.'

It was Lucy who originally chose whippets as a family pet, although David says: 'They say owners choose dogs that look like them – well, I like to think that once upon a time I was a whippet ...'

I came to know David and Lucy when Poppy and my daughter Ella became best friends when they were really young and at school together. It was in David's yard that I first encountered whippets. He told me what great pets they make:

'They are never aggressive, very placid. They're easy to train, they don't moult, they are great with children, other dogs and brilliant around horses and other animals.'

Molly and her predecessors spend their day in the farm yard at David's stables, and he has found their gentle presence is a good, calming influence on the race horses he trains. He also has two Dobermans, Stan and Maud, who live in the yard, as guard dogs, and a collection of other free-range animals, including cats, chickens, two pygmy goats and my namesake, Adam the goat. Adam came originally from my farm, and David chose the name for that reason 'and also because there is a slight ginger tint in his coat'.

I gave David the goat after one of his two pet sheep died.

'When the children were toddlers I took them to see lambs being born at a nearby farm,' he said. 'The farmer moved one newborn lamb into a corner. When I asked why, he said there were too many for the ewe to feed, and they had too many to bottle-feed. So I thought it would be fun for the children if we took it home and bottle-fed it ourselves. A minute or two later another one was put in the corner, so we took that one, too. Then I left quickly before we ended up with any more ...'

David found the sheep were great companions for the race horses, which can be highly strung. When one of the sheep died young, he asked me if I could provide a companion. That's where Adam, a Boer cross goat from Cotswold Farm Park came in.

'He's very much part of the family, along with Libby and Lulu, the two pygmy goats. He's quite an old man by now, but he's not showing much sign of ageing. On a sunny day there's a spot in the yard where all the animals go to sunbathe, and you see them all cuddled up together: goats, cats, dogs and even the chickens. Molly the whippet is always in the mix, she loves snuggling up to the others.'

Since I met David and Lucy's whippets I have encountered another beautiful whippet. Doris Churchley is another family friend: she used to look after our children when Charlie and I were working, and now she moves in to look after our dogs and cats when we go away on holiday. She's part of the family.

When Doris decided she wanted her own dog, she was tempted to have a Labrador: 'That's the breed I grew up with, but I wanted something smaller. I wanted a gentle, placid, loyal dog that likes other animals, because I work with horses. I didn't think of whippets at first, but when I looked into them I realised they fitted the bill completely.'

I remember when Doris brought her puppy, Myrtle, to introduce her to us. She was tiny, and so lovely to look at, a beautiful slate-grey colour with blue eyes. I can easily understand why anyone falls in love with them.

Like David and Lucy, Doris has to share her bed with Myrtle: 'She's under my duvet at the first opportunity. She sleeps curled up by my back, or in the crook of my legs. And, unlike a hot water bottle, she is still warm in the morning. She also loves pregnant women: she lies across their bumps. She's great with children, following them around devotedly. I can understand why they were used to keep children warm in bed, because they love children, and they give off a lot of heat.'

When Doris house-sits for us, Myrtle gets on well with our dogs. 'Dolly, the old Vizsla, used to ignore her, but Boo really loves her. They run around together. She likes all other dogs except other whippets: she gets jealous if I show any attention or affection to another whippet.'

Using dogs for warmth is not confined to whippets: many of today's lap dogs started life as 'comforters', or mobile hot water bottles. However cute dogs like Cavalier King Charles spaniels are, they were only partly chosen as fashion statements. They, and all the other small breeds, enjoyed a lot of popularity among the landed gentry, not only for keeping their owners warm, but also because it was believed they attracted fleas away from their human hosts, back in the days when hygiene wasn't what it is today. Parasites were no respecter of titles or wealth: every seventeenth-century lord and lady had a problem with fleas and lice, and dogs were adopted as allies in the never-ending struggle against infestations, in the belief that the fleas would jump ship onto the dog.

It's probably the most bizarre instance of a job for a dog that I've ever heard about. But it shows that even the smallest, cutest toy dog was, in its own weird way, a working dog. They also serve who only sit on a lap . . .

Afterword

H ow can I summarise my love for dogs? They are so much part of my life and family, and always have been, that it is impossible to think of an existence in which they were not there. I've known a wonderful procession of them, all with different merits and, if I'm honest, sometimes with different faults. But all faithful, loyal, and as devoted to me as I have always been to them.

I'm up early in the morning because of my work on the farm, and the first greeting I get for the day ahead is from the Vizslas in the kitchen, enthusiastic and energetic, thrilled to see me. Then it's outside to let Peg and Pearl out, and another round of tail wagging and sheer delight at the prospect of what lies ahead.

They are workmates, companions, and the greatest friends anyone can have; unquestioning, non-judgmental, and asking for nothing more than food and a bed and as much love as their owner can give them.

I hope in this book I have given a glimpse into not just how much they mean to me, as an individual and as a farmer who relies on them, but how much dogs give, endlessly, to the whole human race. They are our greatest allies.

I, for one, appreciate everything they have brought to my life. I am grateful to you all, my wonderful dogs.

Index

AH indicates Adam Henson.

Picture credits:

Page 9, courtesy of Sophie Cotton. Page 13, courtesy of Clint Coventry.
Page 14, courtesy of Karin Schnichels. Page 14, courtesy of Allen Parton.
Page 15, courtesy of Alan and Fiona Stewart. Page 15, courtesy of Doris
Churchley. Page 16 by Jude Edginton. All other pictures are from the
author's personal collection.

KT-231-134

B51 036 318 9

CHRISTOPHER HIRST is a freelance writer who lives in
London and North Yorkshire. He wrote the witty
el' column in the *Independent* for over a decade and
nks column called '101 Cocktails That Shook The
d'. A contributor on food matters to the *Independent*,
Telegraph and *Intelligent Life*, he was nominated
fiddich Food Writer of the Year in 2005 and runner-
2007.

is far more than a mere cookbook. It's a beautifully
en love letter; the story of a romance that blossomed
he stove. Impossible to put down, elegantly erudite and
n belly-shakingly funny, this is one of the best books
food, cooking, and dare I say it, love, that I've read for
s.'   TOM PARKER BOWLES

ristopher understands that the way to a woman's heart
through her stomach. That is NOT aiming too high.
of that many a true word is spoken ingest.'
                                        KATHY LETTE

have always been charmed and hilariously delighted
Christopher Hirst's musings on cookery and kitchens.
e Bites is brilliant.'   SIMON HOPKINSON

I hugely approve of Mr Hirst.'   JONATHAN MEADES

LOVE BITES

LOVE BITES

MARITAL SKIRMISHES IN THE KITCHEN

CHRISTOPHER HIRST

FOURTH ESTATE · London

First published in Great Britain by
Fourth Estate
A division of HarperCollins*Publishers*
77–85 Fulham Palace Road, London W6 8JB
www.4thestate.co.uk

Copyright © Christopher Hirst 2010

1 3 5 7 9 8 6 4 2

The right of Christopher Hirst to be identified as the author
of this work has been asserted by him in accordance with
the Copyright, Designs and Patents Act 1988

A catalogue record for this book is available from the British Library

ISBN 978-0-00-725550-4

All rights reserved. No part of this publication may be reproduced,
transmitted, or stored in a retrieval system, in any form or by any
means, without permission in writing from Fourth Estate

The author and publishers would like to thank Waitrose Ltd for its
permission to reproduce the recipe for Christmas cake on page 243 and
Fergus Henderson for his permission to reproduce the recipe for seed cake
on page 247, which is taken from *Beyond Nose to Tail* (Bloomsbury, 2007)

Typeset in Adobe Garamond by Birdy Book Design

Printed in Great Britain by Clays Ltd, St Ives plc

Mixed Sources
Product group from well-managed
forests and other controlled sources
FSC   www.fsc.org Cert no. SW-COC-001806
© 1996 Forest Stewardship Council

FSC is a non-profit international organisation established to promote the
responsible management of the world's forests. Products carrying the FSC
label are independently certified to assure consumers that they come
from forests that are managed to meet the social, economic and
ecological needs of present and future generations.

Find out more about HarperCollins and the environment at
www.harpercollins.co.uk/green

To Mrs H, whose real name is Alison

ROTHERHAM LIBRARY SERVICE	
B516318	
Bertrams	09/03/2010
AN	£11.99
BSU	641.5941

Contents

A CULINARY COURTSHIP

GIVEN OUR COMMON INTEREST, it was appropriate that Mrs H (as she then wasn't) and I met in a kitchen. It was at a party in south London, Darling Road to be precise, in 1982. When one thing happily led to another, food emerged as a joint passion. The first meal I ever made for Mrs H was a giant pile of smoked salmon sandwiches. I noticed that they went down well. This was promising. I doubt if a longstanding relationship would have resulted if she had turned out to be one of those females whose main nutritional intake is a breath of air.

The first meal she ever made for me was a Mongolian hot pot. This takes the form of a great plate of raw titbits – slivers of chicken breast, pork and steak, along with prawns, sliced scallops, broccoli florets, mangetouts – that you cook piecemeal in a large pot of stock over a methylated spirit burner. When you've simmered a piece, you eat it. Mongolian hot pot is an ideal dish for a couple in the exploratory stages of courtship. Because you use chopsticks to fish out the various items, there is plenty of scope for intimacy. You might steer your companion towards a succulent piece of steak, while she hands over a juicy prawn. There might be a certain amount of light-hearted competition for a scallop. The culinary foreplay is prolonged but not so heavy on the stomach as to preclude subsequent activity.

The meal was a revelation. My passion for food began when I became passionate about Mrs H. After living in an all-male flat, where food was fuel rather than feast, I was astonished by the flair and generosity of her cooking and also the remarkable amount she spent on ingredients. Not that I was entirely indifferent to food when we met. I don't suppose many men would have proposed the Royal Smithfield Show as a destination for a first date. Somewhat to my surprise, Mrs H expressed keenness to attend this agricultural jamboree. The first thing we saw inside Earls Court was several lamb carcasses suspended over an enclosure containing their living siblings. Mrs H did not seem too alarmed by this vivid depiction of before and after. We bought a pair of pork chops at the show, which she grilled for supper. They were excellent.

Nibble by nibble, our relationship blossomed. We did a certain amount of the restaurant work that courting couples are supposed to go in for. Not that we had many candlelit dinners for two. Economy was a greater priority than romantic surroundings. Restaurants don't come much cheaper or less romantic than Jimmy's, the Greek joint staffed by famously cheerless waiters in Frith Street, Soho, while Poon's on Lisle Street came a close second. Though far from ideal for a tête-à-tête – you ate at shared tables covered by greasy oilcloths – Mrs H was impressed by the robust generosity (she says 'greediness') of my ordering: roast duck, sweet and sour crispy won-tons, oyster and belly pork casserole …

Mostly, we dined at home. Since I spent almost all of my twenties in the pub, I missed out on the prawn cocktail era. Mrs H introduced me to a few delights of that distant time – snails in garlic butter (I was impressed that she owned snail tongs), kidneys in mustard sauce, chocolate mousse and cheese fondue. I'm still fond of her fondue, made in a large Le Creuset pan, though we restrict our intake of this dish, which is of doubtful value for the arteries unless you have spent the day climbing an alp or two, to once or twice a year. In her turn, Mrs H had missed out on certain areas of gastronomy that I regard as essential. I brought pork pie, rhubarb tart and shellfish to her attention. This did not, however, prevent her from refining my technique for moules marinière. 'You don't need great big chunks of onion. Could you chop it finer?'

Through Mrs H, I discovered the difference between proper paella and the Vesta variety. I also enjoyed the revelation that curry could be a pleasure, where you tasted the ingredients, rather than a form of trial by ordeal. She acquainted me with homemade pâté and salads that did not involve floppy lettuce. She even maintains that I didn't like broccoli before we met. I find this hard to believe. I've always been a big fan. 'You haven't! YOU HAVE NOT! And, it's only in the last couple of years that you've eaten curly kale and spring greens.' Well, she may be right on the last point, though I can now see the point of such vegetation. Mrs H also recalls my eruption when she tried serving flowers in a salad, which was fashionable some years ago. 'You objected very strongly and described it as "poncing it up".'

I gained an additional impetus towards culinary matters when I began writing a weekly column called 'The Weasel' in the *Independent*. Though its contents could be anything of a vaguely humorous nature, food and drink began to make a regular appearance. As with any habit, it started innocuously enough. You happen to write a piece about eating muskrat (dark, tough, springy meat not unlike Brillo pad) at a restaurant called Virus in Ghent. Soon after, you find yourself eating betel nut near Euston station, aphrodisiac jam in Paris, illicit ormers in Guernsey …

This new direction for the column bemused some executives on the paper. Objections to the high gustatory content were passed from above ('Can't he write about anything else?'), but I found it difficult to comprehend such griping. After all, what could be more interesting or amusing than food? Indeed, what else is there? Maybe I did ease up on the nosh from time to time, but this only produced an even greater flow of food pieces when I turned the tap back on: setting fire to the kitchen when trying to crisp Ryvita under the grill (they curled and touched the electric element); blowing up the fusebox when I tried to put a fuse on the fridge; making frumenty, the alcoholic porridge that prompted Michael Henchard to sell his wife and child in *The Mayor of Casterbridge* ('Well, I'm not sold on it,' said Mrs H).

Perhaps the real theme, which steadily emerged in

column after column, was the difference between men and women in the kitchen. Or, at any rate, the difference between Mrs H and me in the kitchen. Though I came to spend much time cooking in the kitchen – more, possibly than Mrs H – it remains her bailiwick. Never having been taught the essential rules of the kitchen, such as tidying up and putting the right thing in the right place, I came in for a certain amount of brusque character analysis. Recently, when I foolishly asked Mrs H to refresh my mind concerning my shortcomings in this milieu, it prompted a Niagara-like flow that proved hard to turn off.

Woman on men (i.e. her on me)

Men want a huge amount of praise for anything they do.

Whatever they do, men always create a vast amount of washing-up, but they never think of washing up as they go along.

Men are reluctant to follow recipes in the same way that they are reluctant to ask for directions when they are lost.

Men plunge into cooking without sorting out the ingredients and utensils they will need. Then they can't find what they want. When things are found for them, they never put them away.

Men tend to over-season. They think that if a little is good then a lot will be even better. This particularly applies to salt and Tabasco.

Men give up easily – e.g., if they get a pain in their arm when whisking cakes.

Men disappear if they have to do some work, but they are quite handy for reaching things from high shelves.

Men are not keen on washing burnt pans. (This is simply not true. I'm always washing up pans that Mrs H has managed to fuse food on to.)

Men always want to pinch a bit of a dish that is in the process of being made. They are very keen on eating between meals.

Men fill the dishwasher any old how so it seems packed even though there aren't many items in there.

Following these lacerating comments, it struck me that Mrs H might appreciate a few words of mild correction. Hence:

Man on women (i.e. me on her)

Women are very, very, very bossy.

Women tend to be excessively pedantic about recipes and timings.

Women are very keen on vegetables, even when old and fibrous. They have an inexplicable fondness for purple-sprouting broccoli that is too woody to eat.

Women take a lot of luring into eating oysters. When you finally manage to do this, they can often be sick and look at you reproachfully.

Women are very difficult to get out of kitchen shops. Their favourite reading tends to be the Lakeland catalogue. They spend money like water in such places. I'd never spend £18.99 on a jelly strainer set, though Mrs H says, 'It's worth its weight in gold.'

Women always remember to put on a pinny when cooking. Despite the consequent stains and splotches on my clothes, I would never wear such an emasculating garment.

Women are obsessed with cleanliness to the extent that it imperils our natural resistance to bugs and germs.

When clearing cupboards, women have a tendency to chuck out perfectly good foodstuffs that are only a year or two past their sell-by date.

Women are very willing to eat lobsters and most forms of fish, but show a marked reluctance to kill, gut or scale these creatures.

Women constantly complain that they have not received an equal share of food. They are particularly assiduous in checking the level in their wine glass. 'It's not fair!'

So why did we decide to test our relationship further by cooking the stuff in this book? Lots of food books will give you the recipes, but this one tells you what it was like to make these dishes, and where irritations and cock-ups occurred. We tried a variety of methods and recipes for items ranging from pasta to raspberry jam, pizza to pancakes. While avoiding outré ingredients (OK – we did a hamburger with wagyu beef) and complicated techniques, we aimed to produce versions that were, if not exactly perfect, pretty damn good and capable of being reproduced on the domestic range. From Lady Shaftesbury's hot cheese dip (page 56) to Fergus Henderson's seed cake (page 247), I'd recommend that anyone even vaguely interested in cooking should have a bash. There are, however, some exceptions. Heston Blumenthal's Black Forest gateau is definitely not easy to do. Rocket science is a doddle by comparison. I would never have dreamed of making the damn thing if the features editor of a newspaper had not commissioned me to do so. For sanity's sake, I earnestly entreat you not to try it. Mrs H would say the same about geoduck clams and similar maritime oddities I treated her to in Chapter 11.

Most chapters involve the tutorage of Mrs H. I suppose I could have gone to other authorities for instruction but this would have caused problems. Having experienced several cookery schools over the years, I've come to the conclusion that I'm not very good at being taught things in the kitchen. I claim this is because I'm too much of an anarchist to take orders. 'Actually,' says Mrs H, 'you don't listen when people tell you things.' Well, yes, I do seem to have some kind of mental block when people try to teach me practical skills. (After four years of learning woodwork at school, my sole production was a test-tube rack with three wonky holes.) Having lived with me for twenty-odd years, Mrs H was able to put up with this minor foible. Even so, several dishes were seasoned with salty language and peppery outbursts. But our flare-ups, both verbal and actual, were quickly extinguished. Mostly, it was a rewarding, or at least filling, adventure. Some couples climb Kilimanjaro: we made a pork pie.

1

Cracking the egg

Battle of the boil

HAVING MOVED MY TOOTHBRUSH into Mrs H's house,
I found myself eating very well, though a surprising deficiency in her abilities emerged early in the day. After I'd
cooked the breakfast egg for perhaps a dozen times on the
trot, it occurred to me that Mrs H didn't do boiled eggs.

'Of course I can boil an egg,' she insisted.

'But have you ever done a soft-boiled egg?'

Her resistance crumpled like a toast soldier encountering
a ten-minute egg.

'Well, rarely.'

'When did you last do one?'

'Can't remember. My father was always in charge of egg
boiling. I followed my mother's example.'

'You mean you both just sat there and waited for them
to arrive?'

'Yes. Like chicks in a nest with our beaks open.'

'Just like you do with me?'

'Yes.'

Of course, it was no great hardship to plug this unexpected gap in Mrs H's culinary repertoire. It gave me a *raison d'être* of sorts. But her lack of enthusiasm for this little dish was mystifying. In my view, the breakfast egg is 0-shaped bliss. I formed this opinion at an early age. While other boys invested their spending money on footballs or Ian Allan train-spotting books, I bought a humorous egg-cup etched with the injunction, 'Get cracking!'

Mrs H's take-it-or-leave-it approach to the soft-boiled egg did not prevent her pointing out my occasional failures with some vigour. I concede that it is not a good start to the day when you crack open your egg and find a yolk surrounded by a mainly liquid white. Still, I generally press on and eat the sad swirl. Not so Mrs H. 'I think that's the worst egg you've ever done for me,' she said once, pushing away her untouched breakfast. She was so disturbed that it was several days before she could contemplate another boiled egg.

In order to improve my technique, I began to explore the unexpectedly vexed business of boiling eggs. Though the war between the Big Endians and the Little Endians about the best way to tackle an egg was a Swiftian satire, this stalwart of the breakfast table sparked a vigorous conflict in 1998. The cause of combustion was Delia Smith's advice in her BBC programme *How to Cook*. Her method involves making a pinprick in the big end to prevent cracking, then simmering for 'exactly one minute'. You then remove the pan from the heat and leave the egg in the water, resetting the timer for five or six minutes, depending on whether you want a white that is 'wobbly' or 'completely set'. This advice was described as 'insulting' by fellow telly chef Gary Rhodes. 'I really don't believe the majority of people cannot boil an egg,' he huffed. Obviously, he hadn't met Mrs H.

In 2005, there was a further kerfuffle when Loyd Grossman tested the boiled egg techniques of five chefs for *Waitrose Food Illustrated*. Giorgio Locatelli's method involved constantly stirring the egg in boiling water for six minutes. The resulting centrifuge, he claimed, should keep the yolk exactly in the middle of the boiled egg. Antonio Carluccio insisted that the egg should be boiled for three minutes and then left to stand in the water for thirty seconds. But it was the procedure advocated by Michel Roux of the Waterside Inn at Bray that caused feathers to fly. In his book *Eggs*, he recommends that an egg should be placed in a small pan, covered generously with cold water and set over a medium heat. 'As soon as the water comes to the boil, count up to sixty seconds for a medium egg,' Roux explained to me. 'It requires neither a watch nor an egg timer and it is infallible.' Grossman reported disaster when he attempted this method: 'It was so close to raw that I didn't want to eat it.' I met Roux a few months after this criticism and he was still incandescent about Grossman's comments.

In order to achieve an impartial view, I tried the Roux method using an egg at room temperature. The result was a lightly boiled egg. To achieve a medium set, I had to count for another thirty seconds. Obviously, the time varies depending on the temperature of the egg before it goes into the water and the size of the egg. My main objection to the method is that counting up to sixty or, worse still, ninety is excessively demanding for some of us at breakfast time.

I attempted several methods that claimed to produce the perfect boiled egg, though I drew the line at St Delia's suggestion of simmering for the time it takes to sing three verses of 'Onward Christian Soldiers'. Eventually, I evolved a technique that eschews any form of timer, whether human or mechanical. It involves putting two eggs into simmering water, looking at the digital clock on the oven and adding another four minutes to whatever time is displayed. When this period clicks up, I add a few more seconds for luck, making (I hope) four and a half minutes in all. I then whip out the egg. It works, more or less. The result is usually a nicely set white and liquid but slightly thickened yolk. Mrs H's customary response is 'Very nice'. This is satisfactory, though on her scale of responses it is not as ecstatic as her top accolade, 'Yum'.

Occasionally, for inexplicable reasons, this method produces an underdone egg and accompanying complaints from Mrs H, but I still prefer human approximation to mechanical certainty. 'An egg is always an adventure,' said Oscar Wilde. 'The next one may be different.' In that spirit, I stick to guesswork even if it means a variable outcome at the breakfast table. That's me, living for kicks.

If Mrs H wanted a certain outcome in her boiled egg, she could, of course, break the habit of a lifetime and start doing them herself. Instead, she continues sitting there with beak open. Had she ever considered attempting the break-fast simmer in our two decades together?

'Nope. See what you can get away with if you keep quiet.'

The scramble for success

The boot was on the other foot when it came to scrambled eggs. My inadequacy was brought home when I made some for Mrs H. 'This is fine,' she said, 'as long as you like scrambled eggs that are pale, hard and rubbery.' I scrutinised my effort, which leaked a watery residue that made the underlying toast go soggy.

'It's not all that bad,' I protested, risking a nibble.

'Hmm,' considered Mrs H. 'Perhaps I've had worse scrambled eggs in hotels.' Recalling my encounters with terrible hotel scrambles – friable, evil-smelling, desiccated – I realised that this was not saying very much.

'Chuck it in the bin and buy some more eggs,' said Mrs H.

Swallowing my pride, which was easier than my eggs, I reassessed my scrambling technique. At some point in the past, I'd conceived the idea that speed was of the essence with scrambled eggs. Plenty of heat and plenty of spoon-whirling guaranteed success. Occasionally, I would examine the chewy results of my speed-scramble and ponder, 'This can't be right.'

Mrs H put me right: 'You need four eggs, plenty of butter and plenty of patience.' Of all the culinary lessons imparted by Mrs H in this book, the one that has taken root most effectively, at least in her opinion, is how to do scrambled eggs. 'You've learned to do them very well,' she said, rather like an old master dispatching a talented apprentice into the wide world. 'I like your scrambled eggs as much as mine.' Since then, scrambled eggs have become my default snack. Nothing as simple to cook tastes quite so good.

For two people, five lightly beaten and seasoned eggs are added to a pan that is just warm enough to melt a walnut-sized lump of butter. Cooking at low heat is of the essence. Unlike boiled eggs, poached eggs and soufflés, scrambled eggs demand the near-constant involvement of the cook. They should also be consumed immediately. (That's why the hotel breakfast scramble is usually hopeless.) Nothing seems to happen for ages while you keep stirring. Then, just when you have given up all hope, curds begin to form on the bottom of the pan. These have to be gently broken by the rotating spoon. When the eggs are heading towards setting but still liquid, you add another teaspoon of butter (a splat of cream also works well) and stir again, remove from the heat and serve. The final result should be a slurry, not a set.

If you're trying to do anything else at the same time, especially the manifold demands of the full English breakfast, disaster is likely. But with unceasing attention and quite a lot of butter, you can produce a dish that is luxurious in both taste and texture. It is one of the few items where the amateur can achieve three-star finesse – or nearly. I must admit that Michel Roux's formulation incorporating crab and asparagus tips, which I sampled once at his reataurant in Bray, has the edge on my version. 'There are two schools of scrambled egg,' explained Roux. 'My brother Albert does his for hours in a bain-marie. I do mine over very low gas using a diffuser. His are still half-cooked when mine are finished. Less than three eggs in scrambled egg and you get nothing. Five or six are best.'

My decision not to use a diffuser was assisted by my inability to find the damn thing in our kitchen cupboard. Not that the lowest possible heat is always regarded as a *sine qua non*. In a heretical deviation, Roux's nephew Michel Roux Jr, who is chef at Le Gavroche in Mayfair, dispenses with both diffuser and tiny flame. He recommends 'a medium to high heat' in his recipe for 'the perfect creamy scrambled eggs'. It goes to show that there is no golden rule for a great scramble.

My in-depth research into scrambled eggs was curbed by Mrs H's concern for my arteries. I would have tried Ian Fleming's recipe – his obsession with scrambled eggs is indicated by their repeated appearance as James Bond's breakfast – but requiring six ounces of butter and twelve eggs, it is as potentially lethal as Bond's Walther PPK. Along similar lines, the scrambled egg recipe from the surrealist Francis Picabia in *The Alice B. Toklas Cookbook* calls for eight eggs and half a pound of butter. 'Not a speck less,' insists Toklas, 'rather more if you can bring yourself to it.' Since the result is described as having 'a suave consistency that perhaps only gourmets will appreciate', Mrs H's prohibition was not too painful.

I had better luck with 'Portuguese-style scrambled eggs', one of the variations proposed by Michel Roux. Currently the Sunday breakfast *de choix* at Hirst HQ, it is a good dish to make if you happen to have some meat stock in reserve. (Years ago, I saw a tip in a newspaper about storing concentrated stock in plastic ice-cube bags in the freezer. Aside from being a bit fiddly to achieve – you tend to end up with a lot of stock on the floor – and the tendency of the frozen cubes to get lost in the freezer, it's a fine idea.) The scrambled eggs are served in a soup plate topped with a sprig of grilled cherry tomatoes and fringed by a narrow moat of warm stock. Serve with buttered toast. Mrs H's response is most satisfactory. 'Simply fantastic. It's the very best sort of brasserie food. Just the thing to revive an ailing spirit. Perfect for a late breakfast on a Sunday.'

A dish called scrambled eggs Clamart, which incorporates a sprinkling of fresh peas, sliced mangetouts and sweated lettuce, elicited a similar reaction from Mrs H. 'Yum,' she said, bestowing top gastronomic marks. 'Sweet and crunchy. A perfect spring lunch.' The only drawback is that it is a bit of a faff to do. You cook the peas and mangetouts separately, refresh in cold water, then reheat for twenty seconds before adding to the scrambled eggs with the sweated lettuce. In order not to break the unremitting attention required during the scrambling phase, this requires some deft before-and-after work. By the end, the lettuce isn't the only thing that is sweated.

I came across a robust hybrid in *The Perfect Egg and Other Secrets* by the designer Aldo Buzzi (oddly, the book does not contain much about eggs). Scrambled eggs Frankfurt-style is described as 'more Olympian,

Goethe-esque' than the standard scrambled egg. This is pretty heady stuff at breakfast time, but I gave it a bash. You are directed to use one egg per person and one for the pan. They are whisked with a teaspoonful of water for each egg. Buzzi directs the reader to cook the eggs in 'well-browned butter' over a very low heat. A frying pan seemed to be the best utensil for this, since you have to 'use a spatula to gently move the part that is setting while you make the still liquid part run on to the hottest part of the pan'. Turn off the heat when the eggs have achieved a very light set. The result is a cross between an omelette and scrambled eggs, though lighter and more liquid and glistening than either of them. I followed Buzzi's suggestion of blending in 'well-cooked pepper and tomatoes, in which case what you'll have is a sort of Basque piperade'.

Mrs H was quite taken with it, though her praise came with reservation. 'The tomatoes are nice and fresh, the peppers quite peppery. You've managed to capture the omelette-style scramble. Certainly worth bearing in mind for future, except ...'

'Yes?'

'It might be better for supper than at seven thirty in the morning.'

Poacher's pockets

After two decades of making poached eggs for Mrs H, I came to a sudden realisation. She can't poach for toffee. I mean real poaching with eggs in a pan rather than using an egg poacher. She admits it herself. 'My poached eggs are always rotten compared to yours. Don't know why. One of the great mysteries of life.'

This is an unfortunate culinary omission considering the many admirable applications of the poached egg, a dish that provides its own sauce in a sachet. Hence the word 'poach', from the French *poche* (pocket). What could be nicer or simpler than poached eggs on buttered toast? They're also splendid in a warm salad and in eggs Benedict, which happens to be one of Mrs H's specialities. This is when the egg poacher makes an appearance.

Though some of us might look on this as cheating, it was a method advocated by Mrs Beeton. 'To poach an egg to perfection is rather a difficult operation,' she wrote. 'So for inexperienced cooks, a tin egg-poacher may be purchased, which greatly facilitates this manner of dressing eggs.' People in ancient Rome must have felt the same. A drawing of cooking equipment from Pompeii includes two utensils that look very much like egg poachers (one for four eggs, another for twenty-eight).

My objections to using the poacher involve danger (you are likely to scald your fingers when you remove the little pans from the saucepan), taste (the white of the steamed or buttered egg lacks the pleasing texture of a naturally poached white) and aesthetics. The perfectly round steamed egg is industrial in appearance. It is the kind of egg you get on an Egg McMuffin.

When I imparted my critique to Mrs H, she responded with a delicate yawn. She also pointed out that she never got scalded by the egg poacher because she has the gumption to turn off the gas before removing the egg, unlike others she could mention. However, she agreed that my orthodox version of the poached egg had the edge. Moreover, she expressed willingness to learn.

This reversal of our usual relationship in the kitchen did not prove to be a very happy experience, though we managed the first step of boiling a pan of water without dispute or mishap.

'Get up a good boil,' I pontificated, 'then reduce the heat to a gentle simmer – no bubbles – and break an egg into a cup so we can gently introduce it into the water.'

'What sort of cup?'

'Just a cup.'

'But what kind?'

'What do you mean what kind? A cup from Buckingham Palace! Just get any old cup. Why are you so concerned about cups?'

What she was meaning, it turned out, was the size of cup. When I snatched down a half-pint mug, Mrs H rejected it and used a ramekin to introduce her egg into the water.

'Aren't you supposed to stir the water round so it forms a funnel for the egg?'

'My funnels never last long enough. Just pour your egg in.'

After doing this, she peered sadly into the pan. 'My egg is like a rolling blanket of fog. I told you it would spread.'

'Never mind. Just get it out after four minutes.'

'What with?'

'I usually use the large slotted spoon.'

'Where's that?'

'In the place where we keep slotted spoons!'

'It's not there.'

'Grr!'

Eventually the slotted spoon emerged from its hidey-hole and Mrs H hauled out her dripping creation. 'My poached egg isn't anything like yours,' she groaned. 'Look at that yolk. Completely hard. Mind you, I had a hopeless instructor. You shouted at me.'

'When did I shout?'

'Buckingham Palace! Slotted spoon!' She drew a small figure with black fringe, toothbrush moustache and upraised arm in my notebook. 'How do you think you rated as a teacher?' she continued. 'I'll tell you how many marks you got out of ten.' Mrs H made an O with her forefinger and thumb and squinted at me through the hole.

I felt it was time to return to her poached egg.

'It's quite nice but a bit, er …'

'Watery and all over the place, you mean. I've done them before and they've consistently spread. I can't get them into a nice little lump like you.'

Then I did a poached egg.

'See – that's perfect,' said Mrs H when I got it out. 'It's all nice and round. You can just tell the yolk is going to be perfect. How annoying.'

'I think I might have given you some elderly eggs.'

'You might blame the eggs, but I say rotten maker, rotten teacher.'

Still, I might have been even more demanding as a tutor. Considering the beautiful simplicity of a poached egg, it is remarkable how much complexity some experts have managed to bring to the topic. Culinary titan Joel Robuchon says you should boil your eggs in their shells 'for exactly thirty seconds' before chilling them in iced water and starting an orthodox poach. This is supposed to 'firm up the surface edge of the white a bit', but in my view it indicates a chef who has had a battalion of sous-chefs doing his poaching for him for years.

Michel Roux recommends that you fish your egg out of the pan after one and a half minutes and 'press the outside edge to see if it is properly cooked'. The picture in his book resembles someone pressing home a point by prodding the waistcoat of a rotund gent. 'Now, see here, Carruthers …' If the egg is not sufficiently poached, you put it back in the water. Roux does not say if you have to do more waistcoat-prodding to the egg after its second appearance, though I presume so. Some recipes say that a three-minute boil is sufficient, though I'd advocate four minutes if you stick to a bubble-free simmer. A slotted spoon helps no end when it comes to extracting the egg. Scooping out your egg with an ordinary spoon means waterlogged toast. Some authorities suggest that you should rest the egg on a towel to dry off, rather like a holidaymaker on the beach.

Many recipes suggest a dollop of vinegar in the poaching water to help keep the egg together, but Mrs H doesn't like the resulting vinegar tinge and she could be right. Anyway, a really fresh egg doesn't need any assistance in coagulation.

Culinary scientist Harold McGee dispenses with vinegar since it 'produces shreds and an irregular film over the egg surface'. His solution is to pour off the thin white that causes poached egg untidiness before simmering, but I wouldn't bother. Michel Roux advocates post-poaching tidying. 'Trim the edges with a small knife to make a neat shape. This will also cut off the excess white that inevitably spreads during cooking.' Trimming poached eggs strikes me as cheffiness. As Mrs H will confirm, I am not a great devotee of neatness.

Mrs H's recipe for cheat's eggs Benedict

Our lovely friend Carolyn Hart was so knocked out with this dish, which I served at my birthday brunch party, that she included the recipe in her book called *Cooks' Books*. Because I cooked for around thirty people, it involved the use of an egg poacher (you can handily whack out four servings at a time) and fresh ready-made hollandaise sauce from the supermarket. If the muffins are pre-toasted and kept warm (ditto the bacon), you can rapidly serve quite a crowd, although the quantities given below are per person. I heat the hollandaise in a double boiler at the gentlest simmer whilst poaching the eggs. A child still at the age of pliability is useful for handing round the eggs Benedict to your guests while you try to fend off greedy whatnots demanding seconds. A pitcher or two of Bloody Marys aids the party spirit.

1 toasted muffin
2 grilled rashers of good-quality back bacon (your choice of
  smoked or unsmoked)
1 poached egg
1 generous dollop of gently heated hollandaise sauce

After variously toasting, grilling, gently heating and
poaching the four ingredients, assemble the cheat's eggs
Benedict in this order on top of each other: muffin, bacon,
poached egg, dollop of hollandaise. Don't forget to save
some for yourself.

SEEKING GLORY

DESPITE HAVING SCORED some notable successes in the breakfast area, I began to experience a twinge of dissatisfaction. A boiled egg is fine in its way, but it does not generate the ovations and rave reviews that male cooks crave. It is not enough for our dishes to be nutritious, tasty and satisfying. They should also produce a storm of applause, amazement, even adulation. 'Bravo! Bellissimo! Wunderbar!' Extreme examples of this phenomenon are commonplace in the higher echelons of the gastronomic world. It always strikes me as curious that when, at the end of a banquet, the chef appears from the kitchen, he is greeted with a round of applause. Where else, outside the theatre, does anyone get such acclamation for doing his everyday job? Do we clap a road-layer when he completes a particularly fine bit of motorway? Or the refuse collector when he empties our bins with aplomb?

There was another less egocentric reason for expanding my culinary repertoire. Three years into our relationship, I went freelance and began working from home. Mrs H continued working on the other side of London. On her return journey, she would often call in Reggie Perrin-style, 'Only just reached Victoria. Points failure at Acton. Have pipe and slippers waiting.' It was obviously unfair to expect her to start bashing away in the kitchen when she staggered through the door at 8.30 p.m. My gallantry was given additional impetus by the hunger pangs I began to feel three hours earlier.

Starting with salads, I moved on to pasta, stews and casseroles (all remain gastronomic mainstays at Hirst HQ). Eventually, the day came when I graduated from hob to oven. Like a small, super-heated theatre in the corner of the room, its productions are more likely to elicit acclaim than something scooped from a saucepan. Mrs H was certainly impressed by my efforts. 'I'd come home completely drenched to find the house full of delicious smells and you with a spoon in your mouth having a tasting session. Even though bits of mashing potato were often flying through the air, it was very welcome.'

Mrs H was referring to my slightly feverish construction of fish pie. 'I remember that it always contained large quantities of cockles. A bit odd but rather delicious.' She was also fond of my robust version of coq au vin: 'Your great glug of brandy made it very sustaining. I had to go to bed immediately afterwards.' Pheasant casserole in a Calvados and cream sauce was even more satisfying. 'After a single bowl, I felt as if I might go pop!'

All good stuff that provided much in the way of the requisite congratulation, acclamation, etc. The response to my next production was more ambivalent. While not exactly a flop, it received a mixed review. 'I remember coming home and there was this Desperate Dan-style thing on the kitchen table,' Mrs H recalls. 'It was a vast pie with a patchwork lid. You stood behind it covered in flour and exuding pride from every pore.'

Well, yes, maybe I did generate a hint of righteous self-satisfaction at my first substantial baking achievement. 'It was certainly substantial,' says Mrs H. 'I don't think I've ever seen a bigger pie. In some parts the pastry was very thick, in other parts it was so thin that it disappeared. Still, it tasted OK if you ignored the very doughy bits. My problem was with the inside. I don't like sweet pies and I particularly don't like them filled with rhubarb.'

This is a mystery to me. How can anyone not like rhubarb pie? 'Quite easily,' says Mrs H. 'Rhubarb is quite nice tasting but it collapses into a pink, stringy mush in a pie.'

Her antipathy is supported by one of Britain's greatest food writers. 'Nanny food,' Jane Grigson seethed in her *Fruit Book*. 'Governess food. School-meal food.' In case we haven't got the message, she went on: 'I haven't got over disliking rhubarb, and disliking it still more for being often not so young and a little stringy … Only young pink rhubarb is worth eating.'

Though expounded by two of my favourite authorities, Mrs G and Mrs H, I strongly disagree with this view. We almost always used mature stalks in the most memorable dessert of my childhood. Though somewhat bulkier than Proust's madeleine, a rhubarb pie has the same effect on me. Its combination of bittersweet, tooth-etching filling and juice-infused pastry instantly whisks me back to the West Riding of Yorkshire *circa* 1962. I grew up near the legendary Rhubarb Triangle between Leeds, Wakefield and Morley. Or is it Bradford? Opinions vary about the location of this locale, almost as mysterious as its Bermudan counterpart, but we certainly had several rhubarb plants in the garden of our house in Cleckheaton. In consequence, I ate a lot of rhubarb as a child – almost always in pie form, very occasionally stewed, never under the crunchy awning of a crumble.

If Mrs H was a non-starter in the Rhubarb Pie Appreciation League, I found a more willing recipient in the form of Mrs H's mother. If she was surprised when her daughter's live-in boyfriend started serving her rhubarb pie on a regular basis, she did not express it to me. Admittedly, my Proustian pud did not whisk her back to a Yorkshire childhood, but this was scarcely surprising since she came from Surbiton, Surrey.

2

Rhubarbing

IN HIS BOOK *Rhubarb: The Wondrous Drug*, Clifford Foust, Professor of History at the University of Maryland, explains 'the several advantages' of my home turf of West Yorkshire as the perfect *terroir* for rhubarb. It had 'a climate northerly enough for a lengthy autumn dormancy period' and 'high rainfall for maximum plant development'. The 'smoky and polluted atmosphere' helped 'induce early and full dormancy … for early forcing' and 'urban sludge' provided plentiful fertiliser. No wonder I have rhubarb juice in my veins.

Perhaps the first dish I ever made for myself was chunks of raw rhubarb dipped in sugar. Half a century ago in the West Riding of Yorkshire, we would have been mystified by Jane Grigson's insistence on 'only pink young rhubarb'. This is a 'forced' winter crop grown in large, dark sheds. It tastes great, but why limit yourself to this etiolated stuff when outdoor rhubarb continues to delight the palate throughout summer? Unless you use telegraph-pole-sized rhubarb, you need not fear stringiness. And what if there is a suggestion of the fibrous? Is that going to kill you?

The pie I made as a treat for Mrs H's mother was equipped with a pastry floor, walls and roof, because that's the kind of pie my mother made. I still feel short-changed if I receive a pie, whether sweet or savoury, where the pastry consists only of a lid. Unlike my mother, I cheated by using ready-made pastry, shortcrust because that's what I grew up with, though puff, which Mrs H prefers, is also OK. Either way, a highlight of the pie is the sweetened pink rhubarb juice soaking into the pie floor. You don't get that with rhubarb crumble.

After rolling out the pastry, I used the majority of it to line a large dish. I chopped the rhubarb stalks into cubes and put them into the pie. I then added sugar (a 5:3 ratio of rhubarb to sugar is about right) and installed the roof. As Mrs H points out, it usually required a certain amount of patching. After sealing the joints by pinching, I brushed it with milk and slashed three holes for steam-release as I'd seen my mother do hundreds of times. Emerging from the oven, the pastry patchwork had, I thought, a fine manly vigour. Lumps of rhubarb were visible through the three crevasses.

'Just a small slice for me,' said Mrs H's mum.

While she nibbled, I enlightened her about the mysterious story of rhubarb. For exoticism, its etymology beats everything else in the larder. The 'rhu' bit derives from Rha, the Greek name for the River Volga, where the plant was transported, while 'barb' comes from the Latin *barbarus* (meaning 'foreign', 'strange' and, ironically, 'uncultivated'). This, in turn, came from a Greek onomatopoeic coinage because barbarian speech sounded like 'Ba, ba, ba'. The 'rhubarbing' of film extras is an unconscious return to the plant's distant origins. It was possibly first cultivated in Mongolia by the Tartar tribes of the Gobi Desert. We don't know if anyone told Genghis Khan that rhubarb was nanny food.

'Fancy that,' said Mrs H's mum. 'It was lovely, but I won't have another slice, thank you.'

At our next meeting, I produced another monumental construction. 'I've made you a rhubarb pie,' I announced, a trifle superfluously, as I cut her a chunk.

'Oh, lovely.'

'Did you know that we all come from rhubarb?'

'Really, dear?'

The Zoroastrians, I explained, believed that 'the human race was born of the rhubarb plant'. I gleaned this insight from *The Legendary Cuisine of Of Persia* by Margaret Shaida, who notes that *reevâs*, the Persian name for the plant, comes from a word meaning 'shining light'. The association came about because 'from ancient times, rhubarb has been considered good for cleansing the blood and purifying the system'. Until the eighteenth century, rhubarb was mainly used as a laxative in Britain. Only the root was consumed, with Chinese rhubarb being particularly prized for its cathartic properties. A great rarity by the time it reached here, it cost four times as much as opium in medieval times. I once saw some Chinese rhubarb root in the Fernet-Branca factory in Milan. It took the form of large powdery, purple-brown lumps. Along with forty other wonderfully weird ingredients (white agaric, cinchona, aloes, zedoary, myrrh), it is used to enhance the bitterness of this acerbic potion.

The plant's stalk only became used for culinary purposes with the arrival of Siberian rhubarb in the eighteenth century. Hybrids developed in the nineteenth century combined with the declining price of sugar to make rhubarb a favourite dessert of the Victorians. (You certainly need sugar in rhubarb pie. It's the oxalic acid in rhubarb that makes it such an interesting food.) The types known as Victoria and Royal Albert were developed by Joseph Myatt, evidently an ardent monarchist, in his market gardens in Deptford and Camberwell (the latter is now a park called Myatt's Fields), while the imaginatively named Champagne came from a rival grower called Hawkes in nearby Lewisham. The three heroes of *Three Men in a Boat* (1889) dine off rhubarb pie before setting out on their great adventure. The laxative property of rhubarb continued to be utilised even when the stalks became a foodstuff. In America, rhubarb was known as 'a broom for the system'.

'How interesting,' said Mrs H's mother. 'Actually, I don't know if I'll be able to finish this piece.'

I had no doubt what Mrs H's mum expected the next time she paid a visit. 'Guess what I've made!' I said. Hewing a wedge for her, I returned to our favourite topic. 'Do you know how many cookbooks have been devoted to rhubarb?' The answer is over 300, mostly produced during the 'Rhubarb Craze' that swept Britain and America in the early years of the twentieth century. But for those of us from the

Rhubarb Triangle there is one supreme rhubarb dish. Sadly, my dear mother-in-law is no longer around to enjoy my rhubarb pie. At least, I thought she enjoyed it, though her daughter cast doubt on this.

'It was funny that you always made rhubarb pie when my mother came round.'

'What do you mean, "funny"?'

'You never saw her face when you produced your pies.'

'She enjoyed them!'

'She was too polite to say she wasn't very fond of rhubarb.'

In subsequent years, Mrs H has continued this weird familial objection to rhubarb pie, but she grudgingly agreed to indulge my passion by making some other recipes that involve rhubarb. By way of encouragement, I obtained a volume called *Rhubarb – More Than Just Pies*, published by the University of Alberta Press. They grow a lot of rhubarb in Alberta.

Her preliminary report on rhubarb and ginger mousse was optimistic. 'You simmer sliced rhubarb and orange zest with powdered ginger till the fruit is soft,' she explained. 'Then you add gelatine. When it's half set, you beat egg whites to peaks and fold in to create the mousse. It's got a nice orange and ginger taste that complements the rhubarb. It looks lovely.'

'Should it have separated like this?' I asked after peering into the fridge at four glass beakers containing a murky orange jelly topped by a gnarled-looking mousse of greyish hue.

'It hadn't separated when it went in,' said Mrs H, resentfully. It didn't taste impossibly bad. Just odd. The mousse had a curious texture, like fibre-reinforced resin. It might have been an early experiment in making plastic. It was edible, just about, but not mousse as we know it. The jelly part was tasty but very hard indeed. 'Maybe I used too much gelatine,' groaned Mrs H. 'I used a new kind of gelatine that gives directions for making a litre and I only wanted a pint. I sat there for ages trying to work it out and I think I got it wrong.'

'Do you want to give it another go?'

'No.'

Mrs H thought she might have better luck with savoury rhubarb dishes. Currently, the use of rhubarb as a savoury is very fashionable in trendy restaurants, where, of course, the chefs stick to the wimpy, pink stuff. 'Rhubarb-carrot relish sounds nice,' she said, poring through *Rhubarb – More Than Just Pies*. But it wasn't. Considering the tastiness of the two main ingredients, which were boiled separately in salty water, puréed, then mixed together with butter, the determined blandness of the rhubarb-carrot relish was a disappointment. Maybe they like things bland in Alberta.

'It is slightly reminiscent of aubergine dip,' I said encouragingly. Helped along with Tabasco, it became somewhat more toothsome, but Mrs H would not be consoled. 'Into the bin,' she said.

The nadir of her rhubarb experimentation came with rhubarb relish, consisting of diced rhubarb along with the usual suspects – brown sugar, vinegar, chopped onion and spices. The instructions could barely be simpler: 'Combine all ingredients in a large saucepan and boil until thickened.' So what could go wrong?

'The postman,' said Mrs H.

'The postman?'

'Yes. I did the relish and I was just putting it into jars when the postman rang at the door with lots of parcels for you. While he was giving them to me, a woman came up and said she wanted him to take a letter because the postbox had been sealed. He said he wasn't supposed to take it …'

'What's this got to do with rhubarb?' I asked, feeling we were straying from the point somewhat.

'Hang on! A long discussion followed about where there was an open postbox. The woman said, "I don't know where that is," and the postman reluctantly accepted the letter. Eventually, I brought the parcels back into the house and thought "Oh, hell." I knew something had gone very wrong when I couldn't lift my bailing jug from the bottom of the pan. Look, there it is, stuck fast.'

Yes, there it was. I pulled at the jug. It was like trying to lift the Chrysler Building from the Manhattan bedrock. With the assistance of a kettle of boiling water, I managed to pry the jug from the world's toughest relish. I turned to Mrs H expecting grateful thanks, but all I got was a glum look. Her mouth turned down at both ends like a banana. She pointed at the jars of 'relish' that she had filled before her jar got stuck. The contents were akin to bitumen. It was a sort of rhubarb toffee and might even have been chewable if I'd been able to get any out, but I didn't want to risk my fillings on it.

A few days later, Mrs H returned to the fray. She amended the relish recipe with more onion, more rhubarb and a spoonful of ground allspice, but her major refinement concerned the cooking technique. 'Instead of "boil until thickened", I brought it to the boil then turned it down to a very low simmer and reduced the mixture. Every time I smelled it, I gave it a stir.'

'So how long did that take?'

'I put it on at 8:30 a.m. and finished it at 3:15 p.m.'

The result of the seven-hour simmer was a sticky, brown goo. Sweet-sour but wonderfully rounded, it was excellent. The chunks of rhubarb radiated a profound flavour that tinged on the palate for ages. Maybe it would improve with maturing, but a vintage version of Mrs H's rhubarb relish is unlikely because it is so addictive. Particularly when consumed with pork pie, the contents of a jar can magically disappear in a matter of minutes.

Her next effort concerned a rhubarb sauce intended for pork chops. Made with red wine, vinegar and chicken stock, it looked slightly dubious to me. Fruit with meat (apple with pork, cherries with duck, etc.) is one of my blind spots. I know I should like it, but I feel instinctively drawn to the mustard pot. 'I don't think I'll bother with the sauce,' I announced.

Mrs H took a mouthful of the combination and asserted, 'Well – ner, ner, ner – it goes quite well with the pork.'

After risking a taste, I had to admit that it did. The

sharpness of the sauce, which the wine had made ruby-red, was a perfect foil for the pork chop. Even when the chop had vanished, the sauce was pretty good. Mrs H scribbled in my notebook: 'Mr H said he didn't want any rhubarb on his pork chops, thank you, but he ended up nicking a great spoonful from the serving bowl.'

Even better was her rendition of Persian khoresh, a stew with rhubarb and shoulder of lamb. You may recall that the Persians regarded rhubarb as a holy vegetable, and going by the taste of this they were not far out. 'It's been simmering on top of the stove for about seven hours,' said Mrs H. 'The rhubarb only goes in for the last quarter of an hour.' Each forkful delivered contrasting flavours – the sweetness of the lamb, the tartness of the rhubarb, sweetness again with caramelised onions – which were magically complementary. 'Mmm, this is nice,' I gushed.

After this triumph, I felt it was time for me to have a go at a savoury rhubarb dish. I tried a Gary Rhodes recipe for steamed oysters with rhubarb. Though I am possibly the world's greatest oyster lover, certainly one of the greediest, I was a little hesitant about this weird combination. But Rhodes points out that a sauce of chopped shallots in red wine vinegar (known as mignonette) is a traditional accompaniment to oysters, so he came up with rhubarb softened in red wine vinegar with a touch of sugar as a partner to steamed, buttery oysters.

Inevitably, he calls for '3–4 sticks of forced rhubarb', but I used thin sticks of the ordinary kind. The recipe is a bit fiddly for my liking. Even with shortcuts, I found myself cussing when it came to putting a teensy-weeny pile of rhubarb in each empty shell and placing a steamed, buttery oyster on top of each pile. 'Bloody fiddly, cheffy nonsense.' (I give you an expurgated version.) But, yes, I admit it, the sweetness of the oysters and the sourness of the rhubarb worked remarkably well together.

My final bash at rhubarb came from Robin Lane Fox, biographer of Alexander the Great, who presumably knew a thing or two about rhubarb. According to him (Fox, not Alexander), rhubarb stewed with 'masses of caster sugar', then mixed with the grated rind and juice of an orange and left overnight, is not only 'the supreme recipe' but 'the true king of all English puddings'. It has a very good acidy flavour, but maybe it's more of a delicious accompaniment to stuff like blancmange or yogurt than a pudding as such.

'Mmm. It's very refreshing,' said Mrs H. 'A bit like eating those Haliborange tablets I had as a child.' This was a new one on me, since I had a Haliborange-free childhood, but it was evidently high praise. 'Lovely.'

She also astonished me by reminiscing about another rhubarb dish. 'I rather miss those days when you were always pulling huge, patched pies from the oven.' Mrs H wanted her own Proustian moment.

Mrs H's recipe for lamb khoresh with rhubarb

We make this dish for friends for informal suppers or lunches and it always produces lots of oooh's and ahh's and satisfied slurping noises. Shoulder of lamb has more fat than other cuts but compensates with its sweet flavour. The fat is eventually skimmed off anyway. The herbs complement the lamb in an entirely satisfactory way and the tang of the rhubarb gets the tastebuds going. We usually serve this with a generous quantity of nutty basmati rice, to mop up the juices, and a green salad. Depending on the size of the lamb shoulder and the appetites of the guests, the ingredients below should serve six to eight people.

1.4 kg boned shoulder of lamb
2 large Spanish-type onions
4 tablespoons butter
a generous pinch of saffron
625ml beef stock
4 tablespoons lemon juice
salt and pepper to season
2 bunches of fresh flat-leaf parsley
6–8 sprigs of fresh mint
450g rhubarb, cut into 2.5cm pieces

The khoresh has different cooking times for different stages. I like to think that you are building up the flavours.

Deal with the meat first by chopping the shoulder of lamb into 5cm chunks. Trim off any bits you don't want, but remember you need the fat to flavour the meat. Next chop up the onions and sauté them gently with two tablespoons of the butter in a large flameproof casserole until they are transparent. Once cooked, remove from the pan and set aside. Now turn the heat up a little more and quickly seal the lamb pieces in the casserole, using the pan drippings from the onions to fry and brown the meat. Lower the heat again, then add the saffron strands to the meat and stir well. Now reintroduce the onions to the pan. Add the beef stock and lemon juice. Season with salt and pepper. Bring everything to the boil, then turn the heat down, cover the pan and simmer the khoresh gently for about 1 hour.

While you wait, chop the parsley and mint. Set aside some of the herb mixture for garnish, then sauté the rest of the leaves briefly with the remaining butter and add to the casserole for another 30 minutes.

Add the chopped rhubarb to the casserole for the last 15 minutes. Test the meat for doneness and check the seasoning. The final element of flavour is added when you concentrate the sauce. Use a slotted spoon to remove the meat mix to a serving dish. Keep it warm. Skim the fat from the top of the remaining pan juices and boil the liquid hard until it is reduced by one third. Pour the thickened juices over the meat, and garnish with the saved mint and parsley. Serve with basmati rice and salad.

Mrs H's recipe for savoury rhubarb sauce

Based on a recipe from *Rhubarb: More Than Just Pies*, this was a revelation. Although we served it with pork, I cannot see why it could not accompany other meats. This recipe should be sufficient for four. The pork was grilled and marinated in olive oil and the juice and zest of an orange. We had a fresh spinach and asparagus salad for veg.

4 rhubarb stalks
250ml red wine
125ml red wine vinegar
180ml chicken stock

Chop the rhubarb into smallish pieces and transfer to a saucepan. Mix in the red wine and vinegar and let everything marinate for 30 minutes. Add the chicken stock to the pan and bring everything to a slow boil. Stir the sauce now and again to prevent it sticking. Cook for around 20–30 minutes, by which time the rhubarb should fall apart and the liquid be reduced enough to coat the back of a wooden spoon. Keep the sauce warm until it is ready for use. Spoon it over the meat and wait for the taste explosion.

THE FIRST ERUPTION

THE PUB STEADILY BEGAN to lose its allure, as I stayed in for Mrs H's casseroles and soufflés. During summer, she toiled away over the hibachi, a primitive but effective form of barbecue. As a form of recompense, I attempted a fashionable dish of that time. Mrs H has often recalled it over the years. It was the moment she realised what she had got herself into. Always keen on soups, I decided to attempt French onion soup, regarded as excitingly bohemian twenty-odd years ago. Desiring to bring a whiff of the old Les Halles to the suburbs of south London, I peeled a mass of onions, sliced them into fine discs and started gently frying them in Mrs H's biggest pot. Nothing too unusual there, surely? Except Mrs H came downstairs, poked her head round the kitchen door and asked, 'What on earth are you doing?'

'Making French onion soup.'

'But it's four in the morning.'

'Couldn't sleep.'

'So you decided to make some soup.'

'I was trying to be quiet. Didn't want to wake you.'

'Well, you have.'

'I never knew you could be woken by a smell.'

Afterwards I restricted my soup-making to more social hours.

The main thrust of my culinary proposals concerned the foods of northern England. I was particularly pleased when she showed enthusiasm for pork pie, a delicacy that continues to hold great appeal for me. I had less success in persuading her to enjoy another northern treat. 'No! I am not eating that. It looks revolting.' It was the first sighting of an eruption that became more familiar in subsequent years. Who would have thought that a plate of chopped honeycomb would have prompted such antagonism?

Maybe I should explain that the honeycomb in question was honeycomb tripe. In retrospect, I've come round to her view. Over-bleached and tasteless, English tripe is rubbish, but Italian tripe from veal calves is sensational and French tripe is pretty good. Persisting in my campaign to convert Mrs H, I secured a tin of *tripes à la mode de Caen* (cooked with carrots, onion and leek). While she was otherwise engaged, I opened it, emptied the contents into a saucepan and secreted the telltale tin.

'A bit curious,' she said warily as she tasted a spoonful. Moments later, my ploy ended in disaster. 'Argh! What have you made me eat?'

'It's just a tin of French stew.'

'I've just found a hairy bit.'

'It can't be hairy. There aren't any hairs in tripe.'

'TRIPE!'

It took several minutes for the plaster to stop falling from the ceiling. Even now, Mrs H insists that she found a hairy bit in the French tripe.

I realised that I would have to change tack pretty rapidly if my toothbrush were to retain its position in Mrs H's bathroom. Luckily, I had a sure-fire weapon in my culinary armoury. There was a certain savoury that Mrs H received with such enthusiasm that it would not be overstating the case to describe her reaction as ecstatic. It occurred to me that it would do our relationship no harm if I were to try every known variation of this dish. The path to Mrs H's heart was paved with Welsh rabbit.

3

Rabbiting on

'IT'S MY IDEA OF HEAVEN.' Mrs H's rapturous reception of my cheese on toast could prompt a new direction for theology, though I must admit that my productions in this department are occasionally satanically singed. 'I can't make it at all,' she admits. 'I know it involves Worcestershire sauce and there's a lot of washing-up afterwards, but I don't know your secret method on account of lolling in bed like Lady Muck while you make it.'

Where better to eat toast covered by a blanket of molten cheese than when one is covered by a duvet? It is one of those rare situations where dish mirrors diner. (I can't think of many others. You rarely eat soup in the swimming pool.) I don't want to give the idea that our decadent indulgence of cheese on toast in bed is a frequent occurrence. We only eat it on Sunday mornings and then maybe once a month. Moreover, this sybaritic breakfast is not without drawbacks. Toast crumbs can be a problem. 'But I'm a very neat eater,' insists Mrs H. 'I have to make the bed afterwards to de-crumb your half.' It is also a very rich dish. You can only take a certain amount on board. I once held a dinner party

consisting solely of different kinds of cheese on toast.
Everyone turned greenish around the fourth course.

For some reason, this dish tends to fall into the male
sphere of gastronomic activities. It could be something to
do with a manly partiality for savouries. Something cheesy
on toast forms a traditional finale to the meal in gents' clubs
and chophouses. Very nice it is too, if you happen to have
sufficient space. Maybe I'm in charge of cheese on toast
because I happen to be more intuitively brilliant about the
ingredients and their proportions. Maybe it's because I
allow an extra minute or two under the grill so the seething
cheese attains dark, speckled perfection. However, it has
occurred to me that Mrs H might just have ceded authority
so she can stay in bed while I am grating and grilling in the
kitchen. This was not the cause of our dispute when I asked
Mrs H if she would like some Welsh rabbit.

'Yes,' she replied. 'But it's not rabbit. It's rarebit.'

'Rarebit is a pointless, annoying bit of eighteenth century
gentrification. It just sounds better than rabbit.'

'Well, what does a rabbit have to do with cheese on
toast?'

'Well, what the hell is a rarebit, anyway?'

'Nobody calls it Welsh rabbit. Everyone calls it Welsh
rarebit.'

'Well, everyone is wrong.'

The more I consider Mrs H's explanation for not doing
this dish of disputed nomenclature, the more I think it is
baloney. After all, Welsh rabbit is scarcely Blumenthalesque
in its complexity (though I'm sure Heston could invent an

impossibly complicated version if he put his mind to it). My own formula goes along the following lines. Grate up a quantity of mature Cheddar – though, as we shall see, many other cheeses also work well – and put the result in a bowl, add the yolk of an egg, a few splats of Worcestershire sauce, a generous teaspoon of smooth Dijon mustard and stir well. Lightly toast a few slices of good bread, preferably sourdough. Spread the cheese mixture on the toast. Shove under a hot grill until the topping begins a lava-like bubbling and emits a concentrated aroma of cheesy savouriness. Is any culinary smell more alluring? The point to aim for – and this requires constant vigilance – is when the cheesy mix has melted and gained a dark-brown mottling but the toast has not carbonised too radically round its edge.

'Yum,' said Mrs H as she munched the combination of cheesiness and ooziness and crunchiness and almost-burntness. 'When you come down to it, there's nothing better than Welsh rarebit.'

'Rabbit.'

'I'll do anything for a bit of cheese on toast, as long as it's not too strenuous.'

Crumbs! No wonder I decided to explore every feasible variation of the dish in order to keep the fire of love burning. Or at least lightly toasted.

There turned out to be no shortage of possibilities. A traditional nibble for rich and poor alike, cheese on toast is the great British snack. The French may have their croque monsieur and the Swiss their raclette, but it was toasted cheese that Ben Gunn lusted for during his three years on

Treasure Island. 'But, mate,' the castaway informed Jim Hawkins. 'My heart is sore for Christian diet. You mightn't happen to have a piece of cheese about you, now? No? Well, many's the long night I've dreamed of cheese – toasted, mostly.' Welsh rabbit remains a distinctly British speciality.

A classic formulation appears in Jane Grigson's book *English Food*. Compared to my shortcut version, her 'Welsh rabbit' (note correct name) is a bit complicated. It involves gently warming grated cheese (she suggests Lancashire, Cheddar or Double Gloucester) in a small pan with milk or beer until it melts into 'a thick cream', then adding butter, English mustard and salt and pepper to taste. The result is then heated 'until it is very hot but below boiling point'. You pour it over two slices of toast in a heatproof serving dish. Grigson warns: 'The cheese will overflow the edges of the toast.' The toast is grilled until 'the cheese bubbles and becomes brown in appetising-looking splashes.'

Though this dish shows distinct signs of being a meal rather than a snack – for aforementioned reasons, the view at Hirst HQ is that Welsh rabbit should be something you can eat with your fingers – it came from an authority of such eminence that I gave it a whirl. I decided to do Cheddar with beer. It was a strange sensation to open a bottle of beer at breakfast time (though I dare say one could get used to it). The resulting slurry, tipped over two slices of sourdough toast in a cast-iron pan, didn't do much browning under the grill and the toast became distinctly wilty under the cheese mix. The dish also involved a slight singeing of the fingers and quite a bit more washing-up than my version.

But Grigson's rabbit went down a storm with Mrs H. 'Mmm. I could eat it all day long.' Even the wilting toast escaped censure. 'I quite like the toast soft rather than crunchy. It makes you concentrate on the cheese more.' Maybe due to the beer or the mature Cheddar, Grigson's Welsh rabbit had a profound depth of flavour, addictive yet satisfying. 'Of course, I prefer your eggy version,' Mrs H added diplomatically, 'but this is a real treat.' Milk will probably also work well in the dish. (A friend of mine had a Lancashire grandfather whose favourite meal was grilled cheese with milk. His method was to put milk and bits of cheese on a tin plate, toast it under the grill and mop up the result with bread.)

Keen to keep up the fusillade of cheesy *billets d'amour*, I tried the version advocated by several professional cooks, which involves making the topping first and allowing it to set. Melt a knob of butter in a saucepan, stir in a small quantity of flour, a pinch of mustard powder, a hint of cayenne and a few splats of Worcestershire sauce, then add a good splash of Guinness and half a pound of good grated cheese. When it's turned creamy, turn out the cheesy mixture into a container and leave to set in the fridge. This is then spread on toast and grilled. Cheese-on-toast purists may complain that the protracted nature of this style of Welsh rabbit lacks spontaneity. You have to think ahead. However, it is very quick to make when you have the topping in the fridge, which explains its appeal for chefs.

Most significantly, its intense flavour transported Mrs H to a transcendental plateau of pleasure. 'Coo!'

I turned to the subcontinent for my next variation. Colonel Arthur Robert Kenney-Herbert of the Madras Cavalry was, I'm sorry to say, a rarebit man. In *Culinary Jottings for Madras* (1885), he observes: 'For a really good Welsh rarebit, you should have a sound fresh cheese, not over-strong.' But his other ingredients do not eschew piquancy. You are instructed to mix two ounces grated cheese with one ounce of butter, two egg yolks, a dessert-spoon of English mustard, salt, and a pinch of something called 'Nepaul pepper' (apparently it was along the lines of cayenne, though not quite as strong) until thoroughly smooth. I used Double Gloucester and substituted a tiny amount of cayenne for the mysterious Nepaul stuff. The bright yellow result is spread on toast that has been buttered *on both sides* (the Col's italics) and baked in a buttered pie dish in a really hot oven for ten minutes.

With its brown and gold topping, the result looked tempting. 'It's quite mustardy,' said Mrs H after taking her first nibble. 'In fact, it's very mustardy. Phew!' While not exactly unpalatable, it was an astonishingly robust, take-no-prisoners Victorian snack, somehow both rich and austere. Mrs H quite liked it, but I found the overdose of English mustard slightly queasy-making.

'The Colonel must have liked his food very hot,' said Mrs H. 'It's OK but I don't agree with him that it is a really good Welsh rarebit.'

'Rabbit.'

'Well, he says rarebit.'

Cheesed off with this bickering, I decided to sort out the moniker once and for all. Jane Grigson said that it has to be 'rabbits, not rarebits or rare bits, which are both false etymological refinement'. The *OED* dates Welsh rabbit to 1725, with rarebit appearing sixty years later. In the forthright view of Fowler's *Modern English Usage*, 'Welsh rabbit is amusing and right. Rarebit is stupid and wrong.' According to Peter Graham's *Classic Cheese Cookery*, the 'Welsh' part may have stemmed from that nation's traditional fondness for cheese, which is alluded to in *The Merry Wives of Windsor* (the jealous Frank Ford declares: 'I would rather trust ... the Welshman with my cheese ... than my wife with herself'), but it was probably also a joke against the Welsh. In the unremittingly carnivorous eighteenth century, Welsh rabbit was a substitute for the real thing, ersatz, a bit of a con. If the expression was originally pejorative, the Welsh have had the last laugh. Two other national variants in Hannah Glasse's *The Art of Cookery Made Plain and Easy* (1747), Scotch rabbit (pretty much plain cheese on toast) and English rabbit, have both failed to stay the course.

I decided to make English rabbit as the next volley in my campaign to retain the heart of Mrs H. Hannah Glasse's recipe seems to derive from the medieval dish of sops, which is bits of bread soaked in wine. (In *Richard III*, one of the murderers of the Duke of Clarence says, 'Let's make a sop of him,' before that gruesome business involving a butt of malmsey.) You pour a glass of red wine over a slice of brown toast 'and let it soak the wine up; then cut some cheese very thin, and lay it very thick over the bread, and put it in a tin oven before the fire, and it will be toasted and brown'd presently. Serve it away hot.' Made with Lancashire and Chianti, the snack, not quite as soggy as you might expect, proved to be a mystery mouthful for Mrs H. 'I don't know what the underneath is. Tell me. Tell me.' I cruelly refused to say. Like most females, Mrs H cannot bear the withholding of information. 'Tell me. Tell me! TELL ME!'

Eventually she twigged without me spilling the beans. 'Is it something to do with wine?' The dish caused a diversion of opinion. I thought it was an interesting combination of flavours, slightly like fondue, that delivered a nice, boozy aftertaste. Mrs H was unpersuaded. 'Five out of ten. There's a slight bitterness there that doesn't entirely appeal. It's middling.'

I then tried the Scotch rabbit recipe in Peter Graham's *Classic Cheese Cookery*. This is entirely different from Hannah Glasse's but it does have the merit of being authentically Scotch. It appeared in *The Cook and Housewife's Manual* (1826) by Margaret Dods, the nom-de-plume of Christian Isabel Johnstone, a Peebles pub landlady. Using a cast-iron saucepan over a gentle heat, you stir together five ounces of Stilton (or Gouda) with four tablespoons of stout (Graham recommends Mackeson but I used Guinness), one teaspoon of ready-made English mustard and a lot of black pepper. When transformed into a smooth cream, pour into ramekins and brown under a hot grill. Eat with hot buttered toast. 'Quite nice,' Mrs H hesitated. 'A bit like dunking a biscuit in tea. It's rather drippy. The Stilton is a bit odd.' This was not quite the reaction that I was aiming for. She ate it all though.

Pushing my luck, I then made her another rarity from Graham's book called Irish rarebit. He admits that this dish, which appeared in a First World War cookbook, has no obvious association with Ireland. 'Perhaps the other nationalities had been used up,' he suggests. A combination of grated Cheddar, fried sweet onions, chopped gherkins, fresh herbs and a reduction of 'best vinegar' (I used red wine vinegar) is cooked first in a frying pan and then grilled on toast. Unfortunately, it did not prove to be the food of love. Mrs H was alarmed by the smell ('Poo!') and dismayed by the taste. 'What *are* we eating?' This highly assertive dish was marginally better cold, when its acetic aggression had calmed down. Since cold, vinegary cheese on toast is not renowned as an aphrodisiac, I broadened my research.

The more you look into cheese on toast, the more possibilities you find. Food historian Dorothy Hartley suggested: 'For a rich rabbit, fry the bread in bacon fat.' I didn't put that oily treat in front of Mrs H, but an anchovy-enhanced version from Patricia Michelson's book *The Cheese Room* went down well. Entitled 'A Sort of Welsh Rarebit', the recipe specifies fillets from salted whole anchovies. These are excellent but somewhat hard to locate. I found standard anchovy fillets worked fine. You make anchovy butter, by mashing four anchovy fillets into two ounces of butter. Use it to butter some slices of toast. Pile thin slices of cheese (Michelson suggests Caerphilly) into a dome on the toast, splat on some Worcestershire sauce and grill until the cheese melts and turns gold. 'Rather nice,' said Mrs H. 'Subtle, not too salty. Quite a revelation. I was expecting it to be a bit harsh but it's not strong at all. Very impressive.'

She was even more impressed by a dipping version of cheese on toast. Lady Shaftesbury's toasted cheese, which appears in Jane Grigson's *English Food*, comes from the recipe book of the wife of the Victorian social reformer Anthony Ashley Cooper, 7th Earl of Shaftesbury. However, the dish is not all that grand. 'By the standards of the aristocracy they were poor.' Intended to feed six, Lady Shaftesbury's snack requires rather small quantities: two ounces of butter, seven ounces of grated Cheddar, six tablespoons of cream, two egg yolks, salt and pepper. Impossibly titchy, I thought, but the combination of dairy products is very rich. You don't want much. (A food blogger who ate rather a lot of it reported nightmares.) The ingredients are mixed together in a saucepan and stirred over a low heat until dissolved into a thick cream. You then pour this into six small ovenproof dishes or ramekins and brown under the grill. Serve with toast fingers. Mrs H's reaction: 'Marvellous. Like an individual fondue. Hurray for Lady Shaftesbury!' This was everything I could have hoped for, though I would have preferred 'Hurray for Christopher.'

A CHILLY MOMENT

MY INVASION OF HER KITCHEN was a mixed blessing for Mrs H. Though she saw the advantage when she woke up to scrambled eggs and toast on Sunday mornings, there were a few minor drawbacks arising from my culinary activities. 'There's always a mountain of washing-up to be done after you've done any cooking,' she pointed out. 'And there are breadcrumbs everywhere and bits of kitchen roll. You put infinitesimal bits of cheese and butter back in the fridge and empty chutney jars back in the cupboard.'

I did, however, come in handy for replacing large casseroles on high shelves. It also became evident that my services were required when the lid of Mrs H's elderly chest freezer was forced open by a build-up of pack ice. In my fine manly way, I demolished the ice wall with a wooden steak mallet. There were some comments about the small pools of water that resulted from ricocheting chunks, but I deemed it a job well done.

With surprising speed, the pack ice returned. One day when Mrs H was out at work, I decided that a more radical defrosting of the freezer was required. What was the use of having a man about the place unless he made himself useful? Besides, the cleaving of great lumps of ice from the walls of the freezer was vaguely satisfying. Now I realise that you're not supposed to use a sharp metal object for defrosting freezers, but when did you hear of a snowplough with a wooden blade or an icebreaker with a plastic bow? This was serious, industrial-strength ice, the sort that did for the *Titanic*. After bending several of Mrs H's utensils in the attempt, I found the most effective method of de-icing involved a hammer and chisel.

After dislodging a few berg-sized lumps, I gave a particularly hefty whack and the chisel clunked against the metal wall of the freezer. Worse still, there was the slight but unmistakable hiss of escaping gas. Despite my chilly location, I found myself perspiring freely. I discovered a quarter-inch gash in the side of the freezer. I put my finger over the hole like the Dutch boy and the dyke, and the hissing stopped. Though effective, I recognise that this provided only a temporary solution. In the long term, keeping my hand in the freezer would be a distinct hindrance to my social life. In the short term, my finger was beginning to turn numb. Leaving the ozone-munching chlorofluorocarbons to escape heavenwards, I dashed to the ironmonger's for something to block the hole.

A tube of gunk called 'Chemical Metal' seemed the best bet. Though it made the inside of the freezer smell like a petrochemical plant, the hissing stopped. (It later occurred to me that chewing gum might have sufficed.) I closed the lid and hoped for the best. Peering at the crime scene on the following day, the signs were not good. The ice that had caused the problem in the first place had turned to slush and the long-frozen contents of the freezer were turning distinctly soggy. 'Did …' I remarked over breakfast as casually as possible, 'I mention that I had a bit of an accident yesterday?'

The court of inquiry was uncomfortable and protracted. 'You used a hammer and *chisel*?' For a while, it looked as if my budding hobby of gastronomy was at an end. Peace was eventually restored when I bought a new freezer, my first-ever purchase of white goods. I managed not to destroy this freezer, but I had a slight mishap with a new fridge that we bought soon afterwards. It was all to do with attaching a plug. Yes, it came with a plug attached, but this would not fit where it had to go. So I cut it off, put the flex in the required location and attached a new plug. At least that's what I wanted to do, but the job got more and more complicated. As one thing led to another, I spent the entire day getting ever more embroiled with Mrs H's domestic electrical system. At a late stage in proceedings, when my mind might not have been entirely focused on the job, I found two stray wires that appeared to have no function. I twisted them together, jammed them into the corner of a plug and turned the electricity back on. The result was a blue flash and a massive bang from the fusebox. The resulting loss of electricity involved quite a bit of explaining to Mrs H when she came home. Unfortunately, I didn't have an explanation. Still don't, as a matter of fact. When I took the fragments of ceramic fuse plug that resulted from my mental aberration to an electrical suppliers, the man behind the counter scratched his head and said, 'Never seen anything like this before.'

Unfortunately, another mishap soon followed. Returning home after taking refreshment one night, I decided to restore the tissues by frying up a few links of sausages (Mrs H had gone to bed). Afterwards, I kindly washed up the cast-iron frying pan. This, as it turned out, was not a good idea. 'You've washed up my pan?' exploded Mrs H the following morning.

'Yes. It was dirty.'

'It's my special crêpe pan. You should never, ever wash it up. Just wipe it with a paper towel.'

'What? Even after frying sausages?'

'Sausages? You fried sausages in it?'

Despite my insistence that its admirable qualities would return after a protracted period of non-washing, the crêpe pan never again found favour with Mrs H. She may have had a point. The output of the post-washed pan never had the mottled élan of the pre-washed pan. This unfortunate business had the effect of putting me off pancakes. Making them, I mean. On Shrove Tuesdays, I still sat there like a great red pillar-box receiving consignments of this slender foodstuff, but their manufacture did not appeal. Pondering my lack of pancake proficiency recently, I came to realise that this was a serious omission in my repertoire. I surprised Mrs H with a sudden announcement that I was going to make pancakes. Lots of pancakes.

4

Crêpe souls

'YOU WANT TO MAKE LOTS OF PANCAKES?' Mrs H repeated in a disbelieving tone. 'Er, why?'

Maybe pancakes aren't the most exciting of foods, though some are better than others. A crêpe stall rarely fails to attract my custom, and I am particularly partial to the galette, a Breton speciality made from buckwheat flour. Though pancakes were lifted by the invention of baking powder in the nineteenth century, they remain a primitive dish. As Alan Davidson points out in *The Oxford Companion to Food*, 'The griddle method of cooking is older than oven baking and pancakes are an ancient form.' There is a primal satisfaction about food that is cooked in an instant and consumed an instant after that. This is particularly so with drop scones or Scotch pancakes, eulogised by Davidson ('this excellent pancake'). Where better to start my pancake adventures?

My first renditions of drop scones were a bit too primitive and ancient, but eventually they stopped tasting like shoe soles. Whipped off the pan after a few seconds on each side, there is a delicious contrast between the lightly tanned exterior and the soft, sweet, creamy inside. Davidson insists that these delicacies are 'best eaten warm with butter or jam or both', but in my view the main thing you need with a freshly made drop scone is more drop scones. Especially when a sprinkling of dried fruit is added to the mix, they can be a seriously addictive snack. A frequent treat of my Yorkshire childhood, these sultana-gemmed nibbles have lost none of their appeal.

The main problem with drop scones is when do you have them? Not quite right for breakfast, lunch or dinner, they are perfect for that forgotten delight, the high tea. The only time I've had high tea in recent years was at a Scottish castle, where Scotch pancakes formed part of a massive late afternoon spread. I didn't tackle dinner with my customary gusto. Still, judging by Mrs H's coolness towards these tasty splats ('I haven't cooked them since school and I don't particularly want to start now'), I doubt if I will face this problem very frequently.

The difficulty about time of consumption also applies to the conventional pancake. Once or twice I've eaten them for breakfast in America in the form of a big stack dripping with maple syrup. This oozy construction is so substantial – it resembles the Capitol Records Tower in Hollywood – that you feel like going back to bed immediately afterwards. Pancakes are better eaten later in the day, especially if that day is Shrove Tuesday. While the Latin world enjoys the unfettered orgy of Mardi Gras, the British tuck into pancakes in an atmosphere hazy with particulates. Though I've tried any number of ways with pancakes, I always come back to the traditional partnership of lemon juice and sugar. The lemon counteracts the sweetness of the pancake, while the sugar neutralises the acidity of the lemon. There is also a distinctive combination of sensations: hot pancake, cold lemon juice and the crunch of partially dissolved sugar.

As I remarked, it is customarily Mrs H who stands at the stove on Shrove Tuesday. Wreathed in smoke, she bears a passing resemblance to St Joan. 'I never get to eat one because I'm always making them,' moans this modern martyr. 'I hear noises from the table like a cuckoo: "Feed me. Feed me." By the time I get to eat mine, you've finished and you say "Can I have a bit of yours?" No, I don't like making them. My clothes always smell of oil afterwards. Pancakes are all right but I wouldn't want to do them more than once a year.'

I embarked on my first-ever pancake by making batter, which you have to let stand for an hour or so. Even this most instantaneous of foods demands a degree of forward planning. I used a non-stick frying pan, but the technique came from *The Art of Cookery Made Plain and Easy* by Hannah Glasse (1747): 'Pour in a ladleful of batter, moving the pan round that the batter be all over the pan ... when you think that side is enough, toss it; if you can't, turn it cleverly.' I turned cleverly enough for my pancakes to earn Mrs H's damning-by-faint-praise: 'Quite nice.' The lemon-and-sugar pancake starts light, but ends up as a substantial dessert. The first one disappears as if by magic. Then you take a second and probably a third onboard and begin to feel well ballasted. With this treat as the dessert, it is unwise to have a large quantity of savoury pancakes as the main course. Maybe you shouldn't have savoury pancakes at any time. It is a dish that lies heavy on the plate and heavy in the stomach. Yorkshire puddings without ambition.

'Thank goodness we've got that over with,' Mrs H said after my exploration of the British pancake. 'Crêpes are much better than those doughy things.' Who is going to argue with that? Ever since we had some holidays in Brittany, when I ate them once a day, sometimes twice, I've had a hankering for the crêpe (from the Old French *crespe*, meaning curled) and the buckwheat galette (imaginatively derived from *galet*, a worn pebble good for skimming). The problem with making them at home is that, until recently, we did not have a large enough pan. Though fine for an English pancake, our non-stick frying pan produces only a mini-crêpe. A professional electric crêpe maker, as used on crêpe stalls, costs around £250, which seemed a little excessive to bring back memories of St Malo. The solution materialised when we were mooching round a Le Creuset shop in York. In one corner, I came across a pile of cast-iron crêpe pans. Measuring twenty-six centimetres in diameter, with a lip running round the edge, it had a pleasing heft in the hand and radiated homespun Gallic wholesomeness. From the instant I got it on the hob, I felt sure that my crêpes were going to be the stuff of legend.

Confident that I'd mastered the pancake, I thought that it would not take long to get the knack of the crêpe. In order to learn the rudiments, I took an informal lesson by hanging around a crêpe stall in a French market that visited our corner of London. First, *le patron* lightly lubricated the surface of his electric crêpe-maker with what looked like a large candle. In the centre of the hot plate, he deposited a dollop of crêpe mix and deftly distributed this over the surface of the plate with a T-shaped wooden utensil. It looked like a small version of the wooden rake used by croupiers to rake in roulette chips. When the bottom of the crêpe was cooked, he flipped it over with a spatula and then let the other side cook for a minute or less. Finally, he drizzled an infinitesimal quantity of Grand Marnier (my choice of topping) over the crêpe, folded it twice and handed the fat, multi-layered cone over to me. £3, *s'il vous plait*. Obviously, it was a doddle. As Ken Albala remarks in his book *Pancake: A Global History*, 'Pancakes … are utterly indulgent and completely predictable.'

Unwrapping my Le Creuset crêpe pan from its shrink-wrap, I was assisted by a hole in the plastic. The reason for this hole was because the T-shaped spreading utensil had been removed. Mrs H recalled that the same applied to all the crêpe pans on sale in York. Le Creuset supplied a wooden spatula with the pan, but the company apparently thought that inclusion of a T-shaped utensil would prompt mystified inquiries from UK customers. That it should have been included was evident from the instruction booklet. This directed purchasers: 'Use the *râteau* in a circular motion to spread out the batter.' Aha! So the T-shaped utensil was a *râteau* (a word omitted from my big Oxford-Hachette French/English dictionary). At this point, I should have badgered Le Creuset for a *râteau*, but I thought it would be easy enough to find one in London. This turned out to be a misapprehension. The nearest I got was a shrugging excuse: 'We had some once …' Eventually, on a day-trip to Calais, I bought a *râteau à crêpe* at the Carrefour *hypermarché* for one euro.

At last I was able to use the griddle. Under Mrs H's direction, I proved the pan by slowly heating it, pouring a small puddle of sunflower oil in the centre and wiping round with a kitchen towel until only a sheen remained. 'It seals the pan a bit like a non-stick surface,' explained Mrs H. 'You need to do this if you haven't used the pan for a while. And NEVER wash it up.' Having made my batter an hour or so earlier, I was now ready to tackle my first crêpe. After heating the griddle to the right temperature (water dripped on the pan should evaporate immediately), I was faced with the task of lubrication for crêpe purposes. Here, the booklet indicated another difference in the treatment of French and English customers. In the English text, we are told to 'lightly oil the surface of the pan between each crêpe (half an apple placed on the end of a fork and dipped in the oil is a good way of doing this)' but French readers were told to utilise '*une demi-pomme de terre piquée au bout d'une fourchette*'. A spud seemed to have the greater authenticity for this peasant dish.

After smearing a light coating of sunflower oil on to the griddle with my half-potato-on-a-fork, I poured in a small amount of batter and plied the *râteau* like the bloke in the market. Instant disaster. The mix started cooking and proved impossible to spread. My attempt to use the *râteau* 'in a circular motion' only shifted a tiny bit of the mix. When the first side seemed to be done, I edged the wooden spatula under and flipped it over. The result was a crepe of a disturbingly alien shape, burnt in some areas, under-cooked in the middle. 'The first one is always rotten,' sympathised Mrs H. 'You don't know how much mixture to put in.' The second crêpe was equally bad, while my third one looked like a highly inept English pancake. So much for pancakes being 'completely predictable'.

The Le Creuset booklet suggested that expertise did not come immediately with crêpes: 'Once you have mastered the traditional crêpe recipe, you can experiment with dif-ferent ingredients'. Kate Whiteman's cookbook *Brittany Gastronomique* is more explicit about the tricky craft of the crêpe: '[The batter] is spread outwards in a circular motion using a wood rake. This requires a flexible wrist and a light hand and is definitely not as easy as it looks.' Lacking both flexibility of wrist and lightness of hand, it would obviously take me years of daily crêpe-making to wield the *râteau* with the proficiency of the market man. Mrs H pointed out another deficiency in my approach. 'Your batter needs to be a lot thinner,' said Mrs H. 'It's too floury at present, so your crêpes are too thick.'

Thinning it down helped with the spreading, but the resulting crêpe was *too thin*, more like a crisp than a pan-cake. Though thinness is of the essence with crêpes, I realised that I was not putting enough batter in. Obviously, the lip on the griddle was intended to contain the batter. I also discovered that a paper towel dipped in sunflower oil was better for lightly oiling the pan than any vegetable on a fork. When I finally managed to make an acceptable crêpe with my seventh batch, I felt battered but triumphant. Though it would never be mistaken for a professional rendition, it was pretty much circular and, better still, pretty much edible.

There are no end of crêpe possibilities, both sweet and savoury, but I stuck to the topping I'd enjoyed in the market: Grand Marnier, but more of it. My generously doused version won an ovation from Mrs H. We also tried a smear of Nutella as advocated in Nigella Lawson's *Nigella Express*. This was acceptable in a highly sweet, nutty sort of way, but prodigiously high in calories. Check the ingredients of Nutella and you'll find that it contains a large percentage of vegetable oil. Nigella's suggested accompaniment of whipped cream infused with Fra Angelico (a hazelnut liqueur) does little to reduce the calorific content.

There is one significant exception to my keep-it-simple rule for crêpes. This is the late nineteenth or early twentieth century invention known as crêpes Suzette. It is one of the few instances that a member of the pancake family soars in social esteem (blinis with caviar is another). According to *Larousse Gastronomique*, Henri Charpentier, a French cook working for John D. Rockefeller in the US, claimed to have invented the dish in the Café de Paris, Monte Carlo, in 1896 'as a compliment to the Prince of Wales and his companion, whose first name was Suzette'. In his autobiography, the chef said that the Prince gave him 'a jewelled ring, a Panama hat and a cane' for his creation.

'One taste,' Charpentier insisted, 'would reform a cannibal into a civilised gentleman.'

While Suzette sounds the right sort of name for a 'companion' of the Prince of Wales in Monte Carlo, Larousse says the story is baloney. 'In actual fact, at that date Charpentier was not old enough to be the head waiter serving the prince.' (He would have been sixteen.) John Ayto's *A-Z of Food and Drink* puts us right. The first reference to crêpes Suzette in print was by Escoffier in 1907. His 'Suzette pancakes' was an unflamed dish, as it remains in the recipe offered by Larousse. The encyclopedia notes a bit sniffily that Charpentier 'introduced the fashion for flamed crêpes Suzette to America'.

Though the pancake-loving Suzette remains a mystery, the dedication was no small honour. The tangy orange sauce marries happily with the blandness of the crêpes and, at least, in the Anglo-Saxon version, the flaming brandy provides a dramatic dénouement to a meal. You don't often see the billowing alcoholic explosion from restaurant dessert trolleys these days, but my version of crêpes Suzette – which tested my newfound prowess as a crêpe-maker twelve times over – went down a storm when I did it for some friends. You make the crêpes in advance, roll them up like English pancakes and warm them in the oven before performing the *coup de théâtre* with the flaming brandy. 'Oooh, it's lovely,' said Mrs H. 'Can we start having it instead of pancakes on Pancake Day?' I preened like the dubious Charpentier.

For a savoury pancake, I prefer a galette, which is made

from buckwheat flour. Its flavour is so assertive that many books, including Larousse, suggest a half-and-half mix with wheat flour. The darkness of the flour explains the French name *sarrasin* (Saracen). Over 12,000 tons per year are imported into Brittany for galettes. The batter is pale grey (it looks a bit like mushroom soup) and smells rather nutty. Recipes used to be egg-free, but most modern versions are less austere. Spurning tradition, the galette recipe in *Larousse* includes '5–6 beaten eggs', but I based my recipe on the one in *Brittany Gastronomique*, which requires a single egg for 250g of flour. The ancient Breton mixing technique is described: 'You should beat the batter energetically for at less 15 minutes, slapping it from side to side of the mixing bowl.' I used a hand-held electric whisk for five minutes, which felt quite long enough. The resulting galette was striking in appearance, like a map of dark-brown islands on a light brown sea, edged with lacy filigree. The folding of the galette is different from the crêpe. First, you put a dollop of the savoury filling – two favourites are chopped asparagus in a cheese sauce and shellfish in a cream sauce – in the middle of the galette. Then you fold over an arc of the galette on four sides – about five centimetres left and right, then five centimetres top and bottom – so the result is a squared envelope with the filling visible through a little window.

As with the crêpe, it took me a while to get the knack of galettes, which are thicker and moister. In a less-than-appetising comparison, one Breton writer said galettes are macramé while crêpes are Valenciennes lace. Eventually

I steered a middle course between the soggy dishcloth galette and the so-brittle-it-cracks galette. I even managed to do the fried-egg galette. After cooking one side, you flip it over and break an egg in the middle. The intention is that this cooks through the pancake. When both galette and egg are just about cooked, you fold over the four edges so the yolk appears in the little window. This is all easier said than done. When the galette is cooked, the egg tends to be underdone. When the egg is cooked, the galette is heading for burnt. Still, my effort scored highly with my severest judge. 'Mmm, this is really good,' said Mrs H, when I presented her with a galette filled with an egg and grated Gruyère. 'Lots of potential here. It could be breakfast, lunch or light supper. Do you fancy doing another?'

Somewhat less demanding in construction is the galette with sausage, sold at crêpe stalls in Breton markets. The pancake is simply wrapped round a hot meaty sausage. Mrs H is a big fan. This delicacy is known as the *galette robiquette* after La Robiquette, a district of Rennes noted for the excellence of its bangers. There are a number of rules for the consumption. La Sauvegarde de la Galette Saucisse Bretonne (Society for the Preservation of the Breton Sausage Galette) demands that the sausage should weigh at least 125g, be consumed without mustard, accompanied only by cider and cost no more than two euros. However, local taste is questioned by Kate Whiteman, who advises readers to make sure the galette is hot off the press: 'The Bretons are partial to sizzling hot sausages wrapped in a cold soggy galette.' I haven't tried the cold soggy version, but

I once made the mistake of accepting the offer of a double wrapping of galettes round my sausage. I managed to chomp my way through it but the after-effect is a little hard to describe. Have you ever eaten a blanket?

Mrs H on pancakes, crêpes and galettes

To make any pancake, crêpe or galette, you need to think ahead a bit. At least an hour is required to let the batter mix stand or rest in order to release the starch in the flour to swell and soften. A well-stood batter makes a lighter pancake or crêpe. So make an early start if you have a meal at a certain time in mind. You can make pancakes by hand – using a wooden spoon to beat the mix – but for those who don't want to develop uneven biceps an electric hand-mixer is the gadget you need. A proper crêpe pan (a frying sized pan with a shallow rim) is ideal for batter products as you can flip and turn with greater ease. But you can't beat a decent non-stick pan that is heated to the right temperature.

N.B. I always look upon the first pancake as a bit of a practice run. Sometimes in your haste and response to the clamours from the table to 'get a move on' you find you haven't let the pan heat up properly or the pan hasn't quite become non-stick. The first pancake will also tell you if your batter is too thick or too thin. Add a little extra milk if the batter is too thick. Once you get going, pancakes take no time at all to cook – perhaps 1–2 minutes for the first side and about a minute for the second. Give the batter mix a stir before cooking each pancake – the mix can settle.

Mrs H's recipe for Shrove Tuesday pancakes

This is a standard recipe for the sort of pancake you only have to make once a year – when the price of lemons goes up. A mix with 125g of flour should make about eight pancakes. Alter the ingredients if your table greedily demands more. Because you set up a sort of production line, making this sort of pancake is a smelly business however little fat you try to use for frying – so don't wear your best clothes and keep the windows open.

125g plain flour
a pinch of salt
1 large egg, beaten
300ml milk
a little oil for frying
caster sugar and lemon juice to serve

Begin by sifting the flour and salt into a bowl and make a well in the centre (or as I saw once in an American recipe, 'sink a shaft'). Add the egg and mix in. Next gradually add the milk, drawing the flour in from the sides. Continue whisking until a smooth creamy batter is formed. Let the batter stand for at least 30 minutes. After heating the pan and adding a tiny amount of oil, pour in enough batter to coat the base of the pan. Cook the first side until you see that the centre is drying and the sides crisping. Flip or toss and cook the second side. After turning out on to a plate, sprinkle caster sugar and lemon juice on the pancake and roll up in a sausage shape. Add more sugar and lemon if the diner starts grizzling that you haven't added enough.

Mrs H's recipe for basic crêpes

This crêpe recipe differs from the English pancake because you add melted butter to the mix. Depending on the size of your pan, you should make eight to twelve pancakes.

150g plain flour
3 large eggs
300ml milk
large pinch of salt
55g butter, melted, plus extra for cooking the crêpes

Start by sifting the flour into a large bowl and make a hollow in the centre to hold the liquids. In a smaller bowl, beat the eggs and combine the milk, salt and melted butter. Add this mix to the eggs. Gradually pour the liquid milk/butter/egg mix into the flour well, stirring vigorously to incorporate all the flour – but not so wildly that you swoosh the flour up and over the top of the bowl. Beat until a smooth mixture is achieved – no lumps. The use of an electric hand-held mixer will save time and temper. A thinnish batter is what you want to aim for. Now put the batter mix aside for around an hour to rest. Why not rest yourself as well, since things will get pretty active once you start cooking? Or you can use this time to prepare any filling for the crêpes. When you are ready to cook, heat a frying pan or crêpe pan slowly until it is really hot. Lubricate the pan with the addition of a little hot butter or light oil, then add a ladleful of batter and rotate it in the pan so it spreads evenly. Cook over a medium heat until you notice the edges crisping up and curling slightly. Turn or toss and cook the other side until golden. Turn the crêpe out on to a plate. Add a filling of your choice. Roll the crêpe up or fold over, and deliver to the person with the hungry look on their face.

Mrs H's recipe for buckwheat galettes

Based on the recipe in *Brittany Gastonomique* by Kate Whiteman, this works well. The most difficult part is finding somewhere that sells buckwheat flour. (Hooray for Waitrose.) A light and lacy look to each galette is what you should aim for. I usually get about six to eight galettes per batch with the quantities given. Note, though, that the batter needs a very long resting time. Kate Whiteman suggests overnight, but the mix will separate too much if you let it hang around your kitchen all day too. Cook each galette until the base is a golden brown before flipping. Galettes stack well – which means that the cook can sit down to eat with everyone else. If you make a pile, use non-stick baking parchment to separate the galettes and keep them gently warm in the oven. But not too long or you could end up with a pile of Frisbees.

250g buckwheat flour
1 large egg, beaten
1 teaspoon salt
100ml milk
200ml water
unsalted butter or light oil for cooking the galettes

All batter mixes start in the same way – sift the flour into a mixing bowl. Make a well in the centre, then add the beaten egg and salt, drawing in the flour. Next mix the milk and water and add the liquid a little at a time until the batter is smooth and creamy. You may find that you have to whisk away for a while – it usually takes around 7–8 minutes by hand. As I said before, an electric whisk is invaluable. Then you let the batter rest for at least 2 hours. Before you start cooking the galette, give the batter mix a good stir. Heat a frying pan or crêpe pan slowly until hot. Add a little butter or light oil to lubricate the pan, then pour a ladleful of batter into the pan, swirling as you do so the batter covers the pan evenly. Cook until you spot the edges turning brown, then flip or toss the galette to the other side. Cook this side until golden. Add any fillings – savoury or sweet – and fold in the edges to make a square.

TASTE FOR TRAVEL

During a Sunday night stroll along the seafront of a town on the heel of Italy, we spotted a crowd of young people buying hamburgers from a van with a charcoal grill. It seemed a strangely popular draw. 'Fancy a burger?' I asked Mrs H, though we were planning a more extended meal.

'All right.'

Shoving my way into the throng, I came back with a couple of the inexplicably appealing snacks. 'You're in for a surprise,' I told Mrs H. But before she could take a bite, a tentacle dangled out of her bun. They contained the best octopus I've ever had. A decade on, my mouth waters at the memory of this tender cephalopod surprise.

From our first holiday together on the Greek island of Serifos, where I heroically dived for sea urchins (too gritty to eat), Mrs H became aware that for me foreign food is a major reason for foreign travel. One of the most perplexing things I've ever seen was a stall in a southern French market that catered for the expat market. Its stencilled signs advertised such necessities of Anglo-Saxon cuisine as 'BISTO',

'OXO' and, bizarrely, 'FISH SHOP FISH'. 'CHEDDAR' was also available for those who failed to appreciate the nation's unequalled cheeseboard. The dusty stock seemed precisely calculated to confirm French prejudice about the barbarian appetites of their neighbours across La Manche.

Not all *rosbifs* are so gastronomically insular. I am still racked by regret that the lack of a kitchen during a stay in Barcelona prevented my purchase of the snails that were doing their best to escape from a stall in the splendid Boqueria market on Las Ramblas. We ate snails braised in red wine in a restaurant, but their excellence only served to heighten the pain of my loss. Back home, a way of salvaging something from this missed opportunity occurred to me. 'There are plenty in our garden. Why don't we use those?'

'I think not.' Mrs H shot me a look in a manner that suggested negotiation was not on the cards.

In the course of our travels, a substantial quantity of food makes its way into my luggage, which is inevitably decked with 'HEAVY' stickers when it appears on the airport carousel. I've brought back foie gras from Strasbourg, nutmeg from Grenada (I wish I'd managed some conch), ham from North Carolina, salted anchovies from Collioure and an impressive quantity of tinned sardines from Quiberon in Brittany. 'Quite a good buy,' admitted Mrs H. She was also pleased – if somewhat surprised – by the dozen pots of lox and cream cheese, baked salmon and other fishy salads I acquired in Zabar's, the big, rackety deli on New York's Upper West Side. She was less keen on the plastic bag of saffron I snapped up for a bargain price in the

Old City market in Jerusalem. 'Do we really need a lifetime's supply of turmeric?' Nor did she express fondness for the large lump of *bacalhau* (salt cod) that I brought back from Lisbon. 'It was fantastically smelly and fell out of the cupboard so I threw it away.'

'I wish I'd still got that.'

'Then you should have done something with it. You've still got some tins of that fishy stuff you brought back from Nîmes.' Mrs H is referring to *brandade de morue*, a Provençal dip made with salt cod. I found a shop in Nîmes that sold nothing else. (Raymond at 34 rue Nationale is mentioned in Elizabeth David's *French Provincial Cooking*.) Of course, it would have been unforgivable not to make a heavy investment.

Recalling the fate of the *bacalhau*, I brought back two large tentacles of salted octopus on my next visit to Lisbon. Keen to try this souvenir, I left one soaking in the sink when I went out for the evening. Unfortunately, I forgot to warn Mrs H about its presence. 'I nearly shot through the ceiling,' she told me later. 'I thought it was a dead eel. Not the sort of thing a girl wants to come home to on a dark night.' She was placated somewhat when I barbecued the tentacle. It was delicious in a salty sort of way.

Mrs H has even looked askance at foods that she has requested. Before I went to Mexico she put in an order for dried chilli peppers, which I bought in bulk. In fact, the quantity proved a bit daunting. They are still sitting in a big cool box. This is because someone gave us a warning that the peppers might contain insects we would never get rid of if they escaped into the house. So the lid of the cool box remains tight shut, though I intend to use them one day, possibly in the world's largest chilli con carne. 'Have you thrown them away yet?' Mrs H inquires from time to time.

'I didn't lug them all the way back from Mexico City just to throw them away.'

Equally dismaying was her reaction to the gift I brought back from New Orleans. Though she initially looked pleased at the large, foil-wrapped parcel I pulled from my bag, delight turned to perplexity when she discovered that it contained a vast, circular sandwich. Around a foot in diameter, it was somewhat squashed by its journey of 4,637 miles. 'It's called a muffuletta. There's olive salad in there and salami and mortadella and provolone and ...'

'You've brought me back a squashed sandwich from New Orleans?'

'Yes. It's from this fantastic shop called the Central Grocery on Decatur Street. They wrapped it twice when I said where it was going. It's supposed to be one of the great sandwiches of the world.'

'How lovely.' It turned out to be rather nice in a soggy way, though Mrs H was unimpressed.

There is another American delicacy that I prize above all others. Displaying considerable strength of character, I have never brought it back across the Atlantic. Particularly in America's heartland, where restaurant meals tend to be as mundane as they are vast, it has often been a lifesaver. I have consumed this glory of stateside cuisine from Providence,

Rhode Island, to Carmel, California, and it has rarely failed to satisfy. The dish in question looks pretty similar to the snack we had in Apulia, but in America you don't get octopus in a bun. You get hamburger. I might not have been able to bring American burgers back across the Atlantic, but there was no reason why I couldn't make my own version.

5

Burger king

EATING ONE OR MORE HAMBURGERS a day for two weeks produces some strange effects. I don't mean the alarming physical deterioration recorded in Morgan Spurlock's documentary *Super Size Me*, about consuming Big Macs for thirty days on the trot (he put on 11.1 kilos). It is possible to be spared such ballooning by downsizing the portions and skipping the fries, though you are never actually going to lose weight by eating burgers (the fattiness of the meat is the key to their juiciness). As a consequence of our diet, an outside observer would have seen a household behaving in a bizarrely eccentric fashion. We took to keeping the mincer in the refrigerator. (Yes, the *mincer*, not just the mince.) We grilled food containing ice-cubes. We acquired a slab of beef costing £174.95 per kilo.

We were simply trying to make the best possible hamburger. I'd been making them on and off for years. 'You used to make little round ones like squashed meatballs, then they got bigger over the years,' says Mrs H, who has a better memory for these things than me. The results were only so-so, often on the dry side. I'd eaten far better burgers in the

States and felt an urge to reproduce these paragons of the genre. As a result of our investigations, I am now able to answer a number of significant questions.

Are the best burgers made from steak? No. Do you need to mince your own beef? Usually. Should you press on the hamburger to get singe marks while grilling? No. Was it a mistake to compress our research on this topic into two weeks? Yes.

The reason for this untimely haste is that a magazine accepted my proposal for an article about making the best hamburger. The only drawback about this sponsorship was the deadline, which caused our normally (fairly) balanced diet to go radically haywire. We ate as many hamburgers in a fortnight as we would normally do in five years.

For us, hamburgers are a rare (in both senses) treat. Somehow, they're all the better for being an occasional indulgence. Though I relish a good burger, I can't see the point of most products sold as such. I suspect that I am not alone in being baffled by the success of the Big Mac and everything else sold by the big hamburger chains. I doubt if I've had more than three or four such transient nibbles in my entire life. (They are not a memorable experience.) At its best, the American burger is incomparably superior. A plump disc of minced beef briefly grilled, it has a gently charred crust and a rare, juicy interior. This quintessence of beefiness is more satisfying than many steaks you are liable to encounter.

Mrs H shared my desire to achieve excellence in the hamburger. At least she joined in my intense experimentation.

Later, I discovered that she was not so ardent. 'They're OK,' she said, while waggling her hands in an I-can-take-it-or-leave-it fashion. 'I like the smell, but if I were to have anything minced it would be spicy lamb meatballs with mint and yogurt.' And there was me thinking she had been enjoying them all along. It was like rhubarb and her mum all over again.

In order to assist our experimentation, I acquired an extensive library of burgerology. 'You bored me stupid for weeks with interesting facts on the topic,' Mrs H recalls. 'Did I know that a recipe for Hamburg sausages appeared in Hannah Glasse's cookbook of 1758? Or that Wimpy was originally a character in Popeye? Or that White Castle, the first American hamburger chain, still sells hamburgers from little castles? Zzzzzzzzzzzzzz.'

Hamburger America by George Motz proved to be a particularly entertaining study. Described as a 'State-By-State Guide to 100 Great Burger Joints', it is the result of seven years' research. Typical examples of the prodigious platefuls that Motz took on board were the 'Thurman Burger' of Columbus, Ohio, whose successive strata consist of a twelve-ounce beef patty, grilled onions, lettuce, tomato, sautéd mushrooms, pickle, mayonnaise, half a pound of sliced ham, grilled mozzarella and American cheese, and the 'Seismic Burger' sold in Meers, Oklahoma, with 'one pound of ground longhorn beef topped with cheese, bacon, jalapeño slices ...' Surprisingly, photographs of Motz reveal a man of average dimensions. In his introduction, he warns would-be emulators: 'Embrace moderation.'

Mrs H and I aimed for a much pared-down version of these American gut-busters. It would, we agreed, be gratifying to survive the experience. We determined not only to limit the quantity of beef to around 150g per burger but also to diminish the astonishing quantity of stuff that often joins the meat between top and bottom buns. When Heston Blumenthal attempted to produce the ultimate hamburger for his book *Further Adventures in Search of Perfection*, the result was a towering stack of iceberg lettuce, tomato, grilled cheese and pickle. The painstakingly researched Hestonburger was all but lost towards the bottom. With good reason, such efforts are referred to in the US as 'five-napkin burgers'. By chance, I happened to visit one of the spots where Blumenthal studied burgers. It was a faux grungy joint that had been transplanted from the Bowery and installed on the ground floor of a swanky Manhattan hotel called Le Parker Meridien. Being pretty much unsigned, the burger bar took some finding among the mirrors and the large Damien Hirst (one of his spin paintings, not a bovine work) in the glitzy lobby, but a smoky whiff acted as an olfactory signpost. As Blumenthal says, it was 'a great burger'. Unfortunately, he seemed more impressed by 'the effort that had gone into creating a context for that burger' and did not emulate its restraint in salad/pickle accompaniments.

I knew that a piled-up burger would not go down well with Mrs H. 'I always go for a plain hamburger,' she said. 'A load of slippery things piled up together makes it too challenging to eat.' However, she is keen on tomato ketchup with her burger. At least, I thought she was until I quizzed her about this passion. 'Actually, I don't like it with hamburgers,' she blithely asserted. 'I think it detracts from the meatiness of the burger.'

'Well, why do you reach for the ketchup bottle when we have hamburgers?' I inquired with the lethal suavity of a prosecuting QC.

'I might have a bit of ketchup with half the toasted bun.'

'Ha!'

'But I don't put my halves of the bun together – the ketchup doesn't go on the hamburger! So nuts to you, Mr Nosey Parker.' With that, which was accompanied by an impressive length of stuck-out tongue, she considered herself vindicated.

'But you've always liked gherkins with your burger.'

To my astonishment Mrs H said, 'I don't think I ever had a gherkin before I met you.'

'You're constantly buying them. We only go to Ikea so you can buy the sweet Swedish ones.'

'You're the gherkin addict,' she shot back. 'Who else would trail round New York to visit a pickle stall? It was you who made us catch a cab across Manhattan so we could visit Guss Pickles on the Lower East Side. It was very vinegary and full of men in stained aprons fishing things like giant caterpillars out of plastic barrels. You bought a huge willie-sized pickle and went, "Mmm, lovely." It was all very butch.'

'I bought you a Guss Pickle T-shirt that you never wore.'

'That's because you put it in a plastic bag with your leaky

gherkins, so it smelled of vinegar no matter how often I washed it.'

We did, however, agree about the bun. It shouldn't be too big, but it should be sprinkled with sesame seeds. Having discussed the peripherals, it was time to get down to the meat of the matter.

All hamburger authorities agree that you should mince your own beef. You need to know what you're cooking. Somewhat counter-intuitively, this should not be the best steak cuts. 'Fillet, rib-eye, even rump are too lean,' pontificated Mrs H. 'You want a good bit of fat in the mix to provide juiciness and flavour.' Most American hamburger gurus specify chuck beef. Chuck is a term for shoulder beef, also known in the UK as blade. It contains around 18–25 per cent fat, which is deemed more or less perfect for hamburgers.

Unless you have access to a butcher's powerful mincer, the meat has to be trimmed of connective tissue. 'This is it,' said Mrs H, pointing out some white stringy strips in the meat with the tip of her kitchen knife. 'It's tough, non-fatty stuff that surrounds the muscle fibres of the meat.' Tough is the word. According to Richard Wrangham's book *Catching Fire*, 'Connective tissue is slippery, elastic and strong: the tensile strength of tendons can be half that of aluminium.' Fortunately, connective tissue turns to jelly when heated. So why did I have to cut it out?

'If you don't cut it out,' Mrs H explained, 'it wraps itself round the spindle of your mincer.' That's what happened to Jeffrey Steingarten, food guru of US *Vogue*, when he omitted to take this precaution during his attempt to make the perfect burger. 'The Waring electric meat grinder began to make the sound of fingernails scraping on a blackboard, but amplified a hundred times. We had to buy a new one.'

Its connective tissue safely removed, our meat went into the fridge for an hour to chill again. 'This is to ensure that the fat stays hard while being minced,' explained Mrs H in full didactic flow. 'Otherwise, the blade gets covered in fatty gunge and a horrible pink mousse emerges instead of mince speckled with bits of red and white.'

Judy Rogers of the Zuni Café in San Francisco goes further still: 'Refrigerate the grinder to chill thoroughly. A warm grinder can warm the meat.' For mincing we used our KitchenAid food mixer with (pre-chilled) mincing attachment. It's better to mince the meat twice or even three times to ensure the fat is thoroughly amalgamated. Some experts advocate the addition of salt, fried chopped onions and even a spoonful or two of cream. Steingarten found a report in the *US Journal of Food Science* that said the addition of 10 per cent water (about one and a half tablespoons per burger) 'resulted in higher juiciness, tenderness and over-all palatability'. I also came across a suggestion from James Beard, 'the father of American gastronomy', that the inclusion of an ice-cube in the burger ensures a moist, rare interior.

When it comes to forming the burgers, Harold McGee maintains, 'The gently gathered ground beef in a good hamburger has a delicate quality quite unlike even a tender steak.' The gentle gathering is intended to produce a tasty, crumbly burger. When cooking burgers, what you must not do is what you see short-order cooks doing in American films. You must not press the burger on the grill with your spatula. Though powerfully tempting in a mysterious way, it has the effect of squeezing out the juices. You get a dry burger.

Up to our hocks in advice, we decided to start sizzling. For all our tests, we used our Weber gas barbecue (a ribbed, cast-iron griddle on a gas hob also produces good results). About four to five minutes per side at medium-hot heat produces a medium-rare burger. Just to be perverse, we started with a sample of ready-minced beef, though this wasn't just any old mince. It was Galloway shoulder beef or chuck aged for thirty-five days and sold by Farmer Sharp (a cooperative of Cumbrian farmers) at London's Borough Market. Though we approached it with dubious forks, it hit the bull's eye with our first shot. 'This is quite good, actually,' said Mrs H. 'Really flavoursome. A highly beefy burger.'

So much for never using prepared mince. Our second burger was made from Harrods chuck (£8.50 per kilo). The 'gently gathered' business sounds wacky, but the effect on the taste was perceptible. 'It holds together well and the flavour is pretty good,' said Mrs H. For comparative purposes, we tried chuck from our local butcher (£7.80 per kilo). Mrs H expressed misgivings about the smell. 'It reminds me of school dinners.' But she polished it off happily. We also tried burgers made from rump (dry and lacking in flavour) and hanger steak (better but still on the dry side).

It may seem contradictory, but while cheap beef produces a very good hamburger, so does very, very expensive beef. As a result of my commission, I was sent a 600g chunk of Queensland Wagyu from Harrods. Normally, it would have cost £174.95 per kilo for meat that is 30 per cent fat. Peering in awe at this plutocratic lump, we discovered that it was ribboned and streaked with what looked like pink butter. Fortunately for one's arteries, Wagyu fat is high in (relatively) healthy unsaturates. Even when thoroughly chilled, the meat felt to be melting the moment you started handling it. Mincing this plutocratic fillet seemed lese-majesty of a high order, but the resulting burgers were highly acceptable. Very tasty, immaculately moist, each fragment of meat was imbued with gravy-flavoured fat. 'This is very, very good,' said Mrs H as she nibbled her final fragment. 'You just want a bit more.' Our two 125g burgers cost around £45.

Finally, we tried an adapted version of a burger recipe developed by Heston Blumenthal and his Fat Duck team. We minced a mixture of 50 per cent short rib beef (rich in both fat and flavour, this is a cut that lies on top of the big ribs in an area at the centre on each side of the ribcage) with 25 per cent brisket and 25 per cent chuck. In one of the burgers we hid an ice-cube, to the other we added one and a half tablespoons of water. 'A really excellent beefy taste,' said Mrs H, as she nibbled the results. 'Heston's combination is very good if you can find short rib. It produces a pleasing greasiness.' The additional water resulted in a notably juicy burger. So did the ice-cube, which had the additional bonus of ensuring a rare interior, though commercial operations may get customer complaints concerning the resulting hole. 'Hurrah for the Iceburger!' declared my heroic partner as she dabbed a fragment from her lips. 'We must remember to use ice-cubes when we have hamburgers again. Maybe in five or six years.'

THE SOUND OF FALLING SCALES

'IT WAS THE FIRST THING we ever cooked together,' I reminisced in sentimental mood.

'You mean it was the first thing that you ever got roped into,' blurted Mrs H. 'After years and years spending a good chunk of January with crinkly fingers and the whole house covered in sticky stuff, I decided it was time you lent a hand. Very revealing it was too. You just sat there and moaned.'

'I never moaned.'

'You moaned constantly. It was very revealing about your character. I decided I had a lot to put up with.'

Though marmalade-making at home is often regarded as a symbol of domestic bliss, it did not prove to be very blissful in our case. This was the moment when, with a great clatter, the scales fell from Mrs H's eyes. She was only too willing to itemise my shortcomings as a partner in preserving activities.

'You were resistant to my instructions. You didn't see why you had to sterilise the pots or why you had to chop finely. It was obvious that you didn't know anything about making preserves and it was obvious that you were not a patient man.'

'I'm extremely patient.'

'You're extremely cunning. You say, "Ooh, I can't do that," so I have to do it. You couldn't be bothered to chop peel equally. You wanted to do it any old how. You thought the oranges didn't need scrubbing. You couldn't manage to put all the pips in a muslin bag and tie it on to the pan-handle. So I took over. Now I know you're doing it just to get out of things. Ha, ha, ha! Am I right?'

'Not at all.'

'Yes, I am.'

It was all a long way from our cheese-on-toast-in-bed bliss. But even Mrs H concedes that I am not to blame for her devoting many hours each year to making marmalade, something that she does not particularly like. She started making it for a friend of ours, a marmalade devotee of many years standing. Since he gets through a jar every ten days, he requires thirty-six jars a year.

When she started making marmalade for our friend, I began eating this bittersweet elixir myself. Jolly good it is too. Though I'm not such an addict as he is, I still manage to consume a jar every three weeks or so, making an annual requirement of eighteen jars a year. Mrs H's uncomplaining altruism in filling our joint order for fifty-odd jars would make her a candidate for beatification. At least, it would if this were true – not the altruism but the uncomplaining. She complains about the task long and hard. 'Damn! Ergh! Sticky! Ugh! Horrible!' she mutters while stirring her seething cauldron. Shrouded by clouds of pungent vapour, she might be one of the weird sisters in *Macbeth*. I was unwise enough to point this out at a moment when the rolling boil was at its peak. 'Is that so, matey?' replied Mrs H. 'Well, you can do it next year.'

Of course, she'll forget, I thought. But she didn't. Women have an unfortunate tendency not to forget. So when Seville oranges made their brief appearance in the following year, I was roped in. I realised that our first joint culinary endeavour was not going to be without the occasional release of steam, but it did have one advantage. If Mrs H were ever to throw in the towel, I would be able to have a bash at making the stuff myself. Breakfast without homemade marmalade would be lacking in appeal.

6

Infernal rind

'I WISH IT HAD STAYED PUT IN ARAB COUNTRIES,' said Mrs H. This may seem a strange remark to make about marmalade, the great stalwart of the British breakfast table, but I had just been informing her about its unexpected provenance. First recorded in English in 1480, the word comes from the Portuguese *marmelada*, which refers to quince preserve. Since the finest marmalade is made from Seville oranges, there remains a strong link with the Iberian peninsula. According to *The Book of Marmalade* by food historian C. Anne Wilson, the origin of the preserve lies further south: 'It does look as though Arab food customs and recipes were the original source of this confection in Portugal.'

'Well, that's *really* interesting,' Mrs H responded in an unconvincing way. Strangely, she was more occupied with another aspect of the spread. 'I wonder if kitchens in Portugal get covered in the bloody stuff?' She has a point there. Just a few molecules of marmalade have the magical ability to coat an extraordinary area. The transformation of our kitchen into Chez Sticky takes place each January.

Seville oranges have a brief and immutable season (around three weeks). If you want to make marmalade, you should snap them up as soon as you see them. You should also buy preserving sugar in some quantity because that also tends to disappear. And you need jars to put it in. Most marmalade makers collect jam and pickle jars throughout the year, resulting in a pleasing medley of containers for their output. Since such forward planning is impossible in our house, we tend to buy jars, along with lids with a faux gingham design, circles of waxy paper, labels, etc., from the kitchen company Lakeland.

It is a tricky thing to balance the three elements – Seville oranges, jars and sugar. You always seem to have too much or too little of one of them. With an excess of sugar or jars, you can shove them in a cupboard until next year, but the temptation is to buy more Seville oranges. An excess of oranges involves an emergency foray round local supermarkets to buy more preserving sugar. You could freeze the oranges, but what person with sufficient interest in food to make marmalade will have enough room in their freezer? And so January passes in an endless round of shopping, steaming, stirring, potting and complaining from Mrs H ('My fingers have gone like prunes'), all to make something you can buy in any supermarket.

So why does she bother, especially since she is not a great lover of the stuff? (She will occasionally accept a slice of marmalade on toast and show signs of mild enjoyment, but I have never seen her reach for the pot of her own accord.) The main reason for this annual onslaught is the torrent of compliments that Mrs H receives for her preserve. Most marmalade makers think their stuff is pretty hot stuff – C. Anne Wilson remarks that her own is 'matchless' – and they're usually right. It is not something you can buy in the supermarket. A world away from the one-dimensional sweetness of commercial marmalades, the homemade version does a dance on the tastebuds that hardly any other food can match. With a profound bittersweetness that hints at its exotic origins, it delivers a complex and potent combination of flavours.

But there is a price to be paid for such perfection. Instead of using the food processor to chop up the peel, Mrs H sticks to traditional methods, i.e. a sharp knife. 'In order to ensure that your peel is evenly distributed throughout the jar, it has to be of a uniform length and thickness,' she rather grandly explained. This doesn't happen with a food processor. Taking on the role of time-and-motion expert, I once egged her into using this more efficient way of cutting peel and I never heard the end of it. 'It just chops the peel up any old how,' she blurted accusingly. 'That's all right if you want mushy marmalade. Do you want mushy marmalade?'

For the first time, my role in this annual epic was going to be more than advisory. I was going to get my hands dirty or, rather, sticky. But first they had to be clean. 'Make sure you wash them properly!' ordered the Generalissimo. When I was finally allowed to get my hands on an orange, I discovered that there is quite a bit more to marmalade making than I had thought. Seville oranges are often creased, tough-looking jobs – the Tommy Lee Joneses of the citrus world – and washing them is a tedious prelude before you get down to business. You dig out the stalk, a black warty bit at the top. Then you search for fragments of Sevillian soil wedged in the cracks of the peel. Compensation for this dermatological exploration comes with the fresh, astringent perfume of the zest. Having weighed out three pounds of washed oranges, you bisect them and squeeze out the juice. By far the easiest way of doing this is to use an electric juicer. A cheap one works just as well as the hugely expensive Porsche-designed one I bought in a testosterone-induced moment of madness a few years ago.

A fair amount of juice comes out of fresh Seville oranges, but they're also rich in pips and pith. When you've finished squeezing, you collect the pips from the juicer. You may be forcibly reminded to include any pips that might have been left in the halved orange peels. 'You've left three pips behind!' Mrs H pointed out. It might be considered that a few pips in marmalade would add to its homemade credentials – but apparently not. The pips are placed in the centre in a square of buttercloth muslin. You pull the four corners of the muslin together and tie them with a long piece of string. Our muslin also came from Lakeland. 'Very much recommended,' says Mrs H, who has something of an obsession with Lakeland. 'Their muslin squares are just the right size for the pips.' (Apparently, a clean J-cloth – well, you wouldn't use a dirty one – is also effective.) The resulting little sack goes into the jam pan along with the orange juice. This is because pips are rich in the natural gelling agent known as pectin, which trips off the tongue more easily than its other name, heteropolysaccharide. The pips should save you having to use the commercial pectin known, rather splendidly, as Certo. 'I bet you don't know how to rescue the sack of pips at the end of the boil,' said Mrs H.

'Er, no.'

'I knew you wouldn't. You'd never think of tying the string to the handle of the jam pan. That's why you need a long piece.'

The next step was, to me at least, a surprise. You add six pints of water to the juice. Who would have thought there was water in marmalade? 'You add it to jam as well,' said Mrs H.

'You didn't add it when you were making strawberry jam.'

'Well, that's different. Get on with chopping the peel.'

Ah, yes, I'd forgotten that bit. Unlike normal orange consumption when the peel is chucked away, unless you shove a chunk in each cheek to do a Marlon Brando impression ('You don't even think to call me Godfather'), marmalade-making is a very satisfactory activity for those who detest waste. To chop the peel, you need a short, sharp knife, a chopping board and Radio 4. Bisect each squeezed hemisphere, so you get the peel of a quarter-orange. You then slice this wedge to create ten strips of peel. At least that's how I was directed, but just to show the old anarchic spirit wasn't entirely dead I sometimes did a random amount with some bigger chunks.

'Jolly good fun making marmalade, isn't it?' I announced with resolute buoyancy.

Silence.

Actually, it does get a bit wearing around the tenth quarter-orange peel.

'I knew you'd get fed up,' said Mrs H when she caught me taking a breather. 'And these bits are too big. You'll have to halve them.' I discovered that you need to do the peel-chopping in phases. A cup of coffee or a stare into space with your mouth open is required at regular intervals. It takes maybe an hour – thirty minutes for more dedicated types – to convert the hollow hemispheres from three pounds of oranges into a heap of two-tone strips. The sliced peel goes into the pan of diluted orange juice (with tethered bag of pips), which is brought to the boil on the hob at full blast, then turned down to a simmer for a couple of hours until the peel is soft (it should break up when you press it).

If you nibble the cooked peel at this stage, the effect is a wake-up call for your tastebuds; a profound, startling bitterness with an aftertaste that goes on and on. This orangey bitterness is the backbone of Seville orange marmalade. It is also the zesty powerhouse that propels Cointreau, Grand Marnier and most gins. At the Beefeater gin distillery in London, I once saw sackfuls of dried peel from bitter Spanish oranges that join juniper, orris root and what-have-you among the botanical flavourings. Each year, the company imports three tons of dried orange peel and that is a lot of peel, since it is virtually weightless. Pared from the fruit immediately after picking, the peel is dried on washing lines in the orange grove.

But back to marmalade. When the peel has simmered to softness, you are advised by some authorities, including Mrs H, to leave it in the juice to steep overnight. Or you can just press on. Either way, you have to squeeze the pectin from the bag of pips into the orange juice. After squeezing, Mrs H simmers the bag of pips in a small saucepan of water to extract the last molecule of pectin. This also goes in with the juice. Now comes the moment to add the preserving sugar. Tate & Lyle says it has a larger crystal that 'dissolves more slowly to help make a better product.' Mrs H says it 'helps with the clarity – you don't get so much scum', but some marmalade makers I know achieve excellent results with bog-standard granulated. If you start with three pounds of oranges, the quantity required is six pounds of preserving sugar. Don't add the sugar before the peel is soft. I am earnestly assured by Mrs H that the peel will never get one jot softer from that moment.

While heating the sugary, peel-laden juice to the boil, you have to stir constantly and you have to stir in a certain way. 'Slowly does it,' ordered Mrs H in a parade-ground 'Wait-for-it' growl. 'If you whirl it round in your fine, manly way, you're going to start smashing the peel.' So I stopped whirling. 'But you haven't dissolved the sugar properly.' I started whirling again.

'I think it's dissolved now,' I said after a bit.

'I bet it isn't,' said Mrs H, pinching my spoon. 'There!' she said triumphantly. 'I can feel great crunchy bits at the bottom. You may think it's fine, but do you know what would happen if you didn't dissolve all the sugar?"

'Er, no.'

'It would turn crystalline. That's not good. It might have been fine when you were growing copper sulphate crystals at school but it's not what you want in marmalade. You can tell when the sugar's nearly dissolved because the peel starts to look different. It becomes slightly glassy. That's the fruit hardening up. Also the liquid becomes more transparent.' When the sugar has fully dissolved, the marmalade undergoes the thrilling phase known as the 'rolling boil'. This is quite a bit more than a simmer but somewhat less than a full-blown volcanic boil. It might take some fiddling to achieve the right temperature. 'Do you see it rising up the side?' asked the Generalissimo. 'Well, it shouldn't be doing that.'

The rolling boil in a big pan is rather impressive and a bit scary. The golden goo churns and seethes with hundreds of little bubbles. It's the sort of thing that used to be poured on besieging forces from the top of battlements. Had that thought ever occurred to Mrs H?

'No.'

A foam forms amid the churning orangey boil. The effect is a bit like a film of the surface of the sun. Had that ever struck Mrs H?

'No. Are you stirring properly? You should be stirring with a figure-of-eight movement.' Blimey! Hovering over a steamy pan doing figure-of-eight movements with my wooden spoon was not why I came into the kitchen.

There might have been the possibility of a Spartacus-style revolt by the kitchen slave, but for the fact that you don't have to stir constantly during the rolling boil. Once every five minutes is enough to make sure the bottom bit of the marmalade does not burn, though you have to set the timer to make sure you don't forget. The wonderful bittersweet smell compensates for the tedium of the task. In fact, there are wonderful citrus smells of various kinds throughout the marmalade-making process. (Oil from bergamot, an inedible orange, is used in perfumes and Earl Grey tea.) However, this olfactory magic seems to have palled on Mrs H.

'I find the whole thing extremely banal,' she huffed.

But how long does the rolling boil go on for? C. Anne Wilson and other marmalade authorities say fifteen to twenty minutes. A breeze. But Mrs H says, 'Until it's done.'

'Oh.'

'It depends how much pectin there is in the oranges. This seems to vary with the age of the fruit.'

The procedure to tell if it's done, known as 'the wrinkle test', is like something from the age of alchemy. You put a plate in the fridge to get cold. After, say, fifteen minutes, when you think the marmalade might be done, you dribble a small, golden splat on the plate and shove it back in the fridge to get cold. If the dribble forms wrinkles when you push one edge with your finger, the marmalade is done. If there are no wrinkles, the rolling boil goes on. And on. And on. To the accompaniment of increasingly vehement cussing, Mrs H splats and chills and prods. A deep gloom descends. In the case of the most recalcitrant batches, she reaches for the Certo. Sometimes two bottles go in. She glumly insists that it won't set, but it always seems to. There is a danger during this period that the marmalade will burn or, at any rate, caramelise a bit. The result is a dark, opaque preserve approaching mahogany in hue. In common with other aficionados, particularly males, I favour dark-coloured marmalade, but Mrs H doesn't agree. 'It should be clear and golden. Dark marmalade tastes burnt to me.' After a mere hour or so, which involved twelve lots of figure-of-eight stirs, my marmalade obligingly wrinkled. 'Now we start potting!' I said, with the gung-ho enthusiasm of a wet-behind-the-ears greenhorn.

'Not so fast!' barked the boss. 'First we stir in a bit of butter, which takes away the foam and stops bubbles appearing in the finished marmalade. Then leave it to cool for at least twenty minutes or your peel will rise to the top of the jar when you pot it. Marmalade judges don't like uneven distribution of peel.' Quite right too. Neither do I. I forgot to mention that during the rolling boil you also have to get busy with the jam jars. These have to be thoroughly washed, even if new from Lakeland. A dish-washer helps here. Then the jars are sterilised in the oven at 80°C for half an hour or so to kill off any surviving nasties. All v. tedious, not to mention painful when juggling hot jars from the oven, but v. important in order to avoid green mould growing on top of your marmalade. That doesn't go down well with marmalade judges either. Additionally, Mrs H pointed out, if you pot hot marmalade in cold jars, the dread crystallisation can result.

After twenty minutes has expired, you can start potting. This is where the real stickiness starts. After giving the marmalade a final distributive stir, you start bailing with a jug. To ensure that most of the hot syrup gets into the jar, a wide-mouthed funnel is recommended. The marmalade has a slurry-like quality by this stage, so it doesn't so much pour as tumble from the mug into the funnel. Inevitably, there are many sticky spillages. In the case of my batch, three pounds of oranges and six pounds of sugar (plus the water) produced enough marmalade to fill ten one-pound jars. Mrs H complimented me on the efficiency of my output. 'I was only getting eight jars.' When the jars have cooled, you put a little waxed disc of paper on the surface of the marmalade. This may seem like a needless fussiness, but it helps to prevent product contraction.

After the waxed paper discs, you screw on the gingham-patterned lids. Peering at my jars, Mrs H was impressed by the bright, light gold oranginess of my product. Me too. Its clean tang has converted me from my preference for the mahogany-coloured version. A box of homemade Seville orange marmalade is a highly satisfactory thing to have achieved. It is, however, a dangerous thing to boast to chums about. As soon as you mention your marvellous preserve, the other party invariably says, 'Oh, but I love homemade marmalade!' Or, less politely, 'I could take some of that off your hands.' Before you know where you are, your box has declined to a single jar. On the other hand, it's hard to stay shtum when you've converted fruit to gold.

How to eat marmalade

For some time, I was keen on untoasted brown bread and butter as the foundation for my breakfast marmalade. The combination produces a nice puddingy sensation in the mouth. But I've come round to the more orthodox view that marmalade is best on toast. Spreading it thickly – you can scarcely spread a chunky preserve thinly – on well-buttered toast made from good bread produces a sensational combination of textures and tastes – crunchy, chewy, tart, sweet, luxurious, astringent. It is a grown-up way to start the day.

Marmalade does not have to be the gastronomic equivalent of an alarm clock (though the lure of marmalade on toast is very effective in getting me out of bed). It is possible to enjoy its taste at other times and in other ways than the familiar breakfast spread. A few years ago, I held a competition in my column for the best use for marmalade in recipes or snacks as a way of inducing Mrs H to consume her own output.

Despite the measly prize of one pot of Mrs H's marmalade, the entries flowed in by the sackload. Several of the suggestions, though doubtless highly regarded by the entrants, were less than tempting. I didn't feel any great urge to try Shredded Wheat 'carefully prised open', then spread with marmalade and 'eaten like a sandwich'. Same went for marmalade on bread fried in bacon fat. Someone expressed the view that 'marmalade is quite interesting with lemon-marinaded mackerel fillets fried in butter'. Another suggested spreading marmalade on hot cheese on toast. The combination of marmalade and kippers had several advocates ('lovely!'), who were subsequently supported by David Dimbleby, once shown eagerly tucking into this curious gastronomic partnership on television.

The most frequent and plausible suggestion was for the addition of marmalade to bread and butter pudding. Moreover, it worked with Mrs H, who was finally induced to take on board her own product with some eagerness. The winner was a steamy memory from Arundel: 'One of the ways to my heart in the early days of courtship was for my husband to make a bread and butter pudding. Along with the butter, he would spread the bread with marmalade and shavings of stem ginger. The added zip and zest made it into an erotic delight.'

Though it might not compare for arousal, my favourite dessert incorporating marmalade is ice-cream. I first encountered marmalade ice-cream made by Criterion Ices of Suffolk. Accompanied by a warning ('Beware: It bites back a bit'), this excellent product is flavoured with Frank Cooper's Vintage Marmalade. It prompted me to make ice-cream with Mrs H's marmalade. The palate-tingling result, generously laden with frozen chunks of peel, was one of the best grown-up ice-creams I've ever licked. But you don't have to make Seville orange marmalade to enjoy this treat. 'You can use anything from Rose's lime marmalade to ginger marmalade,' the ice-cream expert Robin Weir once told me. 'Even quite nasty marmalades make great ice-creams.'

Mrs H adored marmalade ice-cream but there is another

marmalade item that she likes even more. The marmalade cocktail was a Twenties invention that has recently been revived as the breakfast cocktail. This may seem a bit early for a drink propelled by a hefty slug of gin and a touch of Cointreau, but Mrs H thinks otherwise. 'It's lovely,' she said. 'What a way to start the day.'

Mrs H's recipe for Seville orange marmalade

If you are a marmalade maker, there is no time in the early part of the year for complacency. You have to be up and at it in no uncertain terms. Seville oranges usually make an appearance around the second or third week in January, but they are around for only four weeks. Try to buy the plumpest-looking fruit, as the pith will contain more pectin and therefore will set better. Our marmalade challenges have occurred when we used drier, end-of-season fruit. When it won't set, I reach for pectin, a natural setting agent. Certo is the leading brand.

I use preserving sugar, as it produces a scum-free set with a brighter colour. Because we make marmalade regularly and in quite large quantities, we have a proper preserving pan, but I also use a large stockpot to boil the water and oranges. Whatever you use, make sure it is tall and wide enough to accommodate the rather frightening 'rolling boil', a bubbling, swirling mass of marmalade that is apt to rise up the sides.

Squeezing the juice can be a laborious task. For years I used one of those wooden squeezers, but then I had a present of an electric juicer – so now this part is easy-peasy (and quite enjoyable). A wide-mouthed jam-making funnel is a useful aid for safely transferring the marmalade into a jar and saves wiping off the dribbles on the outside should you have an unsteady hand.

You will also need the phone number for Lakeland. You will probably run out of jars, lids, wax discs, labels, string or muslin. (In our case, we are likely to have left most of these items in Yorkshire.) Lakeland usually has all these in stock. It also offers an emergency next-day delivery service. As you will see from the recipe, marmalade making takes an age – so set aside plenty of time.

This is a pretty standard recipe that you will find, with a few small variations, in most cookbooks that include marmalade or on bags of preserving sugar. Tried and tested over a century or more, it is based on Imperial weights, so I have included them here. It should make between eight to ten 450g (1lb) jars.

1.4kg Seville oranges (3lb)
juice of 2 lemons
3.4 litres water (6 pints)
2.7kg preserving sugar (6lb)
a small knob of butter

First make sure you have enough glass jars and lids and that they are washed and clean. If you don't want a recipient to discover a little fur coat of mould in your marmalade, you must wash the jars thoroughly in very hot soapy water.

Rinse them well and allow them to dry naturally, or, better still, use a dishwasher. It is also a good idea to place a small plate in the fridge for later use when testing for a set. And make sure you have a sharpened knife for slicing the peel.

Wash the oranges and remove the stalks. Give them a scrub if required. Next, halve the oranges and squeeze out the juice and pips. Do the same with the lemons. Reserve the pips and tie them in a piece of muslin, together with any membrane that has been produced during the squeezing process. Use a long length of string so that you can tie the muslin bag on to the handle of the preserving pan.

The next stage involves slicing the orange peel. (Discard the lemon.) Try to get the segments of peel as even as possible and the same length. I find it easier if I cut each orange in half and then half again. A sharp knife really helps to speed things up. Now place the peel, fruit juices and water in the preserving pan. Tie the muslin bag containing the pips to the handle and plop it into the pan.

Simmer the peel gently until it becomes very soft and the liquid has reduced by about half. It should take about 2 hours to reach this stage. If you can squidge a piece of peel between your finger and thumb, it is soft enough. Remove the muslin bag using its piece of string. Squeeze it well and allow the juice and jelly-like pectin to run into the pan. (At this stage, I warm the clean jars in the oven at 80°C. Cold jars and hot marmalade can result in crystallisation.)

Add the sugar to the pan, heating it gently and stirring until the sugar has completely dissolved. Bring the marmalade to a rolling boil (there should be lots of little bubbles). Maintain this until the setting point has been reached – it should take around 15 minutes. Test for a set by placing a small amount of marmalade on a plate you have chilled in the fridge. Replace in the fridge and check the plate after a minute. If the splat runs all over the plate, the marmalade needs further boiling. If it forms a wrinkle when you press the splat with a finger, you're done.

Take the marmalade off the heat. Stir in a small knob of butter, which has the effect of removing any scum that has formed on the surface. Now let it stand for 20 minutes before potting. Fill the jars right up to the rim – I use a jug and a jam funnel. This can be a very sticky phase, but you have to fill the jars as much as possible. Marmalade shrinks as it cools and you do not want to create a large air space. When it has cooled sufficiently, screw the lids on tightly, and if required, add a label. Then all you have to do is wash up and find somewhere to store all the jars until you are able to give them away. I am compelled to keep a few, since someone in our house likes a bit of marmalade with his breakfast. I rarely eat it – too sticky on the fingers.

Marmalade bread and butter pudding

85g butter, softened
225g good quality white bread, sliced
1 x 454g jar good quality Seville orange marmalade
15g fresh ginger root, peeled and grated
2 large eggs
2 egg yolks
a pinch of salt
1 heaped tablespoon caster sugar
275ml full cream milk
125ml double cream

Butter the bread and spread with marmalade (you will probably use about half a jar). Sprinkle grated ginger over the marmalade. Lay the slices in a buttered baking dish so they overlap. Beat together the eggs and yolks with the salt and sugar and mix in the milk and cream. Pour the egg mixture over the bread slices and leave to soak for 20 minutes. Put into the oven, preheated to 180°C/Gas Mark 4, and bake for 40 minutes until golden brown. This pudding should serve four people.

Marmalade ice-cream

Since this recipe uses raw egg, you should be certain of the freshness and quality of your eggs. It should not be eaten by people who are pregnant or susceptible to infection. To avoid any risk you should first make the egg, sugar and cream into a custard (details in any ice-cream book) and allow to cool. This recipe makes about 1 litre of ice-cream.

3 fresh, free-range egg yolks
300g marmalade
 (chunky Seville orange marmalade works best)
2 tablespoons orange juice
500ml whipping cream
30g caster sugar

Thoroughly amalgamate the egg yolks, marmalade, orange juice, cream and sugar by stirring in a bowl. Pour the contents of the bowl into an ice-cream maker and churn until the mixture has thickened to the consistency of soft whipped cream. Scoop into a plastic container and freeze. Remove from the freezer 20 minutes before serving.

Breakfast cocktail

1 teaspoon orange marmalade
50ml gin
15ml Cointreau
juice of ½ a lemon

To make one cocktail, stir the marmalade with the gin in the base of the shaker until dissolved. Add the other ingredients and shake very vigorously, with ice. Strain into a cocktail glass. The suggestion in one cocktail guide to garnish with a slice of toast on the rim takes the breakfast metaphor too literally.

THE LURE OF THE COOKBOOK

IF MRS H WAS IRKED by the sticky slog of marmalade, a more chronic irritant was my burgeoning collection of cookbooks, which clogged her formerly tidy domain. Alongside her well-thumbed classics appeared works from distant and little known areas of gastronomy. Elizabeth David had to budge over for *Noshe Djan: Afghan Food & Cookery*. Delia was elbowed aside for *The International Squid Cookbook*. Robert Carrier rubbed shoulders with the *Ava Gardner Cookbook* (very sound on macaroni cheese).

'Do we really need a book of recipes from the eighteenth-century navy?' Mrs H grizzled one day. 'I don't really fancy boiled shit.' I should explain that this was not a cloacal expletive from my wife. It is the name of a dish in *Lobscouse & Spotted Dog* by Anne Chotzinoff Grossman and Lisa Grossman Thomas, a gastronomic companion to the seafaring novels of Patrick O'Brian. Boiled shit is exactly what its name suggests: '1oz assorted seabird guano, ¼ cup rainwater. Gather the guano in a large clam shell. Gradually add the water, stirring constantly. Set in a hot sun until it boils. Serves one.' The authors of the book say, 'We made it, but we do not claim to have drunk it.'

In my view, every decent cookbook collection should find room for items that, while not being exactly appetising, are still of interest. Irritatingly preoccupied with the practical, my wife feels differently. In order to dispel Mrs H's urge to ditch *Lobscouse & Spotted Dog*, which happens to be a highly enjoyable culinary adventure, I made lobscouse, a dish that gave the name 'Scouser' to Liverpudlians and is also popular in the ports of the Baltic. (Spotted dog is spotted dick by another name.) With one exception, the ingredients for lobscouse – corned beef, smoked ham, onion, leek, potato and spices – were easily obtained. What I couldn't get hold of was '8 ounces Ship's Biscuit', incorporated in the recipe in crumb form. Though tempted by a tip for beating the dough ('put in a stout bag and repeatedly drive a car over it'), I settled instead for Bath Oliver biscuits. The lobscouse, which proved to be a rather superior version of corned beef hash, went down well with Mrs H. She is a big fan of corned beef hash.

The problem about finding room for several hundred food books was exacerbated by their bulk. Cookbooks tend to be on the big size and the bigger the cook (at least in reputation), the bigger the book. It proved particularly difficult to persuade Mrs H about the merits of my three largest cookbooks. There isn't a single recipe in their collective 2,137 pages that anyone but a mad culinary obsessive would want to attempt. Mrs H staggered when a deliveryman handed over *A Day at elBulli*, by the Spanish culinary genius Ferran Adrià. Unfortunately, its practical value was less than staggering. The 528 pages are bulked out by double-page spreads of dubious value including:

a) a collection of model bulldogs (*bulli* means bulldog);

b) the raking of gravel at the entrance to the restaurant;

c) the delivery of bottles to the recycling bin.

Though the book contains thirty recipes, including such treats as 'preserved tuna oil air' and 'freeze-dried cold white miso foam', a note explained that they were not intended to be attempted by the likes of us: 'The technical level requires specialist equipment ... and professional experience to achieve good results.'

Like the Chrysler Building being overshadowed by the Empire State Building, Adrià's monster was outsized by the 529 pages of Heston Blumenthal's *The Big Fat Duck Cookbook*. Having already essayed his recipes for snail porridge for a newspaper (when we were faxed the recipe from Blumenthal's kitchen, it omitted any indication of when to add the snails) and Black Forest gateau (see page 291), we felt scant desire to have a bash at salmon poached in a liquorice gel, radish ravioli of oyster, etc.

Bigger even than Blumenthal's behemoth was Alain Ducasse's scarcely liftable *Culinary Encyclopaedia*. Contrary to the title, there was very little in its 1,080 pages that appeared feasible for the amateur (even the simplest are complicated in some way – 'crispy country bacon with a truffled salad of pig's head') and an entire section is possibly illegal in the UK, not that I had any desire to eat thrush, whether accompanied by apples, giblet canapés, chanterelles or polenta. It would take a particularly greedy and ruthless gastronome to buy songbirds for the pot.

'You did buy some little birds – very probably songbirds – to eat once,' interjects Mrs H undiplomatically. 'Do you remember that tin?'

Thank you, dear. I'm glad you brought that up. It happened during a brief infatuation with Chinese food. In a rash moment, I bought a tin from a Chinese supermarket that carried not a word of any European language on the label. It felt a bit light. I opened it with a trepidation that turned out to be well merited. Inside, there were half a dozen little birds standing in something congealed.

'Why did you buy it?' asked my wife. 'There's a picture of a nest of birds on the label.'

'I thought it was a trademark.'

No, we didn't, since you ask. The Oriental birds went in the bin untasted.

Anyway, back to books. Instead of the outré and challenging dishes proposed by the three modern masters, I felt the urge to try some recipes from another compendious work. Pioneering but solidly middle-class, it became the foundation stone of British cooking when first published in 1861. But where was I going to find scope for adventure in *Mrs Beeton's Book of Household Management*? Turtle soup was possibly too adventurous ('To make this soup with less difficulty, cut off the head of the turtle the preceding day'). Even mock turtle soup was rather demanding ('half a calf's head'). Prince of Wales's soup with '12 turnips, 1 lump of sugar, 2 spoonfuls of strong veal stock …' was ruled out due to Ms H's aversion to turnips. Sago soup? Mutton pudding? Not quite right for persuading Mrs H about the merits of Mrs B. I'd almost given up hope of turning the culinary clock back 150 years when in section 1,408 I struck gold or, to be precise, white.

Mrs H recalled the moment. '"Blancmange," you said. "Let's do blancmange!" You got out Mrs Beeton and showed me ancient pictures of jellies and blancmange. You got so excited that you took Mrs Beeton off to bed with you. Good grief, I thought, what kind of person gets excited by blancmange?'

7

The joy of blancmange

I CONCEDE THAT THERE may have been more alluring chapter headings in food literature. The word sort of sits there like the substance it describes. Mrs H's reaction when I conceived a desire to make blancmange after coming across several tempting recipes in Mrs Beeton was not encouraging. 'Oh, no, not that horrible cornfloury stuff. I must have been eight when I last had it. I remember that the chocolate one was particularly bad. Brown & Polson have a lot to answer for ...'

'No, I want to do a proper one, a little castle with turrets, like you see in Mrs Beeton.'

'Turrets?'

'Yes, look here. You do it in a mould with sweet and bitter almonds. Where do we get isinglass?'

'Isinglass? Have you come unhinged?' Thus began an epic exploration of blancmange, which went beyond the pages of Mrs Beeton.

Blancmange is the laughing stock of the dinner table. George & Weedon Grossmith utilised the dessert to torment Charles Pooter, the baffled hero of their 1892 masterpiece *The Diary of a Nobody.* 'November 18. I told Sarah not to bring up the BLANC-MANGE for breakfast … In spite of my instructions, that BLANC-MANGE was brought up for supper. To make things worse, there had been an attempt to disguise it, by placing it in a glass bowl with jam round it. I told Carrie, when we were alone, if that BLANC-MANGE were placed on the table again, I would walk out of the home.' Poor Mr Pooter, hounded out by a pud.

Yet the hilarity is misplaced. A properly made blancmange is an impressive and tasty dessert. Tinged with almond and lemon, it is certainly the equal of trendy pannacotta. Moreover, blancmange is endowed with a mysterious and exotic lineage. The word is obviously French – their version is *blancmanger* – and, though it arrived in medieval times, we continue to pronounce this white-food in the French manner.

Blancmange originally referred to a family of substantial medieval dishes, often, though not necessarily, sweetened and usually containing chicken or fish. They were white, but not jellified. According to *Cooking and Dining in Medieval England* by Peter Brears, the recipes all included 'rice cooked to softness, ground with almond milks and either hen or capon, or fish such as lobster, haddock, carp, dace, ray, pike, perch or tench, the whole being … a smooth paste, dished and garnished.' The pale, unresisting result would have been welcome in a pre-denture era. It seems that the French borrowed the word from the Italian *biancomangiare.* The almond element of the dish suggests an Arab origin, but regiments of food historians have tried without success to track down the provenance of blanc-mange. *The Oxford Companion to Food* hedges its bets: 'It seems likely that *blancmanger* does reflect eastern influence, but the exact source and path are obscure.'

Befitting a nation of gastronomic traditionalists, the Italians still eat a *biancomangiare* soup. Pulverised chicken breast is stirred into chicken stock thickened with cream, rice flour and fresh ground almonds. The result is garnished with strips of chicken breast, chopped dill and a few pome-granate seeds. I made this pallid broth for Mrs H and it went down a storm. 'Very good chicken soup,' she said, gazing at the steamy white pond with its gem-like archi-pelago of pomegranate. 'Very rich and creamy, with an interesting range of flavours. Rather memorable. Well worth doing again.'

Blanc-Mange (A Supper Dish)

Despite the merits of this medieval meal-in-itself, blanc-mange (at least in Britain) became identified with the familiar jelly pudding. With the exception of Charles Pooter, the Victorians could not get enough of it. Rightly ignoring Brown & Polson's dire cornflour version invented in 1854, *Mrs Beeton's Book of Household Management* (1861) included a social hierarchy of three tiers of blancmange: 'Blanc-Mange (A Supper Dish)', 'Arrowroot Blanc-Mange (An Inexpensive Supper Dish)' and 'Cheap Blanc-Mange'.

In a moment of rash extravagance, we plumped for

Blanc-Mange (A Supper Dish). Mrs B's recipe requires isinglass, obtained from the swimming bladders of fish, particularly sturgeon, to impart the requisite stiffness, but we sacrificed authenticity and went for gelatine. This is a similar jellifying agent extracted from the bones of cattle and horses. Pig skin also makes a contribution. The transmutation of such gruesome items into the pure transparency of gelatine is one of the stranger gastronomic metamorphoses. (Vegetarians may prefer to try out the carrageen moss pudding described on page 130.) Since Mrs H is an old hand with gelatine, she guided me through the mysteries of blancmange-making.

'Have you got clean hands?' The inquiry might have come from Mrs Beeton herself. (See page 988 of her *Household Management*: '"Cleanliness is next to godliness," saith the proverb.')

'No. I got them specially dirty before I came into the kitchen.'

'I didn't know that we had Mr Clever-Clever in the kitchen.'

You start Blanc-Mange (A Supper Dish) by warming a pint of milk with 'the rind of half a lemon' (we used a zester). The smell was sensational. Calculating the proportion of gelatine to liquid proved problematic, though at first it seemed straightforward. The packet contained fifteen leaves of gelatine – they are moulded with a diamond pattern like very small mullion windows – sufficient to jellify two pints of liquid. So, we needed seven and a half leaves. You chop up the little panes, then soak them and squeeze – a strange, clammy sensation that somehow hints at the organic origin of this ingredient. It was only after completing this task that one of us ('It was me,' says Mrs H) remembered that the recipe also contained one pint of cream, which is added at a later stage. 'So we have to use all fifteen leaves,' I pointed out.

'Doh!' said Mrs H.

When these had been soaked and squeezed, the flaccid gelatine was added to the lemon-infused milk. 'I generally add it in small quantities,' advised Mrs H. 'NOT A GREAT LUMP!' I reduced my speed of addition but not sufficiently. 'You're still putting in great wodges!' Mrs H said the milk should be gently warmed to ensure the gelatine dissolves. This, she added, applies particularly to gelatine in great wodges.

When the gelatine has dissolved, you add pounded almonds, which provides a pleasing link with the dish's medieval prototype. Mrs Beeton's recipe calls for both sweet and bitter almonds. You can buy the sweet ones anywhere, and we acquired the latter in a Chinese supermarket. While I was pounding them in a mortar and pestle (damned hard work – has no one thought of bringing out an electric version?), I was reminded of an expostulation frequently seen in detective yarns when the sleuth would sniff the lips of a corpse: 'The tell-tale smell of bitter almonds. Prussic acid!' This is an old term for hydrogen cyanide. Less lethally, bitter almonds also smell a bit like marzipan. The mixture of pounded bitter almonds and ordinary ground almonds was stirred into the milk. 'I want you to taste the flavour before we slowly bring it to the boil,' said Mrs H.

Never averse to sampling, I had a go. It tasted lemony and almondy. This is only what you would expect, but still rather good. 'Can you see here?' Mrs H added, a few minutes later. 'These little bubbles starting to appear – that means it's just starting to boil.'

'Ah, how interesting. I'd never associated bubbles with boiling before.' But my sarcasm was lost on Mrs H.

'They're not the big bubbles you get when something's boiling. It's *tiny* foam because it's just below boiling. If we were to bung in a thermometer it would be 200°F or something.' (Mrs H shows her age.) She then strained the mixture through a muslin-lined sieve. It emerged in a slow, reluctant stream. 'Just let it drain through.' When the trickle ceased, Mrs H picked up the edges of the muslin so it formed a sort of bag and squeezed out the last remaining drops of milk. I then measured a pint of cream and added it to the strained milk. 'Stir the mixture occasionally until nearly cold,' says Mrs Beeton.

At this point, the recipe entered my specialist area. Mrs Beeton says 'noyeau, maraschino, curaçao or any favourite liqueur, added in small proportions, very much enhances this always favourite dish'. Though we were plumb out of *crème de noyeau* (an almond liqueur), we happened to have both maraschino (a sweet cherry liqueur) and Cointreau (a variant of curaçao). Since we were using two plastic moulds – somewhat like castles though lacking in turrets – I was able to try out both forms of alcoholic enhancement.

All was going swimmingly until Mrs H picked up the

measuring jug. 'Which scale did you use for the milk and cream?'

'That one for half a pint,' I said pointing to a Plimsoll line on the side. 'I did each one twice over.'

'That measures a third of a pint,' she said icily.

'Oh. How will that affect it?'

'I don't know.'

Using two-thirds of the correct quantity of liquid certainly ensured a firm set after a few hours in the fridge. Mrs H picked up one of the moulds, inverted it over a plate and shook it to extract the blancmange. Nothing happened. She shook harder, then harder still. Vibrating in every molecule, she resembled a road-digger with an old-fashioned pneumatic drill. Even though she had taken care to lubricate the mould with almond oil before filling with blancmange mix, as Mrs Beeton suggested, the shaking was singularly unproductive. 'Hmm,' I mused. 'Mrs Beeton says, "It should come out easily."'

'Does she now?'

I took over the shaking. Nothing. Mrs H applied a knife round the side, at first delicately, which still had no effect when she shook, then she really put the knife in, which did the job. Neither of our blancmange castles was quite intact after being coaxed from their moulds, but I maintained that the slightly battered appearance added to their appeal. 'Not too bad,' said Mrs H. 'A little bit chewy. The maraschino blancmange tastes quite strong. I actually prefer the Cointreau. It complements the almond and lemon without taking over.'

Our Victorian dessert worked well when combined with a mixture of soft fruits, though Mrs H thought we had made too much blancmange. 'Two large blancmanges for two people is a bit overwhelming.' We managed to get through quite a lot of these super-strength puds before waving the *blanc* flag. Like Mr Pooter, we found it not quite so appealing on the second day. 'I think blancmange should be eaten on the day you make it,' said Mrs H. 'After that, it shrinks and gets a bit hard.' When we did it again for a dinner party, Mrs H used individual silicone moulds, which performed perfectly at the evacuation stage. Served with a sprinkling of raspberries, the little blancmanges were a huge success with our guests. 'This one is a bit less stiff on account of me putting in the right quantity of milk and cream,' she explained.

Seaside blancmange

There is only one dessert to be found in the 512 pages of Alan Davidson's book *North Atlantic Seafood*. The solitary seafaring pud utilises carrageen (*Chondrus crispus*), a handsome seaweed found particularly in the south-west of Ireland, where the village of Carragheen donated its name (though the spelling changed a bit). You can buy little packets of dried carrageen, which are usually accompanied by a sprinkling of tiny shells. One of the best things about making this dish is watching the desiccated tangles reconstitute as gorgeous fronds of cream and purple in tepid water. It is as though you were gazing into a particularly clean and wholesome rock pool. However, as we shall see, this ingredient can have a certain shock value.

Davidson's recipe is for chocolate carrageen, but I was more interested in carrageen moss pudding, which I had enjoyed at the end of a boozy lunch at Ballymaloe House, near Cork. I remember the carrageen pudding made by Myrtle Allen, doyenne of Hibernian cuisine, as a light, but distinctive blancmange. Maybe I detected a very slight maritime tinge, but, given the circs, my recollection might not be all that accurate.

You don't need much carrageen to make carrageen moss pudding. According to *Irish Traditional Cooking* by Myrtle's daughter-in-law Darina Allen, 'The success of this dish lies in using only just enough carrageen needed to get a set – so you don't taste it in the pudding.' She recommends '8 grams (1 semi-closed fistful)'. Davidson suggested 'two good handfuls', but he described the seaweed tang as 'delicious'. Of course, all this depends on the size of your fist. Mine are on the big side, so one sufficed. I suppose we put 10–12g in the tepid water.

Most recipes tell you to fish out the shells but Mrs H pooh-poohed all that: 'We're going to strain it anyway.' After ten minutes in tepid water, you recover the softened fronds and use them to jellify 900ml milk. The recipe (see page 135) is a bit of a palaver, involving simmering, sieving, adding egg yolk, leaving to cool and folding in egg white. 'It's a leisurely pudding,' observed Mrs H. 'You do something, then you go away, then you come back and do something else, then comes the worrying bit when you see if the wretched thing has set.'

While it was cooling, I tried a bit of the jellified milk. This did not go down well with Mrs H. 'I want that. I want that. That bit you've put in your mouth. There won't be any left.' My explanation that the sampling was purely for research purposes did little to mollify her. But she got even more agitated after accidentally putting her hand on a frond of softened carrageen that had escaped into the sink. 'ARGH!' If she had encountered Tennyson's monstrous Kraken ('Far, far beneath in the abysmal sea,/His ancient, dreamless, uninvaded sleep/The Kraken sleepeth'), the effect could scarcely have been more momentous. 'I did not like that. It felt all slippery, like something horrid you see at the seaside.' This is not a problem you get with Brown & Polson.

After a few hours in the fridge, the carrageen had achieved a light set. 'It doesn't exactly shimmy in the bowl but it does slither around,' said Mrs H. It was a vanilla-speckled mousse without the slightest marine taint. Darina Allen would have approved. 'Do you like it?' inquired Mrs H.

'Well, yes.'

'What's wrong?'

'I expected it to be more assertive.'

'It's very melt-in-the-mouth. There are little puffs of air in it. It's very nice and not too sweet.'

'That's all very well, but little puffs of air are not my idea of pud. I might have preferred more of a seaweed taste. We'll try that next time.'

'Who says there's going to be a next time?'

Mrs H on Mrs Beeton's blancmange

Erase any memories of childhood blancmanges; this dish turned out to be a wonderful surprise. With a subtle, grown-up taste, it has become a favourite dessert. Any berried fruit will go well with it. Use the most Victorian-looking jelly mould you can find for that impressive turreted look. You just can't pull off the same effect with a rabbit shape.

The ingredients listed will be enough to fill a 1.1litre jelly mould. You should be able to buy almond oil from a chemist or a health food shop. This oil aids the release of the blancmange from the mould. You only need a little but make sure any tricky bits are well coated. This recipe was originally based on Imperial weights, so I have included them here.

rind from ½ a large lemon (wash and scrub it well if it is
    unwaxed)
600ml milk (1 pint)
110g caster sugar (4 oz)
35g fine leaf gelatine (or enough to set 600ml/
    1 pint of liquid)
15g ground almonds (½ oz) (or a mixture of sweet and
    bitter almonds, which Mrs Beeton recommends)
600ml double cream (1 pint)
a little almond oil to lubricate the mould

There is quite a leisurely start to the recipe, so begin by taking the rind from the lemon (I use a potato peeler). Pour the milk into a saucepan, add the lemon rind and sugar and place it over a *very* low heat until the milk is well flavoured. You can have a little taste to check. Turn off the heat when you are satisfied with the taste. You should get the smell and tang of the lemon rind.

Next prepare the gelatine according to the instructions on the packet. When it has softened, add the gelatine to the milk mix, making sure it is well dissolved. Then stir in the ground almonds. (Either blanch whole almonds and vigorously pound to a paste, or purchase ready-ground almonds. Both work well.)

Returning the pan to the heat, allow the milk to just come to the boil. Then remove from the heat and strain the liquid through a fine sieve lined with muslin into a jug. (Discard the lemon rind and almond gunk.)

Add the cream and stir the mixture occasionally until it is nearly cold. Let it stand for a few minutes for the mixture to settle. Then carefully pour the mixture into the mould, which should be previously oiled with the almond oil. Avoid pouring in the sediment that has collected in the bottom of the jug (this would spoil the appearance of the blancmange with gritty-looking bits). Put the filled mould into the fridge to firm up.

When the blancmange has set, turn it out of the mould by loosening the edges a little with a knife. Then, placing your serving plate on the top of the mould, invert it, give a vigorous shake and out it should plop. The almond oil gives a glisten to the finished dish.

Mrs Beeton suggests that the flavour of the blancmange can be varied by substituting vanilla or bay leaves for the lemon and almonds. You can also add liqueurs such as Cointreau or maraschino.

Mrs H's recipe for carrageen moss pudding

This is such a surprising dish. How something that looks like a bird's nest can so quickly be transformed into a dish with a delicate sweetened hint of the sea always amazes me. It is a raw egg recipe – so you will have to miss out if you cannot eat eggs in this form. This pudding serves four to six people.

1 tablespoon dried carrageen moss
900ml whole milk
1 fresh, free-range egg
1 tablespoon caster sugar
½ teaspoon vanilla extract

Soak the carrageen in tepid water for 10 minutes. Then strain, put it into a saucepan with the milk and bring slowly to the boil. Put a lid on the saucepan and simmer the carrageen and milk for 20 minutes.

Separate the egg and place the yolk in a bowl. Add the sugar and vanilla essence and whisk together for a few seconds, then pour the milk and carrageen through a strainer on to the egg yolk mixture, whisking all the time. You will need to rub the jelly exuded by the carrageen through the strainer and beat it into the liquid. This should thicken as you beat. Test a sample for set on a saucer. It should set in a couple of minutes. If not, rub more jelly through the strainer. Finally, whisk the egg white to a good stiffness and fold it in gently. Leave the pudding to cool.

Serve chilled with soft brown sugar and cream or some kind of poached fruit compote. Rhubarb works well. Yum.

TOOLS FOR THE JOB

While I may be to blame (mostly) for the accumulation of food books that line the walls of three rooms in our house, I am relatively innocent – well, not quite so guilty – concerning the vast quantity of utensils and cutlery that fills every one of our kitchen cupboards and drawers to bursting. The spectacle of the man of the house swearing furiously, with veins sticking out on his forehead as he tries to heave open a jammed drawer, is a frequent *divertissement* in our house.

Adopting the role of Grand Inquisitor, I put Mrs H in the dock concerning our excess of equipment. 'Why do we have three woks when we rarely, if ever, eat stir-fry?'

'One arrived by default.'

'What do you mean "by default"?'

'I bought the Le Creuset wok in a mad moment. It's a bit too big and heavy for everyday use. The other one is a rather posh Chinese wok. I use it all the time, but not as a wok. I use it for steaming asparagus.'

'And the other wok?'

'I don't count that as a wok. It's more of a saucepan that looks like a wok.'

'What about that metal mallet thing for bashing out steaks? We never use it on steaks.'

'No, but we use it for beef olives.'

'When have we ever had a beef olive?'

Though she admits inheriting a gadget gene from her father, Mrs H sturdily defended her acquisitions. 'I quite like the potato ricer and the jar key for popping the lids off jars. I couldn't live without the slotted spoon, kitchen tongs, digital scales or scissors.'

'But why do we need four pairs of kitchen scissors?'

'We just do. Don't worry about it. After the stick blender, my most important gadget is a skewer. There's no better way of seeing if fish or chicken is done. Anyway, my gadgets are small. Yours are huge, like the electric meat slicer.'

'It's very useful.'

'We only got it because you brought back a ton of salami and cured meat from Italy. And you were responsible for the ice-cream maker and the food mixer and the bread maker and the espresso machine.'

'But we use all those.'

'How about the cataplana thing you brought back from Portugal?'

Well, yes, there was that. When I was on a press trip to Portugal I became obsessed with the desire to acquire a cataplana. Somewhat like a small wok but with a high, hinged lid that is clamped shut during cooking to conserve flavour, it is primarily used for *ameijoas na cataplana*, an excellent stew of pork and clams. When I tracked down a cataplana, my friend Rose Prince, who was also on the trip, predicted: 'You'll never use it.' To prove her wrong, I made *ameijoas na cataplana* the instant I returned. Admittedly, I've never used the cataplana since then, but its day will come.

'Its day will come, huh?' scoffed Mrs H. 'Just like the conical strainer you brought back from Spain to make fish soup. I'm still waiting for my first bowlful. Or the chestnut pan you brought back from France.'

'How can its day come when you chucked it out? '

'We had it for six years and you never used it once. It was purely decorative. Well, as decorative as a rusty frying pan with lots of holes can be.'

Rarely a day passes when I don't regret the loss of the chestnut pan, which you can also use for smoking mussels over a certain kind of pine needle. I feel its lack constantly. Same goes for the salamander that I saw in Languedoc. This is the somewhat fanciful name for a long-handled iron disc that you heat in the fire or on a gas ring. When warmed to red heat, it is used for caramelising the top of the dessert known as *crème catalan*. Outside the shop, I pondered endlessly over this item but was dissuaded by Mrs H. Madness. What could be more vital? I would far sooner have a salamander than our two weedy blowtorches that take an aeon to scorch a crème brûlée. Not that we ever have crème brûlée.

In truth, neither of us feels much restraint where kitchen

gadgets are concerned. We may not have a decent screw-driver in the house, but I know that somewhere (it may take a bit of finding) we have the precise implement to pit an olive, scale a sea bass, shuck an oyster, bisect a lobster, zest a lime, julienne a carrot and extract the pinbones from a trout. Though justified on the erroneous premise that the right tool will transform prowess, these items have a mysterious appeal that is not necessarily linked to practicality. This is evident from Mrs H's wish list. 'Apart from an outdoor hot tub [not strictly speaking a culinary device], I'd really like an outdoor smoker and one of those things for grilling a dozen sardines at the same time, but they're fantastically expensive. And I'd like one of those French hinged moulds for raised pies but they're even more expensive than the sardine rack.'

We may be nuts about kitchen gizmos, but there are a few we don't want. We have survived without toaster, microwave or pressure cooker. Toast seems to have more character when done under the grill. Anyway, it's im-possible to do Welsh rabbit in a toaster. Both of us are indifferent to microwaves, which are more to do with heating than with cooking. Though some people swear by pressure cookers, Mrs H has yet to recover from childhood trauma caused by one. 'My mother had one that scared the living daylights out of me, hissing away like a mad swan.' And I was put off the damn things after a depressing experience in Brittany. We were staying in a holiday cottage with our Parisian friends. One day, I spent a fortune on a free-range, organic poulet noir. Unfortunately, the cottage was not equipped with an oven (a fairly vital culinary gadget in my view), but there was a pressure cooker. A wonderfully fragrant blast of steam emerged when I released the valve. Opening the cooker, I speared the chicken with a fork and lifted it out. The bird was so tender that it tore free of the fork and fell – PLOP! – on to the floor. Our friends looked at each other: '*Cuisine rosbif!*' I recovered an untainted breast of poulet noir and took a nibble. It was utterly tasteless. All the flavour was in the steam.

There is one gadget that, above all others, manages to be irresistibly alluring (at least to foodies) but is scarcely ever used. The idea of a machine to make pasta has a powerful appeal for the food-obsessed, though there is an equally strong reason for not going through the fag of actually using it. You may just have noticed that most supermarkets carry a vast range of pasta. I once heard someone express an eternal truth concerning the pasta machine: 'The first week, you use it three times. The second week, you use it twice. The third week, you use it once. After that, it disappears into a cupboard and you go back to buying pasta from the supermarket.'

The Hirst household didn't even achieve this. We only managed to make pasta twice. The first time, Mrs H's tagliatelle resembled a collection of very short, fat, twisted twigs. They looked like Jiminy Cricket's furled umbrella. The second time, Mrs H attempted to make spinach and ricotta ravioli, which resulted in half a dozen squashed triangles of such unearthly bizarreness that I burst out laughing. Mrs H was so miffed that the pasta machines disappeared into the cupboard. Yes, the plural is intentional. Machines. We managed not to make pasta even though we have two pasta machines. Even in a household that makes a speciality of superfluous culinary equipment, this was ridiculous. Eventually, sheer weight of machinery won the case for homemade pasta. When Mrs H's dudgeon subsided, we returned to the knotty problem of spaghetti, tagliatelle, linguine etc.

8

Slower pasta

THIS IS HOW WE MANAGED to acquire two pasta machines. Mrs H bought me a pasta machine as a birthday present. 'You said you always wanted one,' she said, though I had no memory of ever making such a request. Anyway, I had one now. In its favour, the pasta machine has a pleasing heft. It gleams in a meaningful way and has a solid handle for turning. A very satisfactory gadget – as long as you actually use it. This culinary hurdy-gurdy has two functions. First, there is a stainless steel wringer whose ever-decreasing settings are used for squeezing pasta dough into sheets. Second, rollers can be fitted to cut the sheets into tagliatelle, fettuccine and, less successfully, ravioli. Soon after receiving this unexpected gift, I was given a second pasta machine, which came as an accessory with our KitchenAid food mixer. It works along the same lines as the first, except that it attaches to the drive shaft of the mixer, much like the power take-off on a tractor.

Notwithstanding this excess of pasta machines, we continued buying dried pasta. The chef Rowley Leigh is all in favour of this intransigence. 'The mystery to me is why

anybody bothers at all since the results are usually so dire,'
he wrote about homemade pasta. 'The packet stuff is
usually much better.' Moreover, buying it is a bit easier than
making it. Others have felt the same over the years. In the
eighteenth century, Naples had 280 pasta shops and many
more mobile pasta sellers. It is a shame that the Neapolitan
method of eating spaghetti in the street has died out. It
involved 'raising the strands at arm's length and gradually
lowering them into one's mouth'.

Yet, powerful, even imperative arguments for DIY pasta
have been advanced by two of the finest Italian cooks. 'In
about half an hour you can have [pasta] that has real
personality and you have the satisfaction of knowing all the
ingredients that went into it,' urges Giorgio Locatelli. 'I
promise you, once you get the feel of it, it will seem like
therapy, not a job.' Marcella Hazan goes even further. 'I
don't know of anything you can make in your kitchen that
yields such generous returns on as modest an investment of
time and effort as egg pasta.' I don't think I've encountered
a more persuasive statement in the whole of gastronomy.

Despite feeling Rowley's sceptical eye over my shoulder,
I determined to master homemade pasta. Mrs H, who had
been on a pasta-making course since the Jiminy Cricket
debacle, directed operations. The first step is to make the
dough, which involved sieving 250g of '00' (extra-fine)
pasta flour to make it even more extra fine. This is piled
in a mound in the centre of your work surface. You need
a good deal of work surface when making pasta. The
charming Italian name for this mound is *fontana di farina*

(fountain of flour). You make a well in the middle of the *fontana* and form a little lake by cracking in two eggs and the yolk from a third.

Everything was fine so far, but that was about to change. 'You're not going to like this bit,' Mrs H cackled horribly. 'You're going to go, "Urgh!"' The mixing technique involves plunging a hand into the middle of the lake in order to combine the eggs and the flour. I once saw Locatelli do it with effortless brio. He whirled his fingers a few times like a human whisk and, a moment or two later, the result was a nice, clean blob of dough. When I did it, the flour fountain exploded across the work surface, while the eggs overflowed their crater and headed for freedom. 'Looks rather like Mount Etna,' said Mrs H. This was probably accurate, since she once saw the volcano in eruption, but not very helpful. I managed to dam the yolky rivulets with flour and attempted to start making the dough, but the materials proved remarkably reluctant to combine. Very quickly, my fingers became impossibly caked with egg and flour. I went, 'Urgh!'

My advice in such circs is to use a knife (preferably blunt) to peel your fingers. In order to counter the stickiness, Marcella Hazan has a wise suggestion. (It comes as no surprise to learn she has two PhDs.) She recommends using a fork to scramble the eggs lightly and mix with the flour 'until these are no longer runny'. So do I.

Just when you have given up all hope, the eggs and flour cohere. At this point, you can start kneading. 'First spread a little flour over your work surface and put the dough in the middle,' said Mrs H. 'Use the heels of your palms to press the dough. You have to press and push so you're stretching the dough. Fold it in half from the top, then push and press again. Push, press, fold. Push, press, fold.' The chant might have come from a slave-master on a galley. Had this been the case, there would have been a spot of whip-cracking at this stage, for my efforts were regarded as inadequate. 'No, not like that,' Mrs H tutted. 'At present, you're just pressing down on the dough as if you want to push it through the table. You want to push it from the shoulders rather than the elbows – like a cat having a stretch.'

It took me a while to get the knack. What you have to do is push at the midway point of the lump with the heels of both palms – you push it away, but at the same time slightly downwards – before folding and doing it again. 'That's exactly what I said,' huffed Mrs H. 'Push, press, fold.'

In order to stretch the gluten in the flour, which makes the pasta both strong and elastic, you have to do this for at least ten minutes, which feels like half an hour. But I can see what Locatelli means by 'therapy'. In the end, it is quite satisfying. You feel you've achieved something when the dough suddenly transforms under your hands into a firm, smooth lump with a silky sheen on its surface. For the first time in years, I had learned a new skill. But you don't want to overdo the kneading. Locatelli warns that if you continue beyond this moment, 'You can break the gluten strands.' I felt no urge to keep going one second longer than necessary. When the dough is in tip-top nick, you wrap it in clingfilm and leave it to rest for an hour. (Don't leave it overnight like we did with a second batch. The pasta becomes too relaxed and badly behaved.)

At this point, you have a choice. You can either use a machine to roll out the pasta or tackle it with a vast rolling pin (thirty-two inches is the recommended length). Marcella Hazan says mastering the latter method will endow you with 'one of the most precious skills that a cook can command' and the result will have 'a succulence that no other pasta can match', but it's not simple. She devotes five pages to describing the technique. When I suggested it as a possibility to Mrs H, she rolled her eyes skyward.

We were going to use one of our pasta machines. They are somewhat less demanding than a thirty-two-inch rolling pin. After considering the matter for all of two seconds, Mrs H plumped for the electric-powered pasta roller. (If you haven't got one, you may be better off. Our friend Giorgio Alessio, who makes the best pasta I've ever tasted at his restaurant La Lanterna in Scarborough, advocates the hand-turned machine: 'It give you far more control.') You start by cutting your kneaded lump into a number of manageable pieces. Hazan suggests three times the number of eggs you have used. Though we had used three eggs, we settled for eight bits – yes, I know it should be nine – though six seemed to work OK as well. You flatten your first lump with the palm of your hand until it is about a centimetre thick and feed it into the machine at the No.1 setting. Then you fold the dough in half and feed it in again. According to the KitchenAid instruction book, this stage is repeated 'several times or until the dough is smooth and pliable'. In practice this means three or four times, or you might get fed up with the whole business.

When each lump has been squashed at the No.1 setting, you lay them on a clean tea towel with a *cordon sanitaire* between them to prevent sticking. After this, you simply push each piece through the rollers at progressively higher settings, which produce a progressive diminution of the gaps between the rollers. As we fed the yellow dough through the ever-closer rollers, it resembled first a shirt collar, then a Sixties kipper tie. Occasionally, the dough released a bubble-gum-style pop. When the dough became a silk evening scarf, at setting No.5, it was time to switch to the cutter. This works in much the same way as the roller. For our first batch, we made narrow ribbons of fettuccine. Using the palm of my hand to hold the blonde tresses as they emerged from the cutter, I felt like a hairdresser in some posh salon.

If making pasta became a worthwhile exercise at this point, it was even more persuasive after a brief simmer. Wonderfully resilient on the palate, springy and full of life, it is far superior to shop-bought pasta, whether fresh or dried. In fact, it is so staggeringly good that you pledge never to eat shop-bought pasta again (though, of course, you will). Gillian Riley is probably right when she writes, 'Freshly-made pasta has a delicate flavour and needs little more than a few chopped herbs and a knob of butter, nothing else, not even Parmesan,' though no Parmesan is a step too far for some of us.

In similar vein, Marcella Hazan warns us off coloured pasta, which 'depends for its hues on colouring agents that either communicate no flavour, and therefore have no gastronomic interest, or else impart flavour that lacks freshness'. But sometimes you have to question the dictates of even the greatest gurus. This is especially so if you happen to have a packet of squid ink in the fridge. *Tagliatelle al nero di seppia* is one of the most impressive of all pastas. I mixed the little sachet of cephalopod smokescreen with the eggs before adding to the *fontina di farina*. This startling mixture of hellish black and heavenly white is even messier than the standard *fontina*. Again, you give up all hope it will ever amalgamate but it does eventually. The resulting lump of dough resembles a granite boulder you might find on the beach. 'Lovely squidy flavour,' said Mrs H as she slurped up a strand of Bible-black tagliatelle.

After that, there was no stopping us with coloured pasta. For the green version, you substitute 50g of spinach purée for one egg yolk. As the verdant lumps of dough went into the rollers, it looked as though we were making squashed frog. When the pasta emerged from the roller at the No. 5 setting, it might have been a tie for a particularly decadent club. Red pasta was even more dramatic. This calls for 25g of beetroot purée instead of an egg yolk. The resulting ruby-red tagliatelle is the prettiest food imaginable. Though it faded to a pale pink when boiled (the green pasta is more colour-fast), it was still a most attractive morsel. Combining good looks and great taste, homemade pasta is surprisingly sensual. With the possible exception of the spaghetti scene in *The Lady and the Tramp*, I'd never previously seen pasta as sexy.

Puttanesca sauce

Even if you don't do homemade pasta, you can do home-made pasta sauce. If I may release a bee from my bonnet: NEVER BUY BOTTLED PASTA SAUCE. It is so easy, cheap and enjoyable to make that it is madness to pay money to some TV celeb for his picture on the label. Mrs H prefers the following sauce, which she humorously terms 'whore's drawers', to anything else in my culinary repertoire. The celebrated explanation of 'puttanesca' is that it was a fast cupboard sauce cooked by the prostitutes (*puttana*) of Naples prior to a night on the streets. Unfortunately, the Wikipedia entry scotches this colourful yarn. The sauce was apparently invented in the Fifties by a restaurateur called Sandro Petti on the island of Ischia. He came up with this classic in response to the request of some late-night diners: '*Facci una puttanata qualsiasi*' ('Make any kind of rubbish'). The noun '*puttanata*' means trash or rubbish. Despite this persuasive rebuttal of a carefully nutured myth, this fast, warming sauce is still pretty good if you're heading out for the night. It's best with the narrow spaghetti called spaghettini, but penne also works well. The quantities given below will feed two, rather generously.

1 clove of garlic
1 tin of anchovies in oil
about 24 Kalamata olives
1 dessertspoon capers
¼ teaspoon cayenne pepper
2 x 400g tins of good plum tomatoes
olive oil
250g spaghettini or penne

You make it in a large saucepan (or wok). Finely chop the
garlic and anchovies. Gently fry the garlic in the olive oil
poured from the tin of anchovies. When the garlic has
softened, add the chopped anchovies and fry until dissolved.
Then add the olives (de-stoning prevents subsequent
counting of stones and your partner complaining about her
unfair share), capers, cayenne, the tomatoes and a splash of
olive oil. Bring to the boil, stir, then reduce to a simmer.
Cook over a low heat, stirring occasionally, for an hour or so
(while taking on board a glass or two of Chianti). This
should have the effect of reducing and thickening the sauce.
In another pan, boil the dried pasta according to the
instructions on the packet. When cooked, drain the pasta
and put into a large bowl. Add the puttanesca sauce, mix
thoroughly and serve.

WALKING DOWN THE AISLES

A FEW YEARS AGO, the excessive nature of our food-buying habits was brought home to me by a curious incident that took place in a supermarket near our home. I was hovering round the deli counter, buying a tranche of this and a soupçon of that, when I was addressed by a young fellow behind the counter. 'Excuse me, it's my last day working here,' he announced. 'I'm off to medical school next week. Do you mind if I ask you a question?'

'Well, no, as long as it's not medical.'

'What do you do for a living?'

'I'm a journalist.'

'Oh.'

'Why do you ask?'

'Well, you come in here so often and spend so much on food that we thought ...'

'What?'

'We thought that you must be an eccentric millionaire.'

Yes, we do spend a lot of time and, worse, money in supermarkets. There isn't much alternative to supermarkets if you need to buy food in our bit of London, though there are plenty of them to choose from. I didn't spend so much time there before I met Mrs H. She remembers being bemused by my priorities. 'You would take me to a shop just to look at a jar of Mrs Adler's Old Jerusalem Gefilte Fish. They were horrid floating things that reminded me of specimens in the Path Lab at the Middlesex Hospital. I thought it was very odd.'

And here was me thinking she'd found a kindred spirit. Though we go to the supermarket as a couple, our paths diverge immediately we're inside. Mrs H is more interested in vegetables than me. 'I always follow my little routine,' she says. 'Vegetables, coffee, cat food, milk, cleaning stuff.' Well, where's the fun in that? No wonder I deviate for pleasure and excitement. My little routine goes: oysters, fish, paté, salami, olive oil, cheese, baguettes, wine. It is a banquet that Lucullus might have envied. I bet you wouldn't have found the great Roman gourmet deliberating over Whiskas and Vanish.

After following our well-worn paths like creatures in the forest, we then spend an amazing amount of time looking for each other. That bad-tempered man you've seen furiously stalking up and down the aisles is me. Curiously, Mrs H claims she does exactly the same. 'When we shop together, it takes ages,' she moans. 'I can always track you down eventually. You're either fondling wine bottles or gazing dreamily at the fish counter.'

I do occasionally venture into the veg patch at the supermarket, but Mrs H scrutinises my acquisitions with an eagle eye. 'No, you don't want them,' she said the other day.

'Yes, I do. They're only 49p.'

'We've got tons of shallots, both round ones and banana.'

'I can't spend 49p?'

'No.'

'How come you can spend £70 on a leg of ham and I can't spend 49p?'

'It wasn't £70, it was £57.'

'Well, that's all right, then.'

The whole Serrano ham, which dangled by a hoof in our loft for several months, was a somewhat unusual purchase. We don't buy legs of cured ham all the time. Mrs H bought it for a party. When we eventually tackled it, the ham was a triumph. This was due partly to its quality, but also, if I may say so, to the impressive carving of exquisitely slender rashers (you are supposed to see the knife through the slice) by the author of these words. I would particularly recommend the purchase of a whole Serrano – and the arched wooden gadget that holds it in place – for the man in the kitchen. While engaged in carving, you are briefly transformed into the patrician proprietor of one of the great Sevillian tapas bars like El Rinconcillo or Sol y Sombra, though I'm not sure that I matched their technique. Restaurant critic Terry Durack noted how the owners of the bars did the task 'holding the leg like a cello, gracefully pulling the slender knife across as if it were a bow'.

But the enhancement of my ego was not the main reason

that prompted Mrs H's Iberian investment. The ham was on sale in the cut-price supermarket Lidl, which took over the Safeway premises near us. It might not be the supermarket that we'd choose to have as a neighbour, but it is an *interesting* shop. Mrs H says it's a bit like buying food in Moscow during the Communist era. 'The way it is stocked is highly erratic. You can't rely on finding celery there.' On the other hand, there aren't many supermarkets where you can buy both bratwurst and a unicycle ('the ultimate one-wheeled fun'). I was once tempted by a soldering set. Considering the urban location of this branch, the most bizarre display was an assortment of equestrian equipment. Lidl did not manage to dispose of many horse blankets, though I noticed that the entire stock of training whips (£2.99) had sold out.

One day, while gazing at the blossom-laden elder tree in the churchyard opposite our house, it occurred to me that we were missing out on the biggest supermarket of all. Better still, it is completely free. I decided that we were going to acquire our food from the hedgerow rather than the supermarket. Farewell neon, hello sunlight. Bizarrely, Mrs H did not share my newfound passion for hunter-gathering in the wild – both the wild of North Yorkshire and the slightly less wild of suburban London. 'This hunter-gathering business sends you a bit bonkers,' she grizzled, while probing a bush for blackberries. 'We seem to have spent half the summer falling into ditches.'

There was a scintilla of truth in this outburst. Despite the concomitant stings, scratches and insect bites, foraging is an addictive occupation. Nettles lead to wild garlic, which leads to elderflowers, which lead to blackberries, which lead to hawthorn berries. After discovering how good the results are – nettle and potato soup, wild garlic mayonnaise, elder-flower cordial – you go back for more while the picking is good. Eventually you get used to the bemused glances of passers-by.

Aside from abrasions and the expenditure of much amount of time in processing the fruits of your labours, the main drawback of foraging is the astounding number of pots that result. Though picturesque, the regiment of jars turns a reasonably well-ordered kitchen into a wizard's lair, especially if you have to let them mature for seven years (the recommended maturing period for the elderberry-based Pontack sauce). Still, I'm pretty sure we'll be back in the hedgerow next year – and that's not just because it's free. Try finding nettles or wild garlic leaves in the supermarket. 'Yes, I'd go back,' Mrs H grudgingly agreed. 'But I'd prefer not to do the picking in the park on a Sunday. Wandering round in outsize Marigold gloves looks a bit odd.'

9

A bite on the wild side

Nettles

'I'll be stung to bits. They'll taste gritty and horrid and we'll be going to the lavatory for ages.' Mrs H was not all that desperate to go nettle-hunting, but this reluctance is a mystery to Italians. The food writer Anna Del Conte gives us all a ticking-off: 'It seems a sad waste that these eminently edible weeds should hardly be eaten in a country where they grow in such profusion.' Same goes for Giorgio Locatelli, who once told me about his nation's love of the nettle: 'Italians love getting something for free.'

I used the old silvery tongue to weaken my wife's intransigence. 'No, you won't be stung. Where are your kitchen gloves?'

'Why don't you go picking the wretched things if you're so keen on them?'

For that inquiry I had an answer at the end of my arms. Big hands, you see. Marigolds won't fit. And it was, of course, impossible to go picking these vindictive plants, appropriately known in Somerset as Devil's Leaf, without gloves. The nettle's defence mechanism, ingenious enough for a Bond villain, is a cocktail of poisons including formic acid, which is injected via needles made of silica. This Rosa Klebb of the botanical world wields a glass hypodermic.

Mrs H broadened her attack to the whole notion of foraging. 'Wild food! We'll end up tree hugging and painting ourselves with woad and dancing round the Rollright Stones. Anyway, I bet you can get kitchen gloves to fit even your giant mitts.' She was right, dammit, but the acquisition of my first-ever rubber gloves disproved Richard Mabey's classic text *Food for Free*. I was 75p down before I'd picked a single leaf.

Despite Mabey's observation that nettles are 'widespread and abundant', it proved rather difficult to find a patch in suburban London that met Mrs H's demanding criteria. Those at the roadside were ruled out due to the generous spicing of exhaust fumes, while park nettles were stigmatised by possible canine contributions. No wonder Giorgio Locatelli grows them in his restaurant's garden in Virginia Water, though the suggestion in his book *Made in Italy* that 'the stalks are the part with the sting' suggests that the maestro hasn't had a close encounter with a nettle leaf recently. When we eventually found a thicket of nettles in a dog-free area of our local park, Mrs H insisted on asking permission from the wardens before we started snipping, which scarcely seemed to be in the ruthless survivalist spirit of our forebears.

In the end, it was Mrs H who donned my supersized

Marigolds and did the snipping (more dextrous, don't you know), though I helped by pointing out 'the tops and the young pale green leaves' recommended by Mabey. My invaluable indication of tempting examples of *Urtica dioica* drew a volley of appropriately stinging remarks from the harvester. 'Thanks for pointing that one out. I'd never have spotted a nettle by myself. Ouch! One's got me on the leg. Can't you bring the bag a bit nearer?'

Back home, it was my turn with the rubber gloves. It is very strange to prepare a vegetable that bites back. Each leaf has to be removed from the stalks, which are so fibrous that they were once grown to make cloth. Our bag of nettles required an hour of fastidious pruning. Food for free is only for the time rich. In the course of this activity, I managed to snip a hole in one of the fingers of my new Marigolds. Dealing with this tough, ragged, very untamed plant has a curiously medieval quality. In Pamela Michael's book *Edible Wild Plants & Herbs*, we learn that they were used to treat '30 or 40 ailments of extreme diversity'. Brother Cadfael would have been big on nettles, but how did he manage without rubber gloves?

Left to soak in the kitchen sink, our haul resembled a mini Sargasso Sea. Eerily, the water turned pale pink. Nettle blood. Like our own haemoglobin, the nettle is rich in iron, which constitutes 2.3 per cent of its weight. I washed the soggy leaves two or three times to rid them of grit. Cold water steadily seeped through the hole in my glove. Eventually, the nettles matched the demanding hygiene standards of Mrs H, who regarded food found in the park with deep suspicion. But what the devil should we do with the devil's leaf now?

Most nettle recipes start by making a purée. You boil them for two or three minutes with a splash of salted water in a pan with the lid on, then drain and either purée in the food processor or use the potato masher to mash them with butter. When cooked the nettle loses its sting and darkens to British Racing Green. The result on the palate is hardly earth-shaking. According to Anna Del Conte, the flavour is 'sweet', 'delicate' and 'just discernible' in risotto. Mabey goes further, claiming nettle purée by itself is 'rather insipid – don't expect it to taste like spinach, as is sometimes suggested'. Our nettles tasted mildly herby with a slight, not displeasing metallic tang.

But when incorporated with other ingredients, the well-hidden charm of the nettle emerges. Nettle purée spread on buttered toast topped with a poached egg placated my disgruntled picker. 'What a nice taste – and the colours are lovely.' Nettle risotto, flecked with the plant's intense green, was equally pleasing, but my nettle and potato soup received an even more rapturous reception. I should point out that our substantial intake of nettles did not provoke the dire intestinal consequences predicted by Mrs H, but there was something in what she said. Mabey warns that nettle leaves become 'coarse, unpleasantly bitter and decidedly laxative' after the end of June. By Midsummer Day, you'd better dash if you want to avoid the trots.

Wild garlic

Sometimes, even keen food lovers show reluctance when foraging for certain foodstuffs. This was the case with Mrs H and wild garlic. 'Cor blimey,' she announced in her delicate, lady-like way. 'Talk about a pong. The whiff from that lot would fell an ox.' It wouldn't really, but it would taste quite nice with a bit of braised beef. 'That lot' was a bank of wild garlic in the same park where we got the nettles. Smell aside, it is rather an attractive plant – in his *Dictionary of English Plant Names*, Geoffrey Grigson says it produces 'one of the most beautiful floorings' – with strap-like, pointy leaves and balls of tiny, white, star-shaped flowers that could make an appearance in wedding bouquets, were it not for their distinctive fragrance.

This is indeed very powerful. Especially when you tread on the leaves, it is like the most garlicky dish you've ever eaten, possibly with a top-note of house gas. I remember coming across this assault on the schnoz when roaming as a child in Yorkshire. No, we didn't eat it, though the plant has a long history of adding interest to stews and salads. Its alternative name of ramsons derives from the Old English word *hramsa*. Ramsey in Essex and Ramsbottom in Lancashire were named after wild garlic.

We are so led by the nose that wild garlic smells im-possibly rank to use as a foodstuff. Yet the taste of the leaves is surprisingly delicate, exactly the tinge of garlic that ambitious cooks want to attain with cultivated garlic bulbs. Everyone who has seen Scorsese's *GoodFellas* remembers

the scene where razor-cut slivers of garlic bulb are gently
sautéd for a prison meal. The idea is that the translucent
particles melt into the oil. Apparently it was the technique
used by Scorsese's mother, but in my experience the tiny
strands always shrivel and burn before achieving deli-
quescence.

Mrs H was unpersuaded about wild garlic or ramsons.
'You can go and pick those smelly things yourself.' So I did.
I returned to the park with a plastic bag for more PYO. It
began raining heavily, a possibility that is omitted from
most accounts of foraging. This had the advantage of
removing observers who might have thought that I was
snaffling hyacinths. Fortunately, wild garlic is the easiest of
all wild plants to harvest. It is profuse and lacking in stings
and thorns. I suppose the pong is meant to repel prospective
consumers, though Pamela Michael notes that cows aren't
put off. 'The only disaster I ever experienced with ramsons,'
she writes, 'was on a farm where I worked during the war,
when the cows got into a patch and the whole day's milk
was ruined by the pungent taint of garlic.' After a minute
or two of foraging – just about the ideal length of time for
this task – I'd gathered a bulging bag of leaves. You can also
eat the flowers, stalks (a bit like chives) and bulbs of wild
garlic, though I'm not sure if you should be seen wielding
a trowel in a public park.

For canine and other reasons, it's best to give the leaves
a wipe. (Don't tell Mrs H, but I didn't bother when I found
wild garlic in the middle of a wood, miles from anywhere.)
You can use the leaves for many of the same jobs as bulb

garlic. More, in fact, because the leaves can be used as a salad or for stuffing baked fish. Richard Mabey suggests cutting them in long strips and laying them over sliced tomato. He also conveys the recommendation that they can be added to peanut butter sandwiches, though he doesn't seem to have tried that. Me neither.

The first thing I did with them was garlic bread. Here, wild garlic does the combined work of chopped bulb garlic and parsley. Mrs H admired the appearance of the garlic butter prior to spreading in the baguettes. 'How lovely.' Baked to a crisp gold in the oven, the garlic bread was a definitive version of this venerable dinner party starter. 'Rather excellent,' said Mrs H. 'None of that aggressive bite you get from garlic cloves.'

Following this success, we did no end of wild garlic dishes. It makes a very decent pesto and can be chopped into tomato sauce for pasta. Mrs H used it in a lamb casserole to impressive effect. Wild garlic risotto is outstanding. No wonder the weed has sprouted in food columns and on the menus of posh restaurants. John Gerard's *Herbal* of 1597 suggested that wild garlic 'maye very well be eaten in April and Maie with butter, of such as are of a strong constitution, and labouring men'. Not being among the latter, Mrs H obviously has a strong constitution.

With a fairly long season (Gerard was right there), there seems to be only one problem with wild garlic or ramsons. Since it is free and profuse, you tend to be a bit greedy. I picked bag after bag. We ate wild garlic with pasta, in salads, with couscous and with roast chicken. Mixing the chopped leaves with mayonnaise produces a delicate aioli. If you do the same with soft goat's cheese the result is akin to Boursin, though with a delicate green tinge. V. delish on toast. But mostly I made more and more wild garlic pesto. You can fill your fridge with jars for future use, though this may bring some pungent comments from others who share the fridge.

Elderflower

Going by appearances, few would associate Mrs H with the cocaine trade. Yet this paradigm of middle-class rectitude attracted attention in a local pharmacy by purchasing significant quantities of a substance commonly associated with the purveyors of jazz talc. In case the Metropolitan Police feels the urge to pay a surprise visit to Hirst HQ with a battering ram, I should explain that her acquisition was associated with our research into the consumption of wild plants. The plant in question was not *Erythroxylum coca*, found on the eastern slopes of the Andes, but *Sambucus nigra*, found pretty much everywhere in the UK.

In early summer, this deciduous tree advertises its presence with a gaudy display of creamy-white blooms and an olfactory trumpeting of a heady aroma variously described as 'almost Oriental' and 'muscat-like'. These are the flowers of the elder, for which, as Richard Mabey points out, 'there are probably more uses than any other species of blossom'. It was concentrated elderflower cordial that caused Mrs H to come under the eye of suspicion, but we'll come to that later.

For three weeks or so in early summer, elderflower is everywhere. It must be one of the most profuse shrubs in Britain. Our nearest elder is in the grounds of the church across the road from our house in London. This is not entirely appropriate, since the elder was the object of heathen veneration – the tree was associated with the White Goddess who enraptured Robert Graves – and was therefore anathematised by early Christians. However, it was the luxuriance of the flowery interloper, rather than its pagan significance, that prompted Steve the verger to welcome my appearance with Mrs H's florists' shears. He even offered some empty Communion wine bottles to contain the fruits of our labours.

Five minutes after setting out, I returned with a basket filled with a froth of umbels. My first production run concerned the elderflower drink eulogised by Pamela Michael: 'The best wild flower drink ever.' The first instruction in her recipe is rarely seen in cookbooks: 'Shake the flowers free of insects ...' Shaking the blooms, I felt a little like a priest wielding an aspergillum – the device used for sprinkling holy water – though my blessing failed to disperse the inhabitants. The tiny flies clung on tight and had to be dispatched by the flick of a finger. Soon I had twelve flower heads gyrating in four litres of sugary water sharpened with white wine vinegar and flecked with lemon peel. The effect of this swirling, psychedelic blur of white blossoms, was almost hypnotic. Maybe the elder's pagan reputation is not without justification. Somewhat brusquely, Mrs H roused me from my flower-induced trance.

'What are you peering at?'

'Oh, nothing.'

After twenty-four hours' steeping, I strained my potion. 'So refreshing,' said Mrs H. 'Perfect for a summer day.' After this success, I became a regular sight at the church, snipping the goddess's blooms. I made elder vinegar (I'm still waiting to find a use for this astringent infusion). We had elderflower fritters (not bad but a bit lumpy). Mrs H made elderflower and rhubarb jam. 'Very impressive if you don't mind your jam on the runny side,' she said. 'A lovely pink conserve. It would be great with ice-cream or yogurt.' Her elderflower jelly, which achieved a more resilient set, went well with pork and lamb. Before we had it as a condiment, I sneaked a spoonful and the aftertaste lingered happily for minutes afterwards.

Though very generous in supply, there is a time limit on elderflowers. They should be picked soon after the flowers open. The eighteenth-century cook John Nott wrote: 'Gather your bunches of Elder Flowers just as they are beginning to open, for that is the time of their Perfection … afterwards they grow dead and faint.' Dead and faint isn't quite right. The scent of the mature elderflower is pungent and blowsy. One horticulturalist recommends that they should be picked 'before they develop the feline fragrance of middle age'. Elderflowers are best when they have just opened and the delicately perfumed little flowers are the colour of Cornish cream. Don't bother when they have turned white and whiffy.

I was worried that I'd left it too late when I made my most expensive elderflower product. Elderflower liqueur sounds like one of those drinks made by Miss Marple types in thatched cottages. Such refreshments have the reputation of being ferociously potent and honey-sweetened elderflower liqueur is no exception. Making one bottle of elderflower liqueur requires one bottle of vodka. For some reason that eludes me now, possibly greed, I decided to make two bottles of elderflower liqueur. When I sampled it after making, the taste was worrying.

It was very stalky and powerful. Maybe even a bit feline. Pretty much undrinkable, in fact. It looked like my investment was going down the drain, but one authority recommended storing in the dark for at least two months before drinking. Two months afterwards to the day, I offered a lunchtime sample to Mrs H. 'A fantastic sweet smell like hay.' But was that just to cheer me up? 'It's a nice, straw-coloured liquid.' Then she took a sip. After swallowing, her mouth dropped open and her eyes rolled skywards. This was not because she had been poisoned. It is merely Mrs H's indication of alcoholic strength. 'It's very pleasant and fresh,' she eventually declared. 'Grassy, meadowsweet, outdoorsy – but not like a dung heap.'

'Gratifying to know.'

'Quite summer-like. It would be lovely poured over fruit.' I took a sip. Yes, it was drinkable, just about. It did seem fantastically potent, but that might have been because it was lunchtime. At a subsequent sampling, doubts began to set in. Probably due to an extended steeping of the elderflower in the vodka, it was still a bit stalky. A lot stalky, actually. Still, I pondered, it might be OK in a cocktail. After considerable experimentation, I came up with a successful application. If you ever find yourself stuck with a large quantity of rather rustic elderflower vodka, your best course is to make an elderflower caipirinha. This is quite fitting, since the national drink of Brazil is a rural potion (the name is a diminutive of *caipira*, meaning 'countryman') made with cachaça, agricultural rum. Mrs H claimed that the real caipirinha is 'slightly straw-like', so it seemed a fair bet that my rustic product would work OK. It certainly did with Mrs H. 'Don't suppose there's any chance of another?' Despite this plaudit, we still have one and a half bottles of elderflower vodka lurking in the drinks cupboard.

The greatest success we had with elderflower was a concentrated cordial. Diluted with still or fizzy water, it tasted better – or at least as good – as any of the commercially available versions and was considerably cheaper. So alluring was this quintessence of summer that we decided to make another batch. It was then that Mrs H strayed, very slightly, into the murky world of narcotics.

The recipe involves dissolving 1 kilo of sugar in a pint of boiling water and adding ten elderflower heads and a sliced lemon, along with 25g citric acid, which is required to neutralise the sugar. You just stir it well, leave for 24 hours, strain and bottle. What could be simpler? Except when

Mrs H tried buying citric acid at our local Boots she was informed that the shop didn't stock this harmless ingredient. 'Try an independent chemist,' a Boots salesperson helpfully suggested. At one of those, there was a stock of maybe thirty packets of citric acid. Returning a few days later, when we were making the second batch, Mrs H found three packets remaining. 'Why do you want it?' asked a shop assistant.

'For making elderflower cordial,' said Mrs H. 'Has everyone been making it?'

'You can use citric acid for de-scaling the kettle as well.'

'There must be a lot of de-scaling going on.'

'Well, there may be another reason …'

'What's that?' inquired Mrs H.

'Citric acid is often used for cutting cocaine. That's why Boots don't sell it.'

Blackberries

'One, two, three, four, five,' Mrs H seethed. Her fingers darted into the tangle of a blackberry bush, but she was not counting the fruits of her labours. 'I've now had five nettle stings. Whose idea was this?' I'm sorry to admit that the impetus to go brambling stemmed from a newspaper article about cutting food bills. 'Dine like a king, spend like a pauper,' urged the headline. I'm even sorrier to reveal that the author was a certain C. Hirst. 'September brings blackberries for the hunter-gatherer,' wrote this culinary tightwad. 'This most generous of wild fruits is excellent in crumble, mousse and junket, but never better than when infusing apples in a pie.'

As often transpires with the torrent of advice that pours from newspapers, my well-intentioned words, which happened to be written in the comfort of my London office, turned out to be somewhat wide of the mark when put into practice at a hedgerow in North Yorkshire. Though they looked big and tempting when we spotted the patch a few days earlier, the blackberries had been ruptured and mangled by subsequent downpours.

Moreover, they were not quite as easy to pick as a certain newspaper article suggested. 'The best ones are always just out of reach,' grizzled Mrs H, as she edged through the springy tussocks fringing the bramble. 'It's like walking on an ice floe that might conceal a crevasse. You wouldn't want to fall in.' No, indeed. A few years ago, a helicopter was called in to rescue a North Yorkshire man who had been trapped in a bramble thicket near the sea for two days. The circumstances of this strange ordeal were somewhat mysterious, since it was too early to go brambling. (It emerged that the victim, who had spent some hours in the pub prior to his misadventure, was 'known to the police'.) Despite our endeavours, which resulted in numerous abrasions and an impressive purple smear on my T-shirt, our basket remained depressingly slow to fill. Desirable fruit hung temptingly inches out of reach amid a fearsome forest of thorns. While I was brushing away a cluster of blue-arsed flies, which share the human appetite for black-berries, a gleaming new 4 x 4 drew up alongside. 'They won't be much good after that rain,' announced the driver.

'I need a machete,' I huffed.

'You need someone else to do it for you,' noted my unsought adviser, who roared off chortling at his pleasantry.

After an hour of picking and cussing, we accumulated a kilo of the world's mankiest blackberries. A second stop proved equally unsatisfactory. Displaying an imaginative morbidity that is, I'd venture, not uncommon among females, Mrs H expressed concern about treading on a hidden corpse in the long grass. We managed to increase our haul by another half kilo of equally battered fruit. But it's worth persisting with blackberries. Depending on location, some bushes ripen later than others. Two weeks later, I came across a spot that was glutted with perfect blackberries, which went into a blackberry and apple pie. Since it was on a busy path to the beach, I was puzzled that the irresistible (at least to me), glistening fruit had not been picked. The same indifference seems to apply to apples. Are children now so insulated from nature that they simply don't know that these things are edible? Or does fruit hold no appeal nowadays? How strange that scrumping has to be encouraged.

As well as being free and profuse (sometimes), wild blackberries have much to be said in their favour. They are pleasing in appearance and have an appealing subtle taste. I'm a big fan of crème de mure, the blackberry equivalent of the blackcurrant liqueur crème de cassis. Though lacking the acid tang of blackcurrants, it makes an excellent kir. Wherever you use blackberries – pies, crumbles, jellies, jams, ice cream, sorbet, sauces – an additional splash of crème de mure intensifies the flavour.

Did you know that the blackberry played a part in destroying the TV career of Fanny Cradock? She behaved intolerably to Devon housewife Gwen Troake in Esther Rantzen's 1976 TV programme *The Big Time*. Mrs Troake had won a competition to provide dinner for various bigwigs and wanted to serve duckling with bramble sauce. The belligerent Cradock snapped at this ('What's a bramble?') and everything else that poor Mrs Troake suggested. The viewing public was so offended that the mad old bat was booted off TV for good. In her *Fruit Book*, Jane Grigson says Mrs Troake's sauce goes better with puds.

Our 'runty' (Mrs H's word) blackberries went into a chutney. The bubbling purple stew of blackberry and apple looked more suited to a magician's cauldron than a sauce-pan. The result was then sieved by Mrs H, our resident sieving specialist, before being simmered with sugar. Her five hours' labour in hedgerow and kitchen produced two and a half jars of velvety goo, but it was time well spent – at least in my view.

Hawthorn

Hawthorn berries stood up to the summer storms far better than blackberries. By early September, North Yorkshire hedgerows were aflame with bright red haws. It was only after poring through literature on wild food that I realised they were edible. In my childhood, I had presumed that their main function was to serve as missiles. My father was the usual target, poor chap. However, you can also use them to make a jelly, though reviews are lukewarm. It is variously described as 'moderate' (Richard Mabey) and 'insipid without lemon juice' (Pamela Michael). Chutney appears to be the best bet. Pamela Michael says it is 'delicious with all cold meats and poultry'. We rapidly filled a large punnet with berry-laden twigs. Snip the haws from their stalks, simmer with vinegar for an hour, rub the contents through a sieve, then simmer again with spices and dried fruit. What could be easier? Except that separating a kilo of berries from their stems took us almost two hours.

'Us?' erupted Mrs H. 'You did half an ounce and spent the entire time huffing and puffing and complaining that it was fiddly women's work before packing it in.' When that task was finished, we washed the berries. Floating in the sink, the ruby-like haws reminded me of cranberries I saw being harvested by pump from flooded bogs in Massachusetts. Boiling removed the bright scarlet coats of the haws. Underneath, they were a dull khaki. The task of 'rubbing through a sieve', so easily described, was perhaps the least rewarding culinary task I've ever attempted. Five minutes rubbing the boiled berries into a sieve with a wooden spoon produced less than a teaspoon of purée.

Mrs H proved to be of sterner stuff. After pummelling away for two hours, the haws were transformed into a small pile of brown pulp. 'Cat puke,' she observed. The resulting chutney (two small jars) was a shiny brown, densely granular in texture and pleasantly tasty. You could envisage it being served with fine cheese in a posh restaurant. Only posh joints could afford the labour. While undeniably cheap, hawthorn chutney is the ultimate in Slow Food. 'Would you do them again?' I asked Mrs H.

'Never. Too much fuss.' Then she nibbled the haw condiment with a fragment of blue goat's cheese. 'Well, I might …'

Elderberry

As with elderflowers in spring, we tend to ignore the early autumnal deliveries of elderberries on hedgerows and waste ground. Though there are a host of applications – chutney, wine, ketchup, jelly, autumn pudding – most of the tart fruit tends to go down the throats of birds, particularly starlings. There was one celebrated recipe that I particularly wanted to try. A long-matured elderberry condiment called Pontack sauce is said to be particularly good with liver, though it also goes with game and pork and can be used to bolster gravies. In her book *Preserves*, Pam Corbin describes Pontack sauce as 'kitchen alchemy at its most exciting and rewarding … a secret weapon for the store cupboard that I don't like to be without'.

Its curious name derives from the Pontack's Head, the first de luxe French restaurant in London. This was established in the late seventeenth century by the owner of Château Haut-Brion. For this reason, Richard Mabey suggests that the original recipe for Pontack sauce would have been wine-based, but the cost of Haut-Brion argues against this theory. It wasn't cheap when Jonathan Swift bought a bottle for seven shillings. Today, the 2006 vintage will set you back £348. We decided to use cider vinegar, but there remained a more significant problem. Despite the extraordinary profusion of elder trees in this country – when they're in flower you see one every fifty yards along the side of the A1 – we managed to miss out on the entire crop of elderberries.

We would have picked them in at our place in Yorkshire, but due to deluges they were still dark green when it was time to travel back down south. 'Not to worry,' I said. 'I still have a secret stock down south.' I was thinking of the ecclesiastical tree in London that I plundered for elder-flowers. With berries in mind, I had been somewhat restrained when snipping the blooms. A fat lot of good it did me. The birds had got there first, blast their pecky little beaks. Eventually in the Kent countryside we came across a single bush that had escaped the attention of local starlings. The reason became evident when we tried picking the berries. The tree was at the side of the busiest byway in the Home Counties. Since there was no pavement, the traffic was obliged to detour round the pickers. Many drivers scarcely bothered. Foraging isn't always as healthy a pastime as its advocates suggest.

We ended up with a small bowl of elderberries. Mrs H undertook the somewhat involved process of making Pontack sauce. Her efforts filled a tiny bottle like the one Alice found with the label 'DRINK ME'.

'Is that it?' I said somewhat ungratefully. 'We'll have another bash next year.'

'You mean you'll have a bash next year,' said Mrs H.

Next summer, we extended our summer break in Yorkshire long enough for the elderberries to ripen. On a glorious September day, we saw a bush burdened with gleaming black bunches. Then we found another and another and another. It was a fantastic year for elderberries. Snip, snip, snip went our secateurs. Our harvest was anxiously observed by a flock of starlings perched on power lines like notes on a stave. Back in our house, Mrs H repeated that her involvement with Pontack sauce was at an end. As I've said before, it's funny how women tend not to forget.

'I did it last year,' she announced in a non-negotiable manner.

'But you only made the world's teensiest bottle.'

'Doesn't matter. It's your turn.'

Accepting the unfairness of fate's roulette, I discovered the mysteries of Pontack sauce for myself. The first step is to strip the berries from their fronds. This is not too hard (you use the tines of a dinner fork) as long as you do it outside so the carpet does not gain an archipelago of elderberry blotches. You wash the result, place in a non-reactive container, cover with cider vinegar and leave overnight in an oven at the lowest temperature. In the morning, you strain the marinade through a sieve, mashing the berries with a wooden spoon. The deep maroon extract is more dye than foodstuff. This is simmered with chopped shallots, ginger root and spices for half an hour. Pam Corbin suggests 'perhaps muttering some magic charm while you watch over the dark, bubbling potion'.

'It *does* look like a witch's brew,' said Mrs H. 'Have you done any incantations over it?'

'No, I haven't done any bloody incantations over it.' The one thing I could do without at this stage was humorous comments from non-participants.

After straining again, the murky juice is given a final boil for five minutes, then poured into the empty vinegar bottles, which you have washed, de-labelled, washed again with very hot water and dried in a hot oven to sterilise. In recipes for Pontack sauce, no one mentions the phenomenal amount of washing up involved. Even Sisyphus would find it a bit repetitive.

Mrs H lolled reading on the sofa with the cat on her lap while I strained and washed and huffed and puffed. 'Funny,' she remarked. 'Our usual positions are reversed. You usually sit reading books while I scurry round. How do you like it?'

'Bah!'

'Look, you've frightened the cat.'

My production of Pontack sauce had a final sting in the tail. As I mentioned earlier, it has to be matured before use. Seven years is the traditional period, though Pam Corbin admitted she was 'hard pushed to keep it for seven months'. We tried a spoonful of the tiny bottle that Mrs H made last year. It had become much thicker.

'Crikey!' she said. 'Looks like cough mixture. It tastes

a bit like Worcester sauce. Spicy and tart, but it's got potential.'

Beef gravy enriched with immature Pontack sauce was transformed into something fruity, spicy and rich. 'Rather good,' said Mrs H. 'Nice and Christmassy. I think it's the cloves. It will be brilliant with game.'

Touch wood, it will continue to improve as the years go by. Since I made three litres, we should be able to test this out. As long as I can remember where I put it.

Mushrooms

Mushrooms take up the lion's share of the space in most books on wild food, but in my experience they are not all that easy to find. They are not as profuse as blackberries and do not advertise their presence with the same gaudy display as the elderflower. But this was not the reason that Mrs H resisted my proposal of a wild mushroom hunt. 'Do we have to?' she wailed. 'I've grown quite attached to my liver. I don't want to risk it by eating deathcap.' Pooh-poohing this trifling objection, I loaded the car with penknife, trug, Edmund Garnweidner's *Mushrooms & Toadstools of Britain & Europe* and Mrs H. Though mushroom foraging may have become a popular hobby in the foodie community, our search surprised the genial rustics of Surrey.

'Searchin' for your breakfast?' barked a plum-faced cove from his Jag.

'How lucky you are knowing about mushrooms,' said a

svelte equestrienne. This was some way from the truth, but I do know one or two. After peering at any number of stones, decaying golf balls and other less savoury items, we eventually filled the trug with examples of three unambiguous mushrooms. The Parasol mushroom looks exactly like one of those fashion accessories that appear on the Quality Street tin, while the Penny Bun (the same as the prized Italian porcini) has a close resemblance to the tiny, tasteless rolls that once accompanied soup in restaurants. I yelped like a prospector finding a nugget when we came across one of these mycological treasures, though it had already been extensively nibbled. I took this as confirmation of wholesomeness.

No one would have trouble identifying a Giant Puffball, described by Antonio Carluccio as 'one of the most rewarding as well as the most distinctive' species. In his book *A Passion for Mushrooms*, the great man is pictured carrying several dozen of these monsters. He even found a supermarket basket to carry them home. We found just the one. Though small, it was perfectly oval and gratifyingly heavy.

Back home, I was put in charge of cooking our mushroom feast. 'I'm having nothing to do with them,' declared Mrs H. This was just as well, since a host of wriggling forest fauna fell from the deep gills of the Parasols. Cooked in the manner prescribed by Carluccio – sliced, dipped in beaten egg then breadcrumbs and fried in olive oil – they were light, delicate and juicy. The sautéd Penny Bun was even better, a fungal triumph. For the highlight of our feast,

I decided to fry the Giant Puffball in garlic butter. But when I started slicing it up, I got a surprise. Instead of the pure white flesh I was expecting, it was filled with a stiff, translucent jelly. In the middle, a pale, glaucomatous eye stared back at me. It was my most disturbing encounter with any vegetable life form.

'Come and look at this,' I said to Mrs H.

When she had recovered, we tracked the thing down in the pages of Roger Phillips's pictorial book *Mushrooms*. 'The outer wall of the egg is white to pinkish but there is a thick, gelatinous middle layer held between the membranous inner and outer layers.' I had picked an immature stinkhorn, more graphically described by its Latin name, *Phallus impudicus*. When adult, it would assume its distinctive anthropomorphism and emit 'a strong, sickly offensive smell which attracts flies from large distances'. But this one wasn't going to get the chance to be Lord of the Flies. Despite Phillips's less-than-tempting note, 'The egg stage, which lacks the disgusting smell, is edible though not tasty,' it went in the bin. As the thing stared blankly back at me, I felt like John Hurt. I had brought home the Alien. Oddly enough, Mrs H has preferred to gather her mushrooms in the supermarket since then.

Mrs H's recipe for wild blackberry chutney

This recipe follows a traditional chutney formula and is based on a recipe in Pamela Michael's *Edible Wild Plants & Herbs*. However, because wild blackberries are quite pippy, the chutney is sieved – producing a smooth and glossy product. Pamela Michael recommends this chutney spread thinly in a ham sandwich and she is right. So chuck away the Branston and try this. It is also rather good with game.

Remember to inspect the fruit for spiders or little wormy things that may be lurking. They usually float out after you wash the fruit. The best pan to use for chutney is a preserving pan, as the size allows the necessary evaporation to take place, but a stockpot large enough to take all the ingredients will do.

The test for the 'done-ness' of a chutney occurs when you can pull a wooden spoon across the base of the pan and the chutney momentarily remains where it is (think of Moses parting the Red Sea). Finally, if you wish to use a lid to seal the chutney, it is worth investing in a supply of new ones. The vinegar in chutney can easily eat into the seal if old lids are used.

1.5kg blackberries gathered from the hedgerow
500g onions
500g apples (Bramleys are recommended – if you're using windfall apples, you'll need 1kg because of the brown bits)
1 teaspoon sea salt
1 teaspoon powdered mustard
1 teaspoon ground ginger
1 teaspoon ground mace
¼ teaspoon cayenne pepper
1 litre cider vinegar (I prefer this to malt)
500g soft brown sugar

I always start making jams, marmalade and chutneys with the ritual of washing and warming the glass jars. So wash six to eight jars in hot soapy water and dry in an oven at 70°C. Wash and de-stalk the blackberries, keeping an eye out for any unbidden wildlife and rejecting any runty, unripe or over-ripe fruit. Leave the fruit to drain in a colander. Onions and apples are next: de-skin the onions and peel and core the apples. Chop both into small pieces and place in a large pan along with the salt, spices and blackberries. Finally, add the vinegar. Bring everything to the boil, then turn the heat down and cook gently for around an hour, stirring the chutney occasionally.

Remove the pan from the stove and let the chutney cool a little. Then rub the mixture through a fine sieve or a mouli food mill. Return the blended mix to the pan and add the sugar, heating slowly and stirring the chutney until the sugar is fully dissolved. Now bring the chutney to the boil and cook for 10–15 minutes, or until the chutney is done (see test above).

Pour the chutney into the clean warm jars right up to the rim. Place a waxed disc on the top and either seal with the cellophane and rubber band method or use a new bought lid when the chutney is cold.

Mrs H's recipe for nettle soup

Strip the leaves from the stalks and wash thoroughly. Use kitchen gloves. (Special note in case gentlemen make excuses: yellow rubber gloves in large sizes are widely available.) Fill a saucepan with nettle leaves and add 100ml salted water. Cover the pan and bring the water to the boil for 2 minutes. Then, using a tea towel, hold the lid on to the pan and shake. Return to boil for another minute when the nettles should be wilted. Pour off the water. Add a knob of butter and mash the nettles with a potato masher until pureéd. The rest is a doddle, since it follows the customary way of making soup. I prefer using a stick blender for soups. Soups containing potato can go gluey if you whizz them up in a food processor. This should serve four to six people.

1 onion, finely chopped
50g butter
4 tablespoons nettle purée (prepared as described above)
1 litre chicken stock
1 floury potato such as King Edward, peeled, roughly
　　chopped and washed
salt and pepper
1 tablespoon crème fraîche or double cream
freshly grated nutmeg

Start by gently frying the onion in the butter until transparent and slightly browning, then stir in the nettle purée. Now add the stock and the potato. Simmer until the potato is soft, then liquidise with a stick blender. I prefer to do this briefly so the soup is slightly grainy, but you may like to do it longer for a smoother soup. Finally, season the soup to taste and pour into bowls. Swirl in a dollop of cream or crème fraîche and add a little grated nutmeg to each bowl before serving.

Mrs H's recipe for Pontack sauce

We have high hopes for this sauce. It seems to be a versatile product that can accompany pork, liver, duck and game and can impart flavour to casseroles and gravies. This recipe makes about 1 litre and if you have a small kitchen, open the windows when you reach the boiling stage – the vapours can be eye-watering.

750g elderberries
750ml cider vinegar or red wine (something more
    modestly priced than Château Haut-Brion)
300g shallots, finely chopped
1 teaspoon salt
1 heaped tablespoon black peppercorns
12 whole cloves
4 allspice berries
1 blade of mace
20g root ginger, peeled and finely chopped

After spending a happy hour or two separating the elderberries from their stalks with a fork, give them a good wash and place them in a casserole or large dish with a lid. Pour the vinegar (or wine) over the berries. Cover and leave overnight in a low oven (130°C/Gas Mark ½). The following day, strain the berries through a sieve, pressing with a wooden spoon to extract the maximum juice from the fruits.

Put the juice into a pan with the shallots, salt, peppercorns, spices and ginger. Bring the sauce gently to the boil, then turn down and simmer for 20–30 minutes to reduce the sauce a little.

Remove the pan from the heat and again strain the sauce through a sieve and return to the boil, this time for 5–10 minutes, by which time the sauce should have thickened more. Pour it into a sterilised bottle or jar with a lid and leave it to mature for as long as possible. The prescribed period is seven years, though twelve months can produce a good sauce.

WHINING AND DINING

WE MAY ARGUE OVER AUBERGINES, squabble about shallots and cross swords over cucumbers, but there is one culinary area where peace and harmony reign. We scarcely ever have a heated debate about where we are going out to eat. That's because we don't go eating out …

'Whoa, hold it there,' chips in Mrs H. 'You eat out all the time.'

'I certainly do not.'

'What about you going to Corrigan's last Thursday? Or Café Anglais the week before? And you're never away from St John or the Blue Print. You roll home from lunch in Moro and say, "Have we to have a light supper?" It's usually when I'm absolutely starving.'

'Well, you go out as well.'

'I go to a little Turkish place in Waterloo at Christmas with friends from work. I don't call that incessant going out.'

Anyway, as I was saying, we don't go eating out together as much as we once did. After our early days eating at Poon's, our taste for Chinese meals declined to a once-a-year visit to Chinatown. Same applies to Indian food. We never have takeaways. It seems insane to have an expensive meal made for you when your kitchen cupboards are crammed to overflowing with comestibles.

'I used to like doner kebabs from that place in Croydon,' Mrs H mused wistfully.

'That was before I entered your life. How come you can never remember me taking you out?'

'I do remember you taking me out. You used to buy me a hotdog at Ikea when we were buying stuff for the kitchen. It cost 50p. Wow, how generous. And you'd bite the end off my frankfurter and try and convince me that that was how they came.'

'You believed me as well.'

'I couldn't believe anyone would be so greedy. Why did you do it?'

'Because I like the ends.'

'You like the bit in the middle as well. I'm surprised I got any sausage at all, Mr G. Guts!'

There is, however, one fast-food chain that we have consistently patronised over the years. We used to visit our local Pizza Express after attending a film club that briefly flourished in our area. A pizza and a bottle of Montepulciano was the ideal accompaniment when we discussed *The Seventh Seal* or *À Bout de Souffle* in an earnest, roll-neck jumper sort of way. It went particularly well with *L'Avventura*, *Rocco and His Brothers* and *La Dolce Vita*. We were usually the only people in there and the manageress smiled benignly at her late arrivals as they tucked into a

Four Seasons (me) and a Margherita (Mrs H). We carried on eating there most weeks even though the film club packed up (there is not a big audience down our way for art house cinema, though a dozen turned up for *Belle de Jour*). The main reason was that, like the doner kebab, pizza is a tricky dish to do at home.

Two things made me change my mind about trying to do pizza myself. The first was a revelatory trip to Naples, where we discovered just how stupendous this simple snack could be. 'They are melt-in-the-mouth pizzas,' announced Mrs H after we dined at Da Michele, a Neapolitan shrine to the purist pizza. The second was a nudging remark in the entry on pizza in *The Oxford Companion to Italian Food* by Gillian Riley. Together they started us on the long, hot road to Margheritaville.

10

Pizza excess

'WHY CAN'T WE JUST GO OUT FOR ONE?' said Mrs H when I announced my decision to make pizza at home. 'I suppose I'd better join in or the kitchen will never be usable again.' Her reluctant acquiescence turned to horrified anguish when I added that, in a rash moment of over-confidence, I had asked Pasquale Speziano, the Naples-born chef of Pizza Rustica in Richmond, Surrey, which topped the pizza section in *Restaurant* magazine's 'UK Best Dishes Awards', to assay the results of our heated endeavours. He was visiting Hirst HQ in five days' time.

'You *haven't!*' gasped Mrs H.

But I had. Mrs H was about to receive daily pizza deliveries without even having to pick up the phone.

In case you've ever wondered, the consequence of eating twenty-odd pizzas in five days is a slight but persistent groaning. Our weird diet was inspired by a comment in *The Oxford Companion to Italian Food*. Gillian Riley's entry on pizza, 'a flattened lump of bread dough, usually round, flavoured with whatever comes to hand', concludes with a wagging finger in the direction of her slothful compatriots.

While admitting that pizza should 'really be cooked by professionals in a wood-fired oven', she adds that the dish is 'so easy and cheap to make at home that sending out for a far-from-cheap imitation of the real thing is something to think twice about.'

I have never been tempted to have a pizza from a delivery chain and can count on the fingers of one hand the number of supermarket pizzas that have entered our house. (I grew up in a pre-pizza era that must seem as distant as silent films to the young of today.) Until my recent spell of pizza madness, we have always gone out to eat pizza. This is because my previous attempt at homemade pizza was not, to be brutally honest, a great success. Believing that it might be possible to short-circuit the tedious, messy business of dough-making, I bought a pizza base manufactured by the Napolina food company. Though not quite a genuine homemade pizza, Napolina declared it to be *produtto in Italia*', so I had high hopes.

It was also my first chance to use the pizza stone that came with our Fisher & Paykel oven. Like the oven, it had travelled all the way from New Zealand, so it seemed a shame not to use it. The stone had been in the oven at max (around 300°C) for an hour before I slid on my virtually homemade pizza, coated with tomato purée and dotted with sliced mozzarella. Five minutes later, I presented it to Mrs H. It looked fairly plausible, even if its perfect circularity gave away its factory origin. 'Er …' said Mrs H, after taking her first nibble of my construction. 'It tastes like a digestive biscuit and the topping is completely wrong.

Can we throw it away?' Not all food made in Italy is wonderful.

But that was not the end of the disaster. On the following day, Mrs H asked: 'Did you damp the pizza stone and heat it up very slowly the first time you used it?'

'Eh?'

'You have to prove it so it won't crack.'

'Of course it won't crack,' I said, lifting the much-travelled stone out of the oven. It snapped in two in my hands, again very much like a digestive biscuit. 'I suppose you'd like another?'

'Yes.'

'You know the pizza stone came from New Zealand? It won't be cheap. Are you sure?'

'Yes.'

For my return bout with pizza, I was going to make proper dough and an authentic topping. I also planned to be a bit more careful when heating the replacement stone, which cost in the vicinity of £90. Even so, 'heating' is the operative word when making pizza. You've got to achieve an inferno to make this dish from the land of Dante. When the American food writer Jeffrey Steingarten tried to make the perfect pizza, he was stymied by his oven thermostat, which restricted the temperature to 260°C. His solution was to freeze wet paper towels, which he then wrapped around his oven's heat sensor. 'My oven, believing incorrectly that its temperature was near freezing point, went full blast until thick waves of smoke billowed from every crack, vent and pore,' reported Steingarten in his book *It Must've Been Something I Ate*. 'Inside the oven was a blackened disc of dough pocked with puddles of flaming cheese. I had succeeded beyond all expectations.'

The reason that Steingarten induced his oven to an unfeasible temperature is that he was trying to bake a Neapolitan-style pizza, which requires an oven surface temperature of at least 485°C. Heston Blumenthal's attempt to make the perfect pizza for his book and TV series *In Search of Perfection* was scuppered by his Gaggenau cooker, which threw in the towel at a mere 370°C. His solution was to 'preheat a cast-iron frying pan over a high heat for at least twenty minutes', while simultaneously 'preheating a grill to the highest possible temperature'. He cooked his 'perfect pizza' on the inverted frying pan, which was placed under the grill for ninety seconds. This arrangement sounded more than a little risky to me. Having destroyed my wife's pizza stone in my first endeavour, I didn't fancy destroying our house in my second.

On the other hand, I can understand the motivation behind the unhinged experiments of Steingarten and Blumenthal. It was at Da Michele (1–3 Via Cesare Sersale, Naples) that I ate the best pizza of my life. A hellishly hot, wood-fired stove occupies a good chunk of the white-tiled premises. During Heston Blumenthal's visit to Da Michele (we pizza researchers tend to follow the same well-trodden route), his industrial thermometer merely registered 'Error' when he tried to take the temperature of the oven. It gave up the ghost because the heat topped 500°C. Whipped out after about three or four minutes, my Margherita had an undulating surface like a good Yorkshire pudding. The nodule-like uplands of this landscape were slightly carbonised by the intense heat of the oven, while the valleys were relatively soft. It was the contrasting textures of this miraculously light pizza, along with the sparse, though richly flavoured topping of puréed San Marzano tomatoes (grown in the volcanic Neapolitan soil, they have no peer for flavour) dotted with basil and molten mozzarella that produced such a sublime result.

In fact, it was so good that I followed the example of the gent seated opposite me and ordered a second pizza. This time I went for a Marinara with a topping of tomato purée, sliced garlic, dried oregano and a few anchovy fillets. Having consumed this equally transcendental treat, I stopped ordering pizzas since I had consumed almost the entire menu of Da Michele. With exemplary restraint, it only does three kinds of pizza. Ever since my visit, I have had mild regrets about not having the third type, the folded Margherita or Marinara called calzone (trouser leg), but I'll be back.

During my pizza-making odyssey, I followed Da Michele's example and made nothing but the Marinara (alleged to have sustained Neapolitan mariners on their voyages) and the Margherita (named after the Italian queen who tucked into one in Naples in 1889, a brave snack since the city was racked by cholera at the time). In his introduction to Nikko Amandonico's book *La Pizza*, Ian Thomson insists: 'These [two] are the only authentic pizzas. Everything else is dross.' (Amandonico does not agree or it would have been a very slim volume.)

For our pizza, Mrs H made a dough from reconstituted dried yeast, organic Italian '00' flour (soft and low in fibre), salt and warm water. Left to ferment for an hour, it obligingly rose to twice its size. Mrs H then kneaded it again and left it to rise for a further fifteen minutes. Now came the moment when the ball of dough was transformed into a pizza base. I rolled it out with a rolling pin, turning frequently, though any *pizzaiolo* worth his salt would use his fingers. Perversely, the dough contracted slightly after being rolled, as if shrinking from its fiery fate. Eventually, the slender disc assumed an acceptable shape, like a wonky circle drawn by a toddler.

For the Marinara topping, Mrs H drained a tin of tomatoes, which she pulverised by squeezing. The resulting fragments were distributed over the pizza base. I added a sprinkling of dried oregano, the magical savoury of pizza cuisine, along with a pinch of salt and an anointment of olive oil. The oven containing our new (and proved) pizza stone had been preheated for an hour at its maximum temperature of 300°C and I induced further heat by switching on the oven fan. Using a short-handled pizza shovel, I carefully edged the raw pizza on to the hot stone. Eight minutes later, we nibbled the result. It looked OK, though the crust was cooked to a dark brown. 'Hmm,' said Mrs H, crunching the crisp circumference. 'It looks a bit like a water biscuit.' Yes, it would have been quite a good water biscuit. Unfortunately, it was quite a bad pizza.

On the following day, we went back to the drawing board – or, rather, the nearest Italian deli. We bought a type of Italian '00' flour called Cuor d'Italia made specifically for pizzas, buffalo milk mozzarella, some La Fiammante tinned tomatoes (we were assured that they were akin to the legendary San Marzano), fresh basil and fresh oregano. We also bought a chunk of fresh yeast that smelled like the pub of your dreams. Though not precisely circular – its shape was closer to the Iberian peninsula – our second pizza looked marginally better than No.1 when it came out of the electric oven. This time, the outer crust was a mid-tan, but the base proved to be a bit doughy in the middle. Moreover, the Margherita topping – tomato and mozzarella with a few basil leaves to complete the Italian *tricolore* – displayed a dismaying tendency to slide off the pizza when I lifted it to my mouth. 'I don't remember this happening when I've had pizzas in restaurants,' I said morosely.

'The dough is a bit thicker this time,' Mrs H pointed out. 'I don't think you cooked it enough. There don't seem to be any air bubbles in the base.' More experimentation was called for. We made pizzas with fresh and dried yeast, with buffalo and cows' milk mozzarella (various authorities recommend both kinds), with olive oil in the dough and without, with fresh oregano and dried, with tinned tomatoes, fresh cherry tomatoes and a costly tomato sauce made by the Cipriani company of Harry's Bar fame. Slowly, I gained the knack of making dough (the dough hook on our food mixer helped no end). My topping technique also steadily improved. The pizzette recipe from Giorgio Locatelli's book *Made in Italy* was particularly successful. Topped with the anchovy sauce known as bagna cauda and sliced cherry tomatoes, the mini pizzas swelled up nicely in the oven. 'Absolutely delicious,' said Mrs H. 'But it's more like a crisp Roman pizza than a soft Naples one.' Was lack of heat the problem?

At this point, I decided that it was time to play my trump card. Sitting in our garden is a small wood-fired oven. Made of terracotta, it is called a Beehive. Though not quite the brick stove stipulated by the Associazione Verace Pizza Napoletana, it has been known to produce fairly impressive temperatures. For our next attempt, I got a good blaze going in the Beehive with two bags of logs. While the heat was building to a Vesuvian level, I wielded the rolling pin on my pizza base (shape: Tasmania) and dotted it with halved cherry tomatoes, snipped mozzarella and a splat of oil. When the wood had converted to white ash, I scraped it to one side of the stove. Using a pizza shovel, I introduced my classy-looking pizza on to the floor of the stove with a flashy élan that any Neapolitan *pizzaiolo* might have envied. Everything was going fine until I tried extracting my pizza from the Beehive. One edge brushed against some hot charcoal and burst into flames.

With much huffing and puffing, I managed to quell the blaze. Despite extensive charring round its periphery, the centre of the pizza seemed strangely undercooked. 'I don't think the mozzarella has melted,' said Mrs H, while prodding the tepid cheese.

'Yes, I know that.'

'The dough is not quite cooked under the tomatoes. Do we need to get the heat up?'

'I've been trying to get the heat up, darling,' I said through gritted teeth.

'I wonder if the logs were damp?' Cursing somewhat, I packed the stove with logs carefully selected for irreproachable dryness. This time, it became far hotter, though still nowhere near the incandescence of the hearth in Da Michele. A second pizza (shape: Antarctica) with a Marinara topping fared somewhat better, producing the requisite slightly charred nodules and an undulating base. 'That's a bit more like it,' said Mrs H.

Since Britain's top pizza chef was coming round on the following day, I dashed back to the deli for more supplies. It was not a time for economies. We cleared the entire stock of '00' pizza flour, along with another six tins of La Fiammante tomatoes and six buffalo milk mozzarella (it seemed to work better than cow's milk). In order to guarantee combustion, we bought a small forest of kiln-dried logs from a specialist supplier. In the evening, we drove round to Pizza Rustica in Richmond to taste Pasquale Speziano's prize-winning pizza. Though it was the champ's night off, his deputy's effort was very impressive. 'It's got a lovely texture,' said Mrs H, who, considering the monotony of her recent diet, munched her Margherita with surprising enthusiasm. 'The edges are nice and springy like the pizza we had in Naples.' Peering round the small, open kitchen, I was astonished to find no wood-burning stove. Deaf to the requirements of the Neapolitan pizza, the Richmond authorities had refused to allow a wood oven in the restaurant. The best pizza in the UK had been cooked by electricity.

For Pasquale Speziano's sampling, we decided to make pizzas cooked with both electricity and wood. Prior to his arrival, I loaded the Beehive with logs with the fury of a stoker on an Atlantic liner racing for the Blue Riband. My luxury, kiln-dried wood produced a rather scary heat. Smoke seeped from fissures in the Beehive. Even Steingarten would have been impressed. I was just welcoming the pizza judge into our house when I heard a curious whooping from Mrs H in the garden. Dashing to investigate this alarm call, I found her playing a hose over the Beehive, which was swathed in billows of black smoke. The heat required for the Neapolitan pizza had proved too much for the wooden base supplied with the oven. 'I've remembered why we stopped using it,' said my dripping partner. 'The base caught fire once before.' When the smoke had been quenched apart from a few tenacious eddies, we continued cooking.

Pasquale was elegant, polite and generous. 'Is very good,' said this prince of the pizza when he tried our wood-fired version, which emerged from a somewhat less intense heat than we intended. The pizza from our electric oven drew similar plaudits. 'Very nice.' Pasquale said, 'It is not necessary to use a wood-fired stove for a good pizza.' The dough was the important part, particularly what he charmingly referred to as 'the levitation'. He did not need much urging to give a practical demonstration. In fact, it was impossible to stop him. He whirled a handful or two of flour with a fingernail-sized bit of yeast, a splash of warm water, a dash of olive oil ('Because your London water is too hard!') and a pinch of salt in a bowl. After furious pummelling at blurry speed, a ball of dough magically appeared. More water, more pummelling and the ball of dough was left in its bowl under a damp cloth for about twenty minutes. He then kneaded the expanded dough for a minute, made it into a sphere again and covered it for a further twenty minutes. 'The more levitation you have, the quicker it cooks and the lighter your pizza.'

Instead of using a rolling pin to make the base, Pasquale spread the dough by hand in the prescribed manner of the Associazione Verace Pizza Napoletana. After a few moments of aerial whirling, the pizza base was magically formed. The result was almost perfectly circular. Pasquale pressed his knuckles gently around the circumference to form a raised crust, known as the *cornicione*. 'The shape doesn't matter,' said Pasquale reassuringly as he installed a Margherita topping at lightning speed. 'It's the taste that counts.' His pizza was light, springy and exceedingly edible. 'I have a Margherita for lunch most days,' said Pasquale. And on other days? 'I have a Margherita with a salad on top.'

Though we could not match Pasquale's masterpiece, our pizzas were better than most I've had from pizzerias in Britain. If you can find a deli that stocks the wonderfully silky '00' pizza flour and good tinned tomatoes, you don't need Neapolitan heat to make a quite acceptable pizza. It is a bit more trouble than dialling for a takeaway, but the sight of a homemade pizza, fragrant and steaming from the oven, is considerably more magical than something that arrives on the back of a moped. It transforms a humdrum snack into a thrilling event. We will be making more pizzas, though not on our new pizza stone. I managed to crack that one as well.

Basic pizza dough

This is a recipe where you use your kitchen worktop for making the pizza dough. It makes four medium-sized pizzas. Using an Italian '00' flour manufactured especially for pizzas will give you a dough with a super-smooth texture. It has a fine grind and high gluten content (12–14 per cent protein) and should be available from a good Italian delicatessen. The local Italian deli where we buy the flour also sells fresh yeast, which I prefer to dried (I think it has a faster fermentation). Heat is everything for a pizza – so crank up your oven to its highest point and if you use a pizza stone make sure you prove it beforehand, according to the instructions.

15g fresh yeast
1 teaspoon granulated sugar
250ml lukewarm water
1 tablespoon olive oil
500g Italian pizza flour Tipo '00'
½ teaspoon sea salt

Set your oven temperature as high as it will go (250°C plus, if you can get it).

Start making the pizza dough by first taking a small bowl and mixing the fresh yeast and sugar together until it liquifies, then adding the warm water and olive oil. Put it aside for a few minutes in order to set the fermentation process off. (If using dried yeast, follow the instructions on the packet or tin.) While you are waiting for the lovely yeasty smells to perfume your kitchen, sieve the flour and salt on to a clean work surface. Form it into a mound and make a well in the middle big enough to hold the liquid yeast.

When it is ready, pour the yeasty mix into the well in the flour and either using your hands or a fork bring the flour gradually in from the sides. I quite like using my hands – using a twisty, swirling motion with my fingers – rather like opening a door handle. If using the fork method, finish off by using your hands when the mixture starts to come together (you can dust them to prevent too much sticking). Knead the dough fairly vigorously with both hands, using a stretch and fold method (good exercise for your shoulders) until you have a soft springy dough.

Transfer the dough into a large bowl. Sprinkle a little flour over the top to prevent a crust forming and cover the bowl with a damp tea towel. Leave the dough in a warm place until it has doubled in size. If the temperature is right this should take about 1–2 hours.

When the dough is nicely risen, remove it to a flour-dusted surface and knead it a little more to push the air out (2 minutes). Then divide it up into four small balls and roll, using a rolling pin, or hand form (better because it stretches the gluten) the pizza into a roughly circular shape about 0.5cm thick. Now is the time to turn to your topping. The two simplest – and best – follow.

Pizza Margherita

1 x 400g tin of good plum tomatoes (San Marzano
   tomatoes work best)
5–6 slices of fresh mozzarella (preferably buffalo)
a handful of fresh basil leaves
sea salt and black pepper
olive oil
pizza base (see above)

Preheat your oven as high as it will go. Prove your pizza
stone by dampening it with a wet cloth and placing it in the
oven. (If you haven't a pizza stone, just use an oven tray,
though there is no need to preheat it.)

Drain the tin of tomatoes and crush them with your
hand. Slice the mozzarella and tear the basil leaves.

Assemble the pizza in the following order: spread the
crushed drained tomatoes over the pizza base; arrange the
sliced mozzarella over the tomatoes; top with a scattering of
basil leaves, a scrunch of sea salt and black pepper and a
drizzle of olive oil.

Slide the pizza on to the pizza stone (or oven tray) and
bake in the oven until the cheese has melted, the edges are
golden and the base has crisped up. Add more olive oil and
basil before serving.

Tip: dusting your work surface and the pizza stone with
semolina acts as a non-stick agent and makes transferring
the pizza easier.

Pizza Marinara

1 x 400g tin of good plum tomatoes (San Marzano
    tomatoes work best)
1 clove of garlic, finely chopped
1 teaspoon fresh oregano leaves, roughly chopped or
    ½ teaspoon dried oregano
salt
4 anchovy fillets
2 tablespoons extra virgin olive oil
pizza base (see above)

Preheat your oven as high as it will go and spread the
crushed tomatoes on the pizza base as described in the
previous recipe. Scatter with chopped garlic, oregano and a
good pinch of salt. Add the anchovy fillets and drizzle over
the extra virgin olive oil.

Slide the pizza on to the pizza stone (or oven tray) and
bake in the oven until the edges are golden and the base has
crisped up. Add more olive oil before serving.

DINNER PARTY DUST-UP

WHY IS IT THAT WE HAVE NEVER had a dinner party that was not preceded by a spat, dispute or full-blown eruption? It had been my intention to ponder this phenomenon silently, but I accidentally voiced my query within the hearing of Mrs H. This turned out to be a mistake.

'I'll tell you why,' she announced, after perhaps a thousandth of a second's pause for meditation. 'For some reason, I've got it in my head that a dinner party should be a joint effort. But at the moment when there are a million things to do, you blithely announce that you're going off for a swim or a little nap. This means I get into a dither. Maybe it's because we're not very good at planning. I'm always coming across recipes that say you should start two days ahead, but we usually start in the afternoon of the same day so there is a mad trot round the supermarket. And then you say you have an urgent appointment with the swimming pool or the bed and that's why we have a row.'

'Other people don't seem to have a terrific bust-up before their dinner parties,' I pointed out.

'I can't work out how other people manage to greet you

with a calm smile,' said Mrs H. 'Usually we've just been screeching at one another when the doorbell rings. I suppose we greet people with calm smiles. Except you don't. You tell people, "It's been sheer hell. Never again!"'

If you ask me – not that anyone does – the reason for the stormy atmosphere that boils up before our dinner parties has less to do with preparing the food than with the cleaning and tidying that Mrs H requires. At other people's dinner parties, I'm quite happy whatever the state of the surroundings as long as the food – and, oh yes, the wine – is OK and plentiful. I've been to fine dinner parties where it was necessary to clear the dining table of a thick accretion of newspapers and books before sitting down. Our house, however, has to be scrubbed, polished and burnished to within an inch of its life before the guests arrive.

One mandatory task strikes me as being particularly curious, so I decided to have it out with the Generalissimo. 'Why the hell do I always have to vacuum the stair carpet?'

'It's because I'm usually at work and don't clean up during the week.'

'But why the stairs?'

'Maybe people will want to use the upstairs loo. It's like a throwback to wearing clean knickers in case you're knocked down by an ambulance.'

'Bus.'

'Eh?'

'You mean bus, not ambulance.'

Ignoring my correction, Mrs H pressed on with her analysis. 'One reason I'm obsessed with cleaning up is that people are always expressing opinions about our house in a way that I wouldn't dream of talking about their house. I still remember your friend who looked at our dining room and sniffed, "Well, it's scarcely minimalist."'

I'd argue the point except for the fact that Mrs H is right. On the very day of this discussion, a dinner guest began her critique even before she'd got through the front door: 'The dandelions in your garden are letting the side down.'

'They weren't dandelions, they were aquilegia,' huffed Mrs H in the post-party analysis.

Ironically, flowers can be a cause of dispute between Mrs H and me. 'I like having flowers on the table, but you're always moving them to odd places,' said Mrs H. 'I've sometimes found them in the broom cupboard. And you always pick the wrong time to do things. At the very moment that I'm up to my ears in batter mix, you'll say, "Have I to open the oysters?"'

Once the dinner party is under way, things usually go OK. Though there was the time when the spiced beef wouldn't carve and we ended up with a pile of beefy fragments. And the time when we invited a famous chef and the roast potatoes burnt and the beef went grey because we had one drink too many before the meal. And the time when some guests from west London arrived in a furious temper because south-east London, where we happen to live, is so far from west London. (Of course, it is far nearer from south-east London to west London.) Then there was the time that someone crashed into every car in our street during the cheese course. But even that was a negligible disturbance compared to the ring on the door just as I was carving the pork. The street was full of fire engines. 'Don't worry,' said our neighbour, 'but I thought you should know that the house next door is on fire.'

Customarily, however, the blemishes at our festivities are less cataclysmic.

'You're always putting the wrong cutlery out,' Mrs H recalled. 'We're just sitting down and I'll notice that people have been given serving spoons instead of dessertspoons.'

'Well, you're always forgetting vegetables. How many times have I found a terrine of celeriac mash or pommes dauphinoise in the oven when the meal is finished?'

'Ha! I don't think that you've got much room to talk. How come the wine is ALWAYS at your end of the table? And you never make sure that everyone's glass is filled – except your own, of course.'

'I don't remember people complaining very much.'

'No,' Mrs H was compelled to agree. 'Usually they say it's been very nice.' After a momentary reflection, she added, 'Except for the evening in France when you made everyone eat those shellfish that look like doggy doo.'

Ah, yes, there was that.

11

A selfish feast

IN RETROSPECT, IT MAY HAVE BEEN unwise to entrust me with the food kitty when we stayed with our friends Malcolm and Eileen, who had been lent a villa in southwest France. Let loose amid the oceanic cornucopia of the Toulouse fish market, I instantly dispersed our collective funds of eighty euros on a large quantity of langoustines, crevettes, the small whelks known as *bulots*, crabs, oysters, mussels, scallops and rococo-shelled murex. But my greatest prize was a generous quantity of the Mediterranean sea creature that the *Oxford Companion to Food* says does 'not have a current English name, though it may sometimes be referred to as a "sea squirt".' Known in France as *violets*, their brown, wrinkled appearance has also produced the appellations *figue de mer* and even the oxymoronic *pomme de terre de mer*. These names are on the euphemistic side. Mrs H, who had been the unappreciative recipient of *violets* in the past, insists their brown, wrinkled appearance resembles a canine calling card.

My mountain of shellfish was greeted with amazement and approbation (possibly more the former than the latter).

Apart, that is, from the *violets*, which were regarded with undisguised revulsion by the womenfolk. However, Malcolm expressed wary interest: 'They look a bit like the things inside Daleks.'

'Not to worry, you don't eat the skins,' I cheerily urged. 'You eat the bit inside that looks like scrambled egg.' Enlarging on my theme, I pointed out that smaller *violets* taste sweet with a slight iodine tang, though big ones (they can be twenty centimetres in length) are like solid TCP. In his book *Mediterranean Seafood*, Alan Davidson says, 'It is eaten raw and is pleasant washed down with dry white wine … I have never faced up to a big one.' Edouard Loubet even offers a recipe for 'sea squirts in a germander marinade' in his book *A Chef in Provence*. 'Pretty yummy, huh?' I cajoled. Despite my PR campaign for these gnarly inhabitants of the littoral, the others showed zero sign of being persuaded.

Hacking through the leathery skin of a *violet*, it lived up to its English nickname. Dripping somewhat, I passed an opened sea squirt to Malcolm, who tackled it with a degree of trepidation. 'I like to think of myself as an adventurous eater, but this may be a step too far,' he said. Malcolm's subsequent grimace suggested that the experience had not been one of life's gastronomic highlights. 'It reminds me of something left in a wardrobe with mothballs for many years,' he reported. 'Bloody horrible.'

I tried one just to show that they were 'pleasant washed down with dry white wine'.

'Well, did you enjoy it?' asked Mrs H.

'Not really.'

Far from sympathising, Mrs H stuck the knife in, just as I did to the *violets*. 'Only a silly man would try to inflict such things on his friends,' she said. 'Only a very silly man would buy two dozen of them.' I suggested that they might have been a bit elderly. Even in Languedoc, there seem to be few takers for this Mediterranean treat. I recalled that the *poissonnière* appeared delighted by my desire to corner the Toulouse *violet* market. *The Oxford Companion to Food* concedes that the *violet* is 'not everywhere regarded as edible' and twenty-first century France appears to be heading in this direction. When I suggested to my companions that we should 'get back on that high wire' and buy another batch, the response was a firm negative. Indeed, divorce appeared a distinct prospect.

It grieves me to say that this is not the only occasion when my fervour for all things piscine has produced disharmony. It is not going too far to say that a tug o' war between my tendency to head for the fishmonger's slab in pursuit of the scaly, tentacled and armour-clad and Mrs H's desire to lug me away typifies our relationship. Looking bemused, she has accompanied me on tours of fish markets around the world. We've viewed inky swirls of cephalopods in Athens, mounds of gesticulating crabs in Barcelona, rustling piles of dried haddock in Reykjavik and shoals of tiddlers in Venice. In the spectacular fish market of Muscat, the fish were so fresh they were leaping from the slabs. As far as I am concerned, these are places of the utmost bliss. Our salty blood and tears indicate mankind's marine origins and, if the decision had been left to me, we would never have left. Discovering the mind-boggling variety of sea creatures – and, better still, eating them – takes us back to our murky, primeval origins. Unfortunately, my partner has not been persuaded to share my passion for strange things found in the sea.

This can be literally the case, as with the impressive fish we came across on the beach at Filey, North Yorkshire. It was large, silver and oval, with the big eyes characteristic of deep-ocean dwellers. It was also very dead. Some people had propped it up and were taking photographs of this unusual visitor. I was gazing awestruck when a more knowledgeable pair of strollers arrived. 'That's a Ray's bream,' said one of them. 'Old George caught one and said it was the best fish he'd ever eaten.' With that, his companion snatched up the fish, sniffed it and marched off with it.

I had been formulating the same move, but was restrained by Mrs H. Disappointment turned to consolation when we came across another dead Ray's bream a bit further along the beach. This was also in quite good nick despite being nibbled by seagulls. 'I wonder if …' I started.

'No. Absolutely not. NO!'

Weirdly, she displayed a similar antipathy toward some items sold by Filey's fishmonger, despite their irreproachable freshness. 'You are NOT buying those horrible rubbery things. NO!'

'Rick Stein says "they taste almost like lobster".'

'They're like off-cuts from a tyre factory.'

'Does that mean they're in *Michelin*?'

'Ha! Well, you're not having them.'

'Are you two having a domestic?' inquired the lady behind the counter.

With that, I accepted defeat. I must admit that Rick Stein's tribute to the whelk, which appears in his first book, *English Seafood Cookery* (published in 1988 when he was still 'Richard Stein'), is heavily qualified: 'When freshly boiled in salt water they can taste almost like lobster, albeit a bit tough. But the flavour is variable; sometimes they taste frightful ... I can't say I'm an enthusiast.'

By the time Rick Stein's *Fruits of the Sea* appeared in 1997, he had gained a more wholehearted appreciation of this mollusc. 'I've got a lot of time for whelks,' he confides, before introducing his legion of fans to whelk fritters. A few pages earlier, there is a dish called Chinese whelks with bean sprouts and button mushrooms. 'Thinly sliced and stirred into a Chinese stir-fry,' Stein insists, 'whelks are incredibly good.'

It was this paean that sent me scuttling, alone this time, back to the fishmonger in Filey. I snapped up half a pound of boiled, de-shelled whelks for a couple of quid. Admittedly, the price of Stein's dish began to soar as I acquired other ingredients. Along with the mushrooms and bean sprouts, it required oyster sauce, dry sherry, pak choi, root ginger and hot peppers. Mrs H's response to my whelk-laden shopping trip would have registered high on the Richter scale, but Stein's 'incredibly good' promise placated her, at least temporarily. After slicing and stir-frying as directed, the result didn't look too bad, while the smell was positively tempting. Moreover, the taste was OK – with the exception of one ingredient.

Even when pared into slivers, the whelks remained resolutely whelkish. A couple of minutes after taking her first mouthful, Mrs H announced: 'I'm still chewing.' At my insistence, we chomped on and on. 'Just like school dinners,' said Mrs H. Nearing the bottom of her bowl, she laid aside her spoon. 'I'm feeling a bit queasy,' she groaned. I was forced to admit that I was feeling not unqueasy myself.

Twenty-four hours later, the whelks were still making their presence felt. Rick Stein may have come to venerate the blighters, but as far as I'm concerned, these hardy gastropods crossed the cusp into inedibility. For some reason, the British whelk tends to be a monster. We seem to be so impressed by their mature dimensions that edibility is of little consequence. Maybe British whelk addicts train themselves to absorb these giants in the same way that it is possible to build up a tolerance for arsenic. In France, they sensibly stick to smaller whelks. The *bulots* in garlic sauce I once had in Lille were highly acceptable, even to Mrs H.

It is, I feel, a tribute to the resilience of the human spirit that little more than a year after this episode, I once again found myself seriously contemplating the consumption of a whelk. The reason was a meeting with Fergus Henderson of St John restaurant in Smithfield. In the course of our conversation, the topic of whelks came up (as it might in any discourse between two red-blooded fellows). 'I'm very keen on whelks, but people are reluctant to eat them,' he declared. 'It's very hard to speak for whelks. They have to speak for themselves. People who try them usually like them. You just put some in salty water and get simmering. Can't remember how long. Quite a while. By the end they should be soft and tender and sweet.'

This planted a seed. A week or so later, I came back to Fergus with my proposal for an all-whelk lunch. The chef generously acceded to my proposal, though there was a slight problem. 'We haven't had whelks on the menu for the past year or so. I was sampling one from a new batch when I had a bad moment. You know: Mmmm – errrr – urggh. Luckily, I spat it out. Maybe it's time for them to come back. I've had some quite nice whelk moments.'

Many – possibly most – people may feel that there is no such thing as a nice whelk moment, though someone must be scoffing them because Fergus had a bit of trouble finding some for the Whelkathon, as it came to be known. 'I phoned round the whelkhouses to secure the finest possible whelks. Unfortunately, the south coast didn't have any, but we've got some from Bristol and some more from Ireland. We ended up with about twelve kilos,' he announced, as a small mountain of the blighters was placed before my tasting panel. This consisted of Jeremy Lee of the Blueprint Café and (after being lured with the promise of a bottle of Jo Malone scent) Mrs H.

Boiled briefly then allowed to cool in their own liquor, the whelks were the colour of Cornish cream when prised from their handsome shells. 'A certain amount of chewiness is no bad thing,' declared Fergus. 'But they're terribly sweet and lovely. A quintessentially English dish.'

'They're far more tender than the ones we had in York-shire,' said Mrs H, when she had steeled herself sufficiently to take a nibble. 'But I'm not getting a huge amount of flavour from them.'

'Obviously, you have to develop a relationship with the whelk,' suggested Jeremy. 'I'm very impressed. I like this very well indeed.'

Though we had made scant inroads into the shoal of whelks *au naturel*, the first of the warm whelk dishes arrived. Piled on slices of toast fried in duck fat, this was a dark green slurry of whelks, bacon and laver bread. 'Bacon is a good addition to most things,' said Fergus. 'This is from Old Spot pigs. Very happy bacon.'

'A triumph. I'm very pleasantly surprised,' said Jeremy. 'It may make a few converts. It will certainly refresh memories for old friends of the whelk.'

'I like the bacon,' said Mrs H.

The second dish was described by Fergus as 'chickpeas braised with whelks, chorizo, pig's trotter and a bit of rocket to mix in and keep scurvy at bay'. He assessed a mouthful: 'Hmm. Quite harmonious. There are no bullies here.'

'Very good,' rhapsodised Jeremy. 'The whelk should be ennobled. It's far better than those big clams or Canadian lobsters that are tough as old boots.'

'If you're desperate you could eat whelks,' groaned Mrs H. 'But you'd never choose them before lamb.'

Though there was a lengthy interval before our next encounter with maritime oddities, Mrs H still objected with impressive vigour. 'Good grief! What on earth are those?'

she yelped after seeing the dozen molluscs I had acquired at London's New Billingsgate Market. 'Don't they look rude? I don't like to go near them. CHRIS! One's moving! It's expanding! Eek! I'm off!'

To be fair to Mrs H, the geoduck clam lacks the allure of other shellfish. Our intended supper came in oval, grey shells about fourteen centimetres in length, held shut in rubber-band bondage. At one end of each bivalve, a thick, long cylindrical siphon emerged from between the shells. The floppy protuberance was undeniably, even alarmingly phallic. Cutting off the tumescent siphon and skinning it was one of the more disturbing culinary activities I've ever engaged in. A good deal of disassociation was required. But the anthropomorphic connotations declined as I sliced the siphon into a pile of fleshy rings. Served with soy sauce and wasabi horseradish, the dissected phallus would surely prove irresistible when the moment arrived for supper.

Not everyone does a runner when presented with a geoduck. Pronounced 'gooey-duck', it derives from a word meaning 'dig deep' in the language of the Nisqually tribe of north-west America, who presumably must be fond of eating the creatures. It is also regarded as a delicacy in some Asian cuisines. The ones sold at Billingsgate, which were diver-caught in Scotland, mostly go to Chinese restaurants. Living to an age of 150 or more, geoducks can weigh seven kilos, with a siphon that is a metre in length. The web page devoted to these creatures on Google images, which includes some spectacularly big ones, is jaw-dropping.

Along with the X-rated geoducks lolling in tumescent

splendour, my haul from Billingsgate included a kilo of Indian Ocean anchovies (a kilo is an awful lot of anchovies), a doctor fish, a moonfish (cartoon imperious with an up-thrust jaw, it is also known as the Mussolini fish), a silver pomfret and some home-grown treats in the form of a big bundle of razor clams, a half-kilo of sea-urchins and a large cuttlefish. In the kitchen of Hirst HQ, I started work on the Indian Ocean anchovies, which proved quite a bit harder to deal with than their Mediterranean cousins. For each tiny fish, you had to split open the stomach with your thumbnail, remove the backbone, then take off the head and tail and a spiky dorsal fin. The result was two gorgeous fillets decorated with twin stripes of silver like the chrome trim on a '59 Chevy. Unfortunately, I had 100-odd fish to tackle.

'Time well spent,' said Mrs H when I presented her with anchovy fillets sautéd in butter. 'Mmm, they taste so good. They have a lovely, buttery, caramelised flavour that doesn't really taste of fish.' The fillets were equally excellent after being marinaded overnight in white wine vinegar and a little salt. We ate them as a ceviche with olive oil, slivers of garlic, chopped parsley and lemon zest.

Having previously consumed sea urchins in the Aegean, Mrs H happily tucked in. They are best eaten raw. You snip a hole in the top of the spiny shell, remove the stomach sac and use a teaspoon to eat the five streaks of yellow gonads lining the inside of the shell. They have a delicious, slightly metallic taste of oceanic freshness, akin to oysters, but more profound.

'There's a phenolic hint,' mused Mrs H. 'But it's not unpleasant.' I might also have served the razor clams live, but Mrs H was resolutely opposed to the idea. 'You must cook them. When we ate them live, they wriggled round the plate. It was most off-putting.' Even when they were steamed open and grilled with garlic butter, she had mixed feelings. 'My last one was too big. It's made me feel funny. The smaller one I had before was better. More girly, lovely and sweet.'

The grilled cuttlefish was almost as sweet as a razor clam, but more succulent and satisfying. Perfect barbecue food. The surgeon fish was a disappointment – a bit tasteless, with lots of bones. ('Maybe it's an orthopaedic surgeon fish,' said Mrs H – a joke that may go down well in medical circles.) The Mussolini fish was creamy and delicate, though not as fleshy as its infamous namesake. Firm and sweet, the flesh of the pomfret was like a more solid lemon sole. It also fell off the bone like a flat fish, though it isn't. This treat from the Indian Ocean is worth the trip to Billingsgate in itself. But is it worth purchasing geoducks while you're there? We had the sliced siphon both raw as sashimi and steamed in white wine. I thought the results were OK in a chewy sort of way, but scarcely worth the trauma involved in its preparation. Mrs H was less ambivalent. 'That was disgusting,' she said, after nibbling a geoduck ring in desultory fashion.

'So you wouldn't like it again?'

'What do you think?'

SUET AND STEEL

IN CASE THE *violet*/whelk/geoduck saga gives the impression that I have spent much of our relationship inflicting horrifying foods on my wife, I might point out that it could have been a lot worse for her.

'What about the dumplings?' Mrs H points out.

Ah, yes. At least my obsession was short-lived. We only ate dumplings for a week. Yes, I know it sounds strange, but there was a reason (indignation at an American volume called *A World of Dumplings* that included beef ravioli, Jamaican fish patties, won-ton soup and even Cornish pasty but omitted the British dumpling). We munched away at dumplings both savoury and sweet for lunch and supper, but in my kindly way I spared Mrs H other treats that I discovered in an ancient booklet from the suet-maker Atora. I did not insist on sampling such suety treats as liver-and-rice mould or giblet pudding. Looking back, I'm surprised at my restraint in not serving up Buckinghamshire dumpling (stuffed with liver and bacon) with rice croquettes ('when cold form into attractive shapes'). Despite suffering from a troublesome cough, Mrs H refused another suggestion from the book: 'A teaspoon of Atora, taken in a glass of hot milk at bedtime, is a very soothing and beneficial treatment in the case of a cough or sore throat.'

I knew from bitter experience that an Atora confection called tongue roll would not go down well with Mrs H. She conceived an antipathy towards this tasty offal in student days when her landlady cooked ox-tongue on a regular basis. 'I don't think I've ever got over it,' she recalls with a shudder. 'I once looked in the pan and there was this vast tongue rising and falling in the boiling water. It went gloop, gloop, gloop.' Her attitude is disappointing, since I am fond of ox tongue with a green sauce made from parsley, oil and anchovies. Our friend Jeremy Lee of the Blueprint Café contributed an enticing recipe for this dish to a book called *Eat London*: 'You can steep a few tongues at a time as they don't go off … A modicum of patience is required as the tongues must steep for four or five weeks.' Strangely enough, the idea of having several ox tongues occupying her fridge for a month did not appeal to Mrs H.

In her unreasonable way, Mrs H also jibbed at such tempting dishes as Excited Pig ('a whole skinned salami served upright on a dish containing some very hot coffee mixed with a good deal of eau de cologne'), Simultaneous Ice-Cream ('dairy cream and little squares of raw onion frozen together') and Sicilian Headland (a paste of tuna, apples, olives and nuts spread on cold jam omelette). All come from the *Futurist Cookbook* by Filippo Marinetti (1932). Fortunately, there are less challenging dishes in this work of revolutionary cuisine. I decided that it was necessary and vital to try them at Hirst HQ.

Futurist cuisine is food as manifesto. Iconoclastic, wealthy and belligerent, Marinetti was a preposterous poseur like his hero Mussolini, though his campaigns were knowingly ironic. The Futurist movement came into being when Marinetti crashed his car in 1909. Much like Mr Toad's transformative collision in *The Wind in the Willows* ('Poop-poop!'), he was intoxicated by the experience: 'When I came up – torn, filthy and stinking – from under the capsized car, I felt the white-hot iron of joy deliciously pass through my heart!' Aiming for the polar reverse of the Italy loved by tourists – antique, picturesque, rural – the Futurists adored urban clamour and modernity: 'Long Live Steel!' Their plans encompassed avant-garde headwear (made of cork, glass, sponge and neon tubing), feather-weight aluminium trains and the abolition of cutlery. Their repudiation of pasta caused punch-ups in Italian communities around the world.

Swept up by Marinetti's 100 mph prose ('sing of the vibrant nightly fervour of arsenals and shipyards blazing with violent electric moons …'), I made a Futurist meal that exalted 'the geometric splendour of speed' and 'the aesthetics of the machine'. First course was the Cubist Vegetable Patch (a demanding arrangement of fried carrots, fried celery, pickled silverskin onions and cold boiled peas). 'At least it kept you quiet for an hour while you arranged the ingredients,' said Mrs H. 'The taste wasn't quite as interesting as it looked. Heinz Russian salad without the mayonnaise.' This was followed by the Bombardment of

Adrianopolis (deep-fried rice balls, each containing half an anchovy, three capers, a slice of mozzarella and two olives). 'Quite acceptable, rather like arancini rice balls.'

The dessert course was my *pièce de résistance*. 'Oh,' said Mrs H when she caught a glimpse. 'I was hoping you were not going to do that ridiculous sexist pud.' It was a disappointing reaction. The two impressive mounds of Campari-tinged ricotta, each with a strawberry peeping through at the summit, were, in my opinion, a most persuasive rendition of the dish called Strawberry Breasts. If the spectacle was eye-catching, the taste was slightly odd. 'Er, quite nice,' said Mrs H, 'though I prefer my Campari in Campari and soda.' (Coincidentally, the irresistible little conical bottles containing pre-mixed Campari Soda you see in Italian bars were conceived by Futurist designer Fortunato Depero in 1932.)

In Mrs H's deflating opinion, Futurist dishes were 'the kind of thing a child might make if let loose in the kitchen. They're like recipes from the *Funny Face Cookbook*.' For that reason, I chose not to proceed with Marinetti's recipe for Steel Chicken, which is cold roast chicken filled with '200gms of silver hundreds and thousands'. The nearest I could find in our locale was a cake decoration called Pink 'n' Pretty Sparkles, which was scarcely in keeping with the 'courage and audacity' of Futurism. Still, they might come in handy for our next joint effort in the kitchen. What could be more audacious and courageous than baking a cake?

12

A cake is not just for Christmas

Christmas cake

'Would you like a Christmas cake?' Mrs H's inquiry came as a surprise. We had never made a Christmas cake before, though I am partial to the odd slice. Come to think, I must have eaten several hundredweight of it over the years, mostly made by my mother. Anyway, my response was a big 'YES'.

I have a soft spot for Christmas cake. To be precise, I like the cake bit of the Christmas cake, especially when it is accompanied Yorkshire-style by a chunk of Wensleydale. I'm not desperate about the strata that go on top, though for many people the marzipan and the crunchy icing are the whole point of the thing. I like the gleaming, moist texture of the cake with its whiff of old grog and generous abundance of macerated raisins and sultanas. Not that anyone thinks twice about it, but there is something magical about dried fruit. I dare say I would feel rather differently about these little packages of the warm south if I had to remove the seeds from each fruit as, until quite recently, the cook was obliged to do. Elizabeth David blasted sentimentalists who rhapsodised about the old-fashioned Christmas: 'Have they ever stoned bunch after bunch of raisins hardly yet dry on the stalk, and each one as sticky as a piece of warm toffee?'

But why was Mrs H so inspired by a Waitrose recipe card for Christmas cake with Drambuie-soaked fruits? It would have involved a sudden conversion for her to share my Pickwickian appreciation of Christmas cake. 'I knew that you'd like one,' she said selflessly. Hmm. This did not ring true to me. I like lots of things that she refuses point blank to make. *Tripes à la mode de Caen* is just one example. After close questioning, the truth emerged. It was the 'Drambuie' bit of the recipe that prompted her suggestion. Ever since I wrote a regular column on cocktails, our house has been awash with bottles. She saw the Christmas cake as being a way of empty-ing at least one bottle. Since the cake only required 100ml or one-fifth of a 50cl bottle of Drambuie plus a small amount of the spirit for weekly 'feeding' of the finished cake, her Highland clearance was going to have a pretty marginal effect on my grog hoard. Still, every little helps.

We started with the rather sticky job of quartering soft apricots and prunes and halving glacé cherries. (Actually, it was Mrs H who wielded the scissors: 'A lot quicker and less sticky than a knife.') These went into a big bowl with vine fruit, mixed peel and the juice and zest of an orange. My main job was finding the Drambuie in our over-crowded drinks cabinet. Having only seen service in the production of one cocktail (the Rusty Nail, a favourite refreshment of

Frank Sinatra and The Rat Pack), the bottle was pretty much full. I added 100ml to the fruit for overnight maceration. An alcoholic, orangey aroma rose from the bowl. It smelled so good that I wondered if we should stop the Christmas cake right there.

Ructions started on the following day when Mrs H tried to line the baking tin with baking parchment. 'A bit tricky,' she grizzled. 'My maths let me down when working out the amount of paper I needed.' Worse came when the recipe recommended 'a double thickness of baking parchment round the outside of the tin. This will prevent the cake drying out during cooking.' Though I donated a finger to hold the string in place while Mrs H tied a knot, the paper refused to stay in place. It ruffled like a badly made bed. 'Bloody thing,' huffed Mrs H. 'Hopeless, but I suppose it will do.'

When the butter was creamed with dark muscovado sugar, the result had a pleasant rummy smell like molasses with maybe a hint of pipe baccy. Mrs H was not so fond. 'Not a sweet smell, is it? It's a bit smoky. Poo! I'm a bit suspicious of it.' This last, inadvertent expostulation indicated her true feelings towards the whole project. She was driven more by cupboard cleaning than desire for cake. But I found myself gaining interest as the project advanced. There's a lot to be said for muscovado sugar – tarry, dark, complex. The flavour comes from unrefined sugar cane juice. According to the *OED*, 'muscovado' derives from the Portuguese *mascabado*, meaning 'badly made'. In that case, I for one would not want the sugar made one jot better.

I was caught tasting the macerated fruit. 'That's a glacé cherry you owe me from one of your slices,' said Mrs H. The fruit tasted even better when chopped walnuts were added. For many years I had an antipathy to nuts. 'I think it's a mistake they were ever regarded as edible,' I would blithely assert. 'Really they're bits of wood.' But now I can see the point of nuts. The combination of alcoholic raisins and the dryness of walnut works very well.

I was recalled from my nutty reverie by a crack across the knuckles with the business end of a wooden spoon. 'We're going to add the beaten eggs by degrees into the sugar and butter,' observed Mrs H. 'There's a danger of the mixture curdling if you add eggs too fast. It's a basic thing with cakes. Can you see it looking like sick? Those lumpy-looking bits mean it has curdled. I'll bung in a spoonful of flour.' This antidote arrested the curdling.

The next step was to add the fruit and walnuts. 'Then mix well. Fold in the rest of the flour.' This simple instruction brings to mind the archetypal image of a cook. With one arm she encircles a bowl, while her free hand rotates a spoon like an outboard motor. Looks easy, doesn't it? 'Do you want to have a go?' inquired Mrs H. 'You'll moan. I now know why my mother wanted everyone to stir the Christmas cake. You need a breather from time to time.'

At first it was OK, then it got painful quite quickly. I realised, not for the first time, that I lacked cook's muscles. 'Have you made a wish?' asked Mrs H (though purists might say this only applies to Christmas pud).

'I wish this was finished.'

'There, you've wasted your wish now.'

My wish wasn't answered anyway. I had to carry on stirring.

'Oi! You're just smoothing the top. You're not mixing it. You're just pushing the flour down. You need to sort of twist the spoon. And you have to raise your elbow and twist your wrist. Use your shoulder.' After all this, my arm was really aching. Fortunately, our mix was completed, though Mrs H did a bit more stirring just to indicate the inadequacy of my efforts. Eventually, she shovelled the mixture into the lined cake tin with a silicone spatula. 'The great advantage of silicone,' said Mrs H, 'is that it gathers up every fragment of cake mix so there's not much for anyone to lick out.' Fortunately, she didn't scrape out *every* bit. Sweet and rich, the raw cake tasted of Drambuie, orange and lots of other good things. It might have been a pudding made by a particularly inventive chef. Why the bowl scrapings taste so much better than the finished cake is one of the great mysteries of gastronomy. Using a palette knife, Mrs H smoothed the surface of this luxurious aggregate in the cake tin. 'A bit like a brickie spreading cement on a line of bricks,' I said.

'Well,' retorted Mrs H. 'I've never made a brick wall and neither have you.'

With that, the cake went into the oven. Three to four hours at 150°C. It came out looking brown and happy. (It's funny how a fruit cake seems to smile at you.) For two months, we fed the cake with a dessertspoon of Drambuie on a weekly basis, then it fed us. But first there was the essential task of decoration. Ignoring my offer of Pink 'n' Pretty Sparkles, Mrs H installed a jewel-like encrustation of glacé fruit bought at Fortnum & Mason. The cost must have been eye-watering. 'I won't tell you how much,' she said, which is always a bad sign. 'It's your own fault for not liking icing.' Both Christmas cake and plutocratic topping were delicious beyond words. Sliver by sliver, this opulent creation saw us through the cruellest month of January, accompanied, of course, by a wedge of cheese.

The Victoria sponge sandwich

An entry on Wikipedia says that the name came about because Queen Victoria used to 'favour a slice of the sponge cake for her afternoon tea', though *The Oxford Companion to Food* is more guarded in its explanation, 'named after Queen Victoria'. Mrs H was confident of success since she made one as part of her Domestic Science O level. It's the kind of thing I wish I'd learned for O level instead of Boyle's Law, the ox-bow lake and the Diet of Worms (1521). 'It's just four plus four plus four,' Mrs H reported from Memory Lane (a pre-metric thoroughfare). 'Four ounces each of self-raising flour, caster sugar and butter – plus two eggs.'

'But why have you got two cake tins out?' I inquired.

'Because it's a *sandwich*,' she replied with eyes rolling heavenwards (a familiar rotation when we're together in the kitchen). 'You put one cake on top of the other.' *The Oxford Companion to Food* says different: 'Usually it is cut

in half and spread with jam/or cream to give a sandwich.'
But the schedule for a Yorkshire produce show, where my
mother's Victoria sponge sandwich was once disparaged
(see page 251), declares: 'To be made in two 8-in sandwich
tins.' It seemed wise not to pursue the great Victoria sponge
sandwich dichotomy at this stage. At least the twin cake
approach spares you the tricky business of latitudinal
bisection. I imagine many a Victoria sponge sandwich has
gone awry during this tricky procedure.

'The first thing we do is lots of preparation.'

'Boo!'

Plonking one of the tins on a length of baking parchment, she drew a circle round the base. 'I'm cutting out two
circles of parchment for the bottom of the cake tins. I know
the tins are non-stick but it's best to be sure. You lightly
grease the inside of the tins with butter and then line the
bottom with baking parchment. The idea is that you can
get them out of the tins. And we don't want it to sink in the
middle. If the centre turns out to be too soggy you make it
into a cake with a hole in the middle like a giant Polo. Then
you cover it in icing sugar and claim it is a great invention.'

The first ingredient was four ounces of butter. I cut a
chunk, which proved to be remarkably accurate. 'Four
point four ounces. That's near enough.'

'Make it four ounces exactly.'

Cussing a bit, I cut off a sliver.

'Four ounces exactly!' I announced. 'Give the man a
cigar!'

'Then four ounces of caster sugar. No! Don't shake the

sugar from the bag on to the scale! Use a spoon.' I then added it to the butter in a large bowl. 'While you're at it, you can weigh out four ounces of self-raising flour.' After weighing this, I started adding it to the butter and sugar. 'Oh no!' said Mrs H dramatically. 'Oh dear! Oh dear! Oh dear! Why did you put the flour in?'

'Because you said four plus four plus four.'

'That's just the weighing. Only a nincompoop would put them all in together.' She began fishing out the flour. 'You mix the butter and the sugar, then add the two beaten eggs and only then mix in the flour.'

When operations resumed, my egg whisking proved inadequate. 'You want a good amalgamation. You've still got great gloops of white in there. I usually angle the bowl and keep the fork flatter. You know when it's done because it goes much paler like this, with froth on top.' I began to be grateful that I didn't do an O level in Victoria sponge sandwiches. After an eternity of whisking, I achieved an acceptable paleness. I was then allowed to add half a teaspoon of vanilla extract.

'Now we're all prepared,' said Mrs H in a manner borrowed from her old cookery teacher, 'so we can start mixing with the cake mixer. First we'll mix the butter so it goes lighter.' The food mixer did its stuff on the butter. 'It's called "creaming",' said Mrs H.

'Oh really? I never knew butter had any connection with cream,' I said sarcastically, but it had no effect with Mrs H in full didactic flow. 'When it's creamed, we add the sugar. We're trying to enrobe each bit of sugar in fat. Can you see it changing in texture so it becomes all crumbly? You want to make sure every bit of butter is incorporated. Keep the machine going while we add the whisked egg. Do it a teaspoon at a time so it doesn't curdle.'

After the third or fourth spoonful, I rebelled. Two whisked eggs turns out to be a surprisingly large amount of liquid when you're adding it by the teaspoonful. 'This is infinitely tedious. Are you just doing it for my benefit? Would you really be adding it a teaspoon at a time if I weren't here?'

'Of course I would.'

'It'll take forever. I'll use a dessertspoon.'

'Well, if you know best,' she said and stalked off in a dudgeon.

'Oh, all right. But how would you go on if you were mixing by hand instead of having the cake mixer on? Not having three hands you'd have to stop all the time.'

Mrs H dodged this clever hypothetical. 'Take it from me, there's a reason for all this.' After an age, the egg was incorporated. 'NOW IT'S TIME TO ADD THE FLOUR,' bellowed Mrs H. 'Did you notice that I was talking in capitals? We'll sift the flour – we want to get some air into it – and then fold it in by hand. You do this by cutting and turning.' It didn't go down well when I pointed out that the mixture looked lumpy.

'I HAVEN'T FINISHED YET,' capitalised Mrs H.

'Is the sugar properly mixed in? The mixture sounds scratchy.'

'It'll be perfect,' she said and turned off the cake mixer.

'Can you divide the mixture into the two tins?'

I did it and weighed them to prove the accuracy of my division: 12.6oz and 11oz. In a rare dispensation, Mrs H did not demand the sharing-out of the outstanding 1.6oz. 'Now spread the mix in each of the cake tins with a palette knife. Turn the tin so the mix reaches the edge.'

'This is quite satisfying.' But it is rather reckless to express culinary contentment within earshot of Mrs H.

'Don't handle it too much. You're just moving the middle. Try and get it to the edge. We want the cakes to have the same thickness – no domes in the middle. And there's one more thing.'

'What?'

'You've got some cake mix on your nose.'

After twenty minutes in the oven, the kitchen filled with a buttery smell tinged with vanilla. You could put on ounces just by sniffing. 'You can see it rising and developing a golden colour. Just look in through the window – don't open the oven door.'

'I've just opened the oven door!'

'It's like that bit in *Ghostbusters*: "Don't cross the streams, Ray!"'

Since the door was open, Mrs H gently pressed the top of one cake. 'It's springing back a bit. Nearly done.' Five minutes later, the two slightly mottled sponges were extracted from their tins (not the slightest sign of sticking) and deposited on cooling racks. When they had cooled, I was delegated to spread the raspberry jam. For those new to the twin-cake method of making Victoria sponge sandwiches, here is the procedure. You invert cake A and spread jam on its bottom, then you put cake B on top. The spreading uses around two-thirds of a jar of jam. 'I want it to go right up to the edge,' directed Mrs H. 'You've got too much there. It's a bit thin over here.' When the jammy layer finally gained her seal of approval, I installed the second cake and tapped icing sugar through a tea-strainer on top of the sandwich.

'Looks very nice,' I said immodestly.

'It wouldn't win a prize at the village show,' tutted Mrs H. 'The cake is thicker in the middle than at the side.'

Despite this deficiency, the regal sarnie tasted even better than I expected. Maybe a sponge cake with a jam filling is scarcely the pinnacle of the pâtissier's art, but it was sensationally good. Exquisitely light in texture, the sponge was pleasantly infused with vanilla and delivered a delicious tang of concentrated raspberry. Mind you, you need an exceptional raspberry jam to achieve such transcendental results. May I refer you to pages 273–286?

Seed cake

My mother possibly made seed cake, but I don't remember it and it is a fairly memorable cake. Maybe it is a cake for grown-ups. Softish but not too soft, rich but not impossibly so, it is almost custardy on the palate, with the scattering of caraway seeds providing an occasional, surprising hint of liquorice. It is certainly an adult cake in the version on the menu of St John restaurant in Smithfield, where it arrives accompanied by a large glass of Madeira (19 per cent ABV). Since Madeira packs a punch like the old one-two manoeuvre favoured by boxers in the Fifties, most people have this combo as a form of dessert, but Fergus Henderson, the charming gaffer at St John (yes, he's the same chap who did the Whelkathon. Versatile, you see) prefers it for elevenses.

'The Madeira doesn't mean you have to write the day off,' he told me. 'Of course, you can if you want to – but one glass, or possibly two, gives us a quick jolt, a bit like a firework display. You have a giddy moment and feel restored.' He is adamant that only one pinch of caraway seeds is required in each cake. 'It's the Sultana Bran principle. When I was a child, I was always tempted to add more sultanas to the Sultana Bran, which ruined it.'

He noted that the steady maturing of the seed cake brought variety to his morning ritual. 'The point about seed cake is that it is good fresh from the oven when it is buttery and eggy with a crisp crust. But it is also very good when it is a day old. The sugar comes to the fore and the eggs and butter calm down. It is more grown-up.'

But why partner the seed cake with Madeira? 'It is hard to get the cake down without some form of lubrication and a glass of Madeira is a lot faster than a cup of coffee.' This most amiable of restaurateurs admits that his elevenses campaign has yet to take off. 'I hope others feel the urge to murder a bit of seed cake at eleven o'clock, but usually I'm on my own. Still, someone eats the St John seed cake at some stage in the day. It always goes. You only have to try it once for it to become a habit.'

Quite so. After floating home on a Madeira-scented cloud, I egged Mrs H into making a seed cake. We obtained a jar of caraway seeds. Brown and curved, the seeds (actually, they are tiny dried fruit) look like dark, miniature bananas. The smell was distantly familiar. Eventually, it came to me. Caraway is the main flavouring in kummel, the under-regarded digestif. Though the British use it only in cakes, caraway was once a big deal. It was the first spice plant to be cultivated in Europe and the Germans remain very keen. Caraway crops up in sauerkraut, rye bread and Munster cheese. It is also used to mitigate the fire in the North African pepper sauce harissa. In contradiction to Fergus's less-is-more line on caraway, the label on the Schwartz bottle of caraway seeds declares, 'Use quite generously,' but this turned out to be with vegetables.

Making the cake began with a mad whirl of butter, sugar and a teaspoon of caraway seeds in the food mixer. 'Can you see it going nice and light and fluffy?' asked Mrs H. 'Now we have to add five beaten eggs. Five! That'll make it nice and floppy.'

I felt obliged to make a small warning. 'In his recipe, Fergus says, "Add the eggs little by little to prevent curdling."'

'Aha!' said Mrs H. 'You see, you're taking notice when Fergus says it. If I say it you say, "Poo!"'

I managed to keep quiet when she added the beaten eggs with a dessertspoon. 'You're adding them slowly to keep it light and fluffy. If you were to add them all at once it would slop around and curdle. If it starts to curdle you've got to beat like mad.' With five eggs, the cake mix became almost liquid, a sort of suspension. By this stage, Mrs H was back in lecturing mode. 'Now, we add the flour. Note that we've sieved it first and we're adding it very slowly to prevent lumps.' After being thickened by flour, the mixture was transformed into a sort of batter by the addition of milk.

Like Mrs H, Fergus advocates greasing the baking tin with butter and lining the base and side with baking parchment. The cake mix, an unctuous mix of good things, plopped into the cake tin like concrete at a building site. Fergus's recipe called for a '16 x 10 x 8cm loaf tin'. Mrs H's nearest equivalent was a bit smaller, though just big enough to accommodate the mixture.

'Hope it'll be OK,' said Mrs H warily.

Indeed it was, though the mixture rose during cooking and stood proud out of the tin, supported by the paper lining, by maybe a centimetre. After half an hour (Fergus says '45 minutes') at 180°C, the cake was deemed done. A skewer inserted into the heart of the cake came out without particles adhering. It looked a tempting light brown. I thought that a long fissure on the top added character, but Mrs H tutted and said that a judge would take points off. This judge said it tasted terrific. The richness of the interior was complemented by the slight crunch of the crust. The cake sufficed for ten days of elevenses. No Madeira, though. Fergus is made of tougher stuff than his seedy acolyte.

Mrs H's recipe for Christmas cake

Christmas cake is best made two months before 25th December to allow time for weekly 'feeding' with liquor. This recipe is based on a free cookery card from Waitrose. I was drawn to the recipe not only because it contained Drambuie and would help empty one of the bottles clogging my kitchen cupboard, but also because of the inclusion of apricots and prunes and the rather attractive sugar-paste robin on the icing – which I didn't do in the end. You make the cake in two stages. Day one: soaking the fruit in alcohol (deliciously smelly and a bit sticky). Day two: mixing and cooking. When I found we didn't own a cake tin of the size recommended, day one also involved zipping along to the kitchen shop to buy a square cake tin with a loose base.

I had a request for no marzipan or icing, so I decorated the cake with nuts and glacé fruits. This was a jolly good excuse to visit Fortnum & Mason, where an impeccably charming young man on the glacé fruit counter admirably kept his cool while trying to fish out a rather resistant glacé clementine at my request.

When you finally have a slice of the cake, you will need a slice of good cheese to accompany it. (Apparently this is a Yorkshire tradition, so Wensleydale is in order.)

750g vine fruit mix
250g soft apricots, quartered
200g tub of Italian mixed peel
200g Provençal glacé cherries, halved
100g pitted soft prunes, quartered
grated zest and juice of 1 large orange, plus the zest from
    another orange
100ml Drambuie, plus extra to 'feed' the cake
250g unsalted butter, softened
200g dark muscovado sugar
5 medium eggs, beaten
300g plain flour, sifted
200g walnut pieces
in the absence of marzipan and icing, a selection of nuts
    and glacé fruits for decorating, plus some apricot glaze

The first stage of making the cake is dead easy: just weigh out the dried fruit and put it into a large bowl. (Cut up the prunes and apricots with kitchen scissors – it is quicker and less sticky than using a knife). Then stir in the grated orange zest and juice and the Drambuie. Cover with clingfilm and leave the fruits to soak overnight. Do have a long lingering sniff of the fruits and alcohol before you cover them up. It is a heavenly orangey aroma. (Since I like citrusy things, I added the zest of another orange without any harm to the final cake. I think!)

Next day, start with a bit of preparation: preheat the oven to 150°C/Gas Mark 2. Grease and line the base and sides of a 20cm square (or 23cm diameter round) cake tin with baking parchment so it stands 5cm above the top. Also tie a double thickness of baking parchment around the outside of the tin. This will help prevent the cake from drying out during cooking. (You may need to ask nicely to borrow someone's finger for knot-tying purposes.)

After this you can return to the task of making the cake. In a large bowl, use a hand-held electric whisk to beat together the butter and sugar until it is pale and fluffy. Gradually beat in the beaten egg a little at a time. There is a tendency for the mixture to curdle if you add too much beaten egg at once. If the mixture begins to curdle, add a little more flour. In any case, add a tablespoonful of flour when beating in the last drop of egg.

Add the soaked fruits and walnuts with any remaining liquid from the mix. Stir in the rest of the flour. (This is the arm-aching stage). When thoroughly mixed, spoon the mixture into the cake tin. Use a round-bladed knife to level the top of the mixture. You do not want a domed cake if you plan to ice it.

Stand the tin on a baking tray and bake for 3–4 hours, until cooked through. If the cake starts to get too brown, cover the top with foil.

To check that the cake is cooked, insert a skewer into its centre. If it comes out clean, the cake is done. If there are any smidgens of cake mix glued to the skewer, cook for a while longer but keep an eye on it. Remove the cake from the oven and leave it to cool down completely in the tin.

When the cake is cold, remove the cake from the tin and store with its lining paper, wrapped tightly in foil. Try to keep the cake in a cool place. Don't think you are through with the cake, though. It needs feeding, which you do by unwrapping the foil, making small holes in the cake with a skewer, then drizzling with a couple of tablespoons of Drambuie. Doing this on a weekly basis will help keep the cake moist and adds extra flavour (as well as helping empty the bottle).

As Christmas draws near, decorate the cake. Deviating from the Waitrose recipe I used pecan nuts, glacé kiwi fruit and glacé clementines plus some gold almond dragées. A smearing of apricot glaze fastened them securely to the cake. I also found a bit of ribbon to tie round the side. Then hide in a tin to prevent samples being nibbled before 25th December.

Mrs H's recipe for seed cake

This recipe is taken from *Beyond Nose to Tail* by Fergus
Henderson. Christopher has spent several happy mornings
in the company of Fergus at his St John restaurant nibbling
away at this cake and slugging Madeira for 'elevenses'. Oh,
the hard life of the freelance writer.

260g unsalted butter, softened
260g caster sugar
1 teaspoon caraway seeds
5 large eggs, lightly beaten
120g self-raising flour
150ml full-fat milk

Grease a 16 x 10 x 8cm loaf tin with butter. Line the base
and sides with non-stick baking parchment.

Cream the butter, sugar and caraway seeds together with
a hand-held or stand mixer until they are white and fluffy.
Gradually mix in the beaten eggs, adding them little by little
to prevent curdling. Sift the flour and fold it carefully into
the cake mix with a metal spoon until fully incorporated.
Lastly, add the milk and gently stir in.

Transfer the mixture to the prepared tin and bake in an
oven preheated to 180°C/ Gas Mark 4 for 45 minutes, or
until it is golden brown and a skewer inserted into the
centre comes out clean. (Our cake reached this stage in 30
minutes.) Leave it to cool a little in the tin before turning it
on to a cooling rack. Serve with a glass of Madeira.

Mrs H's recipe for Victoria sponge sandwich

'Four, four, four and two eggs' was the mantra learned from my schooldays, referring of course to ounces. However, since metrification I have had to learn '113g,113g,113g and two eggs' which is a bit of a whatnot to remember. The problem has been solved by doubling the recipe and using larger tins. I can do 225's.

225g butter, softened, plus a liitle extra for greasing
225g caster sugar
4 large eggs
225g self-raising flour, sifted
vanilla extract
raspberry jam for the filling, preferably homemade
icing sugar for dusting

Preheat the oven to 180°C/Gas Mark 4.

Since this recipe involves making two sponge cakes, you'll need two 17.5–20cm cake tins. Grease the cake tins with a little bit of butter and line the bottom of each one with a circle of non-stick baking parchment.

In a large bowl, cream together the butter and sugar until pale and creamy, using an electric hand-held whisk, stand mixer or by hand with a wooden spoon. Beat well to get lots of air into the mixture.

Beat in the eggs one at a time, adding a tablespoon of flour if the mixture curdles. Add a drop of vanilla extract to the beaten egg if you like to enhance the flavour. Fold in the sifted flour using a large metal spoon. Be careful not to over-mix it.

Pour the mixture equally between the two cake tins and level off the top with a spatula. Make a slight dip in the centre with the tip of the spatula if you don't want your cake to be pointed in the middle. Place the tins in the oven and bake for about 20 minutes, or until the cakes spring back when pressed gently with a finger and are pale gold in colour.

Remove the sponge cakes from the oven and take them out of the tins after about 5–10 minutes. Place them on a wire cooling rack, remove the greaseproof paper and leave to cool completely (about half an hour).

Spread raspberry jam on one of the sponges, then sandwich together with the other one. Dust with icing sugar (I use a small sieve) and serve.

JUDICIAL MATTERS

HAVING MANAGED TO AVOID any position of responsibility whatsoever for five decades, it came as something of a surprise when I was made a judge. Sadly, no one called me 'M'lud', though my adjudication was required on matters as significant and onerous as in any court of law. I was co-opted as a judge at the annual show in the North Yorkshire village of Thornton-le-Dale. Country shows are taken very seriously in these parts. As Harry Pearson, an aficionado who wrote a book on such events, remarked, 'The baking section is ruled over by a set of principles so rigid and arcane they make Japanese etiquette look laissez-faire.'

If anything, this is something of an understatement. My mother refused to have anything to do with the produce show in her village following the ruthless verdict on her entry in 'Class 61 One Victoria Sandwich (Raspberry Jam Filling)'. She came second even though hers was the only entry. At the same event, Mrs H suffered annual agonies over 'Class 69 One Shortcake, 6–6.5inch diameter'. The air turned blue as she alternately applied rolling pin and ruler. Her shortcake always expanded by a fatal fraction of an inch and was condemned to ignominious failure.

I was not asked to adjudicate on such demanding matters. After writing about the Thornton-le-Dale show in my column (I was particularly taken with an equine act called the Four Horsemen of the Apocalypse: 'Let's have a great round of applause for Pestilence!'), I was invited to judge 'Class 166 Best Matching Pair of Pigs'. Despite having a great fondness for pigs, I was slightly lacking in technical expertise. This deficiency was remedied by a brief lesson in porcine pulchritude: 'Look out for a good under-line and an even number of teats.' With the assistance of Mrs H, I carefully assessed the two pairs that had been entered. The laurels went to a charming duo of Gloucester Old Spots.

In subsequent years, I was called on to assay scarecrows, fruit liqueurs and children's crafts (a poisoned chalice second only to the bonny baby competition that survives at Rosedale Show near Whitby). Though I continued to accept the judge's badge (the free pen and cold collation lunch contribute to the allure of the post) at Thornton-le-Dale, I missed the Saddlebacks, Great Whites and Berkshires. I like pigs very much. I empathise with their obsession with food and sleep. I admire their cussedness and belligerence. I enjoy the way that pig shows often teeter on the edge of anarchy, with disputing parties having to be separated by their minders (the pig boards used for this purpose often bear the logos of major banking organisations). And, yes, I very much like eating pork.

This aptitude came in handy when I was called back to adjudicate on pigs, albeit post-mortem. Our tasting of 'Class 90 Homemade Pork Sausage' and 'Class 91 Homemade Pork Sausage (Flavoured)' was unexpectedly demanding. The man in charge of the grill mixed up the thirty-odd entries so we were obliged to have a second cook-off. My appreciation of the Four Horsemen of the Apocalypse, especially Famine, was slightly marred by having sixty nibbles of sausage inside me.

The following year, I was gratified that the show organisers had adopted my proposal for an exciting new category, which appeared in the show schedule as 'Class 93 Homemade Pork Pie (max 4in diam.) Tin baked. Hot water crust' and 'Class 94 Homemade Pork Pie (1lb weight approx.) Hand raised. Hot water crust'. Better still, I was asked to judge the porkies.

At Mrs H's urging, we arrived at the show ground in plenty of time. This was just as well. Discovering the location of the six pork pies that had been entered involved a good deal of shuttling between the Produce Tent, the Show Secretary's Tent and the Judges' Lunch Tent, where the tasting was to take place. 'Get a move on,' urged Mrs H in a manner unbefitting the dignity of my office. 'And stop complaining. At least we'll work up a good appetite for the tasting.' An hour's circumnavigation of the show site produced five pies. The sixth had disappeared, presumably to the final resting place of all good pork pies.

As we started our appraisal, a deluge descended. 'Looks like it's set in,' said a fellow judge with grim relish, a condiment much favoured in Yorkshire. Mrs H cut wedges out of the entries, a task that demanded a fair bit of elbow work. 'I feel a bit like King Arthur,' she said, heaving her knife from the heart of a pie. Though the entries shared the attributes of admirably crunchy pastry, nice even walls and tasty jelly, the nature of the meat revealed that only two makers were responsible for all five pies. One favoured lovely chunks of grey pork, the other preferred a fine mince, richly seasoned. Numerous slices were required for me to make my decision. Both approaches had merit and, anyway, I hadn't had any breakfast. By the time I had reached my judgement, the rain had stopped.

'Can I have a bit more?' I requested.

'No, you can't,' said my assistant. 'You don't want to get a prize for being the greediest judge.'

When the flap of anonymity was removed from the entry slips, I discovered that the chunky pies were made by a Mrs Rooke, while the fine-grind pies were the work of Martin, the show chairman (which possibly explains the ready acceptance of my proposal). The two first prizes of £5 were divided between the two entrants. After the success of this introductory bout, the show anticipates an avalanche of homemade pork pies in future years. Possibly, I will be judging fifty rather than five pork pies. Since we in the judiciary are expected to have a profound knowledge of our specialist fields, it became evident that I had to remedy an omission. Though I had devoted a lifetime to eating pork pies, the time had come to make one.

13

Telling porkies

AT ITS BEST, a pork pie is a deeply satisfying combination of tastes and textures. In a Melton Mowbray pie, which should be hand-raised with bulging sides, the pork is uncured, so the cooked meat looks light grey, like a pork chop. It is no coincidence, incidentally, that this Leicestershire town produces both Britain's most characterful cheese (Stilton) and Britain's best pork pies. The whey from the milk went to feed the pigs. In the nineteenth century, pork pies became a favourite snack for the many hunts in the area. Melton Mowbray pies have become my preference, though I'm not averse to a pie containing pink or cured pork.

They're mostly like this in Yorkshire and particularly good when warm. The phrase 'particularly good' doesn't do justice to the pork pies of B. W. Glaves, the butcher in the village of Brompton-by-Sawdon, near Scarborough. When they come hot from the oven, I know of no food more mouth-watering. They are the quintessence of juicy, seasoned porkiness. There are two drawbacks to this mid-morning snack: 1) A juicy dribble always leaks out after your first bite. Despite the safety warning given by Glaves's staff, I customarily spend the rest of the day sporting a huge greasy blotch on my shirt or sweater; 2) It is such a very sustaining snack that you tend to pick at your lunch.

If the pork is the most important element of a pork pie, the crust doesn't come far behind. This should be crisp on the outside and delicately yielding on the inside. A vegetarian friend of mine (admittedly not a very belligerent vegetarian) found this aspect of the pork pie so tempting that she was prone to take a nibble. Then another nibble and another. Before long, she was past the point of no return and polished off the whole crust, leaving just the meat. Her partner used to complain about the distressing spectacle he encountered when peering into the fridge. Instead of the pork pie he was looking forward to, there was something that resembled 'a bald baby's head'.

It may come as a surprise, but there is a third part to a pork pie, almost as significant as the other two. Some recipes don't mention the jelly until the end (Hugh Fearnley-Whittingstall: 'It's a bit like filling a car with petrol …'), but actually it is the bit that you make first. Unless you're Delia. In a bizarre omission, the pork pie recipe on Delia Online doesn't mention jelly at all. Obviously, she didn't grow up eating pork pies. (It comes as no surprise to learn she hails from Woking.) Jelly-making is pretty simple once you've found a butcher who will sell you a pig's trotter or pork knuckle. It's just a long, long simmer with carrot, onion and spices to produce stock, which is then boiled to make a reduction that will set as translucent porky jelly.

When the jelly is done, you can tackle the meat. A survey of pork pie recipes revealed that Jane Grigson, Delia Smith and Hugh Fearnley-Whittingstall recommended a mixture of around four parts shoulder pork to one part green bacon, which Grigson says, 'improves the flavour'. The recipe is therefore midway between the Melton Mowbray pie and the cured pork pie. Grigson maintains the meat should be 'one part fat to two parts lean'. This might be slightly overdoing it. Mark Hix recommends 20–30 per cent fat. Anyway, plenty is required. Like hamburgers, pork pie is not diet food. Where we went wrong was using belly pork in our first joint effort. This was my fault, I admit it. Instead of buying shoulder pork from the butcher, I had a moment of mental aberration and bought belly pork. This can be sensational – some of the most memorable mouthfuls I've ever had were belly pork – but it's not right for a pork pie. There's too much skin (you don't have crackling in a pork pie) and too much connective tissue. (The same white stringy stuff that caused trouble when we were making hamburgers. You may recall that its tensile strength can be half that of aluminium.) It has to be removed so you can chop up the meat. The grisly task fell to me. 'You bought it. You can deal with it,' said Mrs H.

After an hour spent cutting out connective tissue and skin (which both went into the jelly stock), I'd reduced 615g of belly pork to 480g of acceptable pork that had to be cut into cubes for the pie. Even with shoulder, which spares you the task of removing connective tissue, the pork should be chopped up by hand. Delia Smith says you can use 'a processor with the pulse button – you need a chopped rather than a minced effect', but Mrs H was scathing. 'I've tried it and I don't like it. No matter how briefly you pulse, it turns out like sausage meat, too homogenous and compact.'

She demanded a fine cut of both pork and bacon. 'Quarter-inch cubes.' The template she had in mind was the close-textured pork pie made by Mrs Bullivant, a producer who has a farm outside York and sells her pies at farmers' markets in the area. I like her pies as well. Unusually for Yorkshire, her pork is uncured. Inside tremendously tasty pastry, which Mrs H describes as 'the real McCoy', the meat is close-packed, medium-sized chunks. But when I attempted to imitate her chunk-size, my output was deemed too large. 'Here comes the Food Police,' Mrs H declared, pointing out a long strip of bacon that required further attention. When the meat passed this stringent quality control, she seasoned it with fresh sage, allspice and mace. 'I'm being generous with the salt and pepper. As with pâté, you always put in a bit more than you think is necessary.'

'How much?'

'Delia just says "salt and pepper". I'm putting in a teaspoon of salt.'

Both Smith and Grigson also add anchovy sauce. According to the latter, this is used 'in the Melton Mowbray area'. Though I love Alan Davidson's *Oxford Companion to*

Food above all other food books, I'm baffled by his explanation that the pie-makers of the town added anchovy essence 'not only for its flavour but because it was thought to give the meat an attractive pink colour, while pies from other districts were brownish or greyish. In modern pies, which are always pink, the colour is achieved by the use of chemicals.' The only explanation that springs to mind is that Davidson wrote the entry before Melton Mowbray pies enjoyed their recent resurgence. The town's manufacturers may have used anchovy sauce (they tend to be a bit cagey about revealing their seasonings), though it is not mentioned in any of the recipes in *The History of the Melton Mowbray Pork Pie* by Trevor Hickman. We ended up putting in the half-teaspoonful recommended by Smith and Grigson.

Having prepared the meat, it was time to tackle the hot water pastry. Though always rather impressed whenever I heard the name, I hadn't much idea of what it was.

'Weigh out 450 grams of flour!' said Mrs H.

'There you are, 445 grams.'

'Then we need a bit more. Now sift the flour.'

'Oops.'

'Try to get it all in the bowl.'

The hot water part of hot water pastry proved to be rather more thrilling than I expected. The water isn't just hot but boiling and it contains molten lard. It might have been poured on the riff-raff of Paris by Quasimodo from the bell-tower of Notre-Dame. You start by heating a rectangular block of lard in a pan of cold water. As this white island disappears, a puddle of molten lard spreads on the surface of the water. Eventually the lard resembles the remnant of a bar of soap, before vanishing entirely. When the lard and water mixture achieves a white boil, the bubbling emulsion is mixed with the flour.

'You add the flour in a series of trickles,' said Mrs H. 'Trickle, stir. Trickle, stir. Trickle, stir.'

The result was a mess of beige lumps.

'You want to amalgamate the bits and knead it,' she directed.

'Ow!'

'That'll be the boiling fat. It's quite warm.'

Being made of sterner stuff, Mrs H gathered the pastry together and rolled it into a ball. Now came the demanding task of making a leakproof jacket for the pork pie. In Melton Mowbray, they form the crust round a circular wooden block or dolly. It is like a shoe last, but for a pie. Since even our outlandish collection of gadgetry lacked such an item, we used a non-stick pie mould.

'We need to line the mould while the pastry is warm,' urged Mrs H. She quickly rolled out the pastry. With some difficulty she lined the mould.

'It's very keen on falling down, isn't it,' I pointed out.

'It's probably too thin.'

'There's loads of pastry left over.'

'So what about the lid?' said Mrs H with a touch of exasperation. 'How many pork pies have you seen without a lid?' Well, you can get novelty pies topped with cran-berries, onions or even gooseberries, but I thought it wise not to make this point. Mrs H rolled the remaining pastry into a rough circle.

We filled the pastry case with chopped, seasoned pork and put on the lid. Mrs H sealed the joint between lid and walls by pushing her thumb repeatedly round the rim of the mould. For the first time our effort began to look like a pie.

'Make a hole in the top so we can fill the pie with jelly,' said Mrs H. 'I bet you'd forgotten that.'

But it turned out that a hole in the lid was not required. I returned from an outing expecting to see an immaculate cooked pork pie. Instead I was greeted by one of the ruins that Cromwell knocked about a bit. A great chunk of pastry was missing from one side of the pie. 'We made the pastry too thin,' wailed Mrs H. 'It might have been all right if I hadn't dropped it when taking it out of the oven. I should have used oven gloves instead of a tea towel. The mould fell over and the juice leaked out and stuck the pastry to the wall of the mould and I'm fed up with the whole bloody thing.'

The pie smelled very nice though. A lovely cloud of sage and cooked pork hung in the air, so we decided to eat the pie warm. It was very tasty, perhaps a bit too tasty. A very savoury pie. We each had a slice, then another slice, then another and that was the end of the ruined castle. Though we polished it off with gusto, certain reservations remained.

'A bit too salty,' tutted Mrs H. 'I don't think you need salt and bacon and anchovy sauce.'

'I think the bacon was wrong. The pie was neither one thing nor another.'

'It was grey, though.'

'Should we have another go?'

'I think I've had enough of pork pies for the time being.'

When our enthusiasm returned, not to mention our appetites, we resumed the task. For our second effort, we went for pork shoulder, which was much easier than belly. I followed my inclinations and chopped the joint into somewhat larger cubes (between a quarter and half an inch across). No bacon, no anchovy, just salt and pepper and spices. As a pork pie purist, I decided that we should also ditch the herbs. Butchers don't usually bother with them. We had some jelly left over from the first pie. All that remained was the problematic pastry. This time we incorporated milk with the water and lard. Boiling these together produced an interesting lava-lamp effect, with stalagmites of milky water rising into the molten fat before forming a white foam.

The major difference with our second effort was that we did not roll the pastry. This decision was taken after lengthy consideration of pie architecture and crust viability. Rolled pastry produces a thin crust that is liable to leak at the jelly stage. Moreover, Melton Mowbray pies have thick walls.

After cutting off a quarter of the pastry for the lid, I used my hands to form the hot-water pastry into a rough circle about twenty centimetres in diameter. I eased this into the mould so the centre of the circle dipped into the hole. Then came the tricky task of pushing the pastry to the bottom of the mould, so it filled snugly into the joint between the base and the wall. 'Try not to make a hole in the bottom,' said Mrs H.

'I've just made a hole in the bottom.'

After repairing the fissure (it's a good idea to reserve some pastry for patching purposes), I massaged the crust up the wall of the mould. 'Use two fingers and work quickly,' said Mrs H. I fought back the impulse to flourish two fingers in her direction. The difficulty of this task was compounded by the tendency of the pastry to spring back. After some deft fingerwork, the pastry reached the rim of the mould. 'No holes … I think,' said Mrs H. We then filled the pastry with chopped pork. The lid, which I also formed with my hands, then went on top. Well, where else would it go?

When Mrs H suggested decorating our creation, I finally discovered my métier. Hitherto, I have always regarded myself as lacking in any manual talent whatsoever, but somewhat late in life I discovered that I have an innate ability for making tree leaves in pastry. I would have made them in autumnal profusion, but Mrs H said four were enough.

When the pie came out of the oven, we poured in the warm jelly (yes, I remembered the hole) and continued to top up every so often for a few hours. 'Hurray! No cracks,' yelled Mrs H. We let this pie cool before eating. The first slice was a nervous moment, but it came out clean as a whistle. Mrs H expressed satisfaction at the pastry. 'Not too lardy and not too thick. It's not as crisp as a professional pork pie but their crusts can be very greasy.' I liked the meat, a close-packed matrix of chunks set in jelly. 'A pork pie that tastes of pork,' I said, reaching for the chutney. I also discovered that it went extraordinarily well with Tiptree's medlar jelly. A significant part of the pleasure of a pork pie is discovering what goes well with it.

After all this endeavour, would I bother making pork pies at home when rather good ones are available from Glaves the butcher or Mrs Bullivant's market stall? Well, yes, once or twice a year if I felt the urge. 'If I have one criticism, it's that the chunks of pork are still too big,' said Mrs H. 'Now Mrs Bullivant's pies ...' But I was too busy chomping.

Mrs H's recipe for pork pie

One day we will make a hand-raised pork pie. But until then, we remain at the wimp's stage and use a non-stick, loose-bottomed, 11cm pork pie tin. (John Lewis and Lakeland sell them.) I have also hired an oval-shaped game pie tin from our local kitchen shop for our Christmas pie. (Even I cannot bring myself to spend £78.50 on one.) This is our favourite variation, but those who feel so inclined can add a tablespoon of chopped fresh sage and a finely chopped rasher of green back bacon to the pork filling. A note on pig's trotters: OK, the animal may have been squelching around in the soil – but when you buy trotters at the butcher, they are just as clean as the rest of the pig. Your main problem might be getting hold of them. Once we had to join a waiting list for the trotters as our local butcher had an order for a dozen and only bought in one pig a week. 'A pig has only four trotters, love – you'll have to wait.'

Jelly
600ml water
1 pig's trotter (or a pork knuckle)
1 bay leaf
6 peppercorns

Pork filling
600g pork shoulder
a rasher of green back bacon or 2 slices of pancetta
    (optional)
½ teaspoon freshly grated nutmeg
½ teaspoon ground mace
½ teaspoon ground allspice
1 tablespoon chopped fresh sage (optional)
2 teaspoons anchovy essence or 1–2 fresh salted anchovies,
    finely chopped (optional)
salt and black pepper

Hot water crust pastry
50ml warm water
50ml whole milk
150g lard
450g plain flour
salt and black pepper
1 fresh egg yolk, beaten, for glazing the pie

First make the jelly. Bring the water, trotter, bay leaf and peppercorns to the boil, cover the pan with a lid, then simmer until the meat is quite soft and leaving the bone – around 3 hours. Strain the liquid into a basin (I use a muslin square lining a sieve to catch all the little bits), discarding the debris. Leave the liquid to cool, then remove any fat from the top. You should have a flavoursome, slightly cloudy jelly.

Cut the shoulder of pork (and bacon, if using) into small pieces, discarding any connective tissue and gristle. Mix the meat well with the spices (and chopped sage and anchovy essence, if you like). Season well with a pinch of salt and a good grind of black pepper and keep chilled.

To make the pastry, boil the water, milk and lard together until the lard has melted. Pour the boiling liquid on to the flour in a bowl and mix in with a table knife. Remember that it will be quite hot. The pastry should soon come together – when it does, turn it out on to the work surface and knead it a little.

Cut off a quarter of the pastry to make the lid and set aside. Form the rest of the pastry into a ball, pop it into the pork pie tin and begin to work it across the base and evenly up the sides of the tin. (Forming your index and middle finger into a paddle shape helps – rather like an upside-down scout salute). Leave the top of the pastry to overhang the side. Pack the pork filling in loosely, but right to the top of the tin.

Pat the remaining pastry into a circle the same thickness as the pastry sides. And, after brushing the rim of the pastry with beaten egg, pop the lid on the top. Crimp the edges of the pastry together and trim the excess pastry away with a knife. Make a small hole in the centre of the pastry lid. Use the surplus pastry to make leaf shapes or whatever you want. Fix the decoration with a dab of egg glaze and give the whole pie a final brush with the egg.

Bake the pie in the oven at 200°C/Gas Mark 6 for 30 minutes, then reduce the heat to 190°C/Gas Mark 5 for a further hour, or until the pastry is golden brown and the meat is cooked. (Test with a skewer – if it comes out clean with clear juices, the meat is cooked.) When fully cooked, remove the pie from the oven and leave it to cool down a bit before removing it from the tin.

When the pie has cooled completely, turn your attention to the jelly. Reheat it so it returns to liquid and either using a jug with a small lip or a basting syringe, pour the jelly through the hole on the top of the pie. You may need to have several goes to fully fill the pie. Leave the jelly to set before eating.

Tip: a baker told me that should your pastry crust have developed any cracks during baking, use bits of leftover pastry as a temporary bung while you pour in the jelly. Remove when the jelly has set.

Mrs H's recipe for game pie

A game pie is made in a similar way to a pork pie, using a hot water crust pastry and substituting pheasant, partridge, wild boar, venison, etc. for the pork shoulder. The meat is cut into strips and layered with seasonings. I like to add grated zest of an orange. The jelly is flavour-boosted with a celery stalk, carrot and white wine or dry white vermouth. If using whole birds, use the carcasses to make stock.

CASH INTO NOSH

DESPITE A YORKSHIRE TENDENCY towards economy on my side and a southern propensity for dispersing the stuff on Mrs H's, money is something that we rarely argue about, at least when it is spent on food. Is any expenditure more worthwhile than the purchase of pleasurable nutrients? Admittedly, our priorities are somewhat different. Few weeks go by without me buying one or two dozen oysters. Mrs H has a weakness for vegetables – particularly English asparagus, which she buys by the armful during the season, artichokes (both kinds), aubergines, red peppers and the fancier kinds of tomatoes – that can push our greengrocery bill to surprising heights.

We both find it hard – impossible is a more accurate word – to economise on comestibles. Aside from braising cuts and offal, cheap meat is rarely a good idea, still less cheap (meaning elderly) fish. The only bargain that I punt on in a big way is cheese. Reduced price cheese has two advantages: it is cheaper and it is well matured. I buy it by the kilo. One big chunk of something splendid – Appleby Cheshire, Montgomery Cheddar or Wensleydale sheep's milk cheese – makes a much more tempting and impressive cheeseboard than a flotilla of itsy-bitsy wedges.

Curiously, we spend more on food in North Yorkshire than in London, where it is generally more expensive. Crabs, sea trout and salmon (a fiver each if you happen to catch them being landed from the boat) demand to be snapped up. During the game season, when plucked pheasant and partridge are sold in our patch of Yorkshire at £5 per brace, we tend to invest so heavily that it often comes as a slight surprise to the seller that we are not running a restaurant. Sometimes, the northern cornucopia is so tempting that I wish we were, though the first twinge of backache when I'm preparing a meal instantly extinguishes this pipedream.

The odd thing is that when I experience a rare and evanescent urge to be thrifty, the result often ends up being hugely expensive. An example of this occurred prior to our annual summer break in the north. On the brink of departure from Hirst HQ, we gathered vital food supplies from our local Turkish shop. This is not because food is in short supply in North Yorkshire. The reverse is true. However, Turkish supermarkets are a bit of a rarity in the Filey area. I was particularly keen to lay in a large stock of pitta bread. Yes, I know you can get it pretty much anywhere, but the version made by Sofra Bakery of Tottenham is particularly good. It is light, tasty and marbled with carbonised striations. After being sprinkled with water, the pittas puff up on the barbecue like miniature dirigibles. You half expect them to take off and whirl round your head, emitting puffs of steam. At the time of purchase, these edible Zeppelins had another advantage, particularly for the Turkophile Yorkshireman. At £1 for four packets of six, they worked out at 4.16p per pitta.

Or, at least, they should have. While musing in the shop over Mrs H's reaction if I were to buy a hubble-bubble, an assistant started shouting at me. 'Sir, sir, your car! A parking warden!' Dumping my pile of pittas, I dashed. At first, it looked as if I was in the nick of time. The warden was issuing a ticket to another poor blighter. But I'd forgotten that they hunt in packs in South London. A hidden colleague had already stuck the dread notice on my windscreen. Five minutes on a single yellow set me back £50, thus pushing the cost per pitta to an astronomic £2.12.

When we reached our northern base, the world's most expensive pitta breads were utilised in a number of appropriate snacks. We used them for dipping into home-made hummus. They were also filled with the Levantine cold omelette dish known as *eggah* for lunch on the beach. About halfway through my expensive hoard, I felt the urge to switch to the Yorkshire leavened equivalent, which are called breadcakes. These are circular in form, about twelve centimetres in diameter and four centimetres high. More flying saucers than airships, they were a staple of my childhood. Overcoming the hesitation of the outsider, Mrs H has become a convert of sorts. 'A bit like a squashed roll,' she says. At 25p a time, they are considerably more expensive than pitta bread, but this price is not subject to sudden inflation since parking wardens are an easily spotted rarity in our village.

After lunching on breadcakes with a culturally appropriate filling for North Yorkshire (ham and English mustard, roast beef and horseradish) for a couple of days, I returned to the pitta bread. But when I opened the two remaining packs, I experienced an anguish almost as severe as that inflicted by the parking warden. The first pitta was mottled with an archipelago of green and yellow patches of mould. I morosely flipped through the rest like a medieval monk peering into the Book of Lamentations. Each vellum page bore the same unappetising illumination. This second calamity upped the price to £4.25 per pitta. Not good news for a Yorkshireman, though Mrs H pointed out that she paid for both the pitta bread and the fine. 'I don't know what you're moaning about. It cost you, as you would say, "Nowt".'

Despite this reassurance, I have resigned myself to penury due to our outgoings on food. Though I feel boundless admiration and even kinship for certain chefs and food producers, the direction of cash flow delineates the oceanic gulf dividing professional from amateur. They charge. We cough up. Only once have I ever come close (or so I thought) to gaining financial reward for anything I have cooked. In a moment of wild optimism, I saw my raspberry jam as seed capital.

14

Getting the raspberry

IT IS COMMONLY THOUGHT that people engage in jam-making to enjoy the fruits of the sun in colder months, but there is another, less romantic reason why sticky-pawed preservers can be found hovering over steaming pans on the hottest days of the year. The competitive instinct infects this bucolic pastime. As with marmalade, all jam-makers believe their product to be nonpareil. Moreover, they are eager to prove their superiority in that ruthless gladiatorial arena known as the country produce show. Though a placid sort of fellow, I am by no means immune to the lure of the contest. This explains why an entry from C. Hirst was present among the regiment of raspberry jams entered in the 88th Annual Show of Thornton-le-Dale, North Yorkshire. I was in it for the honour, though the prize money (£5, £3, £1) would come in handy. I little realised that this impulse would involve me still being embroiled in competitive conserves twelve months later. You can get stuck with jam.

My rash participation came about when I was alone in Yorkshire. Since Mrs H had been called to London, I made my first-ever batch of raspberry jam under my own steam.

The fruit came from Mr and Mrs Hunter's farm in our village. At their peak in late July and early August, the pick-your-own beds resemble a medieval image of summer bounty. The canes are dotted with fruit in glowing profusion. No pud is better than fresh raspberries 'preferably with sugar and Jersey cream', as Jane Grigson pointed out in her *Fruit Book*, but there is a limit to the amount you can consume. Having reached, possibly surpassed, that point, I felt the urge to try my hand at jam.

You can pick a kilo of fruit in fifteen minutes and that's the hardest bit about making raspberry jam (or so it seemed). According to the formula I obtained from Mrs Hunter, who sells an exemplary version from her farm shop, you gently simmer equal parts raspberries and granulated sugar until the latter has fully dissolved (there must not be the slightest sugary rasp when you stir your spoon). Then you crank up the heat to produce a rolling boil for twenty minutes. At this point, you turn off the heat and pot in sterilised jars. As Mrs Hunter says, 'Raspberry jam cooks itself.'

Nevertheless, I felt that, due to an innate mastery of the art, my very first attempt resulted in a transcendentally excellent example. Set but not excessively so, it was a radiant joy to eye and palate alike. A kilo of raspberries produced around seven jars. It was so easy and the results were so good that I repeated the exercise. Then I did it again. I had thoughts of going into commercial jam-making and even imagined how the label might bear a handsome likeness of the manufacturer along the lines of Newman's Own. Only the reappearance of Mrs H ('Good grief! How are we going to get through all this?') prevented me from jammifying the whole of Mrs Hunter's crop.

I was sure that my raspberry jam would romp home to victory at Thornton-le-Dale, despite the daunting field of eighteen entries. 'Class 5 One Jar Raspberry Jam' is the Grand National of the produce section. When judging was over, I headed confidently for the phalanx of scarlet jars. You may picture my dumbstruck disbelief when I spotted my entry among the also-rans. My jam got the raspberry. As a greenhorn pitting myself against the toughest competition in the world of conserves – Yorkshirewomen who had been making jam before they managed to tie a pinny at the back by themselves – I should scarcely have expected to be among the place money, but the sting was undeniable. It only served me right for the many times I had breezily assessed the efforts of others at Thornton-le-Dale show. 'Judge not lest ye be judged.' Matthew vii.1.

Despite the judicial thumbs-down, I enjoyed my preserve very much. The great plus of raspberry jam is the bite of acid in the fruit that lifts its flavour above others (blackcurrant jam is an equal thrill for the palate). My production run saw me happily through the following year. Jam and bread is my secret vice, a reviving nibble to be consumed when nobody is looking. It's a fairly regular secret vice since I manage to get through twenty-odd jars in the course of a year.

Though primarily a way of preserving fruit for the rest of the year, there is another reason why jam came into being. Because fresh fruit was traditionally regarded with grave suspicion (strawberries were associated with melancholia), simmering with honey and, later, sugar was a way of making it healthy. There is a darker irony about this confection. The British love affair with jam – and, indeed, the word itself – dates from the eighteenth century, when cheap sugar became available from the slave plantations of the West Indies. It was only with the introduction of beet sugar in the nineteenth century, which played a part in the abolition of slavery, that jam became morally acceptable.

Twelve months on from my debacle at Thornton-le-Dale, I decided that radical steps were required. If my previous rendition did not match the stratospheric standards of North Yorkshire jam judges, it was necessary to try a new approach. This time, Mrs H was on hand and we agreed to try the raspberry jam recipe in *Preserves: River Cottage Handbook No.2* by Pam Corbin, formerly a professional jam-maker. It was consoling to learn that even this *maîtresse de confiture* came unstuck in the competitive arena. Ms Corbin describes the 'dismal result' when she entered a pot of strawberry jam in the Uplyme and Lyme Regis Horticultural Show. The strawberry recipe she includes in the book is the result of intense efforts to remedy this catastrophe. (Her secret for 'a wonderful, intense strawberry taste' is the addition of lemon juice.)

Curiously, the book's recipe for raspberry jam comes not from this expert, but from Hugh Fearnley-Whittingstall, the founder/proprietor of River Cottage. It is entitled 'Hugh's prize-winning raspberry fridge jam', though no details are given of the provenance of his triumph. 'Hugh F-W,' writes Ms Corbin, 'thinks the secret of success is to pick the raspberries on a hot, dry day, aiming for a good mixture of ripe and almost-ripe fruit, then to make the jam immediately – to capture the full flavour of the berries.' Well, yes, I did all that (you don't feel much urge to pick on a cold, wet day), but it's not the full story of HFW's innovatory method. The recipe that took the victor's laurels calls for 1.5 kilos of raspberries combined with the staggeringly low quantity of 750g of sugar. HFW uses jam sugar, which includes added pectin. (As you may recall from my adventures with marmalade, pectin is a kind of fruity cement. It helps jams to set, especially when using fruit like apricots and strawberries that are low in natural pectin.) HFW says you should mash half the fruit in a preserving pan with a potato masher, then add the remaining unmashed fruit plus jam sugar. Stir over a low heat until the sugar is dissolved, then 'bring to a rolling boil for exactly five minutes'. It smelled sensational during this brief bubbling. The result was a brilliant red, considerably lighter than my effort of the previous year. This was a good sign. Someone told me that judges tends to favour light-coloured raspberry jam. I was just about to start potting when Mrs H appeared in the kitchen. 'Have you checked the wrinkle point?' she asked.

'The recipe doesn't say anything here about checking the wrinkle point,' I replied acidly.

'If I were you, I'd do the wrinkle test.' I'd previously encountered this infallible analysis when making marmalade.

I deposited a dollop of 'Hugh's prize-winning raspberry fridge jam' on a chilled plate, waited a few moments and prodded. There was not the slightest sign of a wrinkle. It was more of a trickle. Grasping at straws, I hoped the jam would magically thicken after being left overnight in the fridge. In the morning, Mrs W picked up the jar and tilted it. The contents *swirled*. 'That won't win anything in a competition,' she sniffed. I can't remember feeling more disappointed since my defeat at Thornton-le-Dale.

On closer inspection, Pam Corbin's recipe suggested that we should have expected nothing else. 'This light, soft jam is fantastic in cakes or sherry trifles or stirred into creamy rice puddings.' There was nothing about it being 'fantastic' on a bit of bread and butter. The omission was ominous. Obviously, Ms Corbin was not going to rubbish the seigneur of River Cottage, but she seemed to be giving the reader a powerful hint. Reading between the lines, it became clear that HFW's 'prize-winning jam' wasn't jam as such, but a jam-related liquid intended to be used in other dishes.

So where on earth did it win a prize? I decided to apply my investigative skills to the puzzle. I recalled that in HFW's *River Cottage Cookbook* (2001), there is a photo of a certificate from the 1998 Beaminster Summer Show where he scooped third prize for 'Six Different Vegetables'. I therefore tapped 'Beaminster', 'raspberry' and 'Fearnley-Whittingstall' into Google. This produced the River Cottage blog, where HFW preened about his raspberry jam: 'A light boiling produces a loose, almost pourable jam with a fresh, tangy flavour. This version took first prize at the Beaminster summer show, so I must have done something right.'

I gasped. How could it be 'almost pourable' and still be a jam? HFW had actually made something that was more of a sauce or coulis. It certainly would not have won anything in a Women's Institute competition. When I came across a copy of the WI's show guide, entitled 'On with the Show', I instantly turned to the judging instructions on jam. These include the stern specification: 'Consistency jellified, not runny or sticky, no loose liquid or syrup.' The words 'not runny' do not support HFW's cocky, 'I must have done something right.'

Still, his oozy formulation won first prize among the jams at Beaminster, so why not North Yorkshire? I entered a pot made from HFW's dubious recipe in the annual show of the Hunmanby & District Garden Produce Association, which takes place a week before the far larger Thornton-le-Dale event. Giving the judge a bit of a nudge, Mrs H labelled it 'Raspberry Fridge Jam'. Of course, it came nowhere. On reflection, it seems to me that there are two possible reasons for HFW's perplexing success at Beaminster. Either the judges in the West Country are culinary revolutionaries eager to accept avant-garde experimentation in jam-making or they had got some inkling of the celebrity status of the maker. I'm not saying one way or another, but HFW's triumph seems jammy to me.

With three days to go before the 89th Thornton-le-Dale Annual Show, it was time to call on a higher power. I set

Mrs H to work on the HFW jam. 'If it shows no sign of setting, your best bet is to bung in a bottle of Certo,' she said. Mrs H is an ardent believer in this liquid pectin. The label declares: 'Jams made with Certo require less boiling and maintain the full flavour and colour of the fruit.' This proved to be true. When Mrs H produced a jar of the Certo-enriched Fearnley-Whittingstall jam, it looked fantastic. It was the crimson of fresh raspberries, not the maroon of raspberry jam. It also tasted fantastic. Unfortunately, it remained jam of the 'almost pourable' sort.

Once again, we hoped that it would stiffen overnight. Once again, we were disappointed. It did not do any setting whatsoever. Certo made not a scrap of difference. To be fair to Certo, the label does not claim that 'Jams made with Certo require less sugar'. It was time to call on an even higher authority than Mrs H. (They do exist, you know.) Harold McGee's exploration of culinary science *On Food and Cooking* explained the problem. Pectin, he says, is extracted from vegetable cell walls by boiling. 'The long, string-like pectin molecules bind a liquid into a solid by bonding to each other and forming a meshwork that traps the liquid in its interstices. Some fruits, including grapes and most berries, are rich enough in pectin to produce excellent gels on their own.' This explains why recipes for raspberry jam usually require granulated sugar rather than jam sugar, which is pectin enriched.

So why didn't the HFW jam with added pectin do any setting? The answer, according to McGee, is connected with 'the negative electrical charge of pectin molecules'.

'Like poles repel' is one of the very few things I remember from five years of studying physics. Acid in fruit reduces the electrical charge. This should help the pectin to bond. Unfortunately, pectin, which likes to stick to anything but itself, still tends to bond with water molecules. The solution to this quandary is sugar. McGee explains: 'If sugar is added, its highly water-attracting molecules take enough water out of circulation to allow the pectin molecules to reach one another.' In short, you need sugar to make jam. That's why HFW's 'prize-winning jam' isn't jam. 'To thicken a preserve with pectin,' McGee concludes, 'we need acid and sugar: the two substances that fruits specialise in storing. Sounds like a cinch … But as anyone who has tried knows, it's anything but a cinch.' Quite.

We picked punnet after punnet at Mrs Hunter's farm and Mrs H worked furiously to produce a set jam with the fresh flavour of HFW's syrup. I'd say that she worked uncomplainingly but this would not be the truth. As with the marmalade, she complained noisily and at great length. 'Why the hell am I making more jam when we've already got a kitchenful of the stuff?' she inquired. When I pointed out the imminence of the 89th Thornton-le-Dale Annual Show, she used language about the 89th Thornton-le-Dale Annual Show that would be unusual in a food book written by anyone but Anthony Bourdain.

Contrary to my tendency to engage in industrial-scale production, she prefers the small run, maybe four jars at a time. Propelled by irritation at HFW's crowing, she dramatically upped the quantity of both jam sugar and

Certo. The result had not the slightest suggestion of liquidity. Though pleasing in taste, it had the resolute set of brawn. More a jam for slicing than spreading, it was the reverse of HFW's slurry. When I pointed out the minor blemish that it required a bulldozer for spreading, an impressive blast of steam eddied from Mrs H's ears. After cooling sufficiently for operating purposes, this heroine tackled the impossible task of making a set version of HFW jam without a radical increase in the sugar content. It was the jammy equivalent of squaring the circle. On her fifth attempt, she triumphed by slightly increasing the amount of sugar (for 750g of raspberries, she added 400g of jam sugar instead of the suggested 375) and continuing the rolling boil for ten minutes rather than five. The jam had the bright colour and fresh tang of the HFW jam, but passed the wrinkle test with flying colours. When it had cooled, I tried the equally significant test of spreading it on a slice of bread and butter, where it stayed happily in place instead of squirming off and trickling to the floor.

With renewed confidence, we took Mrs H's low-sugar jam to the Produce Tent of the Thornton-le-Dale show. This time, Class 5 contained twenty-two entries. From a discreet distance, we observed a white-coated judge closely scrutinise each jar before tasting a tiny sample. The narrow spatula she used for the purpose was carefully washed in a pot of water before being dipped in the next jar. It was all reassuringly professional, though her intake was molecular compared to my in-depth assessment of pork pies at the same event.

When the barrier came down and the Produce Tent was opened to the public, we casually sauntered towards the phalanx of competing jars. Trying not to look over-eager, we first viewed the neighbouring classes of torpedo-sized marrows, scones like small castles and carrots as long as rapiers. Eventually, we reached Class 5. Prize certificates leaned against three of the jars. I'd like to say that our three weeks' labour, which involved the production of twenty-five jars of raspberry jam, was crowned by glory. But it wasn't. Once again our striving produced zilch. And the same went for Hugh Fearnley-Whittingstall's 'prize-winning jam', which we also entered. This was less of a surprise. He might have done 'something right' in Beaminster, but it wasn't right for Thornton-le-Dale.

At the fag end of August, I decided to test the patience of Mrs H to destruction by making yet another batch of raspberry jam. The reason for this last gasp was a recipe that I came across in Thane Prince's book *Jams & Chutneys*. Displaying the typical modesty of the preserve-maker, it is entitled 'Best-ever Raspberry Jam'. Involving the traditional sugar-to-fruit ratio of 1:1, it requires boiling for a mere 'five to seven minutes'. Mrs Hunter had closed her PYO operation for the season, but she made a special concession for her most obsessively dedicated customer. By this stage, the raspberry canes were parched, brown and blowsy but a few extraordinarily large fruit remained. Fighting off the insects, which have an equal fondness for raspberries, we managed to find a kilo of fruit.

When I put the berries into our preserving pan, Mrs H

pointed out that Thane Prince's recipe required just one pound of raspberries and one pound of granulated sugar. The result would, of course, be two pounds of jam. 'You can't make two pounds of jam if you've just picked a kilo of fruit. It's stark impossible,' I said, heaving a kilo of sugar into the pan.

'You won't get a great load like this to set in seven minutes,' said Mrs H irritatingly. 'I tell you that for free.'

And she was right again, drat it. When I did the wrinkle test after seven minutes' boiling, the jam trickled down the chilled plate. I gave it another four minutes, but the jam still showed no sign of congealment. After a further four minutes – making fifteen minutes in all – it finally displayed sluggishness. As it turned out, my 'great load' only produced three and a half jars. It looked pretty much the same light-red colour as the jam pictured in Thane Prince's book and had exactly the consistency she recommends ('a bit runny'), but the moment of truth had yet to come. It was to be appraised by a judge every bit as discriminating as any at Thornton-le-Dale.

'It's nice and glossy with an excellent set,' said Mrs H. 'Considering it was made from "back-end" fruit, it has a good raspberry taste.'

'Would you say it was supremely excellent?'

'No, but it's quite good jam.' It was only later that I realised I was pretty much back where I started with Mrs Hunter's recipe. See what I mean about getting stuck with jam?

Mrs H's recipe for raspberry jam

We are lucky to have Mr and Mrs Hunter's farm near us in Yorkshire. I've borrowed this recipe from Mrs Hunter. As well as producing tasty eggs, they grow pick-your-own soft fruit, so it means that you can have a happy peaceful time among the canes before the sugary part of making jam. This is the recipe for a jam that sets! It is really easy to make, having only equal quantities of fruit and sugar. It works fine with small batches. You can do as little as two 450g jars. Should you wish to make more, alter the weight of the ingredients as required.

450g freshly picked raspberries
450g granulated sugar

As with all preserves, make sure that your jars are scrupulously washed and dried. Remember to place them in a low oven (80°C) well before you need to pot the jam.

Place the raspberries and sugar in a preserving pan or large saucepan. Stir the fruit gently over a low heat until the sugar has completely dissolved.

Bring the jam to boiling point and boil rapidly for 15–20 minutes, or until a setting point is reached. To test place a small amount on a pre-cooled plate and, after 1–2 minutes, push the surface of your sample with your finger. If the jam wrinkles, it can be potted on. If it fails to pass the 'wrinkle test', boil for another 5 minutes and test again.

Leave the jam to stand for 15 minutes in order to

distribute the fruit evenly, then pour into the warm jars. Fill to the top and allow to cool for another 10 minutes, then place a waxed paper disc on top of the jam. This makes a seal and prevents too much shrinkage. When the jam is completely cool, cover with a screwtop lid. I prefer to use new lids as they have a better seal than recycled ones. If you are aiming for a more traditional look, or want to enter the jam in a competition, cover with a cellophane disc affixed with a rubber band. If you are feeling creative, you could top the jam-pot with a fabric or paper cover. The best-dressed pots last year wore brown paper tied with some brown string and one of those nicely written luggage labels. I'm sorry to say that ours were stored *au naturel* (no label at all) in the cardboard boxes from Lakeland that the pots came in.

RECIPE FOR DISASTER

IN MY EXPERIENCE – and I've got quite a bit in this dept
– a recipe becomes a trial by ordeal because you screw it up
in some way. The reason may be that you measure the
cream inaccurately, you set fire to the pizza or you forget
you're in charge of some baking bread ('I wondered where
the smell was coming from'). Sometimes, however, a recipe
goes right and it is still an unmitigated horror to do. Here
follow examples of both screw-up and intentional torture.

The former occurred when I attempted *sepia con pochas*
(cuttlefish with white beans), from Elisabeth Luard's *The
Food of Spain & Portugal*. It seemed an appropriate dish to
welcome Mrs H back from a work trip to the Costa del Sol.
Another reason for having a bash at this concoction is that
I just happened to have a cuttlefish in the freezer (which
gives you some idea of the contents of the cold store at Hirst
HQ), while in our overflowing store cupboard there was a
packet of dried giant butter beans that I'd purchased at the
Central Market in Athens.

Here are three things you might not know about butter
beans: 1) They originated in tropical America but are

mainly consumed in Greece and Spain; 2) According to *The Cook's Encyclopaedia* by Tom Stobart, they are 'one of the best flavoured of all beans'; 3) They gave the name to the American Forties comedy duo Butterbeans & Susie, best known for a salacious ditty entitled 'I Want a Hot Dog for My Roll'.

After soaking these prodigious legumes for twenty-four hours, I simmered them in white wine and water with gently fried garlic and chopped cuttlefish, as directed by Elisabeth Luard: 'Sprinkle in the oregano, season, put the lid on and leave to cook gently for 20 minutes or so, until the cuttlefish is tender.' After twenty minutes or so, the cuttlefish was tender, but the beans gave cause for concern. They seemed completely unaffected by their braise. Moreover, they produced a daunting rattle in the pan. I fished one out with a spoon and had an experimental nibble. A bullet. Another twenty minutes' simmer produced not the slightest emollience. The beans' granite intransigence remained after a further forty minutes on the hob. In a desperate attempt to induce edibility, I pulled the skin from each bean and gave them another simmer. After an hour, they were marginally chewable but more like biscuits than beans. Having wasted a good chunk of the day on Mrs H's treat, I fed beans and shrivelled cuttlefish into the ever-accepting mouth of the bin.

So what went wrong with the dish that Elisabeth Luard promised was 'unusual but delicious'? A hint appeared in a recipe for prawn salad with haricot beans by Simon Hopkinson: 'Make sure the sell-by date on the dried beans is well advanced, assuring that they are relatively newly dried.' Unfortunately, the traders in Athens market do not put a sell-by date on their produce, but it struck me that I had not been to Athens for three years. My beans were not exactly newly dried.

So what did I do for Mrs H's meal? I still made *sepia con pochas*, but with a bottle of ready-cooked Spanish butter beans from the supermarket and a second frozen cuttlefish (which gives an even better idea of the contents of the Hirst HQ cold store). Mrs H said it was better than anything she had eaten in Andalucia. Over supper, we discussed our varying Spanish experiences. Mrs H told me about Marbella, while I spoke of beans.

For an example of a recipe that goes right and is still excruciating, I refer you to the eight pages of directions for Black Forest gateau in Heston Blumenthal's *In Search of Perfection*. It is a dish that no one in their right mind would want to attempt. I think that can justifiably be said about the twelve-hour grind that it requires. I wonder if anyone else has made Heston's little cake? He obviously thinks his bizarre confection is practicable. Why else would he have included it in two of his books? In case anyone feels tempted by the account in the following chapter, I should point out that it is a complete nightmare. For once, this cliché is spot on. Occasionally, I still dream that I am peering into a cardboard box while wielding a chocolate-filled paint spray gun.

15

Death by chocolate

THE HEART SINKS at the words 'Black Forest gateau', especially if you don't particularly like chocolate. I'm not so desperate about the stuff and Mrs H is even less keen, despite the assiduous efforts of chocolate companies to market their products as a surefire turn-on for females. So why did we make this retro favourite? The answer is that a newspaper asked me to do so.

Along with fish and chips, bangers and mash and spag bol, BFG is one of the dishes that Blumenthal tackled in his book *In Search of Perfection*. His efforts to attain 'the essential character' of these staples involved seeking out the best possible ingredients and applying the outré cooking techniques for which he is famous. Personally, I would sooner have gone for his turbot in batter aerated by soda siphon, but the commissioning editor demanded BFG, which happens to be the most complicated recipe in the book. Obviously, Blumenthal regards his own version as a triumph. It is the only one of the sixteen dishes in *In Search of Perfection* and the sequel volume *Further Adventures in Search of Perfection* that made it into his monumental *Big*

Fat Duck Cookbook (£100). Here the culinary adventurer explains his fondness for this antique confection, 'I like the culinary underdogs … Black Forest gateau seems to be a dessert that no one remembers with affection.' This certainly proved to be the case at Hirst HQ.

Blumenthal's BFG consists of six different layers. Going from the bottom up they are: 1) Madeleine biscuit base covered in cocoa 'wood-effect'; 2) Aerated chocolate; 3) Flourless chocolate sponge; 4) Gelatinised kirsch cream; 5) Chocolate ganache (flavoured fresh cream); 6) Chocolate mousse. Oh, and cherries come into it somewhere. The whole construction is sprayed with chocolate from a paint spray gun. 'To assemble a whole cake in one day would undeniably be a fair amount of work,' Blumenthal warns. 'Better to think of this as architecture and spread out the building tasks. Prepare the chocolate sponge up to a month in advance …' If you are foolhardy enough to want to make Heston's confection it is advisable to follow this leisurely schedule. Unfortunately, in the nutty, hell-for-leather way of newspapers, I had just two days to construct this Teutonic masterpiece. It did not help my mood that I was coming down with flu.

The first day was taken up with assembling a curious variety of equipment and ingredients. With the assistance of Mrs H, I managed to track down a pressurised whipping-cream whipper (a kind of soda siphon with attitude). Made in Austria, the Kisag whipper cost £42.29, plus £24.27 for a box of fifty nitrous oxide charges. Almost seventy quid may seem a little on the high side to make one pud, but

I consoled myself with the thought that I would be able to use the Kisag whipper for the foams that play an important role in Blumenthal's molecular gastronomy. Curiously, this never came to pass. Put us down as gastronomic stick-in-the-muds, but a supper of froth has never appealed.

We found our next bit of culinary kit in Homebase. The paint spray gun cost £31.99. 'Will it take molten choco-late?' Mrs H asked an assistant.

'Dunno,' came the reply. 'Most people use emulsion.' However, the store could not oblige with a 'wood-effect painting tool', possibly since no one in their right mind has desired wood-effect walls since 1973. Unfortunately, the car battery decided to pack in immediately after we made our purchase. Waiting in Homebase car park for the AA and wishing I had a Lemsip, my qualms intensified. 'What the hell are we doing?' I asked Mrs H.

'The whole thing is bonkers,' she replied. 'But we might as well carry on. We've got the whipper thing now.' Restored to mobility, we zoomed to our neighbourhood kitchen shop for the thermal probe Mrs H had seen earlier that day (you need one to ensure milk heats to exactly 75°C during the kirsch cream stage), but someone had gazumped us. Cursing the culinary obsession of the suburban middle classes, I settled for a super-sized thermometer. We bought three tins that almost conformed to Blumenthal's specifi-cation of 'a 5cm deep, 9 x 19cm loaf tin'. We needed three tins because Blumenthal's ingredients are sufficient to make three cakes. (Each stage of what follows was actually done three times but I'll spare you the repetition.) We also acquired a piping bag and nozzles, a melon baller, a non-stick silicone baking sheet and several vacuum-seal storage bags with one-way air valves. By this stage, the equipment bill topped £150. Fortunately, we already possessed the rest of the kit required for this dish: a large Tupperware-style food box, a vacuum cleaner, an atomiser (optional) and a cardboard box.

Blumenthal is equally particular about ingredients. Without these, you are not going to get the full HB-approved experience. Though we had no trouble getting the eighteen eggs, 515ml whipping cream, six plump vanilla pods, 250ml whole milk and two sheets of leaf gelatine, other items were more elusive. We couldn't find Amadei Toscano chocolate, so we settled for Valrhona chocolate sold by the Chocolate Society in Pimlico. Blumenthal specifies '50ml top quality kirsch (e.g. Franz Fies)', and gives an account of his visit to the Franz Fies production plant in the Black Forest. 'I got a real hit of complex, intense cherry smell,' he enthused. 'It was something I definitely wanted to capture in my Black Forest gateau.' After all this, it was slightly irksome to discover that Franz Fies kirsch was not available in Britain. I settled for Lesgrevil kirsch from Waitrose. Similarly, 'top quality sour cherries in syrup (e.g. Amarena Fabbri)' proved a bit thin on the ground in south London. Mrs H came up with morello cherries in syrup from our local Lidl. What could be more Teutonic? Moreover, the label declared them to be 'Premium Quality'.

With a giant plate forming a halo round his egg-like

cranium, Blumenthal is transformed into a culinary saint on the cover of *In Search of Perfection*. Eight hours into making his BFG, I realised he is a devil. He has taken a straightforward recipe, presumably made for centuries by the honest folk of the Black Forest, and endowed it with every fiendish complexity he could devise. He admits it himself, more or less: 'Here it is – a Black Forest gateau composed of six delicious layers ... Lots of layers mean lots of different cooking techniques.' Let me translate Heston's jolly encouragement: every square centimetre of this insanely complex confection involves hours of irritating, finicky, pointless and wholly preposterous labour. Still, it could have been worse. In *The Big Fat Duck Cookbook*, he reveals the research behind his BFG: 'At one point, every inch of the work surface in the development kitchen was covered with miniature versions of classical pastries – jacondes, financiers, dacquoises, génoises, ganaches, parfaits, madeleines, mousses – and the prospect of trying out every combination was daunting.'

Excluding illustrations, the recipe in *In Search of Perfection* runs to eight pages. We peered at the fifty-two stages in a state of shock. Despite this deluge of instruction, we were puzzled by ambiguities. When it came to combining the various strata that constitute the heart of the gateau, there was no explanation of a mysterious white layer that appeared in a photograph of the BFG during construction. Not only was this one of the strata, but it also formed a sort of stucco on the sides. Because it was white, we deduced that it was the gelatinised kirsch cream. The recipe directed us: 'Manoeuvre it on top of the chocolate sponge using a palette knife or fish slice.' But what the hell should we use to put the white sides in place? A brickie's trowel?

Deciding to cross this bridge when we came to it, we made Blumenthal's madeleine biscuit base, the flourless chocolate sponge and the gelatinised kirsch cream, a white jelly that had to chill in the freezer for an hour. To be absolutely honest, Mrs H made them while I had a lie-down. Rising Lazarus-style from my bed, I tackled the 'wood-effect' on the Madeleine biscuit base. Good God! Was I really making a dish that included such decorative frippery? Despite lacking a wood-effect painting tool, I used a spatula to smear the paste of cocoa and water on to the Madeleine biscuit base. The result was a wood-effect veneer whose verisimilitude would have deceived the most ex-perienced Black Forest axeman.

Buoyed by this success, I moved on to the most dramatic element of the entire enterprise – the aerated chocolate. This is where the Kisag cream whipper came into play. After pouring 500g of molten Valrhona milk chocolate into the stainless steel flask, I screwed the top on and charged the device with three cartridges of nitrous oxide. I gave the warm cylinder a vigorous shake, directed its nozzle into a large plastic food box and depressed the stainless steel lever. The hot chocolate erupted into the box (and beyond). It was a highly satisfactory moment, though it cost £66.56 for a two-second spurt.

But there was no time to admire my handiwork. The

next step was to fix the top on the plastic box, put it in one of the vacuum-seal storage bags and evacuate the air from the bag using the (scrupulously cleaned) nozzle of our vacuum cleaner, which I applied to the one-way valve in the bag. You may wonder how I got the air out of the closed plastic box inside the bag? Simple. I followed Blumenthal's ruthless demand for 'a 2.6-litre hard plastic container with a lid (into which you have bored a small hole using a corkscrew)'.

'But it's my best box!' complained Mrs H. Similar expostulations must have been heard from the partners of great inventors throughout the ages. Though the air was sucked out of the bag and, presumably, the box inside, the effect did not conform to Blumenthal's description: 'The chocolate should rise and be riddled with small bubbles.' Despite applying our carefully disinfected vacuum cleaner to the valve several times, the chocolate did not rise. It just sat there. Hoping for the best, I shoved the bag in the fridge. The next job was to make the ganache (a chocolate-flavoured cream stiffened with gelatine) and put it into a piping bag. While that was also cooling in the fridge, we started assembling the BFG. I remembered Heston's injunction: 'Think of this as architecture.' The first job was to line a loaf tin with clingfilm, which is easier said than done. Then you have to spread apricot glaze on the clingfilm at the bottom of the pan, which is even more easier said than done. 'You're going up the sides,' yelped Mrs H.

The next job was to trim the madeleine to fit the base of the loaf tin. Using the madeleine as a template, I cut a rectangle out of the aerated chocolate. (This turned out to be quite a success. It was crunchy and granular with a fair amount of bubbles, but not so many as to make people think we'd just used Aero.) After placing the rectangle of aerated chocolate on the madeleine base, I topped these strata with two lines of chilled ganache. Around the ganache, I placed three rows of Lidl cherries with the delicacy of a Fabergé craftsman. On top of this went chocolate sponge soaked in cherry syrup and kirsch. Finally, I cut out a rectangle of gelatinised kirsch cream and, with some difficulty, managed to place it on top of Blumenthal's Folly, a process akin to nailing jelly to a wall. But that was easy compared to fixing the kirsch cream to the sides of the BFG, a task I delegated to Mrs H.

The basic construction of the pud had taken the best part of a day. Back aching, temper frayed, awash with Lemsip, I totted up how much longer it would take, according to Blumenthal's instructions. Another three hours! My spirits plummeted. Dante's demons could not have devised a more ingenious torment, though this is not Heston's view. 'Do it right and it becomes something wonderful,' he trills like Mary Poppins. 'Food should be fun.' This glib encouragement echoed in my flu-fogged brain as we ploughed on with the futile, fiddly, irksome, brain-numbing complexity.

After being chilled in the freezer, the structure was 'topped off' with chocolate mousse. Once this was set, I used a melon baller to scoop recesses for the final decoration of eight cherries. Then the cake went back into the freezer for an hour. After this, the moment had arrived for the cardboard box. You need the cardboard box as a shield when using the paint sprayer on the BFG. Loaded with a mixture of molten chocolate and groundnut oil (ugh! – you don't want to know the secrets of the professional kitchen), the spraying provided a rare moment of excitement in ten hours of slog. However, this highlight was undermined by the American photographer who was recording our efforts for the newspaper. 'I'm so sorry for you guys,' he said. 'You've been working your asses off all day and it looks like shit. It's funny really.' I could have strangled him, but there was some truth in his observation. The cake was shiny and brown and far from appetising.

Like a mystifying religious rite, Blumenthal's recipe goes on and on. The cake had to go back into the freezer for another twenty minutes. When it came out, the BFG had gained a more appealing matt finish. Blumenthal claims it is 'reminiscent of the close-cropped moss you find on forest boulders'. At this point, I should have bored holes in the top of the BFG and filled them with cherry syrup. But, frankly, I couldn't be arsed. The worm had turned. Similarly, I refused to slit the vanilla pods to form 'decorative stalks' for the embellishing cherries. 'It's a bit tricky,' admitted Mrs H, as she performed this delicate finishing touch. 'I don't think our vanilla pods are plump enough.'

The result of our efforts was three small, rectangular cakes. I placed six cherries (with vanilla 'stalks') into the six little recesses on top of each cake and, as instructed by the young master of the Fat Duck, sprayed kirsch around the room with the atomiser. 'It will magically bring a little of the Black Forest to the dinner table,' claims Blumenthal. Inexplicably, the magic failed to materialise. The final cost of the cakes was in the vicinity of £250. When the photographer had taken a few snaps, we cut into one. It was pretty good – especially if you like chocolate – but very rich. A sliver was sufficient. On the following day, I wrote the feature for the newspaper and went to bed for a week. Eventually, I felt up to having another slice, but the cherries on the remaining Black Forest gateaux had grown a coat of green mould. I chucked them in the bin.

THE FOOD OF LOVE

IF YOU ASK ME, our relationship would have worked just as well if we had both been indifferent about what we ate, though such a state of affairs is hard to imagine. Admittedly, our love of food brought numerous advantages. It gave us something to discuss on car journeys and ensured we had something – often rather a lot – to eat at mealtimes. But, as Mrs H discovered, there was an unexpected drawback to being married to a food writer. On two occasions, I requested her assistance in researching aphrodisiacs. I should explain that this was solely because I had to write articles about them. For some reason, they are a topic of considerable appeal to editors.

There was no problem with asparagus, which Mrs H adores when steamed and served dressed with olive oil and a sprinkle of grated Parmesan ('Yum!'), though its supposed erotic effects do not live up to its erect appearance. Actually, it can have the reverse effect. In P. G. Wodehouse's *Code of the Woosters*, Gussie Fink-Nottle describes the spectacle of his arch enemy Roderick Spode scoffing asparagus: 'Revolting. It alters one's whole conception of man as nature's last word.' Mrs H was also smitten by white truffles, whose eroticism is extolled by Elisabeth Luard in her book *Truffles*: 'Not to put too fine a point on it, the truffle reeks of sex.' We had the good luck to consume these stratospherically priced fungi in some quantity when invited to the truffle town of Moncalvo in Piedmont. 'Earthy and heavenly at the same time,' said Mrs H. We even splashed out 100 euros on a small truffle to bring home, but its thrilling effects went for nought back at Hirst HQ, when Mrs H succumbed to cold, rapidly followed by myself. By the time the colds had gone, so had the potency of the truffle.

Though chickpeas are a male aphrodisiac – according to the *Karma Sutra*, 'If eaten every morning, you will be able to enjoy a hundred women' – my hummus went down very well with Mrs H. 'I think any girl would be impressed if a man made hummus for her. Well, this one would.' Another vegetable with unexpected properties is the onion. In *The Perfumed Garden*, we are informed that when a certain Abu el Heiloukh ate onions 'his member remained erect for thirty uninterrupted days'. Though this is slightly excessive to requirements, my French onion soup has generally gone down well with Mrs H (except when it was made in the small hours).

Other aphrodisiacs were less effective. My rendition of squid sautéd with garlic and chilli, as recommended in *Erotic Cuisine: A Natural History of Aphrodisiac Cookery* by Marilyn Ekdahl Ravicz, did not produce the required effect. I unwisely augmented the recipe with several homegrown chillies of previously untested potency. A Niagara of sweat and a beetroot-red face is not what women generally seek in a bedmate.

Though we were unable to try the sparrows' brains, skink or simmered crane recommended in *Venus in the Kitchen* by Norman Douglas, we were able to get hold of lamb testicles at a Turkish supermarket. The butcher will remove the membrane, but after that you're on your own. With a slight shiver, I sliced the testes in half and followed Douglas's recipe, which, ironically enough, came from the kitchen of a sixteenth-century pontiff. Gently fry in butter with a pinch of saffron. Add a squeeze of lemon before serving. The mousse-like result was less than appetising. Though I doubt if Douglas tried out this dish, Mrs H bravely had a go. 'A bit pale and granular. Doesn't taste of much.' Mrs H's technique with ovine dangly bits was more successful. Once they had been cut into strips and coated with breadcrumbs, they were very tasty. 'But not seductive,' insisted Mrs H. 'Especially when you know how much cholesterol they contain.'

It was high time to spice things up. Black pepper has long been regarded as conducive to a grind. In the ever-encouraging *Karma Sutra*, gents are informed that a pepper and honey anointment on their organ will 'utterly devastate your lady'. Quite. Instead, I procured the Moroccan mixture of spices known as ras-el-hanout (it rather oddly means 'top of the shop') that contains twenty or more spices. According to Paula Wolfert's book *Moroccan Cuisine*, 'The aphrodisiacs (Spanish fly, ash berries, monk's pepper) that appear in most formulae appear to be the reason why the mere mention of this mixture will put a gleam in a Moroccan cook's eye.' Fortunately, the sample I obtained did not contain the telltale blue fragments of the notorious Spanish fly or cantharides. I say fortunately because, contrary to its reputation, Spanish fly is not an aphrodisiac but a potent irritant and poison. The lethal dose is 0.03 grams. A lamb casserole made with a user-friendly version of ras-el-hanout proved to be excellent. 'Unctuous with gentle spices,' said Mrs H, 'but not noticeably sexy.'

Recalling the wise words of Ogden Nash ('Candy is dandy but liquor is quicker'), I mixed Mrs H a cocktail intended to jump-start the engine of love. Two shots of the hazelnut liqueur Fra Angelico, one shot of fresh lemon juice. Shake with ice cubes and serve over crushed ice in a squat glass. Garnish with fresh lemon.

'Mmm,' said Mrs H. 'Can I have another? What's it called?'

'Knicker Dropper Glory.'

'How common.'

At the end of our researches, there was a consensus among participants that the view of aphrodisiacs in *The Oxford Companion to Food* was pretty much spot-on: 'Virtually non-existent ... pathetically feeble ... on a par with finding a crock of gold at the end of a rainbow.' Nevertheless, we have consumed the most esteemed of all aphrodisiacs on a weekly basis for over two decades. For a food that helps to sustain an intimate relationship, may I point you in the direction of the oyster?

16

Shucking revelations

THOUGH MRS H HAS REFUSED to join in several of my gastronomic enthusiasms – she dislikes trifle and is utterly implacable in her opposition to Yorkshire curd tart – I am delighted in my success at pleading the cause of a comestible that many find impossible to contemplate. My favourite of all foods is a cool, fresh oyster. I say 'a' but really I mean 'some', preferably a dozen or so.

When I first met her, Mrs H shared the common British distrust of oysters. 'No, I'd never eaten one before meeting you. Come to think of it, I'd hardly had any fish except for fish fingers.' Though agreeing with Jonathan Swift's view, 'Twas a brave man who first ate an oyster,' Mrs H has overcome her aversion. She tucks in when I open a dozen at home or when I order them in a restaurant. But does she agree that they are the best of all foods?

'I'm not as passionate about them as you are,' she admits warily. 'They're pretty good for you. Not fattening and full of zinc and vitamins, but they're a bit expensive. Really, I only eat them because you eat them – and you eat them all the time. They are quite a companionable thing to eat and it's rather pleasurable watching you eat them with lots of lip-smacking and yum-yumming.' (This may not be a view shared by everyone.) 'But I don't have your homing instinct for oysters – the way that you say, 'Oh, I must have some!' Your little face droops when you can't find any in Waitrose. I will join you, but I usually stop at four if they're alive.'

'You had six yesterday.'

'That's because you cooked them with bacon and dill. I like them that way v. much.'

Yes, I do have them alive, or raw, to put it a little more acceptably, though that swirl of delicate beige flesh lying on the half-shell should certainly be alive. As Mark Kurlansky points out in *The Big Oyster*, 'If the oyster is opened carefully, the diner is eating an animal with a working brain, a stomach, intestines, liver and a still-beating heart.' At their best, the taste is incomparable. It is refreshing, satisfying without being filling, sublimely maritime. Mrs H says, 'They taste of the smell of the sea.' This is a more succinct version of Eleanor Clark's rhapsodic evocation in *The Oysters of Locmariaquer*, best of all oyster books. Describing the native oysters of Brittany, she wrote, 'Music or the colour of the sea are easier to describe ... You are eating the sea, that's it, only the sensation of a gulp of sea water has been wafted out of it by some sorcery, and are on the verge of remembering you don't know what, mermaids or the sudden smell of kelp on the ebb tide or a poem you read once, something connected with the flavour of life itself.' You don't get that with a hamburger.

But raw oysters are not for everyone. Even some shellfish

professionals are not fond. In his book *Edible Seashore*, maritime forager John Wright declares: 'There is nothing wrong with raw ones – for anyone who enjoys sticking their head in a bucket of sea water and taking a deep breath they are a delight.' Like Mrs H, he prefers his oysters to have experienced a touch of heat: 'If there is any fish that tastes better I would be pleased to hear of it ... Cooked oysters are superb.'

In the early days of our relationship, the only time Mrs H and I ate oysters was when we were abroad. A French friend taught Mrs H how to open them with a penknife, so it became her job. 'I remember my jeans getting all wet,' she recalled romantically. 'I opened them on my lap and they leaked all over me.' Recognising that Mrs H's altruism would not last for ever, I took over shucking duties. I go in from the oyster's hinge with a long-bladed oyster knife. You hear a small pop as the bivalve's tight seal, held shut with a force of around 30 lbs, gives way.

When my oyster fever was at its zenith, I lugged the poor girl around the world in pursuit of them. To Brittany, where we ate huge natives known as *fer de cheval* at Cancale and excellent *Belons* at their place of production on the River Belon. To the Bay of Arcachon, a great bite out of the French Atlantic coast where you chew oysters in crumbling shacks. To the Grand Central Oyster Bar in New York, a glorious subterranean temple to the bivalve. To the Davy Byrnes pub in Dublin, where the oysters are great, though Leopold Bloom was not tempted ('Unsightly like a clot of phlegm ... Devil to open them too'). Even to a village called Oyster in Virginia, where no shellfish were available for purchase but the dazzling white roads around the old canning sheds were made of their shells.

On solitary trips to Europe, I would return laden with oysters. I remember bringing them as hand luggage from Amsterdam and watching the overhead locker (not above my seat, of course) for signs of dripping. In pre-Eurostar days, oysters once made me miss the last train to England from Paris. After staying with friends, I made my way to the Gare du Nord, where my main priority was to buy a couple of dozen from one of the restaurants opposite the station. As a result, I was running late, but a quick glance at the departures board told me that I still had plenty of time. When I got to the platform, my train was strangely absent. Puzzled, I returned to the departures board. It was only after looking at it for several minutes that I realised I was actually looking at arrivals. My dash to the right platform made me almost as damp as the oysters. I arrived in time to see the red light at the back of the train disappearing towards Calais. Inexplicably, the greeting back at the apartment of my Parisian friends was a few degrees cooler than when I first arrived. *Non, merci*, they did not desire any *huîtres*.

In Britain, we used to trundle down to Whitstable for oysters. Once I was so desperate to get at them that I managed to prang the car on the central barrier of the M2. It was a relief when oysters steadily became more available in Britain. I and (to a lesser extent) Mrs H tucked in with gusto. The ones we eat 99.9 per cent of the time are long-shelled Pacific oysters, also known as rock oysters or gigas, which, if introduced as youngsters, will happily grow in our waters. Some oyster lovers have shown reluctance to take this interloper to their bosoms and stick to natives. Writing in 1959, Eleanor Clark dismissed Pacific oysters as 'a coarse species ... fast-growing and mostly used in canning'. In 2008, the Irish chef Richard Corrigan continued this disparagement. 'I'm very much an oyster snob ...The native is just perfection. It has to be polished and loved and served on a bed of seaweed or ice, whereas I look at a rock oyster and I think, "Cook you. You're for the deep-fat fryer."'

Yes, the native is rich, sweet and immeasurably satisfying, but they are an expensive rarity (slow to grow and susceptible to disease). Pacific oysters are great for eating at home and cost around one-third the price. Whatever oyster snobs say, a Pacific oyster can be a sensational mouthful when eaten with a squeeze of lemon. Mrs H likes them when they are milky with spat – the French term is *laiteuse* – and, to a lesser extent, so do I, though this self-made sauce is not to everyone's taste. Mrs H is more concerned with size. 'I don't like them if they're too large, like those from Colonel Mustard in Norfolk.' This is true (apart from the name). His oysters were so big that I broke two knives opening them.

Native oysters need no more than a drop of lemon juice (if that) and their preparation is complete. The Pacific oyster stands up to more robust saucing. When embarking on a dozen, I tend to start with lemon, then move on to

Tabasco or Worcestershire sauce, but only one or two drops. Mrs H has tried to wean me off such pungent amendments. But I maintain that, taken in moderation, these condiments work well with the working man's oyster. We both agree that mignonette, the mixture of red wine vinegar and fine chopped shallots often offered with oysters in restaurants, is overwhelming.

In America, a favourite accompaniment for oysters is a compound of tomato ketchup and horseradish. This is because most American oysters are disappointingly bland. There are notable exceptions, such as the tiny Malpeques from Prince Edward Island and Wellfleets from Cape Cod, but the celebrated Bluepoints of New York have only slightly more flavour than Evian. Drenched in tomato ketchup and horseradish and accompanied by the little crackers known as Saltines, they are rather good. Bluepoints are warm water oysters (New York is on the same latitude as Madrid) and grow rapidly without the same saline throughput of their slower-growing cousins in colder waters. The further south you go, the more apparent is this blandness in American oysters. Though I love the Acme Oyster Bar on Iberville Street in New Orleans, where fresh-opened bivalves are slid over to diners across a great marble slab (Dickens would have felt at home here), its oysters from the Mississippi Delta have even less flavour than Bluepoints. Perhaps it is no coincidence that Tabasco is made nearby.

Mrs H's fondness for oysters came to fruition when I started cooking them. Though the raw oyster gets my vote, there is something wonderful about cooked oysters. No other dish offers the same silkiness of texture and depth of flavour. I would cook oysters more frequently if I didn't like raw ones so much.

In Britain, one of the best-known oyster recipes is tagliatelle of oysters and caviar, as served by Marco Pierre White in the late Eighties at Harvey's, the restaurant in Wandsworth that made his name. 'This dish succeeds in every way,' White modestly states in his book *White Heat*. 'It's not enough for a dish to have a great flavour. It's only when the taste of a dish equals its visual appeal that you know you're on to a success. This is one of few dishes I know that actually does that. It's very rare.' When I had this legendary item at Harvey's, an occasion enlivened by the testy chef chasing a photographer down the street, it proved to be pretty and undeniably toothsome, but sadly insubstantial. It consisted of three Pacific oyster shells each containing a few strands of tagliatelle topped by a lightly poached oyster, a small quantity of beurre blanc sauce and a few grains of caviar. It was more of an *amuse-bouche* than a starter. To dull my hunger pangs, I found myself eating the small mounds of mashed potato on which the half-shells were mounted.

The oyster dishes I prefer are much simpler and cooked on the half-shell. They look great and provide their own little bowls when grilled at medium heat or baked. The former is the most natural approach for me, but I've found that cooking the oysters on a tray in the oven for six to eight minutes at 200°C/Gas Mark 6 allows them to firm up without drying out, which sometimes occurs when grilling. The liquor should be drained from the oyster shells before cooking. You can strain it for use in stocks and soups or add it to Bloody Mary, but I usually drink it there and then with a splat of Worcester sauce. 'Are you having a meal before the meal?' inquires Mrs H, whose bat ears can detect a surreptitious slurping from the kitchen. Unlike her limited intake of raw oysters, Mrs H demands equal shares of the cooked ones, particularly the bacon and dill version.

'I suppose it proves what they say,' I said.

'What do they say?'

'About oysters being the food of love.'

'Well, yes.'

'Do you think I should put that in the book?'

'Of course.'

Cooking oysters

Two dozen Pacific oysters at 55p each might not be the cheapest of meals, but no one would worry if a restaurant charged £13 for a starter for four. Once you've mastered the opening of oysters, all these snacks are easy to do. After opening, you might want to free the oyster by cutting the adductor muscle that fastens it to the deep shell and flip it over, though this is not obligatory. How many oysters you cook is up to you, but all should be served with plentiful rounds of baguette. According to Mrs H, these dishes taste 'luxurious, delicious and extraordinary'. A chef could build his reputation on less.

Oysters with bacon and dill

This version delivers the greatest pleasure to Mrs H. It involves putting a fingernail-sized lump of butter on top of each oyster before they go into the oven for 7 minutes at 200°C/Gas Mark 6. When the warm oysters emerge, sprinkle a small quantity of chopped cooked bacon into each one (one back rasher should suffice for three or four oysters) and some chopped dill on top of that. The combination sends Mrs H into paroxysms of ecstasy, although this might be due more to the bacon than the oyster.

Tapas of oysters in hot tomato sauce

Mrs H is also very fond of oysters cooked in a peppery tomato sauce. This should be prepared beforehand. In a small bowl, combine a minced garlic clove, ¼ teaspoon cayenne pepper, 20ml red wine vinegar, 10ml water, a pinch of salt and sufficient tomato purée to thicken up the sauce. After allowing the sauce to meld for 20 minutes, put a teaspoonful on top of each oyster in the half shell. Bake for 7 minutes at 200°C/Gas Mark 6. The result is warm oysters enrobed in hot, spicy tomato – more a soft crust than a sauce.

Oysters baked with shallot and butter

In her fine book *The Art of Simple Food*, Alice Waters of Chez Panisse says that cooked oysters work well with a mixture of chopped shallot, butter, freshly ground black pepper, parsley and grated lemon zest and juice. Place a spoonful of the mixture on to each oyster in the half-shell and bake for 7 minutes at 200°C/Gas Mark 6. The result delivered a pleasing vegetable crunch. 'Oh, I like that – a good discovery,' said Mrs H. 'A bit like eating salad with oysters. It's fresh and green and very lemony.'

Oysters with anchovy butter

This comes from the Grand Central Oyster Bar in New York. For half a dozen oysters gently heat 50g butter with three finely chopped anchovy fillets, ½ teaspoon finely chopped parsley and the juice from ¼ lemon. Put a teaspoon of melted anchovy butter on to each oyster on the half-shell and bake for 7 minutes at 200°C/Gas Mark 6. 'Pretty amazing,' said Mrs H. 'The saltiness of the anchovy somehow wraps itself round the oyster.'

Oysters with Parmesan

Mrs H isn't so keen on this, but I think the combination works well. Open a dozen oysters and pour off the liquor. Free the oysters and flip over in the half shell. Dollop a teaspoon of crème fraîche into each oyster and top with a layer of grated Parmesan. Place side by side on the rack of the grill so they don't fall over and grill for 2 minutes, until the Parmesan forms a crust.

BIBLIOGRAPHY

Adrià, Ferran, *A Day elBulli* (Phaidon, 2008)

Albala, Ken, *Pancake: A Global History* (Reaktion, 2008)

Allen, Darina, *Irish Traditional Cookery* (Kyle Cathie, 2004)

Amandonico, Nikko, *La Pizza* (Mitchell Beazley, 2005)

Ayto, John, *An A-Z of Food & Drink* (Oxford, 2002)

Beeton, Isabella, *Mrs Beeton's Book of Household Management*, first published 1861 (Southover, 1998)

Blumenthal, Heston, *In Search of Perfection* (Bloomsbury, 2006)

——, *Further Adventures in Search of Perfection* (Bloomsbury, 2007)

——, *Big Fat Duck Cook Book* (Bloomsbury, 2008)

Brears, Peter, *Cooking & Dining in Medieval England* (Prospect, 2008)

Buzzi, Aldo, *The Perfect Egg* (Bloomsbury, 2006)

Carluccio, Antonio, *A Passion for Mushrooms* (Pavillion, 1990)

Clark, Eleanor, *The Oysters of Locmariaquer*, first published 1964 (HarperCollins, 1992)

Conran, Terence, and Prescott, Peter, *Eat London* (Conran Octopus, 2007)

Corbin, Pam, *Preserves: River Cottage Handbook No.2* (Bloomsbury, 2008)

Corrigan, Richard, *The Clatter of Forks and Spoons* (Fourth Estate, 2008)

Davidson, Alan, *North Atlantic Seafood*, first published 1979 (Prospect, 2002)

——, *Mediterranean Seafood*, first published 1972 (Prospect, 2002)

——, *The Oxford Companion to Food* (Oxford, 1999)

Del Conte, Anna, *Amaretto, Apple Cake and Artichokes* (Vintage, 2006)

Dods, Margaret, *The Cook and Housewife's Manual* (Margaret Dods, 1826)

Douglas, Norman, *Venus in the Kitchen*, first published 1952 (Bloomsbury, 2002)

Doust, Clifford, *Rhubarb: The Wondrous Drug* (Princeton, 1992)

Ducasse, Alain, *Culinary Encyclopaedia* (Alain Ducasse, 2005)

Edge, John T., *Hamburgers & Fries: An American Story* (Putnam, 2005)

Fearnley-Whittingstall, Hugh, *The River Cottage Meat Book* (Hodder, 2002)

——, *River Cottage Cookbook* (HarperCollins, 2001)

Garnweidner, Edmund, *Mushrooms and Toadstools of Great Britain & Europe* (Collins, 1994)

Glasse, Hannah, *The Art of Cookery Made Plain and Easy*,